COMPARATIVE PERSPECTIVES ON

FORMAL
ORGANIZATIONS

COMPARATIVE PERSPECTIVES ON

FORMAL
ORGANIZATIONS

Edited and with Introduction by

HENRY A. LANDSBERGER

University of North Carolina

LITTLE, BROWN AND COMPANY Boston

LIBRARY OF CONGRESS CATALOG CARD NUMBER 76–91603

FIRST PRINTING

Printed simultaneously in Canada by
Little, Brown & Company (Canada) Limited

PRINTED IN THE UNITED STATES OF AMERICA

TABLE OF CONTENTS

The Satisfaction of Members as Output

COMPARATIVE PERSPECTIVES ON
FORMAL
ORGANIZATIONS

I

Introduction

HENRY A. LANDSBERGER

A Framework for the Cross-Cultural
Analysis of Formal Organizations

THE CONCEPT OF ORGANIZATION

A good conceptual scheme for the cross-cultural comparison of organizations ought to develop out of the application of a general conceptual scheme for the analysis of organizations to the problem of comparative analysis. But there is no general scheme widely accepted by students of organizations, and this introduction is not the place to expand, in detail, on the editor's favorite. We can view the situation more positively, however, for several conceptual approaches and specific concepts are now widely used for analysis, and some of them are relevant to the cross-cultural comparison of organizations. These concepts have been used to organize the readings in this volume.

Chester Barnard, one of the earliest writers on organization, directly or indirectly influenced many later theorists. He conceived of "organization" as only one of several analytical subsystems of a more broadly defined "co-operative system." "Organization" consists only of "a sys-

2 HENRY A. LANDSBERGER

tem of consciously coordinated activities or forces of two or more people,"[1] i.e. their formal role obligations. In addition to organization, the co-operative system includes other subsystems, particularly technology and the personality and values of the individuals involved. In a co-operative system the subsystems are brought into an ordered relationship to achieve "at least one definite end."[2] Barnard emphasized that the functions of the organization are to create, to transform, and to exchange utilities through the processes now regarded as standard in organization theory such as decision-making, communicating, and evaluating.[3] Barnard thus came close to what today would be called the "open systems" or "input — transformation — output" approach to organizations.[4]

Barnard's definitions and conceptualizations are neither easy to grasp nor, perhaps, altogether free from objectionable features. But in the context of comparative analysis Barnard's concepts, and those of others who resemble him, have three considerable merits of which we have made use in this volume. First, the readings are grouped according to whether they emphasize the environment and its inputs into the organization, the organization's internal structure and processes, or the organization's output. Second, Barnard's analysis is valuable because it conceives of technology and personality as external and environmental determinants and causes of "organization." These readings treat technology, personality, and values as influences on organizational structure. But in addition, they recognize that social and political structure and the economic system are important determinants of organizational differences between societies. Third, Barnard appreciated that the formal output of the organization was not its only output, and that other "goods" were "produced" concurrently. The readings also use the idea of multiple outputs.

SOCIETAL CAUSES OF
ORGANIZATIONAL DIFFERENCES

If the internal roles and the structure and processes of organizations, on the one hand, and their outputs, on the other, are the chief "dependent" variables for cross-cultural analysis, then cross-cultural differences must result from differences in other variables that are logically, though not necessarily temporally, antecedent. According to Barnard's crude scheme, these differences in conditions may still be internal to

[1] Chester I. Barnard, *The Functions of the Executive* (Cambridge, Mass.: Harvard University Press, 1938), p. 81.
[2] *Ibid.*, p. 67.
[3] *Ibid.*, p. 240 ff.
[4] For a recent text adopting this approach, see Daniel Katz and Robert L. Kahn, *The Social Psychology of Organizations* (New York: John Wiley, 1966). Herbert A. Simon was one of the creators of the approach in the 1950's.

the co-operative system, at least at the first stage of analysis. For example, a substantial part of Glaser's work on administrators in American and foreign hospitals seeks to answer the question: Why are there more administrative roles in American hospitals? Among the many causes of this phenomenon adduced by Glaser are, first, the greater wealth of American hospitals and second, their more frequent use of expensive and sophisticated equipment. In other words, the abundance of administrative roles is due to the hospital's control of more economic resources as well as a higher level of technology. While the latter is partly a reflection of the wealth of the hospital, it also reflects the availability of technology in American society and is to some extent independent of a hospital's wealth. Indeed, the high level of technology in American hospitals is due in part to the high evaluation, perhaps beyond the point of rationality, of the use of sophisticated gadgetry.

Naturally, factors within the hospital — wealth, technology, and values — are a reflection of factors environmental to the hospital. Yet, the reflection may not be a simple one. For example, while American hospitals receive substantial economic resources from patients, government, and endowments because America as a whole is a rich society — a simple relationship — other organizations such as a church may be rich in economic resources even in a poor society because of value or political power factors that operate in the organization's favor — a complex relationship.

Thus, a frequent way in which cross-cultural differences between societies at large produce differences at the level of organizational roles and organizational processes is by first affecting those subsystems of the entire co-operative system that are not strictly speaking its organization subsystem such as technology, personality, or economic resources. Societies may affect organizational roles and processes initially through their impact on:

1. the resources of which the co-operative system disposes;
2. the co-operative system's technology;
3. the personality and values of the co-operative system's role incumbents, including the informal social relationships that these incumbents establish and that affect organizational role performance; and,
4. the relation of one co-operative system to others.

Where do we look in society for the ultimate causes of these differences? To much the same kind of societal subsystems: to differences in society's (1) economic resources; (2) technological level; (3) values; and, (4) socio-economic, or class and elite system, including professional and career systems.

All of these categories could be divided into dimensions and sub-dimensions ad infinitum but this is not the place to do so. Our attempt here is to integrate the readings contained in this book rather than to produce the most sophisticated possible model for analysis. Nevertheless, the categories of values and socio-economic system are particularly complex, and they need a minimal amount of elaboration since the terms, as they stand, are unrevealing. Our comments will, of course, be directed toward the particular problem facing us: to compare organizations cross-culturally.

Societal Values and Organizations

The description and comparison of cultures, whether according to the values they idealize or according to modal personality structure (motivations, perceptions, etc.) is a vast and rapidly growing field of research. In the first part of this century, speculation took the form of concern with "national character," "patterns of culture," and "basic personality structure." Among more recent endeavors, the best known in this field is Kluckhohn and Strodtbeck's study of "value orientations,"[5] the "pattern variables" postulated by Parsons, Bales, and Shils,[6] Kahl's research on "modernism,"[7] and Inkeles's study of "modernization."[8] The importance of these more recent studies lies in their attempt to map out the domain of values in some definitive, conceptually and empirically exhaustive fashion, and not only to contrast two or three societies that might be of interest to the author at the time of writing.

It might be sufficient for our purposes to focus on those value areas that concern "human nature" and "rationality," to use two of five key terms from Kluckhohn and Strodtbeck's scheme, for the essence of organizations is the role relationship, and more broadly, the problem of interpersonal relations as it affects the rational pursuit of the organization's purpose. But concentration on these broad parts of the value spectrum would be insufficient. For example, "time orientation," a third Kluckhohn-Strodtbeck variable, influences planning, which is an exceedingly important process in organizations, and the "man-nature" orientation, a fourth variable, clearly affects whether persons believe that problems, including those facing organizations, can in principle be overcome.

We find much common ground when we look at those readings included here which stress the importance of differences between societies

[5] Florence Rockwood Kluckhohn and Fred L. Strodtbeck, *Variations in Value Orientations* (Evanston, Ill.: Row, Peterson and Co., 1961).

[6] Talcott Parsons, Robert F. Bales, and Edward A. Shils, *Working Papers in the Theory of Action* (Glencoe, Ill.: Free Press, 1953).

[7] Joseph A. Kahl, *The Measurement of Modernism* (Austin: University of Texas Press, 1968).

[8] Alex Inkeles, "The Modernization of Man," in Myron Weiner (ed.), *Modernization* (New York: Basic Books, 1966).

in values, beliefs, and motivations as causes of differences in organizations. Crozier, Lipset, McClelland, and Williams *et al.* take this approach. Lipset, for example, clearly regards the differential social value placed on individual achievement as critical to an understanding of differences in trade union structure, while McClelland regards it as essential to the study of differences in the vigor of economically productive organizations. Both rate American society higher than other societies in achievement motivation.

Crozier in France, and Williams, Whyte, and Green in Peru — using totally different cultural settings — regard as important the interplay between the nature of superior-subordinate relationships on the one hand, and the tendency to establish strong informal ties with colleagues at the same level, on the other. As compared with both French and Peruvian workers, the American worker is more likely to value and to establish informal group relationships and to see less social distance between himself and his superior. Lipset sees American society as more egalitarian when compared to other societies, but he stresses that the American emphasis on individual achievement leads to less class consciousness at the societal level (and to less "group" formation), however much it may lead to the formation of tight colleague-groups at the organization level. Since Lipset does not deny the American tendency to form cohesive colleague-groups at work, his conclusions do not, therefore, contradict those of others.

McClelland's emphasis on the particularly low desire of Americans for friendship, at least at the executive level, does appear at variance with views of Americans forming strong cliques. Baron and Tropp's analysis even more sharply contradicts the others. They say England, not the United States, emphasizes individual achievement, at least in the educational system; in the United States achievement is superseded by equality.

While authors may agree, therefore, on the kind of societal value dimensions they regard as important to analyze organizations — achievement, egalitarianism, power, affiliation, universalism, neutrality, rationality, trust in others — they may still disagree on where to locate certain societies in relation to each other on these dimensions. Indeed, it would be more accurate to say that there is a good deal of overlap, rather than perfect agreement on the societal value dimensions authors consider important. We purposely highlight the possibility of disagreement in order to make clear that the cross-cultural comparison of organizations still is evolving. Many conflicting interpretations must be reconciled; many conflicting interpretations have not even been recognized. And much even of the agreement may be spurious, due more to the common academic culture of authors than to genuine similarities in the phenomena studied.

Socio-economic Structure and the
Comparative Study of Organizations

To develop a conceptually exhaustive set of dimensions to describe socio-economic structure, applicable to all societies yet meaningful for each one, is even more difficult than to do so for the domain of values and other subjective aspects of society. This is not surprising since even the definition and delimitation of precisely what "social structure" includes is extremely difficult. Nevertheless, there are a number of well-known approaches to the problem, and we have sought to sample them and to show their relevance for the cross-cultural analysis of organizations.

Factor Analysis. One approach to the problem of describing socio-economic structure has been to attempt to reduce to manageable and yet logical proportions the large quantity of published social and economic indices that are extremely important from the point of view of national welfare and policy. Scholars have applied the statistical technique known as factor analysis to critically important data from the realms of (1) economics (income per capita, proportion of the labor force in non-agricultural pursuits); (2) demography (size of population); (3) urbanization (percentage of population living in cities over 100,000); (4) communications (newspaper circulation per capita); (5) culture (religion, linguistic homogeneity); (6) politics (measures of political stability); and (7) education (literacy rate).

The use of factor analysis is subject to much debate no matter what the disciplinary setting. Many writers, for example, do not feel that the available indices reflect what they mean by "social structure." But this approach is important and must be represented. Forward's contribution, which is in principle, if not in statistical fact, a kind of factor analysis, is an example of the application of this approach to the cross-cultural study of bureaucracies.

Ruling Elite. A second approach has regarded the characteristics of a society as substantially influenced by the type of elite that dominates the society, the policies the elite pursues, and the interests it tries to protect. Thus, societies are seen not only as varying along certain quantifiable indices but as differing qualitatively. They are typed by their elites.

This approach is illustrated by the excerpt from *Industrialism and the Industrial Man* by Kerr, Dunlop, Harbison, and Myers. Focusing on the trade union, they see all aspects of that organization as related to the nature of the governing elite. "Inputs" such as the kind of persons the trade union recruits for leadership positions, "internal structure" such as whether or not strong centralized federations exist, and organizational "outputs" such as the amount and type of conflict, and the amount and nature of the union's influence on management, on the state, and on worker-members themselves — all depend on the kind of elite ruling society as a whole.

Centralization. A third approach to the study of social, political, and economic structure might be termed formal or "purely" structural. The degree of centralization in the political and administrative system of a society is an example of a "purely" structural variable which can be used to explain cross-cultural differences in organizations. It plays a major analytical role in the articles by Glaser, Kaplan, Baron and Tropp, Bendix, and Ben-David. Both hospitals and research institutes have larger administrative staffs in the United States than elsewhere, in part because in the more pluralistic and decentralized United States administrative responsibility and, hence, administrative activities are not clearly located at some centralized level above the organization. Similarly, financial support does not come from a single source but from many, and it is uncertain for the American hospital, necessitating an elaborate administrative structure. Baron and Tropp explain the English teacher's greater authority and greater independence from the local community as due to the greater centralization of England's educational system. For Bendix the different degrees of centralization characterizing different societies also play a key explanatory role, for example, in connection with whether or not there is a monolithic managerial ideology, and Ben-David's study of scientific productivity regards competition between organizations as a key explanatory variable.

Udy uses another formal characteristic of social structure to explain organizational differences. Instead of focusing on the degree of vertical centralization, he studies the effect on organizations of different degrees of horizontal institutional integration and interpenetration, "social involvement." For example, he asks if the number of authority levels in organizations is affected by whether or not kinship and political institutions are involved in recruiting members to economic organizations.

As will be readily apparent, writers using "purely" structural variables such as centralization or institutional interpenetration may link these with elite differences, but they do not necessarily do so.

Modernization. A fourth approach to defining social structure has been to think in terms of certain characteristics possessed by a "modernized" society. Sometimes, as in the studies by Riggs and Eisenstadt, though both also allow for elite differences, authors see the modernizing society as having a structure peculiar to itself, different both from the traditional and the already modernized societies. They then trace the effect of this peculiar structure on the functioning of organizations.

Other writers, Fleming, for example, see the modernizing situation as an intermediate state, full of tension, between traditional and modern society. It does not have characteristics peculiar to itself. But once again the author traces the adaptation organizations make to the awkward state of institutional incongruity, caught as they are between the traditional and the modern. Fleming attributes these differences in adaptations for organizations through which political authority is exercised to differences between the original, traditional institutions and the modern pattern that is being approached.

Of course, writers interested in modernization may — indeed, they must — use for their analysis the kinds of variables we have already discussed as well as other environmental variables. In particular, those interested in the relationship between organizations and modernization have studied this problem from the point of view of values and motivations. The modernization of a society, no matter how one defines it, requires the establishment and growth of formal complex organizations in many sectors of society: health, government, and especially the economy. The first question that arises is: What kind of value and attitude commitments does work in complex organizations actually require in comparison to commitments required by the simpler structures of pre-modernized societies?[9]

Are people in societies beginning to modernize "equipped" with the necessary kinds of motivations and attitudes? Until recently, this question has been asked particularly with respect to lower-level employees, especially those in economic organizations. Are workers ready to accept the discipline and the restrictions that are an inevitable part of factory work? Will they accept the new authority structure? Will they respond to economic incentives? Increasingly, findings seem to indicate that new workers, formerly engaged in agriculture, possess the needed values to a far greater extent than had been thought.[10] If they behave as if they are reluctant to accept the obligations and limitations of their low status roles, this is as likely to be due to ineffective managerial personnel policies as it is to workers' values. But this problem has been admirably considered in Faunce and Form's *Comparative Perspectives on Industrial Society* (Boston: Little, Brown and Co., 1969) and we have, therefore, not covered it here.

These four approaches to the study of organizational environment are not at all mutually exclusive. Indeed, the factor-analysis approach is, or should generally be, more a style of measurement employed as a handmaiden to the other approaches than as a conceptually distinct approach in itself.

[9] For a systematic discussion of this question see Wilbert E. Moore and Arnold S. Feldman (eds.), *Labor Commitment and Social Change in Developing Areas* (New York: Social Science Research Council, 1960). See especially part I, pp. 1-77.

[10] See, for example, Peter Gregory, "The Labor Market in Puerto Rico," in Moore and Feldman, *op. cit.*, chapter 9, pp. 136-172.

Occupational Roles. We have left till last, as a kind of appendage because it is not easily related to the other four, the approach to a study of social structure through a study of the structure of professions and occupations. Glaser's study illustrates that an organization — the hospital, in his case — is from one point of view just one part of a professional career that both begins and ends outside the organization. If these careers are differentially structured in different societies, as indeed they are, then organizational roles will differ also, formally and certainly *de facto.* For example, young doctors are less dependent on hospital department chiefs in this country than in others and this affects their relationship to the latter, both formally and in fact. Even after training, the relationship of the established doctor to the hospital is different in this country, where he is only associated with the hospital part-time, than in some countries, where he may be in the hospital either full-time or not at all. Once again, this affects not only relationships with the doctor in charge of some hospital service but also the power of the hospital administrator and the authority of various other groups in the hospital such as nurses.

Baron and Tropp's study of teachers and schools, and Ben-David's of research scientists, can also be interpreted as examples of the effect of a professional career on the roles and output of organizations. As organizations contain more and more professionals—which is precisely what happens as societies become more wealthy and more modern — this effect will become of even greater importance.

Economic Resources

We have illustrated in some detail how the structure of the socio-economic system, variously approached, and how differences in the value system can be used to account for cross-cultural differences in organization. We briefly referred earlier to differences in organizational functioning due to variations in the quantity of wealth available to a society. The studies of Forward and Glaser touch upon this. Indeed, any study that compares organizations from societies differing in wealth must take these differences into consideration even when its primary focus is upon some other causal variable, such as value differences or institutional integration. For example, the fact that in a certain society, government administration and private economic organizations may be poorly differentiated from the kinship system, leading to nepotism and favoritism, may well be not only due to value differences but because in situations of economic scarcity, one looks after family and friends first. In a richer society, they can look after themselves. We shall not elaborate on this point, both because it is relatively obvious and also because few studies have addressed themselves to it. Nevertheless, it is crucial, as Forward illustrates.

Technology

Finally, the amount and type of technology used by a society will greatly affect its organizations. Since higher technological levels create similar technology between societies, technology cannot be the cause of differences, only of similarities. A technological determinist at the societal level who discounts the importance of values and of socio-economic structure and wealth would believe that the United States and Russia are becoming ever more similar in most respects and that their organizations, in particular, will differ little. With reservations, and in a circumscribed way only, Inkeles makes that point.

Theoretically the high degree of association, even if not a perfect one, between wealth and technology implies a choice between wealth-technological determinism and social structure and values. The article by Udy included here shows that no such choice has to be made. He uses both technology and social structure as determinants of organizational differences. He asks: What amount of the variation between organizations can be accounted for by technological factors, and what amount can be accounted for by differences in social structure and in value? Surely we can avoid absolute choices.

THE DEPENDENT VARIABLES: ORGANIZATIONAL STRUCTURE AND OUTPUT

Socio-economic structure, values, wealth, and technology are the four great sources of environmental variables that cause organizations to be different from one society to another. They are the "why" of these differences. But precisely what do they affect? What is different about organizations? In scientific language, what are the dependent variables? We have already listed the two major kinds of dependent variables: internal roles and organizational structure and processes, and the output that results from these processes. Each of these needs a minimal amount of elaboration.

Internal Roles and Organizational Structure

There are two approaches to the study of the internal life of organizations. One is to analyze the basic activities needed to make organizations function: planning, decision-making, implementing, co-ordinating, communicating, and evaluating. These activities may have as their content different task problems[11] such as personnel, finance, and production or its equivalent for hospitals and schools. At the highest levels of the organization all these task problems may be considered simultaneously,

[11] The distinction made here between function and task problems is somewhat, but by no means altogether, similar to that found in Joan Woodward, *Industrial Organization: Theory and Practice* (New York: Oxford University Press, 1965), especially p. 97 *et seq.*

while at lower levels each one is considered in some degree of isolation, perhaps in a department specializing in that task. But the kinds of activities are in principle the same, regardless of the task problem concerned and regardless of the type of organization. Decisions have to be made, implemented, and evaluated.

The second approach is to take the concrete positions in the organization structure involved in the flow of these activities — roles — and analyze their relationship, formal and informal, to other positions in the role-set. Each role, except at the very highest levels, is generally located in one of the task areas of the organization. But once again, the theoretical problems of role relations are in principle similar, no matter what the task area and no matter what the type of organization. There are problems of legitimatizing or otherwise implementing the power of a superior over a subordinate role, of role ambiguity and role conflict, of defining areas of specialization, of roles at the boundary of the organization or of one of its subsystems, and of succession, or who gets to occupy what roles.

Ideally, these two approaches — function and activity, and role — should complement each other and receive approximately equal attention. Certainly their findings ought to be congruent, for a role consists of all the communicating, decision-making, and evaluating activities engaged in and expected from a certain position. And an organization's implementing and planning system derives from that part of a role that concerns implementing or planning.

Particularly when working cross-culturally, sociologists have shown much greater interest in the approach through roles than in the approach through functions. Even when not working cross-culturally, the functional approach has been left predominantly to writers with a professional orientation from business schools or public, hospital, and other kinds of administration.[12] Understandably, these writers approach the analysis of functional activities from a normative rather than an analytical point of view. For example, they are apt to ask how to plan more effectively, rather than ask what are the social or other causes for the existence of the kind of planning and communication system we find in a certain organization or culture, regardless of whether it is effective or not.

Most sociologists who have chosen to investigate a single dependent variable related to internal organizational structure have, therefore, taken some aspect of role as their point of departure. Authors have focused on

---

[12] We are forced to omit subtleties and qualifications. From this particular generalization, for example, we must except a writer like Herbert A. Simon. But other seeming exceptions may not be such upon closer examination. Thus, psychologically oriented studies of decision-making analyze decisions as an individual act, not as an organizational process involving many individuals and having characteristics of its own.

the following authority and power aspects of roles: differences between cultures in justifying authority (Bendix); the size and perquisites of the group wielding authority (Lipset); the extent to which power is desired (McClelland); how many authority levels there are (Udy); the conflict to which the exercise of authority might give rise in a traditional setting (Fleming); how expectations differ between cultures concerning the behavior and attitudes desired of authority figures (Crozier, and Williams *et al.*); and why certain professionals have more authority and independence in one society than another (Glaser, Baron and Tropp). Crozier and Williams *et al.* discuss both authority and colleague relationships and the connection between the two.

While practically all sociologists comparing organizations cross-culturally touch on the problem of authority, they often deal simultaneously with other problems, which we have sought to illustrate in this volume. For example, both Glaser and Kaplan deal with systematic cross-cultural differences in the sheer size of administrative staffs as a subunit of the organization.[13]

A third aspect of internal structure to which authors have paid considerable attention is the normative climate in which decisions are made. Are decision-makers trying to maximize the efficiency of the organization? Are they trying to follow rules? Have they set clear objectives? Are they systematically allocating tasks to different positions? Are they using objective criteria in evaluating problems? In other words, how far do such norms as rationality and efficiency prevail throughout the organization? The selections by Eisenstadt, Fleming, Udy, and Riggs are concerned with these problems.[14]

Output

There is generally little difficulty in identifying what the formal output of an organization is supposed to be. Perhaps precisely for that reason its analysis has once again been rather neglected by sociologists, particularly in making cross-cultural studies. Whether American hospitals cure patients more effectively than British hospitals, its schools educate better or differently, its prisons reform more prisoners, or its factories produce more cars more cheaply, and why all this might be so, has, on the whole, been left to technical specialists. At most, economists have interested themselves in this kind of problem, and while sociologists and psychol-

---

[13] Other excellent studies of this point, statistically elegant and set in the economic sector of society are Seymour Melman, "The Rise of Administrative Overhead in the Manufacturing Industries of the U. S., 1899-1947," *Oxford Economic Papers* (1951), III, pp. 62–112. See also William H. Starbuck, "Sales Volume and Employment in British and American Retail Trade," *Administrative Science Quarterly*, 11 (1966), pp. 345–385.

[14] A classic study in this field of bureaucratic norms is Morroe Berger, *Bureaucracy and Society in Modern Egypt* (Princeton: Princeton University Press, 1957).

ogists have frequently needed productivity data at the level of the individual or the group, they have rarely worked with productivity data at the level of the organization.

The exception to this neglect in the field of comparative organizational analysis has been the investigation of relative scientific productivity. Ben-David's work is an excellent example. Incidentally, it also illustrates, as do several other readings, that role, the organization as a whole, and the even larger societal subsystem — the educational subsystem, for example — are three highly interrelated levels of analysis. In Ben-David's case, the individual university structured itself in certain ways and not in others because the university system as a whole was more or less competitive. This in turn resulted in the greater or lesser productivity of the individual scientist. The product of the scientist can be conceived of as being simultaneously that of the subsystem, the organization, and the individual. It is certainly affected by conditions at all three levels. In the case of the military, invariably unified at the top, the system and the organization are literally co-terminous.

Apart from the formal product, however, sociologists have studied cross-culturally at least two other phenomena that might also be treated as output. One of these is the power the organization uses to intervene in its environment. Admittedly, some of this power is a reflection of society's esteem or lack of esteem of the function the organization performs for society and hence is best regarded as an input.[15] But the power of the military over civil-political processes, and of the public bureaucracy over planning policies, as analyzed by Janowitz and Eisenstadt respectively, is for the most part not simply "accorded" these organizations. This power is rather a product of their internal resources and structure, including their knowledge and technology and the nature of their personnel, and it is best regarded as an output.

The various kinds of satisfactions, or dissatisfactions, that working within an organization produces in its members could also be conceptualized as positve or negative outputs. They are certainly involved in the boundary exchanges in which the organization has to engage in order to acquire resources. In part, the exchange is purely monetary. For example, to pay wages and salaries for human services, the organization obtains money from various sources that, in the case of non-economic organizations, are not confined to the sale of output. Other sources are taxes and donations. Economists concern themselves with comparative

---

[15] A study by Delbert C. Miller, which we were unfortunately not able to include, makes the point that in England, businessmen are less influential in their community than their American colleagues because the economy is less valued. See D. C. Miller, "Industry and Community Power Structure: A Comparative Study of an American and an English City," *American Sociological Review,* 23 (1958), pp. 9-15.

inputs and outputs of a monetary kind such as the analysis of comparative wage structures.[16] But the detailed analysis of satisfactions and dissatisfactions with work, supervisors, and colleagues, career prospects, and even satisfaction with wages, are separate from the analysis of wages themselves. Their study, as organizational outputs, is the province of the sociologist and social psychologist, though they should work far more closely with economists than they do. Two of the readings — that by Inkeles and that by Williams *et al.* — analyze this kind of output cross-culturally.

Finally, organizations in one institutional sector may have a diffuse effect on other institutional sectors. Because these effects are diffuse and usually unintended and not consciously taken into account, and because they take place at the higher level of institutional sectors as a whole, they should perhaps not be called organizational outputs. We have not included them here, but the reader is advised to consider them. For example, a study such as Manning Nash's of the effects on community and family structure of the introduction into an agricultural zone of a factory is of much interest, even though we would be stretching the meaning of words too far to call these effects an output of the factory.[17] But there can be no question of their importance.

These readings are ordered, then, according to whether they emphasize principally inputs (wealth, technology, values, and socio-economic structure), internal processes (authority), or outputs (product, power, and satisfaction). Our classification is necessarily arbitrary, since authors study one of these categories only to clarify the cause or effect of another. Hence, the reader should study each selection while bearing in mind all the concepts we have raised in this introduction.

CRITERIA FOR SELECTION

The intention in putting together this collection of readings was to raise issues additional to those connected with the general input-output model that we have just discussed. The first of these additional issues arises because organizations are usually predominantly located in one or another sector of a society. Cross-cultural comparisons of organizations must always be made, therefore, between organizations located in the same sector of their respective societies. We have selected our readings to include organizations from a wide range of these sectors: the economic, the educational, the scientific, the political and administrative, the military, and the health sectors. If the economic and the political-administrative sectors are overrepresented, it is because we deem them to be socially the most important. If anything, we have given less space

---

[16] See, for example, J. T. Dunlop and M. Rothbaum, "International Comparisons of Wage Structure," *International Labor Review*, 17 (1955), pp. 3-19.

[17] Manning Nash, *Machine Age Maya* (Glencoe, Ill.: Free Press, 1958).

than they deserve to studies of organizations in the economic sector because this and other aspects of industrialization are dealt with in another volume in this series, Faunce and Form's *Comparative Perspectives on Industrial Society.*

Second, we have sought to include selections covering a wide range of geographic areas. Selections consider England (Baron and Tropp), France (Crozier), and Russia (Kaplan). Some of the readings deal with these together with other European countries simultaneously (Ben-David, Bendix, Glaser, Inkeles, Lipset, McClelland). In other selections the focus is on Asia (Riggs), Africa (Fleming), and Latin America (Williams *et al.*). Finally some studies compare societies analytically rather than by culture area (Eisenstadt, Forward, Janowitz, Kerr, and Lipset). We have been especially concerned to cover the so-called highly modernized as well as the modernizing societies and, indeed, we have included one comparative study of complex organizations in traditional, non-industrialized societies (Udy).

Third, we have tried to illustrate the variety of methods that have been used in the cross-cultural study of organizations. Some of the writings employ quantitative techniques, others qualitative. Some authors have analyzed officially available national indices such as Gross National Product and measures of the education level of the population (Forward), while others have used published data to develop their own indices (Ben-David). Still other quantitative studies are based on measures of subjective data such as perceptions and attitudes gathered by the authors themselves (McClelland, Williams *et al.*) or by other investigators (Inkeles). Some of the qualitative studies are careful comparisons of the characteristics of specified cases (Bendix, Kaplan, Lipset) while others, though originally stimulated by specific cases, present broad conceptualizations, models, and ideal types not only of the organizations discussed, but of the societies in which they are set (Eisenstadt, Kerr, Riggs). Many of the authors of qualitative studies use historical data, a technique happily coming again more and more into vogue.

Fourth, we have sought to limit our selection, not to make it more inclusive. With few exceptions, these readings are confined to work that is explicitly comparative and cross-cultural. A study of an organization in some society other than the United States is not, by virtue of that fact, genuinely comparative in orientation. Unfortunately, this has meant that authors from countries other than the United States are underrepresented. Partly because they are less wealthy, they often do not have the resources needed to conduct at least some kinds of multi-country studies. Thus, only scholars from France, Israel, England, and the United States are represented in this volume.

Fifth, we have included at least some writings that emphasize organizational similarities across societies so that the reader is not left with the erroneous impression that cross-cultural comparisons invariably lead to finding differences. In this context, the Inkeles selection balances that by Williams *et al.* Both address themselves to certain subjective reactions to the work situation in complex organizations, but whereas Williams *et al.* find differences, Inkeles finds similarities. There is no direct contradiction between the two results since the authors investigated very different subjective aspects. We wanted to be sure that at least one reading illustrated some underlying similarities of man and his institutions and organizations. The reading by Bendix perhaps illustrates best that there may be both similarities and differences in organizational answers to problems that, in turn, may be both similar and different between two societies.

II

Inputs

Values and Motives as Inputs

In the excerpt from The Achieving Society, *McClelland seeks to answer three questions: Are entrepreneurs in one country drawn from different social classes than in another? Do managers from different countries possess different degrees of the kinds of motivations necessary for organizational success? Does the relation between the social class origin and the motivation of managers vary from country to country? In other words, could it be that in some countries managers drawn from the working class have more of the motivation needed for organizational success than those drawn from the upper and middle classes, while in other countries those drawn from the middle and upper classes possess more? Lipset addresses himself to the same basic problem as McClelland, the "motivational input" of the organization. But whereas McClelland, a psychologist, conceptualizes the problem in terms of psychological "needs," Lipset, a sociologist, does so in terms of socio-cultural "values."*

Both authors are interested, in part, in the same motives. Both regard "achievement" as crucial. Lipset, however, also investigates the effects of "egalitarianism," which has no direct and easy counterpart in McClelland's scheme though it could be related to "n power" and "n affiliation" in complex ways.

*Lipset is less concerned with actually measuring differences in
motivation than is McClelland, but he compensates for this by
elaborating fully on the consequences of differences in motivational inputs for organizational structure and process.*

1   DAVID C. McCLELLAND

Characteristics of Entrepreneurs

SOCIAL CLASS BACKGROUND OF
MANAGERS IN VARIOUS COUNTRIES

Warner and Abegglen (1955), Lipset and Bendix (1959), and others
have intensively pursued the question of what types of social background
American business leaders have been drawn from.[1] They have been
largely interested in determining whether the proportions drawn from
different sources have changed throughout the history of the United
States. The question is important for economic development because
it deals with the sources of managerial talent at different stages or levels
in development. The U.S. studies show in general that 50-80 per cent
of the business élite has come from a middle to upper status background
in a fairly stable proportion over the last 150 years (Lipset and Bendix,
1959, pp. 134-135). The variation in proportions depends on how the

Reprinted by permission of the author and publisher, Van Nostrand Reinhold
Company, from *The Achieving Society* by David C. McClelland © 1961 by
Litton Educational Publishing, Inc., pp. 276-280, 287-292. Works referred to in
the text are identified in the list of references at the end of the selection.

[1] Throughout . . . the terms *entrepreneur, executive, manager,* and the like will
be used interchangeably, despite the ease and clarity with which these roles have
been distinguished by economists and sociologists. The reason is a simple practical
one: while we were able to distinguish clearly . . . what we meant by the *entrepreneurial role,* when it came to picking particular individuals to test, we had no
refined instruments of job analysis available to decide who was really acting in an
entrepreneurial way. Instead we were forced to fall back on job titles, or on occupational statuses; and, in the jumble of terminology used in firms, both here and
abroad, we were able to distinguish only a single very generalized managerial status
in which we could not pick out sub-types with any degree of success. The confusion
adds to error, of course, and once again stresses the fact that while our groupings,
though crude, are generally sufficient to establish the existence of a relationship,
they are by no means precise enough to provide a valid estimate of its extent.

social class categories are defined. Since the percentage of fathers enjoying such high status was smaller several generations ago than today (see Warner and Abegglen, pp. 40, 45), this means in effect that business leaders were drawn from a smaller élite group then than now. Warner and Abegglen (1955, p. 68), also note that the proportion of business leaders who were sons of laborers increased from 7 per cent in 1900 to 15 per cent in 1950, despite the fact that the percentage of such people in the total population remained fairly constant. There is evidence that as the United States has developed, business leaders have been drawn more widely from a less élite group.

TABLE 1. SOCIAL CLASS BACKGROUND OF MANAGERS IN TURKEY, MEXICO, ITALY, U.S. AND POLAND

| | Turkey | | Mexico* | Italy | | U.S. | |
| | Private N = 39 % | Public N = 24 % | Private N = 69 % | Public N = 49 % | Private N = 61 % | Private N = 158 % | Poland N = 25 % |
Social Class							
1-3. Lower	0	4	12	2	8	22	40
4. Lower middle	18	54	30	53	49	26	56
5. Middle	28	25	39	22	26	32	4
6. Upper middle and upper	54	17	19	22	16	20	0

Unclassifiable cases not included (e.g., military or government service backgrounds) or inadequate information.
(1) Unskilled, (2) semiskilled and (3) skilled laborers, foremen, public service workers, and tenant farmers.
(4) Clerical or sales occupations, small farm owners, small business.
(5) Minor professional (e.g., high-school teachers, medical technicians) medium business, and large farms with paid help.
(6) Major professionals, executives, and owners.
*22 salesmen (including managers) from a management course at Mexico City College and a random sample of 47 middle-level executives provided through the courtesy of Dr. Elliott Dantzig of Dando, Mexico City. Median age = 33. All other samples as presented in Table 2.
Courtesy of D. Van Nostrand Company, Inc.

What about the countries we have studied? Are the business leaders in the less developed countries drawn disproportionately from more upper class groups than in the more developed countries? Table 1 summarizes what data we were able to collect on the point. As far as the most underdeveloped country is concerned, Turkey, the expectation is borne out. A very high proportion of the business leaders in the private sector (54 per cent) come from the tiny segment of the Turkish population enjoying the highest occupational status (class 6). Alexander's figures for the Izmir region are not easy to compare directly with these. His industrialists from the private sector also appear to be drawn heavily from the upper end of the socioeconomic scale, but not to such an extreme degree: 17 per cent came from our classes 1-3 and probably somewhere between

50-70 per cent from our classes 5 and 6 (Alexander, 1960, p. 352). The government middle managers from the Istanbul region are drawn more democratically and predominantly from the much more common class 4 background as in other countries. To look at the other extreme for a moment, business executives in the United States, the most developed country, seem to be drawn in fairly equal proportions from all class groups. Our sample from the Advanced Management Program at the Harvard Business School is possibly somewhat less élite than the business leaders studied by others, but it is more comparable to our foreign businessmen. Even so, the percentages do not differ by much from those obtained by other investigators. In the Warner and Abegglen sample 19 per cent of the business leaders come from a blue-collar background (including foremen) vs. 22 per cent for our sample, and 26 per cent were from a class 6 background (professionals, owners of large businesses, major executives) vs. 20 per cent here. Bendix and Lipset report a stable percentage of such men coming from "manual" backgrounds of around 12 per cent (1959, p. 134) which is precisely what our percentage would be if we subtracted the 10 per cent of the group whose fathers were foremen.

The other two non-Communist and less developed countries, Mexico and Italy, are like Turkey in having a smaller percentage of men from blue collar backgrounds than in the United States. They are unlike Turkey, however, in drawing businessmen largely from the middle and lower middle classes. Thus there is support in these data for the commonly held view that outside the United States "access to managerial positions is rigidly restricted" (Harbison and Burgess, quoted in Fayerweather, 1959, p. 100) but not in the extreme form in which the proposition is sometimes stated. The rigidity of restriction is much greater in Turkey than in Italy or Mexico. In fact, it is tempting to see a trend in these data, as the italicized figures show, for increasing proportions of business leaders to be drawn from lower and lower status groups as the country develops more. Going from less to more developed countries the largest percentages of business executives in the private sector are drawn from class 6 for Turkey, class 5 for Mexico, and class 4 for Italy. Then in the most developed country, the United States, significantly more (though not the largest number) are drawn from class 3 and below. However, the trend is no more than suggested by the data because comparable social class identifications in different countries are very hard to make and, furthermore, it is not certain that the managerial groups are exactly comparable.

Poland stands alone among the countries in that a very high proportion of the managers report a working-class background. Probably they exaggerate somewhat since many such men would probably hesitate to admit an upperclass background in a Communist country. But the same bias should in fact be operating somewhat against the employment of such men as managers so that Polish managers may very well be drawn in greater proportions from the lower classes just as the data show. That is, Communist ideology may succeed to some extent in doing what it sets out to do — namely to create a "workers' " state which draws less on men of bourgeois origin. Granick reports (1960, p. 55) similarly that 55 per cent of a group of Russian factory department superintendents (comparable to our middle management groups) stated that they came from blue-collar families (our classes 1-3).

The interesting question is whether this or any other method of recruiting business managers is most likely to draw more efficiently on the supply of enterpreneurial talent (high n Achievement)[2] in a country. Figure 1 has been drawn up in an attempt to shed some light on the problem. Interestingly enough, it shows that the Poles have not gained anything in n Achievement of their managers by recruiting them more from the lower classes because these men have lower n Achievement. The same thing is true of the Turks but in reverse. They recruit managers more heavily from the upper classes but these men also have lower n Achievement. The trends for the private and public Turkish middle managers are identical and have here been combined to give a more stable result. To put it in another way, the correlation between n Achievement and higher social status is positive $(r = .34)$ in Poland and negative $(r = - .23)$ in Turkey, the difference between the two correlations being significant $(t = 2.15, \ p < .05)$. The findings agree fairly well with those for Italy which also show a peak in the n Achievement of managers from a "middle status" background, though it is at a different point (class 5) than in the contrast between Poland and Turkey (class 4).

While the findings are not conclusive, they suggest that the best place to recruit business managers is from the middle classes because they are more apt to have higher n Achievement from that background than if they come from a lower or an upper class background. If we add our tentative generalization for Table 1 to this one, it follows that countries at very low levels of development, like Turkey, are apt to recruit n Achievement talent inefficiently because managers are drawn in such large proportions from the upper class. In a sense they have to create a

---

[2] Need Achievement is measured by means of responses to a set of pictures modified from H. A. Murray's Thematic Apperception Test. This particular set of pictures is numbered 5, 28, 83, 9, 24, and 53 respectively in Atkinson's master list (J. W. Atkinson, ed., *Motives in Fantasy, Action, and Society*, Princeton: D. Van Nostrand Co., 1958, p. 831 ff.). It is fairly well balanced for the three motives it is designed to measure. In the present study the mean scores for each motive are as follows: N = 760 males; 238 from the United States, 162 from Turkey, 281 from Italy, 79 from Poland. Average age = 32. All of business or professional status. Mean n Achievement = 4.69, SD = 5.42. Mean n Affiliation = 4.64, SD = 3.74. Mean n Power = 5.86, SD = 3.52.

FIGURE 1. AVERAGE *N* ACHIEVEMENT LEVELS OF
MIDDLE-LEVEL MANAGERS IN POLAND, TURKEY
AND ITALY AS A FUNCTION OF CLASS BACKGROUND

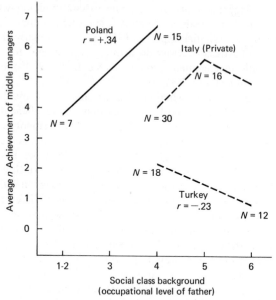

Courtesy of D. Van Nostrand Company, Inc.

larger middle class before they can draw such talent from it. So a vicious
circle is involved: development is necessary to create a larger pool of
middle-class entrepreneurial talent which makes development possible.
The Communist technique of recruiting more heavily from the working
classes does not seem to be more efficient, to judge by the Polish data,
although Communist ideology may have played a part in raising over-all
n Achievement levels in Russia . . . and here among the Poles. . . .

CONTRASTING MOTIVES AND ATTITUDES OF MANAGERS IN MORE AND LESS DEVELOPED COUNTRIES

Much has been written (see Fayerweather, 1959, 1960; Harbison and
Myers, 1959) on how the American business executive differs from his
foreign counterpart. The assumption is usually also explicitly or implicitly made that the American's attitudes are by and large representative
of the best management practices because he is from the country which
has been most successful in the economic sphere. We are in a position
to see how his attitudes compare with those of managers abroad and we
can to some extent escape the charge of ethnocentrism by arranging

countries in order of their level of economic development to discover if the U.S. attitudes are shared most by the next most developed area (Northern Italy), somewhat less by the next developed (Southern Italy), and least by the most underdeveloped country (Turkey). Poland should perhaps be considered in a separate category because good management practices in a Communist-managed economy might conceivably be different.

Table 2 brings together the motivation scores and the attitude items that showed significant trends for the managers from the five areas. To consider the motivational differences first, the decline in *n* Achievement scores from the U.S., to Italy, to Turkey, has already been commented on. It agrees with the level of development of those countries, while the high level of *n* Achievement among the Polish managers suggests that some force, probably patriotism or Communism or both, has been at work to raise it. As for *n* Affiliation, the U.S. executives are lower (combined $p < .05$) than their foreign counterparts (again except for Poland). The finding nicely confirms observations of Fayerweather and others that foreign executives in countries like Mexico and Italy often seem more concerned with adjusting relationships among people than with solving a problem more efficiently, whatever the cost in personal relationships. For example, Fayerweather reports how an American executive working for a U.S. subsidiary in Mexico tried to get his Mexican purchasing agent to do something about the poor quality of some of the parts supplied and the erratic way in which they were delivered. Both problems were costing the company money because the production manager insisted on keeping a high inventory of parts against a rainy day. The difficulty did not seem great to the American: it was a simple matter of getting tough with the supplier, or finding another one. To the Mexican, however, it was more complicated because he was more interested in the personal relationships involved. He wanted to please the American and understood the efficiency problem, but he also felt that the American did not understand how loyal and helpful the supplier had been in a pinch in the past and how much the production manager just wanted a high inventory to feel better (Fayerweather, 1959, pp. 1-3). The data in Table 2 clearly explain the source of these contrasting attitudes, if we compare Italian (in place of Mexican) managers with American ones. Among the latter, concern for achievement is almost double the concern for affiliation whereas among the Italians, the concern for affiliation is significantly higher than the concern for achievement.

Again to quote Fayerweather (1959, p. 73): "In Mexico, very few people are actively opposed to being on time, following plans, or obeying any of the other rules of industrial discipline. When they do not obey them, it is because some conflicting avenue of action appeared and they felt it was more important." One of the main conflicting avenues of

TABLE 2. AVERAGE MOTIVE SCORES AND AGREEMENT
WITH VARIOUS ATTITUDE ITEMS AMONG MANAGERS IN
THE U.S., ITALY, TURKEY, AND POLAND (SCALE = 1 to 7)

Attitude Items	Item No.[1]	U.S. N = 102	Italy (North) N = 41	Italy (South) N = 27	Turkey N = 17-42	Poland N = 31
Mean age		44.8	26.6	29.1	33.5	35.9
Achieved status						
Merit more important than seniority in giving promotions	33	6.67[2]	6.07	5.74	5.41	4.58
Qualified workers should be promoted to managerial jobs	36	6.90	5.85	6.19	4.71	4.74
Pay scale not determined by education	39	5.21	4.78	3.74	3.51	3.06
Average for business items		*6.26*	*5.57*	*5.22*	*4.54*	*4.13*
A man with money can learn good manners without proper upbringing	48	5.52	2.68	3.15	3.93	2.06
Planning, optimism						
Plans work out	42	6.69	5.63	4.52	5.76	4.35
"Market morality"						
Can trust strangers in business	35	6.70	5.41	5.07	6.12	5.97
"Profit" motive						
Corporation not exclusively for profit	50	3.97[3]	1.71	2.56	2.26	3.33
Mean n Achievement score[4]		8.90[3]	4.12	4.26	1.12	6.58
Mean n Affiliation score[4]		4.25[3]	5.15	5.70	5.31	2.16
Mean n Power score[4]		7.01[3]	6.61	5.59	5.93	5.48

Note: The U.S. sample consists of senior executives in the Advanced Management Program at the Harvard Business School (except as noted in note 3 below). The remaining samples are as described in Table 7.2*, except that the Turkish sample includes some middle managers working for the government and a few senior managers (see Table 3).

[1] Item numbers refer to the questionnaire reproduced in full in Appendix VII†. Items have been paraphrased and scored in the direction of "better" management practice for easier comprehension.

[2] Standard deviations for these distributions vary normally between 1.7 and 2.1 so that usually differences between means of the order of magnitude of .7 to 1.0 and 1.2 and up are significant at the .05 and .01 levels respectively.

[3] Middle managers from various companies in the Harvard Business School and the MIT Sloane Fellow Program. Mean age = 34, $N = 38$ for item 50, $N = 67$ for motivation scores.

[4] Standard deviations for the distributions of motivation scores vary around 4.00 ± 1.5 so that differences between the means for different countries of the order of 1.2 to 1.5 and 2.0 are significant at the .05 and .01 levels respectively.

Courtesy of D. Van Nostrand Company, Inc.

* [See David C. McClelland, *The Achieving Society* (Princeton: D. Van Nostrand Co., 1961), p. 262 — Ed]*

† [See *ibid.*, pp. 494-497 — Ed.]

action in Mexico he feels is "the maintenance of personal alliances." If we translate the latter into n Affiliation and Mexico into Italy, our results strongly support this view. . . . In both Mexico and Italy n Affiliation is higher than n Achievement; there is some evidence that these two needs tend to be complementary. In a random sample of 119 cases out of the 760 men tested in all four countries, n Achievement score correlates negatively with n Affiliation score ($r = -.32, p < .01$). Similarly . . . there is a significant negative correlation between the two variables in the children's stories in 1950. . . People who are concerned about interpersonal relationships tend generally to be less concerned about achievement and vice versa.

But we must be wary of overgeneralizing about managers in different foreign countries. While it is true the Turkish managers also show a much greater concern with affiliation than with achievement (although the Turkish children's stories do not), the Polish managers are even less concerned with affiliation than the Americans. Probably the situation will be different in each country and Fayerweather's attempt to treat foreign executives as having a similar personality configuration represents a useful, but demonstrably limited oversimplification. The low n Affiliation of the Polish executives reminds one of descriptions of the severity of Communist production quotas to which interpersonal considerations may have to be sacrificed (Granick, 1960). People with low n Affiliation and high n Achievement might survive better under such pressure. The conclusion is marred, however, by the fact that in retouching the pictures for Polish use, the small family photograph in the draftsman's desk in the second picture was omitted, thus removing an important cue for affiliation-related stories present in the other countries.

The American executives are significantly higher in the need for power, the desire to control the actions of others, than the executives in any other place except Northern Italy, the next most developed region economically speaking. Perhaps here we find a reflection of the popular image of the business tycoon who is interested in building an empire and above all beating the competition. Compare W. H. Whyte's description of his training as a salesman for the Vick Chemical Company in 1940:

> "Fella," he [the supervisor] told me, "you will never sell anything until you learn one simple thing. The man on the other side of the counter is the *enemy*." It was a gladiators' school we were in. Selling may be no less competitive now but in the Vick program, strife was honored far more openly than to-day's climate would permit. Combat was the ideal—combat with the dealer, combat with the "chiselling competitors," combat with each other. (Whyte, 1956, p. 117.)

The word "combat" as an image nicely combines the concern for achievement and power characteristic of American businessmen, according to our results. Sutton *et al.* point out (1956, p. 98) that the American business creed "resists in various ways any image of the business executive as an authoritarian figure of high status" because of the democratic value atmosphere in the United States. In fact it probably masks the power drive in the concept of competition which suggests the image of achievement which is less suspect. Whether n Power is an essential ingredient in managerial success, as we have argued *n* Achievement is, or an accidental feature of the private enterprise system cannot be settled with the information available. The first view is favored by the fact that managers from the next most successful region economically, Northern Italy, may also have a higher *n* Power ($p < .20$) than executives from less economically successful regions; the second is favored by the lack of evidence that managers are higher in *n* Power than professionals and by the evidence presented below that *n* Power is more apt to go with managerial responsibility in the private than the public sector.

To look now at various attitude differences in Table 2, it is clear that belief in rewarding a man directly for what he has accomplished in business (achieved status) is closely associated with the stage of economic development of the region from which the managers are drawn. The average belief in reward solely for performance in business decreases sharply from left to right across the table as level of economic development of the region or country decreases. To take an extreme case, American executives believe to nearly the fullest possible extent that deserving workers should be promoted; Italian managers share the belief almost as fully, especially from the industrialized North. But among the Turks and Poles there is considerable doubt about whether workers should be promoted, because if they are, "it would destroy the respect for authority which the workers must have toward management." Similarly the U.S. managers reject seniority, education, and family upbringing as determinants of a man's standing more firmly than the Italians, who reject them more than the Turks who reject them more than the Poles. The results strongly suggest that belief among managers in a man's right to make his way in the world is at least a strong accompaniment or result of economic development. . . .

The traditional optimism of Americans is also apparent. They strongly believe in making plans because they usually work out while managers abroad are less optimistic, perhaps because in fact their plans don't work out as often. There is something of a vicious circle in scepticism about planning: if you have doubts about its worthwhileness because others don't plan and wreck your plans, then *you* may not plan and may wreck theirs. On the other hand an irrational or unjustified faith in the future may justify itself by creating confidence all around.

The item labeled "market morality" is particularly interesting in view of the importance we assigned to this factor for economic growth. . . . It reads in full: "In business you can only really trust friends and relatives." The Americans disagree almost completely with this sentiment, or (as it is rephrased in Table 2) they believe that you can trust strangers significantly more than do managers in any of the other countries, . . . fair dealings in the market with impersonal, unrelated "others" (i.e. strangers) is one of the necessities of advanced economic organization.

If on the other hand, prices, contracts, supplies, etc. are a function of a multiplicity of particularistic relationships with friends, enemies or *compadres* — in a word, of personal alliances — then economic efficiency is bound to suffer. It is interesting to note that this factor, like *n* Achievement, differentiates the more from the less rapidly developing countries, not only in stories for children but in the attitudes of business executives.

Finally the Americans are less convinced than foreign executives that corporations are *exclusively* for profit. What do they think corporations are for, if not just for making profit? Possibly they are giving some implicit recognition to our point that corporations also satisfy achievement strivings or to a commonly held notion that they have a public service function. Actually the issue should be somewhat complicated for the ideal-type entrepreneur if our psychological analysis of his state of mind is correct. In the pure case, he should be primarily interested in achievement, not money — and not in selfish achievement at that. For if he is interested only in money or personal gain, he is likely to gamble, break the rules of the game or generally act like the competitive individualist that Fayerweather (1959) contends spends his time avoiding, competing with, and outmaneuvering others and thereby creating considerable inefficiency in a firm. If he idealistically expresses no interest in profit, he loses the main measuring stick by which he judges whether the organization is operating efficiently or not. This point is frequently misunderstood both by friends and foes of the private enterprise system. Both imply that profit is important as an *end,* or as an incentive, when actually its major importance is as a criterion or value in terms of which the efficiency of business operations can be judged. The conflict is unconsciously reflected by Fayerweather when he writes:

> Business leaders are generally inclined to accept many responsibilities, both as good citizens and as part of the job of assuring conditions which will be profitable over the long term. But that is not the same as viewing their enterprises as public instruments. Unfortunately, many well-meaning people do harm to their causes by forgetting the profit element and pushing business to act as though contributions to public objectives were its primary concern. . . . [The businessman's] first duty to the public is to keep his business strong (Fayerweather, 1960, p. ix).

Fayerweather seems to be saying, somewhat paradoxically (just as our American executives say in Table 2), that business is for profit, but not exclusively. That is, if businesses are pushed to place other values (i.e. public service) above the profit motive, then they become weak, by inference because they have lost the yardstick that creates efficiency, not because they have lost an incentive system. Despite this emphasis on the importance of profit, he too mentions the businessman's "duty to the public" and the importance of over-all business conditions. Thus there are implicit sanctions invoked against the man who acts exclusively for his own profit to the disregard of all others. The conflict is just as we would expect it to be based on in theoretical analysis of the meaning of profit or money reward to students with high *n* Achievement. . . . It is and should be not exclusively an end in itself but the *measure of achievement*. . . .

References

A. P. Alexander, "Industrial Entrepreneurship in Turkey: Origin and Growth," *Economic Development and Cultural Change*, Volume 8 (1960), pp. 349-365.

J. Fayerweather, *The Executive Overseas*, Syracuse, New York: Syracuse University Press, 1959.

J. Fayerweather, *Management and International Operations*, New York: McGraw-Hill, 1960.

D. Granick, *The Red Executive*, New York: Doubleday, 1960.

F. Harbison and C. A. Myers, *Management in the Industrial World*, New York: McGraw-Hill, 1959.

S. M. Lipset and R. Bendix, *Social Mobility in Industrial Society*, Berkeley and Los Angeles: University of California Press, 1959.

W. L. Warner and J. C. Abegglen, *Occupational Mobility in American Business and Industry*, Minneapolis: University of Minnesota Press, 1955.

M. Weber, *The Theory of Social and Economic Organization*, 1922. (Translated by A. M. Henderson and T. Parsons) New York: Oxford Press, 1947.

W. H. Whyte, *The Organization Man*, New York: Simon and Schuster, 1956.

Trade Unions and Social Structure

Any effort to account for the ways in which American unionism differs
from unionism in northern Europe and Australasia necessarily must deal
with the behavior of the leaders. As recent congressional investigations
and journalistic exposés have made manifest, union officials in this country receive higher salaries, are more wont to engage in practices which
violate conventional morality, and show a lesser regard for the mechanisms of democratic procedure than leaders in the other nations under
discussion here. To a considerable degree these practices, like the political
conservatism, aggressive bargaining policies, and concentration on large
wage differentials discussed earlier, may be related to pressures created by
the emphasis on achievement and equality as national values.

SOCIETAL VALUES AND THE
UNION MOVEMENT

Union Leaders' Job Orientation,
Salaries, and Entrenched Positions

The concept of "business unionism," the dominant ideology of the
American labor movement which perceives unions as fighting for "more"
rather than for social reconstruction, has important consequences in en-

Reprinted by permission of the author and publisher from Seymour Martin
Lipset, "Trade Unions and Social Structure: II," *Industrial Relations*, I (February
1962), pp. 89-102, 108-110. In Part I of the two articles ("Trade Unions and
Social Structure: I," *Industrial Relations*, (October 1961), pp. 75-89), Lipset
describes the fundamental differences in values between the United States and
Western Europe and the effects of these differences on the goals of their
respective labor movements. American society, permeated by the values of individual
achievement and of egalitarianism, has produced workers difficult to organize into
a mass labor movement; once recruited, they have sought concrete economic
benefits for themselves and workers in their own trade or industry. The English
workers, more class-conscious *vis-a-vis* the elite confronting them, sought more
profound social changes and were reluctant to increase wage differentials that would
splinter working class unity. Much of the argument presented in these articles may
also be found in chapter five of Lipset's book, *The First New Nation* (Garden City,
N. Y.: Doubleday-Anchor, 1967).

couraging union leaders to view themselves as bound by the same standards as profit-oriented businessmen, rather than as leaders of a reformist
social movement. Usually the leaders of social movements are expected
to have a "calling," to feel moved by a moral ethic toward serving certain
major social values.

In the early days of many American unions, when they were weak,
often illegitimate, and could yield few rewards in the form of status,
power, or income, their leaders did adhere to some such larger ideology,
often a variant of socialism. This ideology prescribed certain standards of
ethical behavior, of income and style of life. But as American union
leaders shifted from social or socialist unionism to business unionism,
they also changed their values and standards of comparisons. To a considerable extent, those unions which have retained important aspects of
socialist values, such as the United Automobile Workers or the International Ladies Garment Workers Union, are precisely the unions whose
leaders, even with great power, still adhere to the value of relatively low
officer salaries and show great concern over problems of corruption and
civil liberties.[1] To the extent that union office has changed from a "calling" to a "career" as unions have aged and ideology has declined, to that
extent have leaders lost their inhibitions about comparing themselves
with businessmen or widening the discrepancy between their salaries
and those of their members.[2]

The emphasis on ends, especially on pecuniary success, combined with

[1] The two unions which have established external boards to review appeals from
members who feel that they have been deprived of their rights by union officers are
the United Automobile Workers and the Upholsterers International Union. Both
organizations are still led by men who show various signs of retaining large parts
of their early socialist beliefs.

[2] For a more elaborate discussion of these concepts, see Seymour M. Lipset,
Political Man: The Social Bases of Politics (New York: Doubleday, 1960), pp.
383-389. In the U.S., "the gap between the members' wages and the salaries of the
presidents of the larger unions has increased relatively during the 1940's and 1950's.
The heads of the dozen largest unions have salaries ranging from $18,000 to
$60,000, a year, plus ample expense accounts and frequently other perquisites."
Richard Lester, As Unions Mature (Princeton, N.J.: Princeton University Press,
1958), p. 27. For data on union leaders' salaries in three different periods, see C.
Wright Mills, New Men of Power (New York: Harcourt, Brace, 1948), p. 305;
Philip Taft, Structure and Government of Labor Unions (Cambridge, Mass.:
Harvard University Press, 1954), pp. 104–110; and Harry Cohany and Irving P.
Philips, Union Constitution Provisions: Election and Tenure of International Union
Officers, 1958 (Washington, D.C.: U.S. Bureau of Labor Statistics, 1958), pp. 21–
24. A recent study which yields much information on the salaries of European labor
leaders is Walter Galenson, Trade Union Democracy in Western Europe (Berkeley:
University of California Press, 1961). British salaries are reported in H. A. Clegg,
A. J. Killick, and Rex Adams, Trade Union Officers (Oxford: Basil Blackwell,
1961), pp. 55-60.

the absence of the kind of class-consciousness characteristic of more aristocratic societies, has thus served to motivate workers to use the labor
movement itself as an avenue to financial and status gain. The high incomes which many union leaders receive represent their adaptation to
the norm of "getting ahead." The position of union leader is regarded as
legitimate success, not as a sacred trust or way of life. As long as a union
leader has the reputation for "delivering the goods" to his members, they
seem willing to allow him a high salary and sometimes the right to engage
in private business, or even to be corrupt.[3] The success of the International Longshoremen's Association and the Teamsters Union in retaining
or increasing their memberships after being expelled from the AFL-CIO,
and after being publicly castigated by government agencies as corrupt and
ridden by criminal elements, attests to this.[4] The study of the re-election
of Mayor Curley of Boston while under criminal indictment for war
frauds, referred to earlier, may shed some light on the syndrome of attitudes which sustains such corruption. Many of the poorer voters, who
formed the bulk of Curley's support, echoed the phrase: "Curley may
steal from the rich, if you want to call it that, but he gives to the poor,"
and he "gets things done."[5]

The greater perquisites attached to high union office in America, a
seeming consequence of pressure inherent in the achievement-equali-
tarianism syndrome, may also account for the fact that American union
leaders have formally institutionalized dictatorial mechanisms which prevent the possibility of their being defeated for re-election. Although trade
union leaders in all countries have achieved a great deal by moving up
from the machine or bench to the union office, this shift has nowhere
meant as much in terms of money and consequent style of life as in the
United States. Most high-status positions carry with them some security

[3] Some indication of the extent of corruption may be found in a speech by George
Meany, president of the AFL-CIO, in which, discussing the revelations of the U.S.
Senate Committee, he commented: "We thought we knew a few things about trade
union corruption, but we didn't know the half of it, one tenth of it, or the hun-
dredth of it." Reported in the *New York Times*, November 2, 1957, and cited in
Sylvester Petro, *Power Unlimited* (New York: Ronald Press, 1959), p. 146; and
Sidney Lens, *The Crisis of American Labor* (New York: Sagamore Press, 1959),
p. 105. On corruption in American unions see also John Hutchinson, "Corruption
in American Unions," *Political Quarterly*, XXVIII (July-September, 1957), 214-
235; Harold Seidman, *Labor Czars—A History of Labor Racketeering* (New York:
Liverights, 1938); B. C. Roberts, *Unions in America: A British View* (Princeton,
N.J.: Industrial Relations Section, 1959), pp. 59-73; Petro, *op. cit.*, especially pp.
144-181; and Lens, *op. cit.*, pp. 70-132.

[4] See Philip Taft, "The Responses of the Bakers, Longshoremen and Teamsters
to Public Exposure," *Quarterly Journal of Economics*, LXXIV (August, 1960),
393-412.

[5] Jerome S. Bruner and Sheldon J. Korchin, "The Boss and the Vote: Case
Study in City Politics," *Public Opinion Quarterly*, X (Spring, 1946), 19–21.

of tenure, but political positions in democratic societies are insecure by definition. Politicians in most countries may move from electoral defeat to highly paid positions in private capacities, but union leaders customarily cannot do so or are not aware of other opportunities. This means, as I have noted elsewhere, that they are under considerable pressure to find means to protect their source of status. Thus the greater the gap between the rewards of the attained position, that of union leadership, and those from which the leader came and to which he might return on defeat, the greater the pressure to eliminate democratic rights. Within the American labor movement itself those unions in which the gap between leaders and rank and file is narrow in income or in status seem to be much more democratic than those in which the gap is great. Among the unions which fall in this former category are Actor's Equity, the American Newspaper Guild, and the International Typographical Union.[6] Thus the very forces which press for higher rewards of various types for American labor leaders also support and encourage greater restrictions on democratic politics.

It may also be argued that in societies in which deferential values, such as respect for superiors, are strong, union leaders may maintain an oligarchic structure with less strain deriving from membership values than is possible in America. And as I stated in an earlier article:

> Given the assumption that leaders in both [continents] would seek to make their tenure secure, we would expect that American labor leaders would be under greater pressure to formalize dictatorial mechanisms so as to prevent the possibility of their being overthrown. Or, to put it another way, since the values inherent in American society operate to make American union officers more vulnerable than, say, their German counterparts, they would be obliged to act more vigorously and decisively and dictatorially to stabilize their status.[7]

Some evidence that relatively elite societies are more willing to give tenure to union leaders may be found in Great Britain and Sweden, where the principal officers of many national unions are formally chosen for life.[8] Although similar commitments are much less common elsewhere,

[6] See Seymour M. Lipset, Martin Trow, and James S. Coleman, *Union Democracy* (Glencoe, Ill.: Free Press, 1956).

[7] Seymour M. Lipset, "The Political Process in Trade Unions," in Morroe Berger, Theodore Abel, and Charles Page, editors, *Freedom and Control in Modern Society* (New York: Van Nostrand, 1954), pp. 116-117. These two pages present my first efforts to suggest a relationship between societal values and variation in union structures.

[8] In Great Britain, 86 of 127 general secretaries of unions have permanent status. These unions cover 74 per cent of the total membership of the T.U.C. See V. L. Allen, *Power in Trade Unions* (London: Longmans, Green, 1954), p. 215. On Sweden, see Galenson, *op. cit.*, p. 74.

actual opposition to the re-election of national leaders is almost non-existent among most European unions. Lower level leaders and convention delegates may and often do oppose top leadership policies, but such opposition and even successful efforts to change policies by convention vote are rarely linked to an effort to replace the high-ranking officers.

The logic of argument here is similar to that made by many foreign analysts of American stratification who have suggested that precisely because of the antagonism to aristocratic values in the United States, upper class Americans as contrasted with upper class Europeans are more likely to be concerned with the social origins and background characteristics of those with whom they associate at play, in clubs, in school, and so forth. Insecurity, whether stemming from democracy's or equality's denial of permanent status, calls forth defensive reactions on the part of those who would preserve their positions.[9]

The Large Number and Proportion of Paid Union Officials

Perhaps even more important in affecting the varying quality of the internal political life of American and European unions is the difference in the sheer number and proportion of full-time officers. A recent ILO mission of European labor authorities studying American unions was impressed by "the number of paid posts at all levels of union organization," as contrasted with the much lower number in Europe.[10] The most recent available data for various countries is reported in the table below. These indicate one officer for every 300 union members in the United States, while three of the northern European movements, those of Britain, Norway, and Sweden, have one officer for every 1,700 to 2,200 members. (Australia which has one officer for every 900 members will be discussed together with Canada in a later section.)[11]

In Britain, Norway, Sweden, Belgium, and many other European countries, lay union officers and committees, i.e., men working full time at

[9] For a more detailed discussion of this problem in the context of stratification analysis see the references cited in footnote 9 of Part I of "Trade Unions and Social Structure," *Industrial Relations*, I (October, 1961), 78.

[10] Report of a Mission from the International Labour Office, *The Trade Union Situation in the United States* (Geneva: 1960), p. 133. The Swedish economist and sociologist Gunnar Myrdal was startled by the differences between the size of American and European trade union bureaucracies. See his *An American Dilemma* (New York: Harper, 1944), p. 713.

[11] Earlier British estimates are reported in George Cyriax and Robert Oakeshott, *The Bargainers: A Survey of Modern Trade Unionism* (London: Faber and Faber, 1960), p. 133, and in B. C. Roberts, *Trade-Union Government and Administration in Great Britain* (London: Bell, 1956), p. 288.

NUMBERS AND PROPORTIONS OF FULL-TIME UNION
OFFICERS IN VARIOUS COUNTRIES

Country	Total Union Membership	Total Number Full-time Officers	Approximate Ratio of Officers to Members
United States	18,000,000	60,000	1:300
Australia	2,400,000	2,500–2,750	1:900
Great Britain	8,000,000	4,000	1:2,000
Sweden	1,500,000	900	1:1,700
Norway	500,000	240	1:2,200
Denmark	775,000	1,000	1:775

Sources: The American data are from Richard Lester, *As Unions Mature* (Princeton, N.J.: Princeton University Press, 1958), p. 116. The British data are based on an estimate by Hugh Clegg which is an extension of the materials presented in H. A. Clegg, A. J. Killick, and Rex Adams, *Trade Union Officers* (Oxford: Basil Blackwell, 1961), pp. 39, 94. These data, based on a detailed survey of most British unions, report 3,000 full-time officers, 2,600 national officers and 400 branch secretaries, for unions having a total membership of 5,800,000 in 1959. Earlier British estimates are reported in George Cyriax and Robert Oakeshott, *The Bargainers: A Survey of Modern Trade Unionism* (London: Faber and Faber, 1960), p. 133, and in B. C. Roberts, *Trade-Union Government and Administration in Great Britain* (London: Bell, 1956), p. 288. The Australian estimates were furnished by Dr. Tom Truman of the University of Queensland and were obtained from queries sent to union officials. The Norwegian data were gathered by Dr. Stein Rokkan of the Christen Michelsens Institute of Bergen and were supplied by the Norwegian L.O. (labor federation). The 240 Norwegians include 150 elected officers and 90 appointed ones. The Swedish materials were collected by Dr. Ingemar Lindblad of the Swedish Royal Commission on Sound Broadcasting and were secured from officials of the Swedish L.O. Danish data were obtained from officers of Danish unions by Dr. Henning Friis of the Danish National Institute of Social Research. German data which suggest a pattern similar to the British one were collected by Professor Otto Stammer of the Free University of Berlin. They are not presented here since it was not possible to obtain reports from most German unions.

their regular occupations while voluntarily performing union duties, carry out many of the tasks which are performed by full-time union executives and staff men in the United States. National officers clearly cannot have the control over lay subordinates which they have over paid officers, whose tenure in, or advancement up, the union hierarchy usually depends on being in the good graces of the top leaders.[12] To some degree, those who serve as unpaid officers must be men with a sense of mission, who view the movement as something more than an "insurance-policy" and who expect their paid officers to adhere to the values of a social movement. Such lay leaders will clearly remain relatively close in social posi-

[12] "There are strong, dominating personalities at the head of many Scandinavian unions, but power tends to be vested in national committees, most of which include lay members. . . . By all accounts, these rank-and-file men have strong local backing, and are quite capable of standing up to the permanent officers. . . . This pattern of the lay majority on executive boards is quite common in Scandinavia, and is regarded as an important contributor to union democracy." Galenson, *op. cit.,* pp. 74-75.

tion and values to the rank and file.[13] In large measure the perpetuation of serious political debate within union movements such as the British, the Norwegian, or the Belgian, reflects the fact that the many lay leaders are drawn from the ranks of the more idealistic and politically motivated of the membership and are not on a union career ladder.

In the United States, the large number of paid officials at all levels often means that union conventions are to a considerable extent meetings of the full-time local, district, and national leaders. Such meetings are much less likely to create trouble for the national officers than are meetings composed largely of men who are deeply involved in union matters, but who continue to work at their trade. In Britain, to judge from the experience of one union for which data have been reported, the Amalgamated Society of Woodworkers, the majority of resolutions seeking to affect union policy are submitted by "branch officials, that is to say, from keen trade unionists," and most of them concern noneconomic matters.[14] The British Amalgamated Engineering Union, one of the largest in the country, has a lay national committee of 52 members which is authorized to give the full-time executive council "instructions for the ensuing year"; and B. C. Roberts comments that, "This is precisely what it does, and it enforces its constitutional authority on a not always readily compliant executive council . . . [which] is not infrequently prevented from pursuing a wise policy by the powerful national committee."[15] In most British unions, "lay status, that is, holding of no full-time office in the union, and non-membership on the executive council is generally necessary" to be a delegate to a national convention.[16]

Extensive lay involvement in union affairs does not, of course, prevent the paid officials from effectively controlling policy on most matters, most of the time. An analysis of the voting on resolutions at nine British conventions during 1950-1952 indicated that the leaders were defeated on only 31 occasions out of 428 conference votes.[17] But in countries in which most of the secondary leadership are men who work at their trade, national executives are subject to more pressure to conform to conventional

[13] Many of the "lay executive members probably spend more of their time on union business of some kind than working at their trades. . . . In comparison with full-time officers, the bulk of the lay members' incomes does not come from the central funds of the unions. . . ." Hugh A. Clegg, "The Rights of British Trade-Union Members," in Michael Harrington and Paul Jacobs, editors, *Labor in a Free Society* (Berkeley: University of California Press, 1959), p. 133.

[14] Political and Economic Planning, *British Trade Unionism* (London: 1949), p. 29.

[15] Roberts, *Trade Union Government* . . ., pp. 155-156; see also Clegg, *op. cit.*, pp. 132–135.

[16] Roberts, *Trade Union Government* . . ., p. 165.

[17] *Ibid.*, p. 195. This figure may be more significant than it appears, since many, if not most, conference resolutions are noncontroversial.

norms of morality and due-process than when the lower echelons are paid union officers.[18] And even though British top union officers, for example, usually remain in office as long as do the entrenched heads of American organizations, the practice of lay participation all the way to the top permits greater participation in decision-making by the rank-and-file activists, who become unpaid officers, committeemen, and delegates to conventions. Thus Hugh Clegg points to the fact that a major policy of the British unions, the decision made in 1948 to cooperate with the Labor Government's wage restraint policy, was reversed in 1950 "through the gradual process of branch votes and conference decisions in the individual unions. This took place without the wholesale replacement of trade-union executives and officers by opposition leaders. . . ."[19] The same process reoccurred in 1960 when the annual conference of the Trades Union Congress, and subsequently a majority of trade union delegates to the Labor Party conference, voted to support a left-wing foreign policy of unilateral nuclear disarmament. One major union, the Amalgamated Engineering Union, reversed its stand from opposition to support of unilateral disarmament against the advice of its national president, William Carron, who had to go to the two conferences and cast an instructed vote against the policy which he favored.[20]

The fact that union activists, in the form of lay officers and committeemen, have much more influence over the policy of national unions in Britain than in America does not necessarily mean that the British unions more accurately reflect the sentiment of their general membership. The activists are much more likely to be radical than either the rank-and-file

[18] Clegg, op. cit., pp. 133-134. Another interesting consequence of a high proportion of paid officials has been suggested by John Dunlop, in discussing the causes of jurisdictional disputes in the building trades unions in the United States. "The large number of paid union officials at the local level with direct supervision over members at job sites is a feature . . . of workers' organizations in the United States system. 'Professionals' are available to appear at job sites to draw fine lines of jurisdiction. National and local union rivalries are expressed at the work place because the machinery and manpower to express them on the job is available. In other countries . . . few full-time professionals are available to police the rules. . . . Left to themselves on the job site, the workers would engage in fewer and less severe disputes." John T. Dunlop, Industrial Relations Systems (New York: Holt, 1958), pp. 252-253.

[19] Clegg, op. cit., p. 138.

[20] At the Labor Party conference, the A.E.U. resolution was moved by one of the delegates whose first task after taking the floor "was to explain the absence of the union's president, Mr. William Carron, from the rostrum. Mr. Carron, he said, was to have moved the resolution, but he had pleaded a point of conscience. It should not be thought, however, that he was on an unofficial strike." See the Manchester Guardian, October 6, 1960. For a detailed analysis of the factors affecting the way in which the six largest unions voted on this issue, see Alan Fox, "The Unions and Defense," Socialist Commentary, February, 1961, pp. 4-9.

membership as a whole or the national leadership. This was clearly shown in the case of the 1960 debate over unilateral disarmament. A national opinion survey conducted in September 1960, shortly before the Labor Party conference, reported that only 16 per cent of trade union members favored the proposal that Britain unilaterally give up its nuclear weapons, the very policy which was backed by a majority of the delegates representing the trade unions; 83 per cent of rank-and-file union members expressed the opinion that Britain should retain such weapons until other powers agreed to disarm.[21]

Although it is relatively easy to suggest some of the effects of the variation in the proportion of full-time officers on trade union government and behavior, it is much more difficult to explain the source of the variation. Some have suggested that it reflects differences in the income of labor organizations in Europe and America. While this factor undoubtedly plays a role (though Swedish unions are quite well-to-do), the fact remains that American unions began the practice of employing full-time officers and staff members when many of the unions were weak and impoverished. In discussing the American labor movement, the Swedish sociologist and economist Gunnar Myrdal points out that the foreign observer "is struck by the importance played by salaried 'organizers' and the relative unimportance of, or often the lack of, a spontaneous drive from the workers themselves." He suggests that this phenomenon reflects the general "passivity of the masses in America [which] is, of course, a product of the nation's history." Specifically, immigration produced cultural fragmentation and prevented strong interest-group identification, while a very high rate of social mobility drained the working class of its potential leaders.[22]

Although the factors which Myrdal cites may account in part for the relatively low level of "class-consciousness" among American workers, they do not explain the apparent willingness from a very early period in trade union history to pay leaders full-time salaries. As a further factor contributing to this policy, it may be suggested that inherent in the ideology of an equalitarian society like ours, as contrasted with those of countries like Britain and Sweden in which aristocratic values remain

---

[21] The survey, which was conducted for the *Daily Herald* (London), is reported in detail in *Report on a Survey of Opinions Concerning Nuclear Disarmament* (London: Odham's Press, 1960). A survey conducted about the same time by the British Gallup Poll bearing on the same issues, although wording its question differently, also reported relatively little support (24 per cent) among Labor voters for unilateral disarmament. (Gallup did not separate out trade union members in his report.) The Gallup survey is reported in the *Gallup Political Index*, Report No. 9, September, 1960.

[22] Myrdal, *op. cit.*, pp. 713-714.

significant, has been the principle that a man should be paid for his work. The conception that public or social service is performed best when a leader is not paid, or is paid an honorarium, is basically an aristocratic value linked to the concept of noblesse oblige.[23] In Britain, for example, recent parliamentary discussions concerning the salaries of Members of Parliament have explicitly assumed that M. P.'s should not be paid well, because it would be bad if men were attracted to a parliamentary career in order to better themselves economically. European universities have few full-time paid administrators; much of the work which in the United States is done by presidents, chancellors, deans, registrars, university secretaries, and the like, is handled in Britain, Germany, and many other countries by men who are classified primarily as academics but who perform administrative functions in addition to teaching and research. The inhibitions against employing a large number of officials permeate most voluntary associations in the more aristocratic nations of Europe and reflect the historic assumption that such activities should be the "charities" of the privileged classes. The absence of a model of noblesse oblige in an equalitarian society fostered the American belief that such voluntary associations, whether they be the "March of Dimes," social work agencies, or trade unions, should be staffed by men who are paid to do the job. In a sense, therefore, it may be argued that the very emphasis on equalitarianism in America has given rise to the large salaried bureaucracies which permeate voluntary organizations.

In presenting this hypothesis, I do not mean to suggest that historic differences in ultimate values account for the perpetuation and extension of the varying patterns down to the present. Rather, the different values in Europe and America helped to initiate differing early models of behavior, which became institutionalized within varying social structures. The European practice fostered, and in turn has been sustained by, the ideologies, mainly socialist, which the various labor movements adopted. Conversely, in the United States the establishment of the union career ladder made union leaders receptive to incorporating the society's achievement norms into the ideology and practice of the movement, and these norms supported further extension of the practice of maintaining a large and well-paid bureaucracy and leadership core.

There is one major northern European exception to the pattern of few paid union officers — the Danish labor movement. It has one officer for every 775 members, a ratio which is, of course, much lower than that in the United States, but considerably higher than in Norway, Sweden, and

[23] An indicator of traditional British sentiment on this matter can be seen in James Bryce's comment on the fact that legislators are paid in Canada: "The payment of members is inevitable in a country where there is practically no leisure class. . . ." *Modern Democracies* (London: Macmillan, 1921), I, 534.

Britain, or seemingly in the Latin countries of Europe.[24] The most plausible explanations of this difference lie in the greater decentralization of the Danish labor movement and the fact that it has many more craft unions than have Norway and Sweden. As a result of special historical circumstances, the unskilled and semi-skilled became members of the General Laborers Union, an organization which has 40 per cent of the total union membership in the country.[25] The General Laborers Union has been organized on the basis of locals of different occupational groups (building trades workers, longshoremen, truck-drivers, and so forth) and has constantly had to fight off jurisdictional raids from other unions. Given the absence of better educated, skilled workers who elsewhere supply most of the unpaid lay leaders, the General Laborers Union has employed more union officers proportionate to membership than any other union in Europe. Well over half the full-time officers in Denmark are officials of this union, most of them in locals. Thus the actual ratio of officers to union members outside the Laborers Union is probably about one for every 1,000 to 1,200 members, still, of course, lower than in Britain, Sweden, and Norway. Whether the propensity of the other unions to employ officers reflects factors such as the influence of the Laborers or the problems of dealing with jurisdictional disputes is a moot question. Even with suggested interpretations, Denmark must remain an unexplained deviant case which does not fit the expectation.[26]

The Power of Union Leaders and the Decentralized Nature of Power

The greater authority and power centered in the hands of American national union presidents as compared with European leaders, as well as the American union emphasis on the "cult of personality," are undoubtedly related to some of the same value patterns which foster explicit dictatorial practices, if not just other variants of this factor.[27] However, it may be noted that this aspect of American trade union life, as well as

[24] No precise data exist for Italy and France with their diverse labor movements, but information contained in Galenson, *op. cit.*, pp. 9-11, suggests that these organizations have relatively few full-time officials.

[25] The early Danish unions were formed as direct successors of the old journeymen's guilds and hence were pure craft unions.

[26] For a discussion of developments in the Danish unions, see Walter Galenson, *The Danish System of Labor Relations* (Cambridge, Mass.: Harvard University Press, 1952).

[27] The English labor authority, B. C. Roberts, has commented, "Once elected, the power of an American union president generally far exceeds that of any officer of British or Scandinavian unions." *Unions in America . . .*, p. 36; see also, Cyriax and Oakeshott, *op. cit.*, p. 79; Walter Galenson, editor, *Comparative Labor Movements* (New York: Prentice Hall, 1952), p. 121; and Leo Bromwich, *Union Constitutions* (New York: Fund for the Republic, 1959), p. 38.

another very different one, the decentralization of collective bargaining, may be viewed also as an outgrowth of the dominant institutional model of the American political system.[28] As a result of history and size, the United States adopted two distinct institutions, the presidential system — and the federal system. Our principal elections at the national, state, and local levels are for one man, the president, governor, or mayor. Government is largely viewed as the government of the man who holds the key executive office. His cabinet is responsible to him, not to his party, nor to parliamentary colleagues. Hence there is an emphasis on personality and a relative de-emphasis of party or principles. These factors, which have become normative elements in the political sphere, undoubtedly affect the way in which other institutions, such as unions, operate.

The federal system with its relatively strong local government institutions differs from most European central governments, which have much more power than does the American. This system has affected the logic and organization of trade unions, since many of them are involved in various kinds of relations with the centers of political power. If political power for certain major purposes rests on the level of the municipality, this means that unions too must be able to deal with local officials. But probably at least as important as this structural parallelism is the fact that federalism and local self-government have facilitated the maintenance of strong norms of local and regional solidarity and consciousness of difference from other parts of the nation. Business power, also, is comparatively decentralized in the United States. The norms support the institutionalization of competition; this is reflected in the early passage of anti-trust laws and other legislation against unfair restraint of trade. Unions not only have to deal with local political power, but with local business power as well. And business groups in various parts of the country often follow different strategies.[29]

The decentralization and competitiveness of the American economy may also be interpreted as a derivative of the basic value system, as well

[28] American collective bargaining "is perhaps the most decentralized in the world." Arthur M. Ross and Paul T. Hartman, *Changing Patterns of Industrial Conflict* (New York: Wiley, 1960), p. 166. See also, ILO Mission, *op. cit.*, pp. 24-25; Neil Chamberlain, "Collective Bargaining in the United States," in Adolf Sturmthal, editor, *Contemporary Collective Bargaining in Seven Countries* (Ithaca, N.Y.: Institute of International Industrial and Labor Relations, 1957), p. 259; Roberts, *Unions in America . . .*, p. 78; and Lester, *op. cit.*, pp. 23-26.

[29] The ILO Mission points out in the conclusion of its report (p. 146): "Much has been said in this report about the different conditions for trade union activity which are found in different parts of the country. . . . The general public attitude towards trade unions may vary from one state, city or locality to another. Relations with the employers vary in the same way. The relations between the unions and a company may not be the same in all the company's plants in different areas. Unions which are accepted in certain industries in some parts of the country may be opposed in the same industries in other parts."

as of national size and federalism. Thus, there is general agreement among economists that entrepreneurship in America is more dynamic, more willing to engage in risks, more likely to supplant outmoded methods than is true in most if not all of the European nations. This dynamism has been linked to the universalistic economic character of American capitalism, relatively uninhibited by particularistic and traditionalistic values derived from a feudal past and from the more aristocratic class structure which affect much of European industry.

The decentralization of authority may be related to other aspects of union behavior discussed earlier. There are fewer organizational restrictions on union militancy when authority is decentralized. National agreements require centralization of union authority and inhibit locally called strikes. Hence American union militancy may be partly a reflection of the prevalence of local agreements, which, as we have seen, may be regarded as an indirect consequence of the overreaching value system.

The militancy of American unions, which has been derived from attributes and consequences of these basic values, may, in turn, be one of the major factors contributing to the pattern of innovation which characterizes the economy. The editors of the London *Economist* have suggested that the historic propensity of American unions to demand "more" forces employers to find ways to resolve their dilemma by improving productivity.[30] "Thus, there is generated a constant force pushing the employer into installing more labor-saving equipment, into reducing costs in other directions."[31] European unions with their involvement in making national contracts and with their regard for the over-all needs of the polity and economy, concerns which seem in some measure to stem from their political commitments, are less inclined to make "irresponsible" demands or to insist on policies which will adversely affect a sizable part of an industry. Decentralized collective bargaining is in part an *outgrowth* of a dynamic economy in which different portions are advancing at varying rates and in part a *cause* of that very dynamism.

Decentralization of power also facilitates corruption. Corruption in American unions and other institutions is more prevalent on the local than on the national level. Where lower level officials such as union business agents or municipal inspectors deal directly with businessmen

[30] Will Herberg, "When Social Scientists View Labor," *Commentary*, XI (December, 1951), 593.

[31] Roberts, *Unions in America* . . ., p. 102. Sumner Slichter pointed to this phenomenon even earlier: ". . . the tendency for collective bargaining to accelerate technological discovery is undoubtedly one of its most useful effects. . ." *The Challenge of Industrial Relations* (Ithaca, N.Y.: Cornell University Press, 1947), pp. 90-91. American union pressure to raise wages has been a major force "goading management into technical *improvement* and increased capital investment." Sidney Sufrin, *Union Wages and Labor's Earnings* (Syracuse, N.Y.: Syracuse University Press, 1950), p. 86; see also p. 51.

the possibilities of undetected corruption are much greater than in relations among the heads of major organizations.

Political decentralization and strong local governments, as Tocqueville noted well over a century ago, strongly reinforce the norms of individualism which are reflected in the uniquely American pattern of widespread organization and participation in voluntary organizations. Americans are encouraged to press for their objectives through individual or organized group action, not to accept their lot or to hope for remedy from an established upper class or a strong central government. Over time, of course, changes in technology and the nature of social problems have led to increasing centralization of power within government, business, and labor. But it still remains true that, on a comparative scale, American institutions remain decentralized and local units retain considerable autonomy. Hence one has here another example of interrelated supports and consequences of the dominant value system.

Within the labor movement, the emphasis on strong local organizations has, in turn, facilitated the creation of the large numbers of full-time union positions referred to earlier. Thus in its decentralization, as in its conservative politics and militant strike tactics, the American union may be viewed as an outgrowth of the American social system.

ADDITIONAL DIFFERENCES

This analysis of the variations between the American union movement and those of other countries is obviously not intended to be exhaustive. Other significant differences might also be considered. It has been noted, for example, that industrial relations in America tend to be much more legalistic than in most other countries. Unions make more use of lawyers and are involved in considerable litigation. But here again, we touch on an attribute of the larger society; there are proportionately many more practicing lawyers in the United States than in any other country. And it may be suggested that the legalistic and litigious character of America reflects the relative weakness of the traditional forms of social control, of respect for law and authority, which may be found in countries with a more aristocratic tradition.[32]

On a different level, American unions, particularly in recent years, have become involved in administering large-scale welfare activities, e.g., pension funds, health plans, and vacation systems, on a scale found in few other countries, with the possible exception of Israel.[33] On the other

[32] I hope to discuss the varying role of law in egalitarian and aristocratic societies in a subsequent paper.

[33] The Israeli pattern, in large measure, is a consequence of the fact that the Zionist community under the British mandate in Palestine had to establish through private organizations most of the functions normally supplied by the state authority. The Histadruth, the trade union movement, consequently took over responsibility for services such as pensions, medical care, and even schooling.

hand, almost all American unions have eschewed the establishment of joint factory committees (comités d'entreprise), such as exist in many European countries. They do not press for the formal right to participate in or be consulted about production and business policy decisions which is possessed by labor in many countries. Except for a few unions with a socialist background, such as some of the garment workers' organizations, most American unions want to perpetuate a "sharp distinction" between the functions of management and trade unions, a behavior pattern which is consistent with the general value assumption that each group gets as much as it can by conflict or competition, not by cooperation.[34] A group of socialist British labor leaders who visited the United States to study productivity patterns reported their surprise at the American union leaders'

> . . . lack of interest in formal joint consultative machinery, especially as many of them seem well qualified to make an effective contribution to planned efficiency through such machinery. The truth is that most unions do not expect or, we suspect, want to be consulted about the running of a plant. Management, in effect, can do what it likes within the terms of the agreement, but whatever it does is subject to consideration by the union which then decides on appropriate action. There is nothing restrictive about this attitude, even if it is not cooperative. The job of managing is left to management.[35] . . .

CONCLUSION

Any effort at comparative analysis, such as the one here, is necessarily subject to the sins of oversimplification and exaggeration. Oversimplification comes about because, in comparing such complex phenomena as national value systems and national organizational structures, one must necessarily gloss over the internal differences that exist in these phenomena. Exaggeration is also present because any effort to analyze the influence of only one factor on a large range of social behavior, even if that factor is as important as the value system, tends to disregard many other factors which are obviously necessary for the proper understanding of the variations involved. For example, the important economic variables,

[34] Roberts, *Unions in America* . . ., pp. 109-110. George Meany has explicitly stated that labor has no desire for such committees or for codetermination on the German pattern. See Jack Stieber, editor, *U.S. Industrial Relations: The Next Twenty Years* (East Lansing: Michigan State University Press, 1958), p. 16. For a detailed description of the operation of joint committees in one country, see A. Delpérée, "Joint Committees in Belgium," *International Labour Review*, LXXXI (March, 1960), 185-204.

[35] *Trade Unions and Productivity* (London: Trades Union Congress, 1949), p. 57. For a detailed report on the attitudes and behavior of American unions on this question, see *Cooperation in Industry* (Geneva: International Labour Office, 1951), especially pp. 19-32. This book describes practices around the world.

such as differences in past rates of economic growth, in current levels of productivity, and in international market situations, have not been touched on here.

Although the value system has been used as the principal determinant of various aspects of trade union activities, it is obvious that any social system is composed of highly interrelated components and that economic activities and societal value systems are mutually supportive, as Max Weber and many others have stressed. It is when both economic and cultural causes are seen as affecting the structure of trade union activities that the clearest understanding of such activities is obtained.[36]

It is significant that a recent effort, discussed in the first part of this paper, by a group of labor economists to provide a conceptual framework for the comparative study of industrialization suggests hypotheses about the sources of variation in trade union behavior similar to those presented here.[37] The four economists, Kerr, Dunlop, Harbison, and Myers, differentiate societal systems according to the character of the elites in charge of the industrialization process. Specifically, they distinguish between three elite groups: (1) the "dynastic-feudal," which is drawn from the aristocracy, is "oriented toward the past," and "cherishes the family, the church, the military, and the national state";[38] (2) the "middle-class," which is drawn from the existing commercial groups, "is economically individualistic and politically egalitarian," and believes that "each man's responsibility begins and ends with the injunction to make the best use of his opportunities";[39] and (3) the "revolutionary-intellectual," which is "self-appointed to sweep away the old order and to push industrialization at the fastest possible pace."[40]

All the nations discussed in this paper would probably fall into the category of those which industrialized under the leadership of a "middle-class elite." However, I would suggest that the characteristics which distinguish the middle-class elite pattern from the dynastic-feudal one in

[36] Joseph Schumpeter saw the link between society and economy on yet another level than the one presented in this paper. He argued that the political values of the lower strata and of the society as a whole are set in large part by the intellectuals of a nation. "Under-employed and frustrated intellectuals" undermine the solidarity of a society. In the United States, however, he suggested that "the scheme of values that arose from the national task of developing the economic possibilities of the country drew nearly all the brains into business and impressed the businessman's attitudes upon the soul of the nation." *Capitalism, Socialism, and Democracy* (New York: Harper, 1950), p. 331.

[37] Clark Kerr, John T. Dunlop, Frederick Harbison, and Charles A. Myers, *Industrialism and Industrial Man* (Cambridge, Mass.: Harvard University Press, 1960). An earlier statement of the theory is presented in Dunlop, *op. cit.*, pp. 307-389.

[38] *Ibid.*, p. 318; Kerr and others, *op. cit.*, pp. 52-53.

[39] *Ibid.*, p. 55; Dunlop, *op. cit.*, p. 318.

[40] *Loc. cit.*; Kerr and others, *op. cit.*, pp. 59-61.

the model of the four economists are similar to those which separate North America and Australasia from northwestern Europe. That is, the United States, Canada, and Australasia have been industrialized completely under the leadership of the commercial classes, while the countries of northwestern Europe have to some extent been developed by an elite which included a large part of the traditional aristocracy. Hence, it may be argued that the differences between the labor movements emerging in newly industrializing countries under "dynastic-feudal" leadership and those in countries led by the middle class should be similar to the differences found within the North Atlantic-Australasian "culture area."

The four economists suggest that in countries dominated by dynastic-feudal elites the leaders of unions will be ideologically motivated, there will be relatively little concern with developing local union organization, the union structure will probably be highly centralized in a national federation, there will be little variety of structural forms, unions will have limited funds, and industrial conflict will be repressed. Conversely, the economists argue that in the countries dominated by middle-class elites one should expect to find leaders who are less concerned with political ideology, strong local units, considerable variety of union form (e.g., craft, industrial, and general unions), a union full-time career "ladder on which leadership starts at the bottom," unions which "tend to be relatively well financed by dues," "labor organizations which are bargaining institutions primarily," and considerable "industrial conflict [which is regarded] . . . as little more than an extension of the market mechanism, a corollary of the freedom to buy and sell labor services."[41]

The relative similarity between the two sets of findings, one dealing with industrializing culture areas and the other with the most developed and mature industrialized areas, suggests that a focus on the key organizing principles of complex systems, whether these be initially described in terms of the character of their dominant economic class or in terms of their value systems, is a fruitful way to account for variations in the internal patterns of behavior of various societies.

But while the principal contribution of comparative analysis is to permit the elaboration and testing of hypotheses concerning complex social systems, it has another less ambitious function, which those who may reject the first as intellectually unattainable should be able to accept. A look at the same institution in varying cultural contexts is basic to any effort to understand why it has the character that it does. To understand the American labor movement, American religion, American law, or any other institution, it is necessary to know how it differs from the comparable institution in other cultures. Only when one knows what is

[41] Dunlop, *op. cit.*, pp. 324-327; Kerr and others, *op. cit.*, pp. 222-223.

unique on a comparative scale, can one begin to ask significant questions about causal relationships within a country. The analysis of union behavior is an excellent example of the way in which a growing concern with comparative research has greatly increased understanding of an American institution.

Technology and Social Structure

Values and motives are not, of course, the only external influences on the internal structure and operation of organizations. The structure of organizations — roughly equivalent to what Udy terms "the administrative system" — is affected also by other "institutional systems" in the society and by the "technological system" adopted by the organization. The complex relationship between these three is examined in the article by Udy.

The article by Bendix really defies categorization in any one of our three major rubrics of input, structure, output, for it covers all three. It asks: how do different societies reconcile the structural fact *that authority and subordination exist in their organizations with certain* values *such as egalitarianism that exist in society at large? Bendix answers that they do so by creating ideologies that vary according to the stage of development of the country (and hence the precise nature of the authority problem its organizations face), and differences in social values and social structure between countries. According to our scheme, social values and social structure are conceptually a kind of input, and the ideologies are a kind of organizational output.*

Technical and Institutional Factors in
Production Organization: A Preliminary Model

While it is true that administrative structure is likely to be strongly influenced by technical exigencies as well as by the institutional setting, at the same time, existing systematic models of organization are largely restricted to variations in the internal workings of administrative structures.[1] For many purposes this is indeed quite appropriate, but often the absence of explicit technical and institutional variables from organizational models is severely felt.

Two fairly common examples may be cited: The first is the frequent necessity, *faute de mieux*, of using the essentially residual concept "informal organization" as an explanatory variable where institutional conditions are actually involved. The second, on the technical side, is the difficulty in accounting for — if not the frequent lack of recognition of — differences in patterns of job satisfaction among workers engaged in different types of technical activity.[2] Both instances, and others like them, point to the need for systematic organizational models which explicitly introduce technical and institutional variables as influencing administration. It is the purpose of this paper to develop and test a preliminary model of this type.

Specifically, the unit to be described is the *production organization;* that is, any social group manifestly (though not necessarily exclusively) engaged in producing material goods from raw materials. Since any such organization is carrying on a technological process in a social setting, it will be oriented not only to an *administrative system* (a system of role

Reprinted by permission of the author and publisher from Stanley H. Udy, Jr., "Technical and Institutional Factors in Production Organization: A Preliminary Model," *The American Journal of Sociology*, LXVII (November 1961), pp. 247-254.

[1] See, however, James G. March and Herbert A. Simon, *Organizations* (New York: John Wiley & Sons, 1958); Talcott Parsons, *Structure and Process in Modern Societies* (Glencoe, Ill.: Free Press, 1960), pp. 16-96.

[2] Robert Blauner, "Work Satisfaction and Industrial Trends in Modern Society," in W. Galenson and S. M. Lipset (eds.), *Labor and Trade Unionism* (New York: John Wiley & Sons, 1960), pp. 339-60.

expectations defining interactive relationships among members), but also
to a *technical system* (a system of activities performed on raw materials
by members), and an *institutional system* (a system of norms and roles
through which participation and motivation to work are institutionalized
and carried out).[3] Our model, essentially, attempts to show how certain
aspects of administrative structure are shaped by certain technical and
institutional influences, in the course of production. The model in no
sense purports to be exhaustive; the purpose here, rather, is to demon-
strate the feasibility of the method with a view toward further work on
a more complete version. The empirical basis of the analysis is a sample
of thirty production organizations in thirty different societies, using data
drawn from the Human Relations Area Files, supplemented by additional
ethnographic materials.[4]

DEFINITIONS

The particular aspect of the technical system which will concern us is
the *flow of production*; that is, the pattern of spatial and/or temporal
division of labor among work positions differentiated in the same process.[5]
Three principal dimensions of the flow of production are: *specialization*
(the differentiation of activities performed simultaneously); *specification*
(the differentiation of sequential sets of specialized activities over time);
and *combined effort* (the manifest rhythmic integration of simultaneous
activity).[6] For the thirty cases studied it proved possible to construct
process charts from the ethnographic descriptions. The degree of specialization could thus be measured in each case by the maximum number
of specialized activities ever performed at once in the process; the degree
of specification, by the number of sets of such activities temporally differ-

[3] Parsons, *op. cit.*, pp. 60-65.

[4] This sample represents all those cases employed in an earlier comparative study
of work organization on which adequate data were available for present purposes.
The following societies are represented here: Aleut, Andamanese, Atayal, Azande,
Bemba, Betsileo, Buka, Cambodian, Central Chinese, Crow, Dahomean, Haitian,
Hopi, Jukun, Kabyle, Karen, Kikuyu, Li, Lobi, Maanyan, Malekulan, Mam,
Mbundu, Navaho, Ojibwa, Paiute, Sanpoil, Siriono, Sotho, Tibetan (for details
on methods of selection and bibliography see Stanley H. Udy, Jr., *Organization of
Work: A Comparative Analysis of Production among Nonindustrial Peoples* [New
Haven: HRAF Press, 1959]).

[5] Arnold S. Feldman and Wilbert E. Moore, "The Work Place," in W. E.
Moore and A. S. Feldman (eds.), *Labor Commitment and Social Change in Developing Areas* (New York: Social Science Research Council, 1960), p. 27.

[6] Max Weber, *The Theory of Social and Economic Organization*, trans. A. M.
Henderson and T. Parsons (New York: Oxford University Press, 1947), pp.
225-26; Karl Bücher, *Die Entstehung der Volkswirtschaft* (Tübingen: J. C. B.
Mohr, 1920-21), Vol. I, chap. viii-ix; W. G. Ireson and E. L. Grant, *Handbook
of Industrial Engineering and Management* (Englewood Cliffs, New Jersey:
Prentice-Hall, 1955), pp. 291-92.

entiated in the process; and the degree of combined effort, by its presence at any point (1) or its absence at all points (0). The total *technical complexity* of any flow of production is defined as the arithmetic sum of these three quantities.

We shall consider two dimensions of administrative systems: *authority* (institutionalized power over the actions of others); and *rationality* (in this context, role expectations based on planning for the announced objectives of the organization). Organization charts were reconstructed from the descriptions of the cases, and the amount of authority was measured in each case by counting the number of hierarchical levels. Similarly, the data permitted classification of the organizations studied into three ranks of increasing rationality, depending on whether none, one, or both of the following characteristics were reported present; (a) limited objectives (announced objectives limited to production); (b) segmental participation (participation based on any kind of mutual limited agreement).

On the institutional level we shall be concerned with two dimensions of production organization: social involvement and the scope of the reward. Any production organization is socially involved to the degree that participation and motivation are institutionalized through expectations and obligations existing independently of the production situation. The organizations studied were ranked into six categories of presumed increasing social involvement, as follows:

1. Participation of all members voluntary, in the sense of no socially prescribed sanctions attached to non-participation.

2. Agreement to participate voluntary for all members, but participation obligatory in terms of an agreement, once such agreement is made.

3. Participation of a permanent core of members required on the basis of kinship and/or political obligations, but not continuously for each separate occasion; participation of temporary auxiliary members the same as category 2 above.

4. Participation of all members as in the permanent core of category 3.

5. Participation of a permanent core of members as in the permanent core of category 3; participation of temporary auxiliary members based on institutionalized reciprocity, without option to refuse.

6. Participation of all members required on the basis of kinship and/or political obligations, continuously required on each separate occasion and sanctioned legitimately by force if necessary.

The above rank order was devised by asking: "To what extent do members or potential members have the option to refuse to participate?" Category 1 is clearly the "most voluntary" from this standpoint. Initial membership is also voluntary for category 2, but members must remain members once they have agreed to participate. In categories 3 through 6, on the other hand, all or a major part of the membership is ascriptive; one may not refuse to participate. Category 3 is ranked below category 4 because it contains an element of option; category 5 is ranked above category 4 because it involves compulsory reciprocity in addition to kinship and/or political criteria. Category 6 is ranked above categories 3, 4, and 5 because participation is continuously (rather than just usually) required and may be compelled by force.

One might reasonably dispute the relative ranking of categories 4 and 5, on the ground that kinship and political ties are stronger than the convention of reciprocity. Inversion of these two categories in the analysis produced no change in the over-all results beyond a slight lowering of a few τ values. (It is hoped that any other possible alterations in the ordering appear as unreasonable to the reader as they do to the author, for when they are made the outcome is severely disrupted.)

The institutionalization of participation and motivation may also (or alternatively) center on some type of reward system, a reward being any material object accruing to some party as a consequence of production by a given production organization and a reward system being the pattern of allocation of rewards relative to the membership of the organization. The scope of the system of any production organization will be deemed broad or narrow to the degree that motivation to participate and work is or is not, respectively, expected on the basis of rewards received by the organizational membership. A rough ranking could be achieved of the organizations studied, on the basis of the number of different aspects of participation of members which entered into determination of the type or quantity of rewards. The following situations were counted, and the organizations ranked in presumed order of increasing scope of reward system, according to the number of the situations: differential allocation of rewards on the basis of proprietorship (control over possession of the means of production); differential rewards in the office by organization; differential rewards according to performance (quantity and/or quality of work done); allocation of rewards to members doing physical work on raw material; absence of contributions by members lower in the hierarchy to those of higher authority.

THE MODEL: PROPOSITIONS AND FINDINGS

Figure 1 illustrates the proposed model schematically. The boxes represent variables already defined, with lines and arrows indicating causal patterns and alleged causal direction. Plus and minus signs denote positive and negative relationships, respectively; dotted lines indicate relationships which apply only to complex organizations, as that concept is defined below.

FIGURE 1. INTERRELATIONS AMONG TECHNICAL, INSTITUTIONAL, AND ADMINISTRATIVE FACTORS IN PRODUCTION ORGANIZATIONS

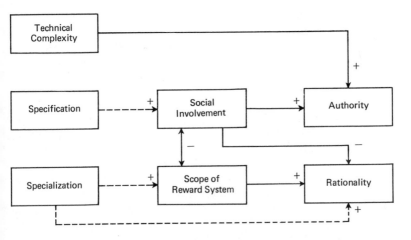

TECHNICAL COMPLEXITY AND AUTHORITY

The relationship between technical complexity and authority is contextual, relative to the other relationships in the model. In an earlier paper I discussed in some detail two assumptions.[7] From these assumptions — (1) that technical complexity plus one is a valid measure of the number of items to which administrative attention must be given in order to assure production flow, and (2) that five such items is the maximum effective limit of the human span of attention — it follows that:

1. Organizations having a technical complexity of five or more tend to possess at least three levels of authority.

The results in Table 1 confirm this hypothesis; a similar result was reported in the earlier paper.

TABLE 1.

	Authority >3	Authority <3
Technical complexity $\geqslant 5$	9	1
Technical complexity <5	1	19
$Q = +.98$ $x^2 = 18.01$ $p < .001$		

[7] Stanley H. Udy, Jr., "The Structure of Authority in Nonindustrial Production Organizations," *American Journal of Sociology*, LXIV (May, 1959), 582-84.

The argument maintains only that technical complexity determines a minimum amount of authority consistent with gross effectiveness. Presumably, other circumstances may have the effect of increasing the number of levels of authority beyond the technical minimum and also, conceivably, of decreasing the number of levels, presumably at the expense of effectiveness. Over-all technical complexity thus emerges as essentially a base line relative to which other effects alleged by the model must be observed. It is not, however, continuous in its effects; it serves, rather, to differentiate organizations into types. Accordingly, in the remainder of the analysis, we shall distinguish between simple organizations (where technical complexity is less than five) and complex organizations (where technical complexity is five or greater). The findings appear not only to justify the establishment of different base lines but also to indicate that other qualitative distinctions are involved as well.

As Figure 1 suggests, not only does total technical complexity have this effect on the structure of authority, but two components of technical complexity — specification and specialization — are alleged to have in and of themselves separate effects on other aspects of organization. The implied formal properties of the system demand some clarification. Technical complexity requires administrative attention, which, in turn, "generates" a minimal structure of authority. For present purposes it is assumed that it makes no difference whether the attention required results from specification, specialization, or, for that matter, combined effort — insofar as the direct relationship with authority is concerned. However, specification in itself is alleged to affect social involvement through a different, essentially ecological and adaptive mechanism quite independent of its generation of a need for integrative administrative attention. Similarly, specialization per se is alleged to affect rationality and the scope of rewards through a mechanism which is different from its contribution to the required level of over-all administrative attention. It thus would appear proper to treat technical complexity, specification, and specialization as three separate variables, provided one bears in mind that from a purely formal standpoint (1) a high level of technical complexity implies as a minimum a high level of either specification or specialization, with attendant consequences, and (2) a low level of technical complexity severely restricts the possible ranges of variation of both specification and specialization.

SPECIFICATION, SOCIAL INVOLVEMENT, AND AUTHORITY

One would expect specification to have organizational consequences quite independent of its effect as a component of technical complexity, on the basis of ecological reasoning. For specification per se involves (1) redefinition of proximate organizational objectives, and (2) reallocation of personnel and resources. It is in the social setting of the organization that objectives are ultimately evaluated and personnel and resources procured. Consequently one would expect specification in particular to involve adaptive problems vis-à-vis the external environment. Therefore:

2. The more specification, the more social involvement.

As alleged in the model, social involvement in turn tends to lead to an expansion in the number of levels of authority beyond the technical minimum. Any organization is faced with the problem of legitimating the authority system. In a socially involved administrative system, general differences in societal status are carried over into the organization and act as a basis for such institutionalization; differences in authority are perceived as legitimate on external social grounds. When legitimation of authority occurs in this way, however, the social selection of the status system is presumably governed by the conditions of proposition 1. The number of levels differentiated in the external system must be at least as great as the technically required minimum; otherwise the organization will not be effective. There is, however, no technical reason why the external status system cannot distinguish more levels than the minimum requirement. If it does, under conditions of social involvement, such "extra" levels will presumably also be carried over into the administrative system. Under the assumption that a one-to-one correspondence between minimum technical requirements and number of levels of status in any available external system is unlikely, one therefore infers that:

3. The more social involvement, the more levels of authority, over and above the technical minimum.

Table 2 shows the results of a rank correlation test of propositions 2 and 3. The results are generally consistent with the hypotheses but indicate that social involvement is affected by specification only under conditions of complexity. In part, this would have to be true on purely formal grounds, inasmuch as specification cannot by definition vary greatly in simple organizations. Such variation as it does exhibit, however, appears to have little or no relationship to social involvement; furthermore, simple organizations are just as socially involved as complex ones (the average rank is 3.3 for each type). The implication is that specification controls social involvement under conditions of complexity; whereas social involvement can vary independently under conditions of simplicity. Evidently simple organizations are indeed so simple from a technical viewpoint that operations can be carried on effectively regardless of the mode of institutionalization. Maintenance of a given pattern of interdependence among substructures is essentially not a problem.

As regards social involvement and authority, the fact that the correla-

TABLE 2. SPECIFICATION, SOCIAL INVOLVEMENT, AND
AUTHORITY (ZERO-ORDER VALUES OF KENDALL'S τ)

	Entire Sample (N = 30)	Simple Organizations (N = 20)	Complex Organizations (N = 10)
Specification/Social involvement	+ .31	+ .10	+ .90
Social involvement/Authority	+ .28	+ .41	+ .81

tions appear higher for both simple and complex organizations separately than for the entire sample lends support to the alleged status of over-all technical complexity as a variable of the context. It also appears that the correlation is higher for complex than for simple organizations. This again may be interpreted as indicating that complexity increases the salience of organizational solidarity; where operations are relatively simple, organization can be quite loosely knit and still be adequate to the task at hand. But as complexity increases, the degree of interdependence among substructures becomes greater. Such broad interpretations can, of course, hardly rest on these findings alone. They are mentioned at this point, however, because they are also suggested by findings elsewhere in the model.

SPECIALIZATION, SCOPE OF REWARDS AND RATIONALITY

Like specification, specialization also has organizational consequences of its own which are independent of its effects as a component of over-all technical complexity. For a large number of specialized activities implies an emphasis on specificity of administrative roles if structural co-operation is to occur. This suggests explicit agreement in the organization as to what the members are supposed to be doing. Therefore:

4. The more specialization, the more rationality.

As the number of specialized activities increases, furthermore, the problem of differentiating the persons performing them becomes increasingly acute. Presumably this could be done by means of social involvement. Indeed, certain social criteria of assignment of roles are well known to be universal, such as division of labor on the basis of sex. Unlike the case of specification, however, there is no mechanism involved in specialization per se which would tend to bring the organization into contact with its external setting and hence actually produce more social involvement as specialization increases (the actual τ value is − .11). If social involvement is already present for some other reason, it presumably can provide a basis for differentiation and assignment of roles, but if not, there is no reason to believe that it will be produced by anything inherent in specialization. An alternative mode of differentiation, internal to the organization and hence subject to the effects of specialization, is the attachment of differential rewards to positions and activities. Hence, assuming the model to be exhaustive:

5. The greater the degree of specialization, the greater the scope of the system of rewards.

A reward system which is broad in scope links organizational activity directly to personal motivation and hence supports incentives to organized planning. Therefore:

6. The more extensive the system of rewards, the more rationality.

These hypotheses were likewise tested by rank correlation, with the results shown in Table 3. Again, the results are generally consistent with the hypotheses, but with the suggestion again that administration is not a technical problem in simple organizations. Also, the relationships appear less pronounced than in the previous series, suggesting that possibly the model is open to more question at these points.

TABLE 3. SPECIALIZATION, RATIONALITY, AND SCOPE OF REWARD SYSTEM (ZERO-ORDER VALUES OF KENDALL'S τ)

	Entire Sample (N = 30)	*Simple Organizations* (N = 20)	*Complex Organizations* (N = 10)
Specialization/Rationality	+ .23	+ .05	+ .39
Specialization/Scope	+ .21	+ .07	+ .41
Scope/Rationality	+ .44	+ .41	+ .33

SOCIAL INVOLVEMENT, SCOPE OF REWARDS AND RATIONALITY

Social involvement and a system of rewards emerge as potentially competing ways of institutionalizing administrative activity. It appears that under some circumstances social involvement overrides rewards or renders them superfluous, while under others the opposite is true. Rewards, for example, can be removed by forcible action and work still compelled, if enough social involvement is present. It is also conceivable that social involvement can be adequate to differentiate roles, thus rendering differentiation by rewards unnecessary, at least on cognitive grounds. On the other hand, a broadening scope of rewards can undermine a traditional system of obligations, as for example in the case of the introduction of general media of exchange in folk society. Thus, apparently for a variety of reasons:

7. Social involvement and scope of the system of rewards vary inversely in a reciprocal causal relationship.

Social involvement by definition implies the introduction of ascriptive elements into recruitment and assignment. Therefore:

8. The more social involvement, the less rationality.

Rank correlation of the variables in propositions 7 and 8 yields the results shown in Table 4. Again the relationships seem more marked in the case of complex organization, particularly as regards social involvement and scope of rewards. The inverse relationship between social involvement and rationality on the other hand seems ubiquitous. Complex organizations appear to be neither more or less socially involved nor more or less rational than do simple organizations. The average rank of social involvement for both types is 3.3, and the average rank of rationality, 1.8. However, complex organizations appear possibly to possess systems of rewards of somewhat broader scope than do simple ones (the average ranks are 3.8 and 3.1, respectively). This may indicate that rewards do not begin to interact with social involvement until they reach some minimal threshold of importance.

TABLE 4. SOCIAL INVOLVEMENT, SCOPE OF REWARD SYSTEM, AND RATIONALITY (ZERO-ORDER VALUES OF KENDALL'S τ)

	Entire Sample (N = 30)	Simple Organizations (N = 20)	Complex Organizations (N = 10)
Social involvement/Scope	− .34	− .36	− .61
Social involvement/Rationality	− .89	− .87	− .94

The results by and large sustain the realistic character of the model proposed, particularly in the case of complex organizations. In simple organizations, certain of the proposed relationships are attenuated or disappear entirely. This might be because (1) the technical system is so simple that virtually any administrative form can adapt to it; (2) organizational solidarity becomes more important as complexity increases; and (3) the scope of rewards is too narrow in simple organizations to be felt in terms of social involvement.

Alternative explanations, equally consistent with the empirical findings, are of course possible. One could, for example, maintain that rational planning can rid the organization of social involvement, that social involvement produces specification, and so forth. We have alleged those which seem most plausible in view of existing theory and research. For example, in view of the fact that social involvement stems from the setting within which rationality takes place, it seems plausible that it influences rationality, rather than the other way around, at least most of the time. This contention is also in accord with most findings on human relations. It is easier to explain the differences in specification and social involvement between simple and complex organizations if one assumes the explanation of cause and effect posited in the model, although it may well be true that under certain conditions socially involved organizations "invent" extra specified tasks to fill idle time if the system is already complex. As regards the including of additional arrows in the model, given the present data, one must again rely largely on verbal theoretical reasoning. The presence of tied ranks, as well as the numbers of cases, ruled out the possibility of partial correlation; the fact that the data could not defensibly be converted to interval ordinal scales unfortunately ruled out causal analysis of the type proposed by Simon and Blalock — a method of analysis which otherwise would seem particularly appropriate.[8] It should, however, perhaps be noted that when all variables are correlated, the τ values for relationships not alleged by the model are in all instances lower than those where direct causal relationships are alleged.

This rough model illustrates the relevance of technical and institutional features to certain aspects of administrative structure. Furthermore, if the relationships alleged are correct, they suggest the existence of certain endemic organizational problems and tensions, and also indicate further research possibilities. The interplay of social involvement, rationality, and scope of reward system would appear to be of particular interest, especially if some measure of the efficiency of performance could be added to the model. Assuming that rationality "produces" efficiency, organizations involving a great diversity of specified tasks which are also highly specialized would be expected to face rather severe difficulties. It is possible that such difficulties are minimized through certain systems of rewards. Similarly, the technical complexity-authority-social involvement-rationality set of interrelations seems of particular relevance to problems of "human relations."[9] In any event, it is hoped that the model proposed may prove useful in ordering data in cases where technical and institutional conditions have a bearing upon administration.

[8] Herbert A. Simon, *Models of Man* (New York: John Wiley & Sons, 1957), pp. 37-49; H. M. Blalock, Jr., "Correlation and Causality: The Multivariate Case," *Social Forces*, XXXIX (March, 1961), 246-51; also see Blalock's *Social Statistics* (New York: McGraw-Hill Book Co., 1960), chap. xix.

[9] Stanley H. Udy, Jr., " 'Bureaucracy' and 'Rationality' in Weber's Organization Theory: An Empirical Study," *American Sociological Review*, XXIV (December, 1959), 791-95.

Industrialization, Ideologies, and Social Structure

Since World War II American social scientists have become preoccupied with the industrialization of underdeveloped areas. Considering the recent history of our disciplines, this is a relatively novel undertaking insofar as it involves the study of social change in complex social structures on a comparative basis. One approach to such a study consists in the selection of a social problem encountered in several societies but resolved differently in each. In a recent publication I used this approach by examining the authority relationship between employers and workers and the ideologies of management which justify that authority.[1] The present paper considers some implications of this analysis.

The first part of this essay summarizes the changes of ideology that have occurred in Anglo-American and in Russian civilization over a two-hundred year period. The second part deals with the historical significance of ideologies of management, and the third part with the theoretical implications of a study that treats such ideologies as an index of social structure. In the fourth part I turn to the problem of bureaucratization and to the difference between totalitarian and non-totalitarian forms of subordination in industry.

CHANGES IN IDEOLOGY

At the inception of industrialization in England an ideology of traditionalism prevailed; John Stuart Mill called it the "theory of dependence." According to this view the laboring poor are children, who must be governed, who should not be allowed to think for themselves, who must perform their assigned tasks obediently and with alacrity, who must show deference to their superiors, and who — if they only conduct them-

Reprinted by permission of the author and the American Sociological Association from the *American Sociological Review*, 24 (October 1959), pp. 613-623. This article is a revised text of the MacIver Lecture delivered before the District of Columbia Sociological Society, February 3, 1959.
[1]Reinhard Bendix, *Work and Authority in Industry*, New York: Wiley, 1956.

selves virtuously — will be protected by their betters against the vicissitudes of life. This interpretation of authority is self-confirming and self-serving.[2] But it sets up the presumption that the dependence of the poor and the responsibility of the rich are the valid moral rules of the social order. In the course of industrial development these ideas were gradually modified. As the responsibility of the rich was increasingly rejected by the advocates of laissez-faire, the dependence of the poor was turned from an inevitable into a self-imposed fate. As it was "demonstrated" that the rich cannot care for the poor without decreasing the national wealth, it was also asserted that by abstinence and exertion the poor can better their lot. The same virtues which in the 18th century were extolled so that the lowly will not aspire above their station were praised by the middle of the 19th century because they enable a man to raise himself by his own efforts.

In England, and even more in America, this praise of effort led toward the end of the 19th century to an apotheosis of the struggle for existence. The militant language of an ethics of the jungle was applied to the relations between employers and workers. Riches and poverty merely reflect differences of ability and effort. The employer's success is evidence of his fitness for survival, and as such justifies his absolute authority over the enterprise. This assertion of authority has a clear-cut meaning only as long as most managerial functions are in the hands of one man. The idea becomes ambiguous as the use of expertise in the management of enterprises increases and the managerial function becomes subdivided and specialized. Yet the idea of the employer's absolute authority over his enterprise coincided with the "scientific management" movement which sought to give him expert advice on what to do with that authority. It may be suggested, therefore, that the doctrines of Social Darwinism gradually lost their appeal, in part because changes in industrial organization gave rise to a changing imagery of men in industry. From the Gilded Age to the 1920s, workers and managers were self-evident failures or successes in a struggle for survival, in which they were the recalcitrant objects or the exasperated originators of managerial commands. Today they have become individuals-in-groups whose skills must be improved and allocated systematically and whose productivity must be maximized by appropriate attention to their psychological makeup. Thus, over the past two hundred years, managerial ideologies in Anglo-American civilization have changed from the "theory of dependence" to laissez-faire, to Social Darwinism, and finally to the "human relations" approach.

---

[2] The laboring poor are asked to prove their virtue by their obedience, but they are also told that their dependence results from a natural inferiority. Similarly, the ruling classes are said to be responsible for the deserving poor, and if they do not meet this responsibility, it is only, they say, because the poor who suffer are not deserving.

In the Russian development we also find the assertion of paternal authority and of child-like dependence, and in much the same terms as in England. But in Russia this ideology of traditionalism was a very different thing from what it was in England because of the Tsar's assertion of supreme authority over all the people. This authority remained intact regardless of how many privileges the Tsar granted to the landlords and regardless of how rarely he interfered in fact with the use and abuse of these privileges. Ideologically the Tsar maintained his preeminence through repeated assertions concerning his paternal care and responsibility for all of "his" people. Through repeated petitions and sporadic revolts the people used this Tsarist claim in order to obtain redress for their grievances against landlords and employers. Finally, because of the early centralization of authority under the Muscovite rulers, the whole distribution of wealth and rank among the aristocracy turned upon the competition for favors at the Court and hence reenforced the Tsar's supremacy.[3]

During the second half of the 19th century this pattern of Tsarist autocracy had far-reaching consequences. The dislocations incident to the emancipation of the serfs (1861) and the development of industry brought in their train assertions of absolute authority by the employers, efforts of the workers to organize themselves, and sporadic attempts of the government to regulate the relationship between them. Although ostensibly acting on an equitable basis, the government in fact supported the employers against the workers. Much of this is again broadly familiar from the English experience; but Russia's historical legacies prevented the shift in ideology which has been described for England. As long as Tsarist autocracy remained intact neither the rejection of responsibility by the Tsar and the ruling strata nor the demand for the self-dependence of the workers developed. Instead, the Tsar and his officials continued to espouse the ideology of traditionalism. Quite consistently, Tsarist officials sought to superintend both employers and workers in order to mitigate or suppress the struggles between them. That is, the officials aided *and* curbed the employers' exercise of authority as well as the workers' efforts to formulate grievances and organize protest movements.

Tsarist autocracy was overthrown in the Russian revolutions of 1905

[3] In Russia the landed aristocracy never succeeded in making itself the unavoidable intermediary between the ruler and the people in contrast with Western Europe, where the ruler's administrative and juridical authority in effect ended at the boundaries of the estate, though this contrast merely states the end-result of protracted struggles over the division of authority. Cf. Max Weber, *Wirtschaft und Gesellschaft*, Tuebingen: Mohr, 1925, II, Chapter 7 and esp. pp. 720-723, and Otto Hintze, "Weltgeschichtliche Bedingungen der Repräsentativverfassung," *Historische Zeitschrift*, 143 (1931), pp. 1-47.

and 1917. Although vast differences were brought about by the revolution, the managerial ideology of Tsarism lived on in a modified form. In theory, Tsarist officials had regarded employers and workers as equally subject to the will of the Tsar; loyal submission to that will was the mark of good citizenship. In theory, Lenin believed that all workers were equal participants in the management of industry and government; their loyal submission to the Communist party represented their best interest and expressed their sovereign will. The logic of Lenin's as of the Tsarist position is that under a sovereign authority the same person or organization can and should perform both subordinate and superordinate functions. For example, Soviet labor unions approach the ideal of workers' control of industry when they are called upon to participate in the management of industry. But they also function in a managerial capacity when they inculcate labor discipline among their members under the authoritative direction of the Communist Party.

Ideologically this position is defended on the ground that the party represents the historical interests of the proletariat against the short-run interests of individuals and factions. In this orientation one can still see survivals of Tsarist autocracy since all wisdom and responsibility reside in a small group or indeed in one man who, like the Tsar, knows better than private persons what is the good of all, and cannot but wish the well-being of the people. But there is also an important difference. The leaders of the Russian revolution were faced with the task of developing self-discipline and initiative among workers if a suitable industrial workforce was to become available.[4] They proceeded to inculcate these qualities by the direct or indirect subordination of everyone to the discipline of the Communist party. This policy continued the Tsarist tradition by making all matters the object of organizational manipulation rather than of personal striving; but it also represented a break with the past in that it was no longer restricted to personal submission. I shall have more to say on this subject in the fourth part of this paper.

HISTORICAL SIGNIFICANCE
OF IDEOLOGICAL CHANGE

What are the historical implications of this analysis of managerial ideologies? Ruling groups everywhere, including the rulers of developing industrial societies, justify their good fortune as well as the ill fortune of those subject to their authority. Their self-serving arguments may not appear as a promising field of research; in fact, the whole development of industrialization has been accompanied by an intellectual rejection of such

---

[4] Lenin's statement that "the Russian is a bad worker" and his advocacy of the Taylor system and of electrification as the road to socialism are indicative of the fact that the problems of complex industrial organizations came to the fore at once.

ideologies as unworthy of consideration. Yet the fact is that all industrialization involves the organization of enterprises in which a few command
and many obey; and the ideas developed by the few and the many, I
believe, may be considered a symptom of changing class relations and
hence as a clue to an understanding of industrial societies.[5]

Historically, ideologies of management became significant in the transition from a pre-industrial to an industrial society. The authority exercised by employers was recognized as distinct from the authority of
government. This was a novel experience even in Western Europe where
there was precedent for such autonomy in other institutions, because the
industrial entrepreneurs were "new men" rather than a ruling class
buttressed by tradition. This was also the period during which the discipline of sociology originated. Under the impact of the French revolution society came to be conceived in terms of forces that are independent
from, as well as antagonistic to, the formal institutions of the body
politic. Some early elaborations of this key idea enable us to see the
historical significance of ideologies of management.

The authority of employers rests on the contractual acquisition of
property, which the 18th century philosophers made the conceptual
basis of the social order. In Rousseau's view that order can be and ought
to be based on a general will which presupposes that the individual acts
for the whole community. In such a society, as George Herbert Mead
has pointed out, ". . . the citizen can give laws only to the extent that his
volitions are an expression of the rights which he recognizes in others,
. . . [and] which the others recognize in him. . . ."[6] This approach
provides a model for a society based on consent so that the power of
rule-making is exercised by all and for all. This foundation of society upon
a "general will" was directly related to the institution of property. As
Mead has stated,

> If one wills to possess that which is his own so that he has absolute
> control over it as property, he does so on the assumption that everyone
> else will possess his own property and exercise absolute control over it.
> That is, the individual wills his control over his property only in so far
> as he wills the same sort of control for everyone else over property.[7]

Thus, the idea of a reciprocal recognition of rights specifically presupposed the equality of citizens as property-owners.

This implication gave pause to some 18th and 19th century philosophers. They noted that the reciprocity of rights among property owners

[5] See Bendix, *Work and Authority*, pp. xvii-xviii, 1-2.

[6] George Herbert Mead, *Movements of Thought in the Nineteenth Century*,
Chicago: University of Chicago Press, 1936, p. 21.

[7] *Ibid.*, p. 17.

based on freedom of contract does not apply to the relations between employers and workers. As early as 1807 the German philosopher Hegel formulated the problematic nature of this relationship in a manner which anticipates the modern psychology of the self, just as Rousseau's "general will" anticipates the sociological analysis of interaction. Hegel maintains that men come to a recognition of themselves through a process whereby each accepts the self-recognition of the other and is in turn accepted by him. That is, each man's sense of identity depends upon his acceptance of the identity of others and upon their acceptance of himself. In Hegel's view this reciprocity is lacking in the relation between master and servant. The master does not act towards himself as he acts towards the servant; and the servant does not do towards others what his servitude makes him do against himself. In this way the mutuality of recognition is destroyed and the relations between master and servant become one-sided and unequal.[8]

In Western Europe this inequality of the employment-relationship coincided with the ideological and institutional decline of traditional subordination. Yet while the old justifications of subordination crumbled and new aspirations were awakened among the masses of the people, their experience of inequality continued. According to Tocqueville this problem had a differential impact upon masters and servants. In the secret persuasion of his mind the master continues to think of himself as superior; but he no longer recognizes any paternal responsibilities toward the servant. Still, he wants his servants to be content with their servile condition. In effect, the master wishes to enjoy the age-old privileges without acknowledging their concomitant obligations; and the servant rebels against his subordination, which is no longer a divine obligation and is not yet perceived as a contractual obligation.

> Then it is that [in] the dwelling of every citizen . . . a secret and internal warfare is going on between powers ever rivals and suspicious of each other: the master is ill-natured and weak, the servant ill-natured and intractable; the one constantly attempts to evade by unfair restrictions his obligation to protect and to remunerate, the other his obligation to obey. The reins of domestic government dangle between them, to be snatched at by one or the other. The lines that divide authority from oppression, liberty from license, and right from might are to their eyes so jumbled together and confused that no one knows exactly what

---

[8] Georg Friedrich Wilhelm Hegel, *Phänomenologie des Geistes*, Leipzig: Felix Mainer, 1928, pp. 143, 147. My paraphrasing attempts to convey Hegel's meaning without use of his language. The relevant passages are readily accessible in C. J. Friedrich, editor, *The Philosophy of Hegel*, New York: Modern Library, 1953, pp. 399-410.

he is or what he may be or what he ought to be. Such a condition is not democracy, but revolution.[9]

In the 19th century men like Hegel, Tocqueville, and Lorenz von Stein pointed out that the spread of equalitarian ideas was causing a transition in the relations between masters and servants. This transition may be called a crisis of aspirations. In Tocqueville's words the servants "consent to serve and they blush to obey. . . . [They] rebel in their hearts against a subordination to which they have subjected themselves. . . . They are inclined to consider him who orders them as an unjust usurper of their own rights."[10] As a consequence most European countries witnessed the rise of a "fourth estate" which struggled against existing legal liabilities and for basic civil rights, above all the right to suffrage. In a parliamentary debate on Chartism, Disraeli remarked that this struggle was invested with a degree of sentiment usually absent from merely economic or political contests. To the extent that such complex movements can be characterized by a common denominator this sentiment referred, I think, to the workers' quest for a public recognition of their equal status as citizens.[11] Where this and other civil rights became accepted, such recognition compensated for the continued social and economic subordination of the workers and thus assuaged the crisis of aspirations. Moreover, the political utilization of these civil rights could lead to a recognition of basic social rights which today is embodied in the institutions of social welfare characteristic of many Western democracies.[12] The initial crisis of aspirations continued, on the other hand, where civil rights were rejected or where their acceptance was postponed for too long, leading either to an eventual revolutionary upheaval as in Tsarist Russia, or to a more or less damaging exacerbation of class-relations as in Italy and France.

My hypothesis is that the break with the traditional subordination of the people gave rise to a generic problem of many industrial societies.[13]

[9] Alexis de Tocqueville, *Democracy in America*, New York: Vintage Books, 1945, II, p. 195. Some phrases in the preceding paragraph are also taken from this chapter of Tocqueville's work.

[10] *Ibid.*

[11] See Bendix, *Work and Authority*, pp. 34-46, 150-162. I deal with this aspect in more detail in a forthcoming monograph on *Class Relations and European Industrialization.*

[12] For a perceptive analysis of this development see T. H. Marshall, *Citizenship and Social Class*, Cambridge: At the University Press, 1950, Chapter 1. The statement in the text refers specifically to England. Social rights have been instituted in other ways, sometimes in order to withhold the establishment of civil rights as in Imperial Germany.

[13] An expanded statement of this point will be found in my article "A Study of Managerial Ideologies," *Economic Devolpment and Cultural Change*, 5 (January, 1957), pp. 118-128.

The question of 19th century Europe concerned the terms on which a society undergoing industrialization will incorporate its newly recruited industrial work force within the economic and political community of the nation. Ideologies of management are significant because they contribute to each country's answer to this question. In England the workers were invited to become their own masters, if they did not wish to obey; in Russia they were told that their subordination was less onerous than it seemed, because their own superiors were also servants of the almighty Tsar.

THEORETICAL SIGNIFICANCE OF IDEOLOGIES

What are the theoretical implications of this approach? Ideologies of management may be considered indexes of the flexibility or rigidity with which the dominant groups in the two countries were prepared to meet the challenge from below. This "preparedness" or collective tendency to act is analogous to the concept of character-structure in the individual: it may be defined as an "inner capacity" for recreating similar lines of action under more or less identical conditions.[14] The ideologies of management, which reflect this "inner capacity," naturally provoke new challenges and these in turn lead to new managerial responses, so that at the societal level there is a replication of the action-reaction process so typical of interaction among individuals.

An analysis of this process must deal with those explicitly formulated ideas that are as close as possible to the collective experience of employers and workers. This social philosophizing of and for the ordinary man as a participant occurs at a level somewhere between his attitudes as an individual and the sophisticated formulations of the social theorist. Such philosophizing is exemplified by what Andrew Ure wrote in his *Philosophy of Manufacturers* or by what the publicity-men for General Motors say in their pamphlet *Man to Man on the Job*. However, the serious analysis of such documents is at variance with the prevailing tendency to dismiss them as obviously biased and hence unworthy of consideration on their own terms. Marx, it may be recalled, reserved some of his choicest invective for his characterization of Ure's book, and in this respect Marx was a forerunner of the intellectuals born in the 1850s and 1860s. Freud, Durkheim, Pareto, and others shared with Marx the search

---

[14] The quoted phrase occurs in Burckhardt's definition of the objective of culture-history, which "goes to the heart of past mankind [because] it declares what mankind *was, wanted, thought, perceived,* and *was able to do.* In this way culture history deals with what is constant, and in the end this constant appears greater and more important than the momentary, a quality appears to be greater and more instructive than an action. For actions are only the individual expressions of a certain inner capacity, which is always able to recreate these same actions. Goals and presuppositions are, therefore, as important as events." See Jacob Burckhardt, *Griechische Kulturgeschichte*, Stuttgart: Kroener, 1952, Vol. I, p. 6.

for some underlying principle or force that could explain the manifest beliefs and actions making up the external record of individual and collective behavior.[15] Many writers of this generation were less interested in what a man said, than in why he said it. Accordingly, ideologies of management might be dismissed because they *merely* express a class-interest, or because they do not reveal the *real* attitudes of the employers, or because they disguise *actual* exploitative practices, or because all this talk tells us nothing about man's behavior or about his personality structure. These various objections have in common an intellectual preoccupation with covert forces that can explain the manifest content of the social world.

Modern social science owes to this intellectual tradition many important insights, but also many of its aberrations. Where the phenomena of the social world are treated merely as the reflection of "hidden forces," speculation easily becomes uncontrolled with the result that observable evidence is dismissed from consideration as being "irrelevant" or "uninteresting" on theoretical grounds. The difficulty is familiar in Marx's theory of history which encouraged him to treat whole series of facts as epiphenomena, such as the "false consciousness" of the workers that was bound to be superseded in the course of history. Similarly, the Freudian approach tends to devalue a behavioristic study of social life because it deals with the appearance rather than the underlying motivations of social action. Again, the use of organic analogies in the study of society treats all actions as dependent adjustments to other actions (or environmental conditions); consequently this approach devalues all deliberate and all innovative activity, since upon analysis such activity will be revealed as yet another dependent adjustment. In in-expert hands all of these approaches lead to a cavalier construction of the evidence which can always be more easily imputed to the "underlying determinants" than analyzed in detail on its own ground.

Yet human experience occurs at this phenomenological level — and the study of ideologies of management illustrates that it can also provide an approach to our understanding of the social structure.[16] The managerial interpretations of the authority relationship in economic enterprises together with the workers' contrast-conception concerning their

[15] Cf. H. Stuart Hughes, *Consciousness and Society*, New York: Knopf, 1958, which gives a perceptive analysis of this "generation."

[16] By "ideologies" I do not refer to attitudes of the type that can be elicited in a questionnaire study, but to the "constant process of formulation and reformulation by which spokesmen identified with a social group seek to articulate what they sense to be its shared understandings." See *Work and Authority*, p. xxii. I call these articulations "ideologies" in the specific sense of "ideas considered in the context of group-action." All ideas may be analyzed from this viewpoint; hence I depart from the identification of "ideologies" with false or misleading ideas.

collective position in an emerging industrial society constitute a composite image of class relations which has changed over time and which also differs from country to country. This aspect of the changing social structure may be studied by examining each ideological position in terms of its logical corollaries as these relate to the authority of the employers and in a wider sense to the class position of employers and workers in the society. Where these corollaries create major problems for the complacent self-interest of the group, one may expect the development of tensions, and perhaps of change, ideologically and institutionally.[17]

Such ideologies, and this is a second level of analysis, are in part expediential rationalizations for the problems confronting the entrepreneur, and in part the result of historically cumulative response-patterns among social groups. In this way ideologies are formulated through the constant interplay between current contingencies and historical legacies. As Marx put it, "men make their own history," but they do so "under circumstances directly given and transmitted from the past." (Marxian dogmatism consistently sacrificed the first to the second part of this generalization.[18] Accordingly, ideologies of management can be explained only in part as rationalizations of self-interest; they also result from the legacy of institutions and ideas which is "adopted" by each generation much as a child "adopts" the grammar of his native language. Historical legacies are thus a part of the social structure: they should not be excluded from a discipline that focuses attention upon the persistence of group-structures. In the following section an attempt is made to show

---

[17] For example, at the turn of the century American employers asserted their absolute authority over the workers but this assertion lacked content until the bureaucratization of industry brought to the fore experts who worked out methods for the exercise of authority. Again, the Tsar's assertion of authority over all the people inadvertently encouraged the peasants to appeal to the Tsar for redress of grievances. This procedure is adapted from that used by Max Weber in his sociology of religion.

[18] The sentence immediately following this quotation reads: "The tradition of all the dead generations weighs like a nightmare on the brain of the living." See Karl Marx, *The 18th Brumaire of Louis Bonaparte*, New York: International Publishers, n.d., p. 13. I do not accept this polemical exaggeration, since traditions are enabling as well as disabling, but the emphasis upon the impact of cultural tradition on current ideologies is more in line with the facts than the effort to explain the latter solely in terms of the problems the businessman encounters in his work. Such an interpretation leads to an elimination of ideological changes, and of differences between ideologies, since all ideologies are in this sense responses to the strains endemic in modern society. Cf. Francis X. Sutton et al., *The American Business Creed*, Cambridge: Harvard University Press, 1956, *passim*, where the change of business ideologies over time is denied and where these idealogies are explained in exactly the same terms as nationalism and anti-capitalism. See also the comments of Leland Jenks, "Business Ideologies," *Explorations of Entrepreneurial History*, 10 (October, 1957), pp. 1-7.

the link between historical legacies and the structure of industrial societies by relating ideologies of management to the bureaucratization of industry.

IDEOLOGIES, INDUSTRIAL BUREAUCRACY, AND TOTALITARIANISM

Since the 18th century Anglo-American and Russian civilizations have witnessed a growing managerial concern with the attitudes as well as the productivity of workers. It is possible to relate this change of ideology to a large number of the developments which comprise the transition from an early to a mature industrial society. The changing structure of industrial organizations was only one of these developments. Yet the bureaucratization of economic enterprises is of special importance for any attempt to "interpret the difference of fact and ideology between a totalitarian and nontotalitarian form of subordination in economic enterprises."[19] Bureaucratization is also especially suitable for a comparative study of authority relations in industry, since it involves processes that are directly comparable in two such different civilizations as England and Russia. This choice of focus deliberately eschews a comprehensive theory of society in favor of selecting a problem which, if suitable for comparative analysis, will also lead to an analysis of social structures. For, if comparable groups in different societies confront and over time resolve a common problem, then a comparative analysis of their divergent resolutions will reveal the divergence of social structures in a process of change.[20]

Problems of a systematic management of labor come to the fore where the increasing complexity of economic enterprises makes their operation more and more dependent upon an *ethic of work performance*. This ethic involves a degree of steady intensity of work, reasonable accuracy, and a compliance with general rules and specific orders that falls somewhere between blind obedience and unpredictable caprice. Where personal supervision is replaced by impersonal rules the efficiency of an organization will vary with the degree to which these attributes of work-performance are realized, and this realization is part of the on-going bureaucratization of economic enterprises. That is to say, management subjects the conditions of employment to an impersonal systematization, while the employees seek to modify the implementation of the rules as their personal interests and their commitment (or lack of commitment)

---

[19] *Work and Authority*, p. xx.

[20] Here again I am indebted to the work of Max Weber, although more to what he did in his own studies than to what he wrote about them in his methodology. See my forthcoming *Max Weber, An Intellectual Portrait*, New York: Doubleday, 1960, Chapter 8.

to the goals of the organization dictate. As everyone knows, there is no more effective means of organizational sabotage than a letter-perfect compliance with all the rules and a consistent refusal of the employees to use their own judgment. "Beyond what commands can effect and supervision can control, beyond what incentives can induce and penalties prevent, there exists an exercise of discretion important even in relatively menial jobs, which managers of economic enterprises seek to enlist for the achievement of managerial ends."[21] In the literature on organizations this exercise of discretion by subordinates is known by a number of terms: Veblen called it the "withdrawal of efficiency"; Max Weber referred to it as the bureaucratic tendency towards secrecy; Herbert Simon might call it the "zone of non-acceptance." I have suggested the phrase "strategies of independence" so as to get away from the negative connotations of the other terms, since the exercise of discretion may serve to achieve, as well as to subvert, the goals of an organization.

Now, the great difference between totalitarian and nontotalitarian forms of subordination consists in the managerial handling of this generic attribute of all authority relations. The historical legacies of some Western countries have encouraged management to presuppose the existence of a common universe of discourse between superiors and subordinates, and this presupposition is related to the successful resolution of the crisis of aspirations. From the evangelism and the tough-minded laissez-faire approach of 18th century England to the latest refinement of the "human relations" approach, managerial appeals have been addressed to the good faith of subordinates in order to enlist their cooperation. Whether such good faith existed is less important than that such appeals were made, though it is probable that in England and the United States large masses of workers in one way or another accepted managerial authority as legitimate even if they were indifferent to, or rejected, the managerial appeals themselves.[22] In Russia, on the other hand, historical legacies did *not* encourage management (under the Tsars) to presuppose the existence of a common universe of discourse between superiors and subordinates. From the time of Peter the Great to the period of rapid industrial growth in the last decades preceding World

[21] *Work and Authority*, p. 251. To avoid a possible misunderstanding I add that this assertion, which is elaborated in *ibid.*, pp. 244-251, is in my judgment compatible with the endeavor to put managerial decision-making on a more scientific basis. The substitution of machine methods for manual operations is obviously an on-going process that has greatly curtailed the areas of possible discretion, although machine methods also create new opportunities for discretionary judgments. But while these methods and organizational manipulations may curtail and reallocate the areas in which discretion is possible or desired, and may in this way achieve greater efficiency, they cannot, I believe, eliminate discretion.

[22] Cf. *Work and Authority*, pp. 248-249, for a fuller statement.

War I managerial appeals were addressed to the workers' duty of obedience towards all those in positions of authority. Whether or not the workers actually developed a sense of duty the appeals presupposed that they had not. Accordingly, officials and managers did not rely on the good faith among their subordinates, but attempted instead to eliminate the subordinates' strategies of independence.

This managerial refusal to accept the tacit evasion of rules and norms or the uncontrolled exercise of judgment is related to a specific type of bureaucratization which constitutes the fundamental principle of totalitarian government. In such a regime the will of the highest party authorities is absolute in the interest of their substantive objectives. The party may disregard not only all formal procedures by which laws are validated but also its own previous rulings; and where norms may be changed at a moment's notice, the rule of law is destroyed. Totalitarianism also does away with the principle of a single line of authority. Instead of relying on an enactment of laws and on the supervision of their execution from the top, totalitarian regimes use the heirarchy of the party in order to expedite and control at each step the execution of orders through the regular administrative channels. This may be seen as the major device by which such regimes seek to prevent officials from escaping inspection while compelling them to use their expertise in an intensified effort to implement the orders of the regime. A totalitarian government is based, therefore, on two interlocking hierarchies of authority. The work of every factory, of every governmental office, of every unit of the army or the secret police, as well as every cultural or social organization, is programmed, coordinated, and supervised by some agency of government. But it is also propagandized, expedited, criticized, spied upon, and incorporated in special campaigns by an agency of the totalitarian party, which is separately responsible to the higher party authorities.

The rationale of this principle of a double government can be stated within the framework of Max Weber's analysis of bureaucracy. An ideally functioning bureaucracy in his sense is the most efficient method of solving large-scale organizational tasks. But this is true only *if* these tasks involve a more or less stable orientation towards norms which seek to maintain the rule of law and to achieve an equitable administration of affairs. These conditions are absent where tasks are assigned by an omnipotent *and* revolutionary authority. Under the simulated combat conditions of a totalitarian regime the norms that govern conduct do not stay put for any length of time, although each norm in turn will be the basis of an unremitting drive for prodigies of achievement. In response, subordinates will tend to use their devices of concealment for the sake of systematic, if tacit, strategies of independence. They will do so not only for reasons of convenience, but because the demands made upon them by the regime are "irrational" from the viewpoint of expert knowledge and systematic procedure.[23] The party, on the other hand, seeks to prevent the types of concealment that make such collective strategies possible by putting every worker and official under maximum pressure to utilize their expertise to the fullest extent. This is the rationale of a double hierarchy of government, which places a party functionary at the side of every work unit in order to prevent concealment and to apply pressure. The two hierarchies would be required, even if all key positions in government and industry were filled by party functionaries. For a functionary turned worker or official would still be responsible for "overfulfilling" the plan, while the new party functionary would still be charged with keeping that official under pressure and surveillance.[24]

In this way totalitarianism replaces the old system of stratification by a new one based on criteria of activism and party orthodoxy. The ethic of work performance on which this regime relies is not the product of century-long growth as in the West, but of material incentives and of a political supervision that seeks to prevent evasion from below as well as from above. For example, the collective "bargaining" agreements of Soviet industry are in fact declarations of loyalty in which individuals and groups pledge themselves publicly to an overfulfillment of the plan, while the subsequent organization of public confessionals, the manipulation of status differences between activists and others, the principle of collective leadership, and further devices seek to maximize performance and prevent the "withdrawal of efficiency." The individual subordinate is surrounded almost literally. Aside from ordinary incentives he is controlled by his superior and by the party agitator who stands at the side of his superior; but he is also controlled "from below" in the sense that the social pressures of his peer group are manipulated by party agitators and their agents. This institutionalization of suspicion and the consequent elimination of privacy are justified on the ground that the

[23] Hence they will do so even for the purpose of achieving the objectives of the party itself. Cf. Joseph Berliner, *Factory and Manager in the USSR*, Cambridge: Harvard University Press, 1957, which documents that the most successful Soviet managers use the systematic subversion of authoritative commands for the purpose of realizing the ends of these commands as well as for their personal convenience. This fact suggests that "good faith" can be inculcated in many ways, even by the systematic distrust of all subordinates, provided of course that the distrust has a higher rationale, such as the utopian and nationalist ideology of Russian Communism.

[24] A case study of totalitarianism in the context of industrial relations is contained in *Work and Authority*, Chapter 5. For a more generalized treatment of this approach to totalitarianism, cf. Bendix, "The Cultural and Political Setting of Economic Rationality in Western and in Eastern Europe," in the forthcoming Gregory Grossman, editor, *Economic Calculation and Organization in Eastern Europe*, Berkeley: University of California Press.

party "represents" the masses, spearheads the drive for Russian industrialization, and leads the cause of world communism.

SUMMARY

The purpose of this paper is to state the case for a comparative analysis of social structures, which pays attention to the historical continuity of societies as well as to the concatenation of group structures and deliberate, self-interested action in the process of social change. In lieu of abstract considerations I have tried to make this case by analyzing some implications of ideologies of management in the course of industrialization.

The change of ideologies of management during the last two centuries in Anglo-American and in Russian civilization was similar in so far as it can be characterized as an increased managerial concern with the attitudes of workers that presumably account for their differential productivity. This overall similarity coincides, however, with a fundamental divergence. In Western civilization the authority relations between employers and workers remained a more or less autonomous realm of group activity even where the "human relations" approach has replaced the earlier individualism. In Russia, the employment relationship has been subjected throughout to a superordinate authority which regulated the conduct of employers and workers and which could transform superiors into subordinates or (more rarely) subordinates into superiors, when governmental policies seemed to warrant such action.

This comparison of ideologies of management is significant for specific historical reasons in addition to the fact that authority relations in economic enterprises are a universal attribute of industrialization and hence lend themselves to a comparative analysis. Ideologies of management became significant when the equalitarianism of property owners, brought to the fore by the French revolution and by the legal codifications which followed, was contrasted with the inequality of the employment relationship. A heightened awareness of this inequality coincided with the decline of a traditional subordination of the lower classes and hence with a rise of aspirations for social and political as well as for legal equality. In England these demands for equal rights of citizenship on the part of the lower classes eventuated in a painful but peaceful reconstitution of class relations; in Russia, the same demands were rejected and finally led to the revolutions of 1905 and 1917.

The comparative study of ideologies of management is of theoretical as well as of historical interest. Such ideologies may be considered indexes of a readiness to act, which together with the ideological responses of other groups, can provide us with a clue to the class relations of a society. Ideologies, it is assumed, are an integral part of culture, which should be analyzed on its own terms as an index of the social structure, much as the neurotic symptoms of an individual are analyzed as an index of his personality. It is further assumed that such ideologies are expediential rationalizations of what are taken to be the material interests of a group, but that such rationalizations tend to be circumscribed by the historical legacies which are a part of a country's developing social structure.

Although ideologies of management can be treated as a clue to class relations, it is also worthwhile to relate them to other aspects of the social structure. One such aspect, which is especially suitable for a comparison of totalitarian and non-totalitarian regimes, is the fact that all industrial enterprises undergo a process of bureaucratization and all bureaucracy involves the use of discretion in the execution of commands. Comparison between the Anglo-American and the Russian tradition reveals that in the two cases managerial appeals have differed in terms of whether or not they have presupposed the good faith of subordinates. Where that supposition has not been made, the drive for industrialization takes the specific form of a double hierarchy of government which is designed to apply maximum pressure on subordinates and to forestall their evasion of commands by supplementing executive with political controls at every point in the chain of command.

Both English and American and Russian industrialization have been marked by bureaucratization, and bureaucratization certainly threatens the development of initiative.[25] But the Soviet case also illustrates that this threat many provoke countermeasures. One might speak of an institutionalization of initiative in the totalitarian party and one can speculate that the dynamic drive of the Soviet regime might be jeopardized by too much relaxation of a Cold War which appears to justify that drive. This is, I submit, the new context in which the comparative study of ideologies of management will continue to be an intellectual challenge.

Political and Economic Structure

Kerr, Dunlop, Harbison, and Myers do not deny the causal potency of values, technology, and social structure but highlight an aspect of the environment affecting organizations that are

---

[25] Cf. Joseph Schumpeter, *Capitalism, Socialism and Democracy*, New York: Harper, 1950, where this theme is elaborated.

very relevant today. They emphasize as the key determinant of organizations the nature of the governing elites of each society and the policies they pursue with respect to certain critical decisions all elites must make if they wish to stimulate development. Since these elites and their policies and interests differ from country to country, so will the structure, methods, and goals of the major societal organizations. Kerr, Dunlop, Harbison, and Myers examine variations in the labor movement. They find five major types of elites that influence society: the dynastic-traditional (as in pre-Revolutionary Russia); the middle class (the United Kingdom, the United States); the revolutionary-intellectual (Cuba); the nationalist (Egypt); and the colonial (India prior to 1948, Europe's African colonies).

Baron and Tropp seek to explain differences in the nature of school teachers' authority by comparing the United States and England. In drawing attention to the influence of community and family on the teacher, they are reminiscent of Udy's stress on the effect of the environment's "institutional system" on the organization. But in going on to discuss differences in the whole structure of the educational system as a cause of differences in teacher authority, Baron and Tropp draw our attention to the fact that any organization is a part of a societal sector. The concept of societal sector is admittedly vague, but it is important nonetheless. Like the economic sector, the educational sector has its own structure, which varies from society to society and affects the structure of the specific organizations within it. Finally, Baron and Tropp see the teacher's authority in the school organization affected by the characteristics of the professional organizations to which the teacher belongs.

Anyone not familiar with the statistical concepts of "correlation" and "factor analysis" might have difficulty understanding the selection by Forward. But it is included precisely because the statistical analysis of cross-cultural indices is being employed with increasing frequency. Even apart from its methodological interest, the argument of the article is valuable, for it emphasizes the importance of a society's level of income in determining the characteristics of at least an organization such as a government bureaucracy. It also highlights the importance of other aspects of development, especially political development and the development of communications.

CLARK KERR, JOHN T. DUNLOP,
FREDERICK H. HARBISON, AND
CHARLES A. MYERS

*The Impact of Modernizing Elites
on Worker Organizations*

WORKER ORGANIZATIONS
AND THE ELITES

In the community led by each ideal type of industrializing elite distinctive worker organizations develop in conformity to the elite's grand strategy of the great transition and reinforcing its other policies. Industrialization everywhere creates organizations of workers, but they differ widely in their functions, structure, leadership, and ideology. Indeed, the term "labor organizations" is used here rather than "labor unions" to emphasize more generality and to avoid implications of forms and functions peculiar to the middle-class ideal type.

The general relationship between each of the ideal types of elites and the labor organizations which arise in the societies they seek to industrialize may be briefly characterized at the outset. The dominant labor organizations in the dynastic-led society remain foreign to the elite; they do not fit nor do they readily conform to the paternal view of the elite. The labor organizations of the middle-class elite conform and are consonant with the market. In the industrialization program of the revolutionary intellectuals the labor organizations are consistent with and conform to the state. The labor organizations of the colonial elite are not congenial to the dominant elite; they tend to be nationalist and press for independence. They are foreign to the colonialist vision of industrialization. The labor organizations under the nationalist elite are beset by a deep dilemma and divided loyalties in shaping their policies, as is developed in a later section of this chapter. These general relationships between the ideal types of elites and their labor organizations suggest that greatest conflict and tension would characterize the dynastic and colonial-led industrialization.

This section describes in turn the labor organizations which arise under each of the ideal type of elites. The labor organizations are described in terms of a list of seven features: (1) the view workers take of managers,[1] (2) the functions of labor organizations, (3) the extent of competition among labor organizations, (4) the structure of these organizations, (5) their sources of funds, (6) the sources of leadership; and (7) their ideology. Chart 1 summarizes the characteristics of labor organizations arising under the various ideal types of industrializing elites.

The Dynastic Elite

The dynastic community is characterized by workers personally dependent upon the enterprise manager. The worker looks to the paternal manager for guidance in personal, economic and social problems; community affairs are not properly his concern, but the province of the paternal elite.

The dynastic elite does not in principle encourage labor organizations. At the plant level, organizations of workers supplement and help to administer the paternal activities of the managers and the state, but they provide little effective constraint on the decisions of management. At the industry level they provide a broad form of minimum regulation which the enterprise managers often find congenial to the support of cartels or associations. These standards have little relevance to actual plant conditions, and there is little connection between the plant level and the industry level of workers' organizations. In the society led by the dynastic elite, political organizations of workers emerge which often have only indirect connections with the plant and industry levels of workers' organizations, and they seek detailed government regulation of compensation and working conditions to offset plant and industry-level weaknesses and division of workers. These political organizations also seek to challenge the established elite and conduct political demonstrations.

In the traditional society led by the dynastic elite there are frequently deep social distinctions, religious, racial, nationalist, linguistic, and political party divisions among workers. There tends to be multiple representation of workers at the plant level, as in workers' councils, and at the industry level, as in negotiations for agreements signed by several overlapping workers' organizations. Among these organizations at the plant and industry level, and in political activities, there may be keen rivalry and competition. In the absence of exclusive jurisdiction or ex-

---

[1] In a consistent and stable industrial relations system these attitudes are the converse of the views of managers toward industrial workers. [See Chapter 7 of Kerr, *et al.*, *op. cit.*]

clusive representation for the majority organization, the rivalry is limited since it need not end in extinction for any of the competitors. Majority rule does not apply with the winner-take-all. Changing conditions lead to relative shifts in workers' support, but the existence of the organizations is not endangered. There may also be keen competition between organizations at the plant level and at the national level over the distribution of functions. Any competition among workers' organizations is lamented; it is tolerated as an unavoided consequence of historical divisions in the traditional society.

The dynastic elite tends to build organizations which provide minimum regulation on an industry basis, without a direct line of control to the plant level. The labor organization is constricted on the one hand by work-level groups, such as workers' councils, over which it has little, if any, control, and the political organs which seek regulative legislation. The labor organization operates in a relatively narrow corridor between plant groups and the political parties. There is strong internal confederation control which may be further limited by rival confederations.

The operations of labor organizations, as any other, are much influenced by the funds at their disposal and the source of their finances. Under the dynastic elite labor organizations tend to be relatively poorly financed. There are a variety of competitors for support by the workers — work-level organizations, national level groups, and political parties — and their access to workers for funds is not often coordinated. The paternal characteristics of the system are not congenial to large dues payments. The focus of the society around the family, state, and religion is not congenial to the financial support of vigorous voluntary associations. Labor organizations do not place a high preference upon building strong financial positions in view of their major activities. Labor organizations are a movement, and movements are not primarily concerned with finances. At times the government may provide some resources in the form of buildings, a subsidy for the operation of labor exchanges, or social insurance services, or pay the salaries of some leaders who may fill some nominal public function in exchange for loyalty.

Leadership of labor organizations may be drawn from the ranks or from intellectuals outside the organizations or be imposed from a party or subject to government approval. The leadership of labor organizations in the country under the dynastic elite tends to be drawn from those ideologically oriented toward political activities and from intellectuals. The activities of the labor organizations, as opposed to works councils and enterprise or plant bodies, are primarily at the industry and national level. The emphasis upon social policy and law places a relative premium upon learning. The absence of plant level problems as a concern in these organizations decreases the need for leadership more familiar

CHART 1. WORKER ORGANIZATIONS AND THE ELITES

Industrializing Elite	Dynastic	Middle-Class	Revolutionary-Intellectuals	Colonials	Nationalists
View toward workers	Personally dependent upon managers in time of need.	Independent workers.	Class of dependent workers.	Dependent upon foreigners.	Partners in the new nation.
Functions of workers' organizations	Social functions at plant level; little constraint upon management. Provides minimum industry conditions by legislation. Political activity challenges the elite.	Regulates management at the local and industry level. Independent political activity accepted. Does not challenge the elite.	Instrument of party to educate, lead workers and to stimulate production. No political activity except through the party.	Largely a part of the independence and nationalist movement.	Confronts the conflicting objectives of economic development and protection of workers.
Competition among workers' organizations	Limited rivalry at the plant level and the distribution of functions between the local and industry levels. No exclusive representation.	Exclusive representation and keen competition. Some rivalry between plant and industry levels over allocation of functions.	No rivalry or competition allowed.	Divided by ideological, tactical, regional and personal leadership factions.	Tendency for consolidation among organizations recognized as loyal by nationalistic elite. Advantage over those not so recognized.

Structure of worker organizations	Relatively large number of industrial unions. Centralized confederation often limited by rival confederations. Unions perform narrow range of functions.	A variety of structural forms. Confederations not so centralized. Organizations perform a wide range of functions.	A few industrial unions. Centralized confederation. Organizations perform a narrow range of functions.	A wide variety of structures. Organizations not well developed, often personal.	Tendency toward industrial unions with one confederation acceptable to elite.
Sources of funds	Meager resources from irregular dues payments and indirect government allowances. Financial success not highly regarded by workers' organizations.	Substantial resources secured by regular dues; regulatory functions require administrative organizations and large budgets.	Substantial resources secured by assessment of all workers; financial resources present no problem with support of regime.	Meager funds often raised outside workers' organizations.	Funds often secured indirectly from government in addition to meager dues. Officers receive other salaries.
Sources of leadership	Intellectuals and those ideologically oriented toward political activity. The leader's income position is often insecure.	The ranks through lower levels of workers' organizations. They have an established career.	Reliable party leaders with experience in worker organizations. They have an established career.	Nationalist and independence leaders. Intellectuals with a personal following.	National leaders and intellectuals except where confined to manual workers.
Ideology	Class-conscious and revolutionary except for a minority.	Reformist.	Preserve the true revolution.	Independence.	Nationalism.

with the actual work processes. The income of such leaders may not always depend solely upon the labor organization, but may be based also upon political activity, legal practice, journalism, and other activities. It should not be inferred that leaders do not arise from the ranks, but the dynastic arrangements tend to favor the intellectual type for labor leadership.

The labor organizations which emerge in the course of industrialization under each ideal type of elite tend to develop a distinctive ideology or view of their place in the community. Under the dynastic elite the dominant labor organizations tend to be class-conscious and revolutionary; they advocate the drastic overhaul of the traditional society. There may also be labor organizations, particularly organized along religious lines, which are more loyal to the traditional society.

The Middle-Class Elite

The middle-class case is characterized by the independent worker. While the worker is required to follow the directions of management at the work place, as are workers everywhere, his personal affairs are his own concern within a system of rules, and in community life his vote is the equal of the manager's.

The middle-class elite is more readily reconciled to the principle of workers' organizations than the dynastic elite and supports the principle of their affirmative public value. At the plant and industry level the organizations regulate relationships with managements. There is closer coordination and often direct lines of authority in these workers' organizations between the industry and the plant level; in some cases this authority extends to a single national center, as in Sweden, at least on some questions. The political organization of workers is less concerned with detailed regulation of managements and more preoccupied with community issues. The middle-class elite regards such organized political activity as legitimate, and the workers' political organizations are less dedicated to challenge or to displace the industrializing elite.

In the society led by the middle class there is typically supposed to be one workers' organization for each type of worker by craft or industry. The scope of labor organizations often conforms to the contour of the market. There tends to be competition among contending organizations since the triumph of one means the loss of recognition to the rivals among a particular group of workers, at least for a period. A degree of competition among workers' organizations, moreover, is regarded as an affirmative good to stimulate more responsiveness to the wishes of the workers. There is relatively little overt competition, however, between organizations over the distribution of functions at the plant and industry levels, although there is internal tension in workers' organizations over the extent of centralization and decentralization of functions.

The labor organizations under the middle-class-led industrialization tend to build a variety of unions: craft, industrial, and general. The range of functions is broad, not constricted by other forms of worker organizations. The diversity in structure represents a response to a gradual historical development, to a lesser degree of confederation centralization, and to a greater responsiveness to the preferences of particular sectors and groups of workers. It also reflects an economy with more reliance upon the market mechanism under which the pattern of union growth may have had to conform to market constraints to survive. The powers of the confederation often tend to be lesser than in the other ideal types; the principles of decentralization and autonomy are highly regarded values.

The country led by the middle-class elite develops labor organizations that tend to be relatively well financed by dues regularly collected from the membership. The labor organizations seek to build strong financial positions, partly to provide more effective services to the members and partly to provide security in case of struggle with managements. The labor organizations typically receive little, if any, support or subsidy from the government (save in a few cases related to social services). Financial independence from government is a cherished value. The emphasis upon regulatory functions, in constraining management through rules at the work place, operates to create modern administrative organizations which require large-scale budgets.

The leadership of labor organizations in the middle-class-led country tends to be drawn almost exclusively from the ranks of workers. The predominate concern with rules constricting enterprise managers and the direct interest in the immediate work place necessarily place a premium upon leadership seasoned in the practical operating problems of enterprises. The intellectual would be out of place. The more direct organizational tie between plant and industry or confederation levels of workers' organizations creates more of a ladder on which leadership starts at the bottom. Full-time officers arise who regard the labor organizations as a career; they are in a sense professionals or bureaucrats of the labor organizations with a primary concern for administering and negotiating agreements with professionals in management.

The middle-class elite leads a society in which labor organizations are bargaining institutions primarily; they are mildly reformist in their ideology and attitudes toward the larger community.

The Revolutionary Intellectual

This elite regards workers as a dependent class. Industrial workers as a group are subject to managerial direction which is regarded as an expression of the elite leadership. The personal conditions of individual workers are not the concern of managers, and workers do not look to them personally, as with the dynastic elite, but the rules of the work place are paternal rather than market oriented. In community affairs the worker is to look to the leadership of the party.

The revolutionary intellectual elite regards organizations of workers at the plant or industry level as its own preserve. The purpose of the workers' organizations is less to constrain managements than to educate, to stimulate production, and to lead the industrial workers on behalf of the ruling elite. They are agents of the state to insure industrial production. Independent political organization or activity is precluded except through and under the direction of the party.

In the society led by the revolutionary intellectuals there is no room for competition between contending labor organizations at the plant level, nor is there any contention over functions to be performed by rival workers' organizations. Since the organization of workers is an instrument of the ruling party to educate and to lead workers, discordant tones serve no purpose and are not tolerated. Labor organizations are agents of the state; and there is only one state. A degree of tension may arise between plant-level representatives and those higher in the hierarchy. Competition among workers' organizations, however, is seen only as an evil, weakening the regime.

The revolutionary intellectual elite tends to create a limited number of labor organizations, industrial in form, with a high degree of centralization over district and local groups and at the confederation level. The structure reflects the deliberate design of labor organizations by the elite rather than more gradual evolution or conformance to the market. This structure also reflects the function of the organizations: to serve as the organ of education and communication between the party and the industrial workers and to stimulate industrial output. This narrow range of functions reflects a design in which the party and the state fulfill the functions of regulating or constraining managers which is elsewhere performed by labor organizations and the market. This type of organizational structure may be vulnerable to the rise of plant-level worker organizations from below as illustrated by works councils in Hungary.

In the country led by the revolutionary intellectual elite, labor organizations are relatively well financed by assessments levied upon all workers. The organizations are particularly well supplied with buildings appropriate to their status as an arm of the regime. Finances and resources are no problem.

The leadership of the labor organizations in the revolutionary-intellectual-led country tends to be drawn from reliable party leaders, many of whom have devoted a career to the work of the party in labor organizations. They are financially secure and are in a sense (with a different type of assignment) professionals or bureaucrats of the labor organization and the party. They are concerned with the administration and implementation of policy and ideology developed by the party.

Labor organizations under the revolutionary intellectuals have no ideology apart from the ruling elite. They seek to preserve the true revolution envisaged by the elite.

The Colonial Elite

The indigenous worker is envisaged as personally dependent upon the foreign manager as the agent of the colonial power. The role of labor organizations of indigenous workers tends to be largely a part of the nationalist and independence movement. After a country has passed through the portals of political independence, the dilemma of the function of labor organizations arises with perplexing urgency. There is, of course, the purpose to "consolidate independence," to "liquidate the evil remains of colonialism," and to push for the more practical objectives, in foreign firms particularly, of training local citizens to replace foreigners in managerial, technical, and highly skilled positions. The dilemmas which confront labor organizations in the newly industrializing countries are explored in a later section of this chapter.

Labor organizations under the colonial elite tend to be united on the theme of independence, but they are likely to be divided on a wide range of ideological, regional, and tactical grounds, as well as on the basis of personal leadership. The rivalry is one of slogans, programmes, and personal leadership rather than of representation or constraints on management. Under the colonial elite the workers' organizations among the indigenous workers tend to reflect a wide variety of structures. Organizations are not well developed, and they are often the reflection of personal leadership.

Labor organizations have no systematic dues collection, and they are poorly supplied with funds. Their funds may come largely from other nationalist groups. The leaders of labor organizations in the colonial community are drawn from the nationalist and independence movement; they tend to be intellectuals with a personal following. The ideology of these labor organizations is built around independence and anti-colonialism.

Nationalist Leaders

Workers in the new nationalist state regard foreign managers as a lingering vestige of colonialism and indigenous managers ideally as partners in the new nation.

The nationalist leader seeks the support of the rising group of industrial workers and is concerned to insure their reliability. Industrial workers are a strategic group to the nationalist elite. The elite tends to bestow favors upon reliable organizations and to assist in the opposition to rivals for worker support in exchange for subordination to the nationalist objectives.

This elite tends to develop more explicit and more advanced organizational structures than under the colonial elite, largely industrial in form. The tendency is to adopt the organizational forms of labor organizations from some more economically advanced country held in high prestige by the nationalist elite. The nationalist elites tend to promote reliable and loyal labor organizations and encourage the collection of membership dues for them. These dues may even be required of all workers. The elite may also provide funds directly for local organizations, and it may support reliable groups by government grants to worker education and by employment on public payrolls of a number of leaders of labor organizations.

The reliable leadership of labor organizations is drawn from nationalist leaders in the first generation after independence. The leadership includes many intellectuals responsive to the nationalist elite, except in cases in which leadership is specifically confined to manual workers. The ideology of labor organizations under the nationalist elites is that of partners in development.

THE DILEMMAS OF LABOR ORGANIZATIONS IN EARLY INDUSTRIALIZATION

Labor organizations in newly industrializing countries, particularly with a new nationalist elite, confront four questions of fundamental significance to the elites and to the labor organizations:

(1) *Wages vs. Capital Formation.* There are conflicting claims of economic development and immediately improved wages and other benefits for workers. The nationalist labor leaders' dedication to industrialization, which requires increased savings, conflicts with the labor organizations' declared purpose and their often promised gains from independence, to provide immediately improved wages and working conditions. Within some limits, higher wages may increase worker productivity, but this is likely to be a narrow and a difficult range of wage policy to find.[2]

(2) *Strikes vs. Production.* The nationalist labor leader must choose again on strike policy. Strike action tends to decrease production where successful and may make development investments less attractive to foreign investors, but strike action may be necessary to achieve economic objectives of the labor organization, to build disciplined labor organizations, and to retain the interest of the membership.

[2] Harvey Leibenstein, *Economic Backwardness and Economic Growth, Studies in the Theory of Economic Development* (New York: John Wiley and Sons, 1957), pp. 62-76.

(3) *Grievance-handling vs. Discipline.* Individual workers and small groups in an emerging industrial work force have numerous complaints, grievances, and frustrations. The national labor leader must choose in some degree between supporting the immediate reactions and grievances of workers or supporting the insistence upon higher standards of discipline, a faster pace, training, and production which are vital to economic development.

(4) *Organizational Prestige vs. Political Subservience.* The labor organization is often long on political influence and short on economic power. It must weigh the costs of faithful support and dependence on a political party or government against the benefits of governmental recognition and support in a variety of ways, including exclusive labor rights and favoritism in treating rival labor organizations and outright financial support. The immediate attractiveness of a strong legal position in dealing with managements, members, and rivals and financial solvency is to be balanced against the loss in independence of action in being subservient to the government.

These basic policy decisions, which are most difficult for labor organizations in a country led by a democratic and middle-class elite, present few difficulties for the labor organizations under the revolutionary intellectual elite. Economic development takes first priority over wage increases; production cannot be interfered with by strikes; labor organizations are designed to increase labor productivity, and they are always subservient to the party and government. There is more of a problem in a country under the dynastic elite, but in the main wages cannot be raised very much in the face of the slow rate of development, and strikes are little more than demonstrations. The labor movement cannot secure many concessions from the government or ruling elite, although individual leaders or factions of labor organizations may secure benefits in exchange for political support.

It is easy to understand why many leaders of industrializing countries and their labor organizations in countries outside the Eastern orbit find the choices posed above to be very hard, and they talk of ways to develop labor organizations that will make a more affirmative contribution to the national objective of industrialization. Neither the elite nor the leaders of labor organizations find congenial the traditional model of the "free trade union" drawn from advanced Western countries. As Dr. Nkrumah has said, ". . . . The trade union movement has a great part to play and a far wider task to perform than merely the safeguarding of the conditions and wages of its members."[3] The debate and the experi-

[3] Quoted in R. B. Davison, "Labour Relations in Ghana," *The Annals of the American Academy of Political and Social Sciences* (March 1957), p. 139.

mentation over the role of labor organizations in recently industrializing countries is one of the focal points of the competition among groups for leadership in the process of industrialization.

The distinctive characteristics of the labor organizations created in the industrialization process by each ideal type of elite (see Chart 1) indicate the interdependence of each separate feature. The functions exercised by labor organizations, for instance, are closely related to their structure, leadership, financial arrangements, and ideology. Further, the labor organizations that arise in a society in transition led by an ideal type of elite fit into the full range of policies of that industrializing elite. The universals of worker protest and organization are molded to conform and contribute to the grand strategy of the industrializing elite.

6   GEORGE BARON AND
         ASHER TROPP

Teachers in England and America

The purpose of this study is to examine schoolteachers in England and America, in relation to the social contexts within which they are placed in their respective countries. Such an analysis presents certain difficulties, the most important being the incomplete nature of the available data. The majority of the research work in both countries has concentrated on the social origins of teachers,[1] the attitudes toward the teaching profession of potential students and their parents, criteria of success in teach-

Reprinted with the permission of The Macmillan Company from *Education, Economy and Society* by A. H. Halsey, Jean Floud, and C. Arnold Anderson (eds.). © by the Free Press of Glencoe, Inc. 1961.

[1] In the not far distant past the term "teacher" in England (at least as far as men were concerned) was associated with the elementary school system and its offshoots. Now, however, and in this study, it is used to cover all teachers in primary and secondary schools of whatever kind. In America, on the other hand, "teacher" has always had a more general significance and it may be necessary to point out that its use here does not embrace teachers in universities, colleges, and other institutions of higher education.

ing, and the activities of professional associations.[2] In America, although not in England, a great deal of work has been carried out on the position of the teacher in the local community and more recently on teacher-administrator relationships. The American work in these latter fields has been more substantial, partly because there are more sociologists interested in the sociology of education in America, but mainly because the whole field of teacher-community relationships represents a social problem in America affecting the whole success of the educational enterprise.[3] Education in America is a function of the local community, whereas in England, as we shall see later, there is a more widely diffused national responsibility. This crucial fact by itself does a great deal to explain the different position of the teacher in the two countries.

Ideally, comparison should await the results of similar research carried out with similar methods in the two countries. However, we hope in this paper to reveal gaps in the material and stimulate further thought and work. Our focus is on one dimension of the position of the teacher, which we consider decisive—the nature of the *authority* with which the teacher is vested in the two countries.[4]

This approach is adopted for two reasons: first, because the authority an occupation possesses determines the role it can play within the society of which it is a part and its adaptability when faced by new pressures and demands; second, because the understanding of American and English society largely depends upon an appreciation of how authority is distributed throughout the social structure of both countries.

Our approach to the topic is threefold: We begin by discussing the

[2] See "The Sociology of Education: A Trend Report and Bibliography," *Current Sociology*, VIII (1958), No. 3, 189-91, 224-5, for a bibliography and review of the literature.

[3] "The public schools in American society are among our most locally centered, indigenous social institutions. In spite of increasing state and federal financial support, the schools generally remain locally controlled and extremely sensitive to local public opinion." G. W. Blackwell, "A Sociologist on School-Community Relationships," *Annals of the American Academy of Political and Social Science*, CCCII (Nov., 1955), 134.

[4] We are using "authority" in the same sense as H. A. Simon in *Administrative Behavior* (New York: Macmillan Co., 1954), pp. 125-28. "'Authority' may be defined as the power to make decisions which guide the actions of another. . . . We shall use 'authority' broadly, and comprehend under it all situations where suggestions are accepted without any critical review or consideration." See also E. C. Hughes, *Men and their Work* (Glencoe, Ill.: Free Press, 1958), chap. vi, who distinguishes between "licence" and "mandate"—"an occupation consists, in part, of a successful claim of some people to *licence* to carry out certain activities which others may not, and to do so in exchange for money, goods or services. Those who have such licence will, if they have any sense of self-consciousness and solidarity, also claim a *mandate* to define what is proper conduct of others toward the matters concerned with their work."

relationship of the school in both countries to two other major social groupings—community and family. Second, we describe the main relevant differences between the English and American educational structure and their consequences for teachers in the two countries. We then turn to the distribution of authority within the distinctively professional organizational and occupational groupings of English and American teachers and their relation to national and local interest groups.

SCHOOL AND COMMUNITY
IN ENGLAND AND AMERICA

In England, as in Europe generally, the teaching profession has a dual origin. On the one hand, it stems from the needs of what are traditionally ranked as the "learned professions," that is, the church, the law, and medicine; on the other, it has grown out of the increasingly elaborate provision, by national governments, of universal schooling. In both cases, the teacher has always been linked with sources of authority external to his immediate environment. At all times in England, behind the local grammar school have stood the universities of Oxford and Cambridge; behind the elementary school, the great religious voluntary societies in the nineteenth century and, from the 1830's, a central government department (now the Ministry of Education). In America, the situation has been quite different. National consciousness is at least as strong as in England and often more overtly expressed, but the necessity for each pioneering community to organize its own affairs made education a local responsibility in a way in which it has never been in England.[5]

Compare the following statements by American and English educators. First, George S. Counts:

> That system [of common schools] was not imposed from above by a strong central government or an influential intellectual class. Rather were its foundations laid by relatively untutored farmers who established one-room district schools in rural neighborhoods as they moved across the continent.[6]

Second, Sir Fred Clarke:

> . . . the mass of the English people have never yet evolved genuine schools of their own. Schools have always been provided for them from above, in a form and with a content of studies that suited the ruling interests.[7]

[5] This generalization would not hold good in other parts of the United Kingdom. For example, Scottish education, though now highly centralized, was at one time very much the concern of each individual parish.

[6] George S. Counts, *Education and American Civilization* (New York: Teachers College, 1952), p. 454.

[7] Sir Fred Clarke, *Education and Social Change* (London: Sheldon Press, 1940), p. 30.

The essential difference is perhaps to be summed up as follows: whereas in England it is the teacher who represents to the community in which he works "nationally" accepted values, in America it is the community that interprets to the teacher the task he is to perform.[8] This difference is of supreme importance, because if it can be accepted it explains fundamental differences in the behavior of teachers as a professional body in each country. It explains, at least in England, why the *content* of what is taught in the schools is virtually never discussed save in professional gatherings of educators, whereas in America constant efforts are made, through citizen committees and parent-teacher associations, to insure that what is done in the schools is done with the "authority" of lay opinion.

The distinction suggested is, of course, expressed in formal governmental structures. In England, whilst education and hence teachers are the concern of local education authorities, the powers of the latter are exercised under the close supervision and control of the Minister of Education. For example, local education authorities have virtually no control over what they pay their teachers, since nationwide salary scales are settled by statutory negotiating bodies, superannuation is a matter for parliamentary legislation, and conditions of service (tenure, sick benefit) are nationally agreed. There can be no question in England, therefore, of local campaigns to improve or reduce salaries. In America, on the other hand, the conditions of service enjoyed by a teacher can vary very considerably from state to state and from district to district. One consequence is that there is, unlike England, a very considerable literature dealing with the internal comparison of conditions of service in different regions produced by teachers associations in America.[9]

Further differences emerge in the field of national and local politics. As already indicated, education in England is very much a national con-

---

[8] This is put best by W. W. Charters, "It is possible that something which we shall call a 'margin of tolerance' describes the school-community relationship. Citizens of each community may delegate to school personnel the freedom to educate youth according to their professional consciences but freedom within certain well-defined (or ill-defined) bounds. The boundary is composed of values dear to the particular community. If school personnel over-step the boundary, crisis ensues and community values enter into the determination of school affairs. The margin of tolerance allowed the school may be narrower or broader in different communities . . . however unreasonable or irrelevant the components of the boundary line may seem, *the community is in a position to enforce them.*" "Social Class Analysis and the Control of Public Education," *Harvard Educational Review*, XXIII (Fall, 1953), 268-83.

[9] National salary scales, a national superannuation scheme and agreed procedures relating to tenure emerged only slowly as a result of strenuous efforts on the part of teachers' associations and ultimately pressure exercised on the local education authorities by the central government. See A. Tropp, *The School Teachers* (London: Heinemann, 1957).

cern and, as such is a matter for debate between and within the major political parties and within parliament itself. At the local level, education is not administered by "school boards" but by "local authorities," which, besides being concerned with education, are responsible for the whole range of country and city administration.[10] Borough and county council elections are generally fought on party lines, councillors are looked upon as representing national political parties, and party "discipline" is strictly maintained. Citizens or groups with grievances or suggestions about educational matters can of course use normal pressure techniques on their local councillors, but they face men and women whose outlook is not limited to education alone, but who are firmly anchored within political parties. To vote against a particular member of the education committee means a change in basic political allegiance and, in England as in America, such a step is not taken lightly.[11] This involvement with political as well as with national- and local-government agencies contributes, paradoxically enough, to the *insulation* of the school system from direct social pressures. This insulation is not a matter of accident. From 1870 to 1902, in England and Wales, each area had its own school board, providing elementary schools and schooling according to the regulations of a central Education Department but with a considerable amount of freedom. The Education Act of 1902 abolished these school boards, which numbered several thousands, and brought education within the scope of the all-purpose local government bodies that have since served as local education authorities. There was a whole complex of reasons for abolishing the school boards — educational, administrative, and legal — but one pronounced motive was the desire to "insulate" the schools from popular pressure at the local level.[12]

[10] See *Annals of the American Academy of Political and Social Science*, CCCII, (Nov., 1955), 74-99, for accounts of the working of educational administration in England.

[11] Occasionally, it is true, "independent" and "rate-payer" candidates are elected to local councils but rarely on a strictly education "ticket."

[12] See Tropp, *op. cit.*, chap. x. Also E. Eaglesham, *From School Board to Local Authority* (London: Routledge and Kegan Paul, 1956), p. 179.

Compare T. L. Reller on the early history of American education: "There was a strong desire to have the schools close to the people and not too readily responsive to those in positions of influence and power in government. . . . Popular control was intended to ensure an educational program which would provide a basis for a more perfect union rather than for the enhancement of the power of any one group, including public officials. . . . Local government was believed to be "corrupt," and many people wished to remove the schools from this corruption. . . . The legal concept that education was a function of the state supported those who were anxious to eliminate local governmental control of education because of corruption: it was argued that the state should establish separate and independent local Boards of Education to provide and maintain the educational service." "Changing Scenes—

Conservative, Labour, and Liberal parties alike have consistently held to the view that the content of education and methods of instruction are not matters for popular debate and decision, but should be left in the hands of teachers themselves and of other professional educators. This being so, individuals or groups seeking to "use" the schools for their own purposes are confronted, not by the hastily constructed defenses of the teacher or of a single school or school board, as in America, but by the massive disregard of experienced politicians and administrators.[13] This willing delegation of educational issues to educators is possible because the latter form a coherent and predictable element in the authority structure that moulds English society.

It is not only the size and relative insulation of the educational authority that is important, but also the nature of the community itself. Teacher-community relations in large urban areas in both England and America are different from similar relations in small towns. But not only is England a more highly urbanized country, with 40 per cent of the population living in six great conurbations, but there is no real equivalent to the American small-town life described so often by sociologists and novelists. The teacher is not under such close and continuous scrutiny.[14] What is more, while there are constant complaints by American educators that teachers play little part in voluntary associations and

---

Changing Issues," *Annals of the American Academy of Political and Social Science,* CCCII (Nov., 1955), 3.

[13] Note the attitude of an extremely distinguished English educational administrator, W. O. Lester-Smith. "A noteworthy feature of English life today is the large number of associations formed to propagate or combat particular causes. Many of them attach great importance to influencing the young, some even have junior sections of their organisation. They are constantly—one or other of them—asking Education Authorities to countenance their lectures or circularise their literature. . . . The normal practice of Local Authorities is to turn a deaf ear to such requests, but they do from time to time make exceptions to their rule." W. O. Lester-Smith, *To Whom Do Schools Belong?* (Oxford: Basil Blackwell, 1946), p. 20.

[14] There is a good deal of evidence that community pressure on teacher behavior is declining in the U.S.A., e.g., "The rather rigidly circumscribed life of the teacher in the community has been loosened somewhat partly because of the shortage of teachers, partly because of changes in standards for the culture at large. It is not often possible, for example, to enforce prewar prohibitions against dancing, dating, social drinking, smoking, card-playing, and similar activities, particularly when these activities are socially approved for other professional and managerial groups. Yet some pressures do remain . . . a sizable minority of teachers . . . do feel pressures and a lack of freedom to behave and participate like other professionals." H. Grobman and V. A. Hines, "Private Life of the Teacher," in L. J. Stiles (ed.), *The Teacher's Role in American Society* (14th Yearbook of the John Dewey Society; 1957). But see also D. Riesman *Constraint and Variety in American Education* (New York: Doubleday and Co., 1958), p. 125; and W. S. Elsbree *The American Teacher* (New York: American Book Co., 1939), p. 540.

while they are often debarred from engaging in political life,[15] in England teachers play an extremely important part in all forms of voluntary associations, including political parties.[16] Thus, teachers are in a key position to ward off local attacks on the schools and are indeed, as we shall see later, the most powerful interest group acting in the educational field on both the local and the national level.

The relation between the school and the family also differs in the two countries. In America, for the most part, the parents hand over their child to the school system but maintain a continuous scrutiny over his progress. In England, "interference" by the parents in the school is resisted both by teachers and by educational administrators. Parents' associations and parent-teacher associations are becoming increasingly common, but they limit their activities to social functions and to meetings at which school policy is explained but not debated. As H. S. Becker has shown, there is a fundamental difference between American and English practice. In the lower-class schools he studied in Chicago, there had developed, quite informally, an amazingly strong self-protective code.

> No principal or teacher ought ever to admit that anyone on the school staff has done anything wrong . . . for to admit such a thing would be to admit the parents into the power structure of the school . . . parents and other outsiders are allowed to see the schools in action only when there is plenty of warning and a "show" of some kind has been prepared for them.[17]

Becker sees this system of defense as growing up only in schools that

---

[15] "Many teachers are required by contract or school board regulations to adjure not only politics but all things that might be construed as political. And doubtless even where there are no written regulations, there may be unwritten regulations. . . . The proportion of teachers in legislative bodies is insignificant. . . . Teachers have not been conspicuously in the fore in leading intelligent discussions of political affairs or of speaking out in support of the rights of others. Teachers have been conspicuous by their relative absence even in such non-partisan citizen groups as the League of Women Voters." H. Grobman and V. A. Hines, "Teacher as a Citizen," in L. J. Stiles, *ibid*. See also W. B. Brookover, A *Sociology of Education* (New York: American Book Co., 1955), pp. 238-40.

[16] C. F. G. Masterman wrote of the English teaching profession in 1909 that they were "everywhere taking the lead in public and quasi-public activities. They appear as the mainstay of the political machine in suburban districts, serving upon the municipal bodies, in work, clear-headed and efficient; the leaders in the churches and chapels, and their various social organizations. They are taking up the position in the urban districts which for many generations was occupied by the country clergy in the rural districts." *The Condition of England* (London: Methuen, 1909), p. 83. This general description is still true.

[17] H. S. Becker "Schools and Systems of Social Status," *Phylon*, XVI (1955), 159-70.

are "very likely to be attacked at almost any time by the parents of their pupils, for not doing their job well enough or in the right way, for using improper disciplinary measures, and so on." It should be noted that Becker works on the assumption that schools normally accept parents' criticisms and informal inspection. It is for this reason that lower-class schools have to develop special defensive mechanisms. In England, no such constructed and conscious mechanisms are necessary, because the school is already so *insulated* by the nature of the total institutional structure of which it is a part.

Bolstering the authority of the teacher in England is his own intellectual separation from the majority of the parents. Throughout his school life and subsequent training, the English teacher lives in a world that progressively removes him from the non-selected mass, that places him first in a grammar school in which he receives a grounding in "liberal" subjects and later in a college or university with essentially intellectual purposes. He feels, therefore, in a way not felt by the American teacher, that he has been linked, although remotely, with a world of scholarship, both literary and scientific, which gives him authority in dealing with parents, businessmen, and others, and with their possible criticisms or suggestions relating to his work. In large measure he is right in his assumption since, in England, where education for the larger part of the population ceases at the age of fifteen, the teacher will have had more education than all except a minority of parents.[18] In America, he faces a large number of graduate parents with their own expertise. Howard Becker and David Riesman have shown that in America it is the more highly educated and upper-class parents who are most ready to challenge the teacher's authority.[19] There are two other points to bear in mind in connection with this argument. The first is the different attitude toward the intellectual and the scholar in England and America. The teacher in England shares in the higher esteem of the intellectual. In America, the periodic attacks on intellectuals have involved the teacher as well. Second, the attachment of teachers in Eng-

[18] "Both parents of two-thirds of the boys and girls who attended selective schools (grammar schools and technical schools) themselves left school at 14, which was in their day the legal minimum leaving-age. Only 12 per cent of the boys and girls came from homes where both parents had had a longer education than the legal minimum." United Kingdom. Ministry of Education. *15 to 18. A Report of the Central Advisory Council for Education (England)* Vol. I. *Report.* pp. 8-9. (London: Her Majesty's Stationery Office, 1959).

[19] See H. S. Becker, *op. cit.* Also H. S. Becker, "The Career of the Chicago Public School Teacher," *American Journal of Sociology,* LVII (March, 1952), 470-77. "The Teacher in the Authority System of the Public School," *Journal of Educational Sociology,* XXVII, No. 3, 128-41; D. Riesman, "Teachers and Changing Expectations," *Harvard Educational Review,* Spring, 1954.

land to the world of scholarship and their removal from the "masses" have been a deliberate aim of powerful education administrators.[20]

ENGLISH AND AMERICAN TEACHERS IN THE EDUCATIONAL STRUCTURES OF THE TWO COUNTRIES

Let us now turn aside from these general considerations of the English and American teacher in relation to the societies in which they live and examine the specific positions they respectively occupy within the *educational* structures of the two countries.

The task of the American teacher is to provide for each child an education in no sense inferior to that provided for any other; differentiation in the quality of the service offered is unacceptable in a social situation in which schools are traditionally maintained by the equal contributions of each member of the community. The role of the teacher, therefore, is not concerned with selection; it is limited to the giving of guidance and advice, and even this tends to become a specialized function supported by administrative techniques. In short, decision-making is assumed to lie, not with the teacher, but with parents, students, or community; and it is for the teacher to meet the needs thus made evident.

Much of what has been said accords also with the overt purposes of the English educational system. Here, however, the basis for determining what provision shall be made for any individual child is not his simple status as a junior citizen, equal to all other junior citizens, but his qualities as an individual. Indeed, the 1944 Act stresses the age, ability, and aptitude of each individual child as the touchstone for deciding upon the educational provision to be made for him. From this it is clear that the assessment of ability and aptitude, and selection based upon performance, is implicit in the English approach. Moreover, selection and decision is placed, not with the community or the family, but with the educational system itself.[21] Hence, it is the teacher within the educational system, and not the parent within the community, who is in touch with the sources of authority. It is for him to judge whether or not a child can tackle work of a certain kind or level, to place him in an appropriate group for teaching purposes and, as he moves from primary to secondary education, to add his judgment to the results of

[20] See Tropp, *op. cit.*, pp. 13-15, 177-78. It should be emphasized that the aim of introducing the teacher (recruited from the working and lower-middle classes) to the world of "culture" and separating him from the parents was in order that he should be able to act as a "missionary" to his class.

[21] Certain relatively minor powers of decision as regards the choice of a school of an appropriate religious denomination are reserved to the parent but not powers as regards the kind of secular instruction his child receives.

standardized and other tests of performance. Within the secondary school, whether it be selective or not, the teacher is able, by reason of the typical structure of an English school, to determine educational opportunities more finally than is the American teacher by the typical structure of the American school.

A further distinction between the educational structures in which American and the English teachers work lies in the differing concepts of the "educational administrator." By and large, the American school superintendent is responsibile to his school board for all aspects of the education given in the schools of a city or district; school principals are his subordinates, and he is expected to give leadership, whether autocratic or democratic in nature, in purely educational topics, such as curriculum-building and the evolution of appropriate teaching methods.[22] In England, the domains of the teacher and the administrator are much more distinct. The functions of the latter are to provide the conditions under which education can take place, to insure that schools are built and equipped, that teachers are appointed, and that public money made available for education is properly accounted for. As an educator, his functions are to advise his committee on the large-scale planning of school provision, but not in developing a particular educational philosophy. Although the "Director of Education" of an English L.E.A. is an extremely influential person, the pivot of the English school system, indeed, is the headmaster or headmistress,[23] who is not, like the American principal, looked upon as an administrator, but as a teacher. The distinction is reinforced by him or her being appointed by a Board of Governors or Managers.[24] Moreover, professional opinion requires that a headmaster once appointed, should be given full freedom as regards the internal organization of his school, its time-table, its syllabuses, and its out-of-school activities. Whilst he is expected to seek his governors' consent to major changes and is expected to listen to their suggestions and comments, he is not expected to shape his policy to fit the educational theories of his lay advisers. His "authority" derives not from them but from well-established sources within the educational structure, notably the universities, which, through their control of major school

---

[22] See N. Gross, *Who Runs Our Schools?* (New York: John Wiley and Sons, 1958), for a discussion of the role of school superintendent.

[23] G. Baron, "Some Aspects of the 'Headmaster Tradition,' " *University of Leeds Institute of Education. Researches and Studies*, No. 14 (June, 1956).

[24] To preserve the individuality of each school, it is customary in England for education committees to appoint governors (for secondary schools) and managers (for primary schools). Such governing bodies are composed partly of committee members and partly of other persons nominated because of their interest in local politics or education. Thus, each school has its "board," which protects it from undue interference by the committee and its officers, but which is limited by them in its own powers.

examinations and their more recently acquired responsibilities for teacher-training, lend their considerable prestige to the underwriting of what is done in the schools.

The division between administration and teaching results, in effect, in their being considered as forming two distinct careers. That is, the ambitious young man in England must decide early whether he is to remain a schoolteacher and strive for a headmastership or whether he is to seek a subordinate post in an education office and work up the administrative hierarchy. It is virtually unknown for a headmaster, for example, to be appointed to a senior administrative post, as it would be felt that his experience was inappropriate. It should be noted, however, that the teaching profession has been sufficiently influential to insist that *senior* administrative officers should have had some actual teaching experience early in their careers.

The third aspect of the educational structure is more difficult to define. In America, there is on the one hand the world of "education" of the elementary schools, the high schools, and the college, and on the other hand, that of the "higher learning," represented by the great postgraduate schools and research organizations. In England, groupings are on a different basis. Here, universities and *selective* secondary schools (that is, publicly maintained grammar schools and independent "public" schools) form very much their own world; and non-selective secondary schools, primary schools, and, to some extent, teacher-training colleges, another. There are two reasons for the English situation: the first is the obvious one—that the duality of the educational system, already mentioned and corresponding to the social-class structure, still persists; the second, closely connected with it, is that teachers in selective secondary schools and in universities in England have virtually identical preparation for their work. That is, the sixth-form English master follows the same courses at his university as those followed by the young university teacher. There is no question of him taking a composite degree with some elements of pedagogy and some elements of English and thus being marked as a high-school teacher of English. His professional training will be limited to one year of professional study after his main university course has been completed. As a result, he identifies himself very closely with the university approach to his subject.

STRUCTURE OF THE TEACHING PROFESSION IN ENGLAND AND AMERICA

We now consider the structure of the teaching profession itself, in each of the two countries, in terms of the formal organization that American and English teachers have set up to defend and promote their general and specific interests.

In America, there is a sharp line to be drawn between the *education association* and the *teachers union*. The former brings together teachers, principals, superintendents, and other professional workers within local and state units; and the great majority of such regional associations form the vast federal structure known as the National Education Association.[25] The teachers unions in America, of which the leading example is the American Federation of Teachers, are more specifically concerned with salaries, superannuation, and other matters relating to conditions of service. Moreover, superintendents are excluded from membership, and the participation of principals and other supervisory personnel is carefully legislated. Most important of all, the American Federation of Teachers is affiliated with the trade-union movement as a whole, in the form of the Combined American Federation of Labor and the Congress of Industrial Organizations.

Developments in England have taken a very different course, partly because of the more readily accepted separation of teaching and administrative functions already discussed and partly because the local administrator emerged after the teachers had already organized themselves.[26]

While teachers in the higher selective forms of secondary education still belong to separate and independent associations for headmasters and headmistresses, assistant masters and assistant mistresses, the National Union of Teachers, which is open to all teachers, is by far the largest of the professional associations. There are separate and distinct associations for teachers engaged in various forms of further education and for lecturers in teacher-training institutions. These separate associations do for particular purposes act in coalition and concert. Administrative officers have their own associations.

Despite its name, the National Union of Teachers is not a trade union and is not affiliated with the trade-union movement nor are any of the

[25] For details and comments on the American teachers unions, see M. Lieberman, *Education as a Profession* (Englewood Cliffs, N.J.: Prentice Hall, Inc., 1956); Commission on Educational Reconstruction, *Organizing the Teaching Profession: The Story of the American Federation of Teachers* (Free Press: Glencoe, Ill., 1955); E. B. Wesley, *NEA: The First Hundred Years* (New York: Harper and Bros., 1957); W. B. Brookover, *op. cit.*, pp. 260-61; W. S. Elsbree, *op cit.*, chap. xxxiii.

[26] Until 1870, the administrative officers concerned with education operated at national level, as members of the Department of Education and the national inspectorate or as secretaries and officials of voluntary societies of national scope. Local control was largely in the hands of local clergy or other amateurs. It was their dependence upon remote sources of authority and their independence of such sources in other respects that made the coming together of various local and denominational bodies of teachers in 1870 and the formation of the National Union of Elementary School Teachers (later the National Union of Teachers) possible. Similarly, secondary schoolteachers came together in their own organizations before any body of officials concerned with secondary education at a local level had come into being.

other teacher associations. Nevertheless, they all draw to a considerable extent upon the "authority" that underlies the concept of trade unionism and that grows out of the assumption that the conditions of service of workers should be settled by collective bargaining. The nationwide salary scales are settled by negotiations between representatives of the main teacher associations and representatives of the local education authorities, subject to the approval of the Minister of Education.

TEACHERS IN THE SOCIAL STRUCTURE

Through their membership in voluntary associations, political parties, local councils (both as elected members and as co-opted members of education committees),[27] and parliament, teachers are strategically placed in Great Britain to represent the views of their profession. The other great interest groups, which play such an important part in American education — business, labor, religious, and patriotic groups[28] — play a different role in England. Business is of course strongly represented in the Conservative party and labor in the Labour party and businessmen and trade unionists will be found in almost all education committees. Both the Federation of British Industries and the Trades Union Congress have, in the past, developed schemes for educational reconstruction, including even curriculum reforms, and pressed them on political parties and governments. But apart from this they have never sought to interfere with the day-to-day work of individual schools. The Church of England was sufficiently influential, because of its constitutional status, to contend, throughout the nineteenth century, with public bodies for the control of a wide area of elementary education. Even during the period leading up to the passing of the 1944 Education Act it was strong enough to insist on an extension of the teaching of "undenominational" religion in every grant aided school. In schools under the control of the religious bodies (Anglican, Catholic, or Jewish), 75 per cent of capital investment and all running expenses are provided by the state, and religious tests can be imposed on a proportion, but not all, of the teachers. In the publicly provided school (65 per cent of the whole) the conscience rights of teachers occupying all positions are fully secured, but the position of a head teacher is a delicate one since an "act of

[27] Teachers may serve on "any committee appointed for the purposes of the enactments relating to education" (The Education Act, 1946, s.10), but they may not become members of the *local education authority* that actually employs them.
[28] See H. K. Beale, *Are American Teachers Free?* (New York: Charles Scribner's Sons, 1936); Brookover, *op. cit.*, pp. 60-71; M. Starr, *Labor Looks at Education* (Cambridge, Mass.: Harvard University Press, 1946); F. Sparks, "What Management Wants from Our Schools," *Studies in Higher Education*, (Lafayette, Ind.: Purdue University Press, 1944); W. Gellerman, *The American Legion as Educator* (Teachers College Contributions to Education, No. 743; New York: Columbia University Press, 1938).

worship" is required daily, by law, in every school, and is part of the assembly invariably presided over by the headmaster or headmistress. In many schools, and particularly in those with long-standing religious connections, the headmaster or headmistress accepts considerable responsibility for the religious instruction of the older pupils and even prepares them for entry into, or confirmation in, a church. This aspect of the professional life of the teacher in England has no counterpart in the case of the American public-school teacher. The relationship between teachers and the church has not always been amicable, but after the religious settlement of the 1944 Act a state of affairs appears to have been reached where the teacher draws upon the authority of the church while remaining independent of it. Finally, one should note the almost complete absence of pressure from patriotic associations. There have been minor incidents concerning Communist teachers and attempts to strengthen teaching of commonwealth history but these pressures have been far less serious in the life of the English teacher than the American.

The greater authority of the teachers in the English educational structure and their insulation from external pressures is reflected in the classroom situation. There is less need for the British teacher to seek the consensus of his pupils. Parents are either active or passive supporters of teachers in their disciplinary problems, and in the selective grammar schools the system of external public examinations unites teachers and pupils in a common effort to outwit the examiners. Inside the English school there is a gradual drawing of boys and girls, according to age and capacity, into the core of authority within each school. The younger children are given responsibility for things (e.g., duster and chalk); and the older, for the behavior of younger children (e.g., as prefects), or for organizations (e.g., teams and clubs). This differs from the American approach, which rather seeks to minimize age and status differences and to emphasize *sharing* in the *making* of authority through group decisions, rather than to emphasize the *distribution* of authority drawn from custom and tradition. The English teacher is far more cautious in the place that he accords to school and form councils as authority-creating instruments.

As earlier suggested, what has been attempted in this discussion is an examination of the English and American teacher seen within three overlapping frames of reference in which their relationship to major sources of social, educational, and professional authority may be studied. It is true that such an approach obscures the dynamic role of education in relation to social change in modern society. On the other hand, preliminary analysis of this nature is essential if detailed empirical studies are to be effectively planned and interpreted.

7   JOHN FORWARD

Toward An Empirical Framework
For Comparative Studies in
Public Administration

INTRODUCTION

In recent years, increasing interest has been shown in the ecological
approach to the study of comparative administration. The basic premise
of this approach is that bureaucracy may be regarded as one of several
basic institutions in a society and that in order to fully understand its
structure and function, it must be studied in the context of its interrela-
tionships with other institutions. In system theory terms, bureaucracy
as a social institution is continually interacting with the economic, political and socio-cultural systems in a society and is both a modifying
influence on these systems as well as being modified by them.

Many notable attempts have been made recently to develop specific
theoretical models for the ecology of public administration. However, one
disturbing feature, which is shared by most models, is that they are based
solely upon intuitive and *a priori* assumptions concerning the relationship of bureaucracy to other societal systems. Consequently, although
these models may make important contributions in terms of descriptive
analysis and imaginative classificatory schema, their development towards
explanatory theory is hampered by a serious lack of empirical background.

At this early stage in the development of the field, it might be
useful to give some consideration to the problem of finding types of
analysis which are best suited to the task of developing an adequate
empirical basis for ecological models given the limited quantity and
quality of available data. This problem has been largely neglected in the
construction of existing models, but it is of some importance for the
development of a body of explanatory theory in ecological study.

AN EMPIRICAL FOUNDATION
FOR ECOLOGICAL STUDIES

In any new field of investigation, the preliminary data which are gathered tend to be somewhat general and subject to a high degree of error. Concepts are imprecise and lacking in operational definition, the measuring instruments are crude and still to be refined and strong stable relationships between variables are difficult to establish. What is needed at this stage is a method of analysis which is capable of producing some degree of order to the seemingly disordered collection of observations. One particular set of methods which has been successfully applied to this task in other fields is correlational analysis. Correlational techniques, such as factor analysis, can be used to determine an initial patterning among a large number of different variables. It is this pattern of relationships which may serve as an empirical foundation for theory construction and model-building.

Perhaps the utility of correlational analysis for the present stage of development in ecological studies will become more evident if the expected outcomes of such an analysis are considered. The following points may serve also as an outline for the analysis to be presented in this study.

A. *The Initial Selection of Variables*

All theoretical models require an initial selection of variables for consideration from a large number of possible choices. Whereas this selection process is largely implicit or intuitive in current ecological model-building, correlational analysis provides a procedure which is both explicit and empirical. By correlating a large number of variables with any criterion variable of interest, it is possible to order all variables in terms of the relative strength of their association with the criterion variable. On the basis of this empirical ordering, variables may be selected or ignored according to whether they show a high or low degree of relationship with the criterion variable. In the construction of ecological models, selection of variables could be accomplished by using some measure of bureaucracy as the criterion variable.

B. *The Empirical Determination of Factors*

On intuitive grounds, a factor refers to an abstract category of classification which unites and gives meaning to any particular set of variables. In existing models, several factors are set up initially and then variables are assigned to these factors. Correlational or factor analysis reverses this procedure.

An empirical factor is defined as a set of variables which correlate more highly with each other than with all other variables outside the set. By constructing a complete intercorrelation matrix, certain factoring techniques can be applied in order to determine what empirical factors best order the data under consideration. In this manner, factors are defined on the basis of the empirical patterning of the variables, rather than on the basis of pre-conceived assumptions concerning ecological classification.

C. *The Specification of Ecological Variables*

Once the factors or underlying dimensions have been extracted, variables can be given various factor weightings which represent the relative contribution they make to several different factors. As a hypothetical example, we might expect that an advanced degree of urbanization would have a high factor loading on the economic factor, but we might also find that it contributes substantially to the socio-cultural and communications factors.

The significance of this procedure for model-building is twofold. Firstly, it provides an empirical specification of the relationships between variables and factors and secondly, it allows us to give a more precise empirical meaning to any given ecological variable.

Finally, the pattern of relationships which emerges from the analysis may suggest a number of hypotheses for further testing. It may be found, for example, that literacy rate is not directly related to the extent of bureaucratic development, but that the relationship is mediated indirectly through several other variables, such as economic development, educational attainment or newspaper circulation. It should be noted that correlational analysis demonstrates an association between two variables and not a causal sequence. However, it does provide an empirical basis for the formulation of causal hypotheses for further investigation by other methods.

Before proceeding to the analysis outlined above, some discussion of available data is necessary.

NOTES ON AVAILABLE DATA AND METHODOLOGY

In their book, *World Handbook of Political and Social Indicators* (1964), Russett *et al.* have used extant statistical records to rank-order a large number of countries on a selected set of system variables. The correlational analysis at the end of the book is similar in many respects to the type of analysis suggested here. Unfortunately, this set of data is not appropriate for the present study, since it does not contain any measures of bureaucracy and its exclusive dependence on statistical records precludes the measurement of many variables of interest for studies in comparative public administration.

A second set of data, Banks and Textor's computer printout, *A Cross*

Polity Survey, is more appropriate for this study, since it does contain one measure of bureaucracy as well as a number of ecological variables of direct relevance for comparative studies in administration (Banks and Textor, 1963). Although a full discussion of the Banks and Textor data will not be presented here, the following points are of some importance for the development of an empirical framework for ecological studies.

A. *An Empirical Framework for Ecological Models*

The Banks and Textor data covers what is claimed to be an exhaustive sampling of world polities and so the measures generated represent highly generalized trends across all world polities. It is for this and the following reasons that I have chosen to speak of developing an empirical framework, rather than an ecological model, on the basis of this data.

The main guidelines for the ecological study of comparative administration were first presented by Robert Dahl almost two decades ago (1947). In this seminal paper, Dahl particularly stressed the need to limit the scope of ecological studies to the unique patterning of system variables within one society only. This approach has been followed by Riggs in his monograph, *The Ecology of Public Administration* (1961), in which he has selected three countries and limited his analysis to each of these countries respectively.

While recognizing the validity of this approach for the development of specific ecological models, there may still be some value in developing a universal and generalizable framework for comparative studies. Before we can specify what is unique to the ecological pattern of a single country, it will be necessary to know what constitutes the general features of the pattern.

B. *A Measure of Bureaucracy*

The measure of bureaucracy used in this study is the one included in Banks and Textor's set of variables. Although this measure is subject to an unknown degree of error in that it is based on the subjective ratings of experts in the field and despite its ambiguous definition, it is the only measure available. Each polity in their sample has been classified into one of the following categories:

Modern	generally effective and responsible civil service, performing in a functionally specific, non-ascriptive social context;
Semi-modern	largely rationalized bureaucratic structure of limited efficiency because of shortage of skilled personnel, inadequate recruitment criteria, excessive intrusion of non-administrative organs, or partially non-congruent social institutions;

| *Transitional* | largely rationalized ex-colonial bureaucratic structure in the process of personnel nationalization and adaptation to the servicing or restructuring of autochthonous social institutions; |
| *Traditional* | largely non-rationalized bureaucratic structure performing in the context of ascriptive or deferential stratification system. |

(Banks and Textor, p. 112-113)

Banks and Textor present a printout for all the significant cross-breaks using the 'Modern' and 'Semi-modern' versus 'Transitional' and 'Traditional' split on the bureaucratic measure. Statistically, the Chi-square and Fisher-exact statistics are used to give an indication of the relative strength of a relationship between any two variables. However, since the value of Chi-square varies with different sample sizes and the Fisher-exact values are often so close to zero that only .000 is reported, these statistics are unsuitable for the purposes of ordering the variables in terms of the degree of their association with the bureaucratic measure. To overcome these difficulties, all Chi-square values at or beyond the .05 level of significance were converted to coefficients of contingency, which corrects for sample size and may be read like the usual correlation coefficient.

This procedure made it possible to rank order all selected variables in terms of the strength of their relation to the measure of bureaucracy. The result may be seen in Table 1. In this table, it is seen that the variable, "Historically or Significantly Westernized" best differentiates the polities with either Modern or Semi-modern bureaucracies from those with either Transitional or Traditional bureaucracies (Rank 1, c.c. = .582). On the other hand, the variable ranked as number 25, "System Style Is More Mobilizational" is least related to the measure of bureaucracy (c.c. = .176). For convenience, in this study reference will be made to the rank number of the variable and the Banks and Textor variable number is included for reference use by the reader only.

A CORRELATIONAL ANALYSIS

Bureaucracy and the Relative Importance of Ecological Variables

Existing ecological models include a number of different system variables, political, socio-cultural or economic. However, since they lack the necessary empirical basis, the problem of assessing the relative importance for different systems to the development and maintenance of bureaucracy must remain at the level of intuition. At this level, some degree of bias due to these implicit or explicit assumptions is inevitable. For example, although Riggs includes at least five different systems in his "Sala Model," he appears to give a predominantly socio-cultural emphasis to his interpretations of the roles which salas, clects and nepotism play in the bureaucratic structures of prismatic societies. On the other hand, a model like Dorsey's "Information-Energy Model" places a great deal of weight on economic and technological factors, but gives little consideration to social and political factors (Riggs, 1962; Dorsey, 1962).

If the variables in Table 1 are examined in terms of the relative degree of their associations with the bureaucratic measure, many interesting features may be observed which may, or may not, support existing assumptions concerning the relative importance of various ecological variables for the existence of an advance bureaucracy. A few of these features are discussed below.

TABLE 1. CROSS-BREAKS FOR BANKS AND TEXTOR'S MEASURE OF BUREAUCRACY, (NO. 180); MODERN AND SEMI-MODERN VS. TRANSITIONAL AND TRADITIONAL (VARIABLES RANK ORDERED BY DEGREE OF CORRELATION)

Rank No.	B&T V. No.	C.C. Value	Variable Description and Cross-Break Split
1	75	.582	Historically or Significantly Westernized (vs. Opposite)
2	29	.559	High Urbanization (vs. Low)
3	117	.531	Interest Articulation by Associational Groups Is Significant. Moderate or Limited (vs. Negligible)
4	45	.518	Literacy Rate Is Above 50% (vs. below 50%)
5	43	.515	Economic Development Status Is Very High, High or Low (vs. Very Low)
6	30	.506	Agricultural Population Is Very Low, Low or Medium (vs. High)
7	85	.490	Political Modernization Is Advanced (vs. Transitional)
8	164	.453	Leadership Charisma Is Negligible (vs. Significant)
9	36	.450	C.N.P. Per Capita Is High or Medium (vs. Low or Very Low)
10	89	.430	Ideological Orientation Is Conventional (vs. Other)
11	54	.424	Newspaper Circulation Is 100 or more per 1,000 persons (vs. Less)
12	107	.389	Autonomous Groups Fully Tolerated in Politics (vs. Not)
13	105	.387	Electoral System Is Competitive (vs. Partly or Not)
14	101	.381	Representative Character of the Regime Is Polyarchic (vs. Not)
15	175	.379	Legislature Is Fully or Partially Effective (vs. Opposite)
16	99	.372	Government Stability present from World War II (vs. Opposite)
17	125	.366	Interest Articulation by Anomic Groups Is Infrequent (vs. Opposite)
18	68	.349	Linguistically Homogeneous (vs. Heterogeneous)
19	34	.349	Gross G.N.P. is Very High, High, Medium or Low (vs. Very Low)
20	153	.338	Party System Is Stable (vs. Moderately or Unstable)
21	26	.319	Population Density Is High, Medium (vs. Low)
22	114	.261	Sectionalism Is Negligible (vs. Extreme or Moderate)
23	111	.225	Political Enculturation Is High or Medium (vs. Less)
24	66	.193	Religiously Homogeneous (vs. Heterogeneous)
25	92	.176	System Style Is Mobilizational (vs. Less)

A. *Bureaucracy and Economic Variables:* In general, the economic indices in Table 1 are ranked high on the list. These are, "Economic Development Status" (rank 5, c.c. = .515) and "G.N.P. Per Capita" (rank 9, c.c. = .450). If the ratio of agricultural to non-agricultural population is interpreted as an indicator of industrial development, this measure also ranks with the main economic indices (rank 6, c.c. = .506). It is possible that the degree of westernization, (rank 1) and urbanization (rank 2) reflect, among other things, a relatively advanced state of economic development.

These observations serve to supplement the results of an analysis by Russett and his colleagues, in that they found that economic factors play a vital role in the development of almost all the major institutions in a society (Russett, 1964). Although Russett did not include a measure of bureaucracy in his analysis, these results show that it is no exception to this finding.

B. *Bureaucracy and Communication Variables:* There are few variables which are direct indicators of the communication system in these data, but those which do appear are closely related to the measure of bureaucracy. "Literacy Rate" (rank 4, c.c. = .518) and "Newspaper Circulation" (rank 11, c.c. = .424) are probably the most explicit indices of communication capacity, with the degree of westernization and urbanization again serving as indirect measures. In view of the importance of a developed system of communications for effective bureaucratic performance, it is surprising that, with one or two notable exceptions, communication variables have been largely neglected in current ecological model-building.

C. *Bureaucracy and Socio-cultural Variables:* The features of interest here are not so much the relationships which did occur, but some expected relationships which failed to show up strongly. For example, one might expect that homogeneity of language would be a socio-cultural measure which would correlate highly with effective bureaucracy, since it may represent a more basic homogeneity of values and it would certainly reduce the communication barriers inherent in a polylingual society. However, this variable is seen as relatively unimportant in the list (rank 18, c.c. = .349). A related variable, religious homogeneity, is also low on the list (rank 24, c.c. = .193). Again, one might expect that the degree of sectionalism which exists would be more closely related to the measure of bureaucracy than it is (rank 22, c.c. = .261).

D. *Bureaucracy and Political Variables:* Some people have proposed that a stable and representative political system is a necessary precondition for the development and maintenance of effective bureaucracy (cf. Friedrich, 1950). However, in Table 1 the measure of governmental stability used by Banks and Textor appears well down the list (rank 16, c.c. = .372), as do many of the indicators of representative government (cf. variables ranked 13, 14, 15 and 20).

The political indices most closely related to the bureaucratic measure are "Interest Articulation by Associational Groups" (rank 3, c.c. = .531), "Ideological Orientation Is Conventional" (rank 10, c.c. = .430) and "Leadership Charisma Is Negligible" (rank 8, c.c. = .453), all of which represent factors other than the purely political. Eisenstadt (1959) and Riggs (1961) have both placed some importance on the necessity of associationalism, as opposed to ascriptivism, as a socio-political basis for effective bureaucracy. Interest articulation by associational groups is a compromisable process which can be mediated through the bureaucratic structure, whereas the uncompromising demands of closed and conflicting ascriptive groups present what are often insuperable difficulties for effective bureaucratic performance.

In general, the data appear to support the assumption that it is effective bureaucracy which is the pre-condition for representative and stable government, rather than *vice versa*. Effective bureaucracy is seen to be highly dependent on a relatively advanced level of economic development, literacy, urbanization and communication capacity, all of which appear higher on the list in Table 1 than many of the direct indices of representative government.

The Empirical Determination of Ecological Factors

By utilizing other parts of the Banks and Textor printout data, it would be possible to construct a complete intercorrelation matrix which included all the variables in Table 1. In order to determine what factors account for the greatest amount of the variance in such a matrix, several different factoring techniques could be applied. One method which is suitable for our purpose is the technique of "unfolding the matrix," developed by Coombs (1964). However, the services of a large computer would be required to factor a matrix of the size contemplated here, and since the necessary time and money were not available at the time of writing, a full-scale analysis of the data was not possible. Instead, for the purposes of illustration, a smaller matrix consisting of twelve representative variables has been constructed and unfolded by hand. (see Table 2 for the matrix).

The unfolding of the smaller matrix produced four fairly distinct factors and one residual factor. These factors are represented in tabular form for discussion in the next section. It should be noted that, although the factors have been given descriptive labels, such as political and economic, that these labels are somewhat arbitrary and open to various interpretations. What is actually represented by these factors are the empirically determined underlying dimensions which best order the data in Table 2.

TABLE 2. INTERCORRELATION MATRIX OF 12 SELECTED VARIABLES FROM TABLE 1

	Bureaucracy Modern or Semi-modern	Westernized (1)	Associational Grps. (3)	Literacy (4)	Economic Devel. (5)	G.N.P. Per Cap. (9)	Ideology Conventional (10)	Newspapers 100+ (11)	Autonomous Grps. Tolerated (12)	Linguist. Homog. (18)	Political Encult. (23)	Urbanization (2)
Bureaucracy Modern or Semi-Modern	—											
Westernized (1)	.582	—										
Associational Grps (3)	.531	.588	—									
Literacy (4)	.518	.555	.442	—								
Economic Develop. (5)	.515	.572	.490	.542	—							
G.N.P. Per Cap. (9)	.450	.534	.446	.559	.602	—						
Ideology Conventional (10)	.430	.564	.546	.471	.540	.485	—					
Newspapers, 100 + (11)	.424	.496	.367	.560	.514	.610	.488	—				
Autonomous Grps Tolerated (12)	.389	.510	Not Given	.418	.465	.470	.600	.423	—			
Linguistically Homogeneous (18)	.349	.318	.256	.338	.233	.258	.350	.312	.254	—		
Political Enculturation (23)	.010	.245	Not Given	.291	.246	.238	.286	.287	Given	.256	—	
Urbanization (2)	.559	.554	.542	.511	.603	.537	.505	.498	.407	.383	.179	—

Interrelationships Among Factors and Ecological Variables

In the discussion of the factors which follows, attention is directed to the following considerations.

In accordance with the rules for correlational analysis presented earlier, each factor can be examined in terms of whether the core variables intercorrelate more highly with each other than with variables outside the set, and also, whether the core variables order all other variables in a similar manner.

Since factors may be thought of as mediating the relationships between different ecological variables and bureaucracy, it will be of interest to observe how closely each factor relates to the bureaucratic measure.

By observing the position of any given variable in the overall pattern of relationships, it is possible to trace not only its direct relationship with the bureaucratic measure, but also how this relationship is mediated indirectly through other factors and associated variables. This aspect of the analysis is a source for hypothesis formulation concerning the specific relationships between different variables.

Finally, by considering the relative contribution which any given variable makes to several different factors, it is possible to give a more determinative empirical meaning to the variable in question.

These considerations serve as a framework for the discussion of the factors which are presented below.

A. *The Economic Factor:* The following table shows the lists of intercorrelations for the two core economic variables, "Economic Development Status"[1] and "Per Capita Gross National Product."[2] If a more complete specification of any variable is desired, reference may be made to the variable description in Table 1 by means of the rank numbers preceding the variables listed below.

It is observed that the two key economic variables correlate highly (.602) and that they order their respective lists of intercorrelates similarly, thus forming the core of the economic factor.

Although the relative rank of the bureaucratic measure is low on both lists, when it is compared with the other factors in terms of the values of the contingency coefficients, its relationship with the economic factor

---

[1] In terms of the Banks and Textor definition and the specific crossbreak used here, those polities which are rated high on "Economic Development Status" are those with "self-sustaining" or "sustained" economic growth, or those which have a reasonable prospect of achieving this status by the mid-1970's (see Banks and Textor, p. 65).

[2] Polities rated as "High" on "Per Capita Gross National Product" by Banks and Textor are those with $600 G.N.P. Per Capita or more (See Banks and Textor, p. 63).

is one of the highest. An examination of the variables which correlate highly with the core economic variables suggest a number of hypotheses of interest.

Economic Development Status

		Variable	Value
	(2)	Urbanization	.603
*	(9)	G.N.P. Per Capita	.602
	(1)	Westernization	.572
	(4)	Literacy Rate	.542
	(10)	Ideology Is Conventional	.540
**	(—)	Bureaucracy Modern/Semi.	.515
	(11)	Newspaper Circulation	.514
	(3)	Associational Groups	.490
	(12)	Autonomous Groups Tol.	.465
	(23)	Political Enculturation	.246
	(18)	Linguistic Homogeneity	.233

Per Capita G.N.P

		Variable	Value
	(11)	Newspaper Circulation	.610
*	(5)	Economic Development	.602
	(4)	Literacy Rate	.559
	(2)	Urbanization	.537
	(1)	Westernization	.534
	(10)	Ideology Conventional	.485
	(12)	Autonomous Groups Tol.	.470
	(3)	Associational Groups	.463
**	(—)	Bureaucracy Modern/Semi.	.450
	(18)	Linguistic Homogeneity	.285
	(23)	Political Enculturation	.238

* Core variable correlation
** Bureaucratic measure

The high ranking of Literacy Rate on both lists may indicate the necessity of an advanced degree of economic development for the operation and maintenance of a wide-scale educational system. All relationships are circular to some extent, but the relatively high literacy rate, together with some degree of consumer power, (G.N.P. Per Capita) might explain why Newspaper Circulation is so closely related to the economic factor. It is not surprising to see that Urbanization is ranked high on both lists, since it points to the possibility that there exists some degree of industrialization, or at least some centralization of commercial activities in a society. The moderate relationship of Westernization to the economic factor is probably redundant in that it contributes only those aspects of Westernization which are reflected already in the variables above.

In view of the high value of many of the intercorrelations in this table, it may be concluded that the economic factor, together with those variables it mediates most strongly, is of considerable importance for the development and maintenance of effective bureaucracy.

B. *The Communication Factor:* The two core variables for the communication factor are, "Literacy Rate"[3] and "Newspaper Circulation."[4]

Literacy Rate

*	(11)	Newspaper Circulation	.560
	(9)	G.N.P. Per Capita	.559
	(1)	Westernization	.555
	(5)	Economic Development	.524
**	(—)	Bureaucracy Modern/Semi.	.518
	(2)	Urbanization	.511
	(10)	Ideology Conventional	.471
	(3)	Associational Groups	.442
	(12)	Autonomous Groups Tol.	.418
	(18)	Linguistic Homogeneity	.338
	(23)	Political Enculturation	.291

Newspaper Circulation

	(9)	G.N.P. Per Capita	.610
*	(4)	Literacy Rate	.560
	(5)	Economic Development	.514
	(2)	Urbanization	.498
	(1)	Westernization	.496
	(10)	Ideology Conventional	.488
**	(—)	Bureaucracy Modern/Semi.	.424
	(12)	Autonomous Groups Tol.	.423
	(3)	Associational Groups	.367
	(18)	Linguistic Homogeneity	.312
	(23)	Political Enculturation	.287

* Core variable correlation
** Bureaucratic measure

The communication factor is so similar to the economic factor that there is little reason to separate them on empirical grounds. Both factors order the variables in much the same manner and are similarly related to the bureaucratic measure. However, since many of the variables used in this study are of such a general nature as to permit multiple interpretations, it is convenient to treat them as separate factors for the purpose of discussion.

[3] In terms of Banks and Textor's classification and the specific cross-break used, polities with a literacy rate of 50% or better are rated as high (see Banks and Textor, p. 66).
[4] Polities rated as high in "Newspaper Circulation" by Banks and Textor are those with a circulation of 100 or more per 1,000 persons (see Banks and Textor, p. 69).

It has already been hypothesized that the strong set of relationships between Literacy Rate, Newspaper Circulation and G.N.P. Per Capita has significance for effective bureaucratic performance insofar as it is mediated by the economic factor. However, the same set of relationships has significance for bureaucracy in the degree to which they reflect upon the capacities of a society's communications system. The necessity for having effective means of mass communication and a public which is capable of receiving and transmitting written communications has generally been overlooked in ecological studies which seek to specify the prerequisites for effective public administration. The variable Urbanization may also have a somewhat different meaning for the communication factor than it had for the economic factor in that it reflects the communication advantages which are inherent in the social and geographical propinquity to be found in centers of high population concentration.

Even though these hypothesized relationships are heavily dependent upon economic variables, it is apparent that the communication factor does have an independent contribution of some importance to make to the effective performance of administrative systems.

C. *The Political Factor:* The following are the two core variables and their intercorrelations for what has been labelled the "political factor." The core variables are "Ideological Orientation Is Conventional"[5] and "Autonomous Groups Are Tolerated in Politics."[6]

The two core variables correlate highly and order all other variables in a similar way. However, of all the factors presented, the political factor is the least related to the bureaucratic measure which appears at the bottom of both lists. Since this relationship is relatively weak in its more direct form, it is all the more important that the more indirect relationships be examined. A few hypotheses concerning indirect relations between bureaucracy and the political factor are presented below.

The variable, "Associational Groups," is closely related to the core political variable, "Ideology Is Conventional." Although Banks and Textor do not present a printout table for it, it is also possible that the degree of interest articulation by associational groups and the degree to which autonomous groups are tolerated in politics is also highly related. If this is so, the following relationships are hypothesized.

[5] By Banks and Textor's definition, polities are "conventional," rather than "doctrinal," "developmental," "situational" or "traditional," in ideological orientation if, "there exist conventionalized procedures for the achieving and legitimization of new or changed power relationships, even though access to the conventions in question is effectively denied a majority of the population" (see Banks and Textor, p. 80).

[6] Banks and Textor rate polities highly on the variable, Freedom of Group Opposition" if, ". . . autonomous groups [are] free to enter politics and able to oppose the government." (see Banks and Textor, p. 87).

Ideological Orientation is Conventional

*	(12)	Autonomous Groups Tol.	.600
	(1)	Westernization	.564
	(3)	Associational Groups	.546
	(5)	Economic Development	.540
	(2)	Urbanization	.505
	(11)	Newspaper Circulation	.488
	(9)	G.N.P. Per Capita	.485
	(4)	Literacy Rate	.471
**	(−)	Bureaucracy Modern/Semi.	.430
	(18)	Linguistic Homogeneity	.350

Autonomous Groups are Tolerated in Politics

*	(10)	Ideology Conventional	.600
	(1)	Westernization	.510
	(9)	G.N.P. Per Capita	.470
	(5)	Economic Development	.465
	(11)	Newspaper Circulation	.423
	(4)	Literacy Rate	.418
	(2)	Urbanization	.407
**	(−)	Bureaucracy Modern/Semi.	.389
	(18)	Linguistic Homogeneity	.254

(Data missing: Assoc. Grps.)

* Core variable correlation
** Bureaucratic measure

The political significance of associationalism is that it provides a compromisable basis for interest articulation which, when linked with an advanced degree of economic development, is likely to be related to the reduction of sharp differences in ideological orientation within a society. This set of conditions would help to provide a political environment in which autonomous groups are more likely to be tolerated. The significance of this for public bureaucracy is ambiguous since, while it may create a more complex set of authority and responsibility relationships, it is also clear that a stabilized and routinized political situation is a more congenial environment for the effective functioning of bureaucracy.

D. *A Socio-political Factor:* The two key variables which constitute the core of the fourth empirical factor are "Historically or Significantly Westernized"[7] and "Interest Articulation by Associational Groups."[8] Although it is not clear what descriptive label is most appropriate for this factor, for the purposes of discussion, it is tentatively

[7] For Banks and Textor, the label "historically western" refers to those polities which are located within the limits of the old Ottoman Empire with the addition of Greece. "Significantly westernized" presumably refers to polities outside this area which are either derivative, or have been profoundly influenced by historically western polities (see Banks and Textor, p. 75).

[8] The main characteristics of associational groups are, ". . . explicit representation

labelled as a socio-political factor. The intercorrelates of the two key variables are presented below.

The requirements that the two core variables intercorrelate highly and that they order other variables similarly are adequately met. It is also observed that the bureaucratic measure shows a fairly high degree of correlation on both core variables, particularly the variable Westernization. However, due to its rather general and ambiguous definition, it is unclear what the socio-political significance of Westernization is for the development and maintenance of advanced public bureaucracy. However, the strong relationship between Westernization and Interest Articulation by Associational Groups may give some clues for hypothesis formulation.

Westernization

*	(3)	Associational Groups	.588
**	(−)	Bureaucracy Modern/Semi.	.582
	(5)	Economic Development	.572
	(10)	Ideology Conventional	.564
	(4)	Literacy Rate	.555
	(2)	Urbanization	.554
	(9)	G.N.P. Per Capita	.534
	(11)	Newspaper Circulation	.496
	(18)	Linguistic Homogeneity	.318

Interest Articulation by Associational Groups

*	(1)	Westernization	.588
	(10)	Ideology Conventional	.546
	(2)	Urbanization	.542
**	(−)	Bureaucracy Modern/Semi.	.531
	(5)	Economic Development	.490
	(9)	G.N.P. Per Capita	.463
	(4)	Literacy Rate	.422
	(11)	Newspaper Circulation	.367
	(18)	Linguistic Homogeneity	.256

* Core variable correlation
** Bureaucratic measure

Interest articulation through associational groups is primarily a political process, but the basis for the existence of associational groups is mainly socio-cultural. The possible contributions which westernization makes to this basis may consist of the advanced degree of economic development and urbanization which is related to westernization. Increased

---

of the interests of a particular group, orderly procedures for the formulation of interests and demands and the transmission of these demands to other political structures, such as political parties, legislatures, bureaucracies" (see Banks and Textor, p. 89).

industrial urbanization may indicate the rise of secularization in a society following the break-down of geographically dispersed and localized ascriptive groupings and this is possibly an important pre-condition for the development of associational groups. In turn, the significance of associational groups for effective bureaucratic performance has been mentioned earlier in that it provides a compromisable basis for the demands made by different groups upon bureaucracy, whereas the exclusive and conflicting demands of ascriptive groups present great difficulties for public administration. Westernization also makes other indirect contributions to the bureaucratic measure through its high association with literacy rate and the existence of a conventional ideological orientation, both of which have been discussed earlier.

CONCLUSION

The correlational analysis presented in this study is admittedly a very limited sample of what might have been accomplished if a full-scale analysis had been possible. However, it may have served to illustrate some potential contributions which a full-scale empirical framework would have to make to the development of specific models of the ecology of public administration. In conclusion, some of these contributions are summarized.

One of the first tasks of model-building is the selection of variables for inclusion in the model. The present study has demonstrated that, by means of correlational techniques, a selection from a large number of variables can be made on objective grounds rather than on *ad hoc* and intuitive bases.

Another preliminary task in the construction of models is the definition of analytic terms and categories which are to be used in the formulation of basic assumptions and propositions. In models of the ecology of public administration, these terms will include the definition of basic institutional structures in society, such as the economic, political and socio-cultural systems. In this study, these systems have been defined empirically through the use of factor analysis. In factor analysis, the empirical factors which represent institutional systems are based on the pattern of relationships which emerges from the intercorrelations among a large set of variables. This procedure has many advantages over the usual method of first defining the systems intuitively and then assigning variables to the systems in terms of the intuitive definitions.

Many of the ecological variables used in current models are of such a general nature that a precise definition of them is difficult and their significance for bureaucracy is unclear. In factor analysis, it is possible to give a more complete specification to any variable by observing its relationship with other factors and associated variables. In the analysis presented here, for example, the degree of urbanization is seen to con-

116 John Forward

tribute substantially to several different factors. This suggests that the usual definition of urbanization in terms of population density is a highly general one which could probably be broken down into more specific components. Different terms could be given to different aspects of urbanization, insofar as it has economic, political or socio-cultural significance for bureaucracy. Another example is that the variable "Interest Articulation by Associational Groups" was found to have socio-cultural significance for bureaucracy in addition to the political meaning which is normally attributed to it.

Once the selection of variables and the formulation of basic assumptions and propositions have been achieved in model-building, the long process of hypothesis derivation and testing can begin. The present study has shown that correlational analysis may make an important contribution to this aspect of model-building also. Some examples of hypotheses which were suggested by the patterning of the variables emerging from the sample analysis in this study are to be found in the discussion sections dealing with the four main factors which were extracted.

Finally, the task of developing specific models for the unique patterning of ecological variables within one particular society is facilitated by knowing what are the features which are general to all societies. This universal patterning of ecological relationships would be provided by the empirical framework which has been suggested and illustrated in this study.

References

Banks, A. S. and Textor, R. B., *A Cross-Polity Survey* (Cambridge: M.I.T. Press), 1963.

Coombs, C. H., *A Theory of Data* (New York: Wiley), 1964.

Dahl, Robert A., "The Science of Public Administration: Three Problems," *Public Administration Review*, Vol. 7 (1947), pp. 1-11.

Dorsey, J. T., Jr., "An Information-Energy Model," in Ferrel Heady and Sybil L. Stokes (eds.), *Papers in Comparative Administration* (Ann Arbor: Institute of Public Administration), 1962.

Eisenstadt, S. N., "Bureaucracy, Bureaucratization and Debureaucratization," in [N. Raphaeli, *Readings in Comparative Public Administration* (Boston: Allyn and Bacon), 1967].

Friedrich, Carl J., *Constitutional Government and Democracy* (Boston: Ginn and Company), 1949.

Riggs, Fred W., "An Ecological Approach: The 'Sala' Model," in [N. Raphaeli, *Readings in Comparative Public Administration* (Boston: Allyn and Bacon), 1967].

———, *The Ecology of Public Administration* (New Delhi: Asia Publishing House), 1961.

Russett, B. M., Alker, H. R., Deutch, K. W. and Lasswell, H. D., *World Handbook of Political and Social Indicators* (New Haven: Yale University Press), 1964.

III

Internal Structure

Subunit Size

The similarity of Kaplan's and Glaser's themes is extraordinary. Kaplan, comparing research institutes in the United States and the Soviet Union, discusses the relative size and the degree of authority of their organizational subunits dedicated specifically to administrative tasks. Glaser, contrasting the United States and Europe, does the same for hospitals. Both, therefore, necessarily deal also with the amount of administrative authority retained by the professional — scientists in one case, doctors in the other. Both authors conclude that the structure of the economic environment from which their respective organizations must obtain resources exerts an enormous influence both on organization structure itself and on the structure of the larger systems of which each organization is a part. But the different career structures that obtain in each country, the different values attached to administrative tasks, recruitment patterns, and many other factors also influence organization structure.

Research Administration and the Administrator: U.S.S.R. and U.S.

In a recent paper I described the newly emerging role of the research administrator in the U.S. and tried to analyze a number of conflicting definitions and problems that stem primarily from the organizational structure in which the role is embedded.[1] During the summer of 1959, an attempt was made to compare these findings on the American research administrator with the situation of the Soviet research administrator. Some preliminary results of this comparative study are reported in this paper.[2]

After a brief description of the study in the U.S.S.R., I will outline a typical large-scale Soviet medical research organization. The administrator is located in this structure and his role is then described and compared with that of his counterpart in American research organizations. Although there are many similarities between these two roles in the two societies, some basic differences emerge, which are of potential significance for both the concrete study of research organization and for organizational theory generally. In a later section of the paper, some of the factors that may account for this basic difference are explored. Finally, some implications of this analysis are discussed.

Reprinted by permission of the author and publisher from the *Administrative Science Quarterly*, 6 (June 1961), pp. 51-72.

[1] Norman Kaplan, "The Role of the Research Administrator," *Administrative Science Quarterly*, 4 (1959), 20-42.

[2] Revision and extension of a paper read at the 127th annual meeting of the American Association for the Advancement of Science, December, 1960. Some of the ideas were initially developed in a lecture on "Comparative Research Organization," delivered at the Fifth Institute on Research and Development Administration, American University, Washington, D. C., April, 1960. This investigation is part of a larger series of studies on the organization of scientific research. Grateful acknowledgment is made for the support of these studies by a Public Health Service research grant (RG 5289), from the National Institutes of Health, Division of Research Grants, U.S. Public Health Service.

DESCRIPTION OF THE STUDY

One of the most important objectives of the study in the U.S.S.R. was to obtain data on the organizational structures and practices in research institutes that would permit comparisons with results previously found in the U.S. The study was therefore restricted to research institutes in the medical field, and especially those concentrating on cancer research, so as to examine roughly similar types of organizations engaged in roughly similar activities in both the U.S.S.R. and the U.S.

In all, I interviewed the director or deputy director, as well as a number of department heads and other scientists, in thirteen medical institutes located in Moscow, Leningrad, and elsewhere in the U.S.S.R.[3] Interviews were frequently conducted in a mixture of English, French, and German, as well as Russian. Sometimes we relied on interpreters almost entirely, and in general, either lay or scientific interpreters were almost always available. A qualitative interview guide was used, and on the whole the cooperation in answering questions very specifically was exemplary. Most of the interviews lasted a minimum of two hours, and many were much longer. In a few instances it was possible to conduct several interviews with the same person on successive days.

Most of the organizations visited were under the jurisdiction of the Academy of Medical Sciences, and the majority of these were concerned primarily with cancer research.[4] The smallest institute had over two hundred people while the largest had over a thousand research workers

[3] Most of the Soviet institutes visited were selected prior to my arrival in the U.S.S.R. on the basis of available knowledge here concerning their focus on medical research generally, and on cancer problems in particular. I am particularly grateful for the advice and suggestions offered by the late Dr. C. P. Rhoads, director of the Sloan-Kettering Institute, and Dr. John R. Heller, then director of the National Cancer Institute, and now president of the Memorial Sloan-Kettering Cancer Center. The selection of institutes, as well as initial contact with their directors prior to my arrival in the U.S.S.R., was greatly facilitated by the availability of an excellent document compiled by David P. Gelfand, *A Directory of Medical and Biological Research Institutes of the U.S.S.R.* (U.S. Public Health Service Publication No. 587; Washington, 1958). Finally, Mrs. Galina V. Zarechnak, of the National Library of Medicine, very kindly made available a prepublication draft of her study of the history and organization of the Soviet Academy of Medical Sciences, which provided valuable background information helpful in the selection procedure as well as in the subsequent interviews with Soviet medical scientists.

[4] I am pleased to record my gratitude to the institute directors, vice-directors, and other Soviet scientists who helped me to explore some of these problems of research organization. I am especially grateful to Professor S. A. Sarkisov, a member of the Presidium of the Academy of Medical Sciences, and Professor N. N. Blokhin, the director of the Institute of Experimental Pathology and Therapy of Cancer in Moscow (Dr. Blokhin has since become the President of the Academy of Medical Sciences), for their help in facilitating my visits and interviews, and in general, for enhancing my welcome at the various medical institutes in the U.S.S.R.

including auxiliary staff. In size, scope, and nature of specific research activities, these institutes were not unlike many to be found in many parts of the U.S.

STRUCTURE OF A RESEARCH INSTITUTE

As one might expect where most of the institutes studied are under the jurisdiction of a single organization, namely the Academy of Medical Sciences, the basic structure tends to be the same in most of the institutes.[5] Differences were, of course, encountered but these appear to be related primarily to differences in size and especially to differences in emphasis with respect to clinical operations. In this section the basic outline of the structure encountered in most research institutes is described in general terms. No claim is made that this structure is typical of all medical research institutes in the U.S.S.R., let alone all scientific research institutes. My interviews lead me to believe, however, that the deviations and differences which may exist in other research institutes are not basic ones. This will necessarily be an exploratory account, since the primary purpose here is to locate the role of research administration and the administrator.

The director is the chief executive of the research institute and has over-all responsibility for the conduct of the research program and the maintenance of the research institute and its staff. He is appointed by the Presidium of the Academy of Medical Sciences for a three-year term which is renewable indefinitely. Directly below him in the organizational hierarchy is the deputy director or vice-director and typically the title contains the phrase "for research." He assists the director, acts for the institute in his absence, and has primary responsibility for the conduct and co-ordination of the scientific program of the institute. Below the vice-director are the departments into which the institute is divided with the department heads or chiefs reporting directly to the vice-director. The number of departments as well as their composition depends upon the size of the institute and the scope of its program. Below the department heads, one is likely to find a number of laboratories with the laboratory chiefs reporting directly to the department heads.

The basic outline of this type of structure is very familiar and certainly resembles that of most larger medical research institutes in the U.S. and many European countries. Parenthetically, it might be noted that I saw only one organization chart at all the institutes visited, although

[5] For a general, and somewhat critical, review of the history and organization of the Academy of Medical Sciences based primarily on Soviet documentary sources, see: Galina V. Zarechnak, *Academy of Medical Sciences of the U.S.S.R.; History and Organization, 1944-1949* (Public Health Monograph No. 63; Washington, 1960). See especially her charts and descriptions of Soviet research institutes, pp. 12 ff.

most of the directors with whom I talked were quite willing to help me draw one up.

Two other elements are always present in the organizational structure and should be described in some detail. The first is the Scientific Council (*Soviet*) which is nominally responsible for the over-all research plan of the institute, evaluating progress of the institute and of individuals, and in general dealing with any organizational or scientific problems that may arise. The director of the institute is the chairman of the Council which is made up of all or most of the department heads. The Party is represented formally on this Council by the secretary of the local Trade Union of Scientific Workers who is normally one of the regular scientists on the staff. Senior scientists who may not be department heads may also be on the Council. In addition, at least two eminent scientists, usually in related fields, but always from other institutes, are also members of this Council. The total number of members varies, of course, according to the size of the institute, and most of the ones about which information is available vary from about twelve to about thirty-five members. The frequency of meetings varies from institute to institute, but in general there are regularly scheduled meetings once or twice a month although they may occur as often as once a week.

The Council appears to combine in a single group the functions normally incorporated in two separate groups in most scientific research institutes in the U.S. One function is that of executive committee for the institute as a whole, which in the U.S. would be composed typically of department heads, the vice-director for research, and the director as chairman, as in the U.S.S.R. The second function is typically carried out by a separate group in many institutes in the U.S. and is called a scientific council made up of scientists who are not regular members of the organization, but who are invited once or twice a year (or perhaps more frequently) to evaluate the scientific work of the institute. This scientific council in most U.S. institutes has no operating functions. It is difficult to know whether the scientific council in the U.S.S.R. institute would appear above the director's box on an organization chart, or whether it would more appropriately be on the same level as that of the director, with a dotted line denoting a primarily advisory function.

Finally, we turn to the position of the research administrator. Every institute visited has such a person and the title is usually a variant of "vice-director for administration" or simply "director of administration." As in most U.S. organizations, he has primary responsibility for finances, supplies, apparatus, equipment, furniture, repairs, maintenance, and other such service activities. The size of his staff tends to vary with the size of the institute as a whole and in some of the larger institutes the administrator may have a staff of over thirty persons working in a number of separate departments. The administrator's position in the organizational hierarchy is also difficult to locate precisely. He reports to the director of the institute but he has very little if anything to do with any other scientists. Although he reports directly to the chief executive, he is not a part of the executive committee nor is he typically considered a member of the executive hierarchy. Interestingly enough, I did not meet him personally at most of the institutes visited, with one or two exceptions, when the director wanted a precise figure or fact I had asked about and he consulted the administrator. With this background, it is now possible to examine the role of the research administrator in more detail.

ROLE OF RESEARCH ADMINISTRATOR

As already noted, the administrator reports directly to the director of the research institute and may have a fairly large staff. Furthermore, he is responsible for more or less the same kinds of activities as is his counterpart in the U.S. Some differences begin to appear as we note that the Soviet administrator is typically trained in what would be the American equivalent of business accounting and business procedures. It is not considered essential, or even desirable (as it is frequently considered here in the U.S.), that he have a scientific background or that he come from the ranks of the scientists. This difference becomes somewhat accentuated when we note his absence in greeting a foreign visitor, where the analogous situation in an American institution would find the administrator one of the more important men present at such a meeting. This is particularly to be expected when the visitor is more interested in problems of organization than in the substantive content of the work of the institute.

It is at first surprising to hear him referred to as the "bookkeeper" and his job described essentially as a bookkeeping one with few if any policy-making responsibilities. This term as used there implies more than simply the keeping of the financial books, referring also to "keeping the books" on maintenance, equipment, and so on. In many respects, we find that he occupies a position sometimes designated in American organizations as that of chief clerk. He has administrative responsibility for the clerks who work under him but has no other decision-making functions.

It is not surprising, therefore, to find that typically he is paid considerably less than most of the research scientists — normally only somewhat above the research technician with no advanced training. While laboratory technicians may earn approximately twelve to fifteen hundred rubles per month and the director of a research institute may have a base salary of at least five to six thousand rubles a month, the chief administrator earns approximately twelve hundred to two thousand rubles per month.[6] The range for the administrator indicates primarily the differences in size of organization and length of experience. A researcher starting out with the first advanced degree probably earns about eighteen hundred to two thousand rubles a month. In short, there can be little doubt that the chief administrator, who is referred to as the bookkeeper and whose duties correspond to those of a chief clerk, is in fact paid as one would expect a bookkeeper or chief clerk to be paid compared with the more technically trained research scientists in the research hierarchy.

For the research administrator there is little or no conflict concerning authority and control over science and scientists. These are exercised by the scientists themselves and not by a lay administrator. The Soviet administrator, when compared to his American counterpart, occupies quite a subordinate position in the research organization, despite the fact that the two have essentially the same titles and many of the same functions in a research organization.

The American research administrator is paid a good deal more than most American scientists in the same research organization and frequently is paid nearly as much as many senior scientists. In the organizational hierarchy, he is always at or near the top of the organizational structure. Although his duties may correspond very closely to those described for the Soviet administrator on a formal basis, the American administrator has many decision-making functions, overtly or covertly.[7] Many of these, incidentally, seem to stem from the unwillingness of the research director to make the decisions himself. The American research director often feels that he has little time for purely administrative decisions, and furthermore, the administrator is often thought to be better equipped to make them. In the U.S. it is often considered desirable for an administrator to have a scientific background, and not infrequently chief administrators in research organizations are recruited from the ranks of scientists. The American administrator is definitely a public figure and in fact serves to save the research director's time in public relations. He frequently exercises authority over scientists with regard to the kind of equipment they can get, space allotment, and adherence to budgets, although much of his authority is exercised in-

[6] These are 1959 rubles. It is difficult to translate these earnings into terms which permit suitable comparisons with the U.S. Furthermore, it is unnecessary to do so for our purposes here since the object is to show that the administrator's salary tends to be much closer to that of technician or beginning scientists, and not, as in the U.S., closer to that of the senior scientists, associate directors, or even department heads.

[7] The observations on the role and status of the American research administrator are drawn largely from an earlier paper. Cf. Norman Kaplan, *op. cit.*

directly, frequently with the budget or some such impersonal instrument as the indirect mechanism employed.[8]

Finally, when the American administrator is not a scientist, it is not very likely that he can move up much higher in the scientific research institute. This is, of course, similar to the Soviet situation. But frequently the American administrator, even without scientific training, who moves out of the scientific realm whether in the same organization (e.g. an industrial firm or the government) or whether from an organization in one institutional sphere to another, can move up very high in the organizational heirarchy by virtue of his *expertise* as an administrator.

In sum, the American research administrator is better paid, compared with his Soviet counterpart and with scientists in the research organization. He enjoys much higher prestige in America and, of course, he is the source of many more conflicts and problems in a research organization.[9]

This brief description indicates some vital differences in the role of the research administrator in the U.S. and the U.S.S.R. Since we are dealing with essentially similar types of organizational structures and with organizations concerned with roughly similar problems, handled in approximately the same way, and whose over-all size is roughly comparable, we are faced with the question: Why is the role of the Soviet administrator so very different? We are amazed that the Soviet administrator occupies such a subordinate position in the research organization compared with the American administrator. Of course, we could with equal validity ask the question: Why does the American administrator occupy such a superordinate position in the research organization relative to his Soviet counterpart? Asking the question both ways raises interesting subsidiary problems, some of which are considered in the remaining sections of this paper.

POSSIBLE EXPLANATORY FACTORS

As an American commenting on the Soviet scene, it seems to make sense to try to amplify the question in terms of Soviet experiences first. The first obvious question is what happens to all the administrative tasks? Obviously, the American administrator and his staff have much to keep them busy; in fact, they always seem overburdened with a variety of administrative problems. Who takes care of these problems in the Soviet research institute?

This seemingly simple and obvious question turns out, of course, to be fairly complex upon closer examination. For one thing, we must ask whether there is the same "amount" of administrative work and detail

[8] Kaplan, *ibid.*, p. 33.

[9] *Ibid.*; for other evidence see E. Orowan, "Our Universities and Scientific Creativity," *Bulletin of Atomic Scientists*, 15 (1959), 237-238; L. Kowarski, "Psychology and Structure of Large Scale Physical Research," *ibid.*, 5 (1949); A. M. Brues, "The New Emotionalism in Research," *ibid.*, 11 (1955).

in the Soviet and American research institutes. We must also inquire whether the Soviet administrator has approximately the same kinds of duties but simply a lower status, or whether he has lower-status duties and a lower status as a consequence.

We are almost forced to start with the notion that the Soviet scientists, as compared with their American counterparts, tend to view the content and the boundaries of research administration differently. The Soviet view of the research administrator essentially restricts him to a bookkeeping function and in terms of administrative theory, might be labeled the pure execution of policy.[10] The American view of the chief administrator is often much broader. The hypothetical distinction between the execution of policy and the formulation of policy often does not work out in practice. Furthermore, the American scientist's tendency to delegate any problem that he considers essentially nonscientific results in a concept of the chief administrator's role as essentially residual — it becomes in effect all things and all functions which the director or the other top scientists are unwilling, unable, or reluctant to do themselves. In return for the alleged freedom resulting from a broadly conceived view of administration, the American scientist-director must also give up some of the areas of decision making which at the same time he continues to feel are still his prerogative; hence the almost continual underlying conflict between the administrator and the scientists in many American research organizations.

In the U.S.S.R., and for that matter in most of the rest of Europe, the scientist and the director of scientific research organizations appear to be much less reluctant than their American counterparts to assume

[10] See, for example, the discussion by Herbert Simon, where he questions the distinction (attributed to Frank J. Goodnow) between policy and administrative processes, "Recent Advances in Organization Theory," in *Research Frontiers in Politics and Government,* (Washington, 1955), esp. pp. 24-26. This kind of distinction has been emphasized by many political scientists commenting on the alleged stability and resilience of the civil service apparatus in Great Britain, France, and other nations in the face of marked changes in the political leadership of the state. This thesis is explicitly challenged in a brilliant analysis of the Nazi Germany case by Frederic S. Burin, "Bureaucracy and National Socialism: A Reconsideration of Weberian Theory," in Robert K. Merton *et al.*, eds., *Reader in Bureaucracy* (Glencoe, 1952), pp. 33-47.

To our knowledge, the distinction between the formulation and the (mere) execution of policy has been confined almost exclusively to the political sphere. It has not been studied adequately in other kinds of large nongovernmental organizations. Is there, for example, a "neutral" apparatus in large corporations which remains essentially intact in the face of sharp changes in the leadership and control of the company? Our analysis here points to the possibility that the Soviets effectively avoid the problems which may arise if the distinction is recognized insofar as the scientists keep administrative policy-making functions for themselves rather than delegating these and by downgrading the administrator to the level of a chief clerk.

administrative duties which have a bearing on the conduct of the research.[11] They cheerfully delegate keeping the books and other financial personnel records, and similar bookkeeping-type operations to a chief clerk, who is called a research administrator. But most other so-called nonresearch duties the Soviet scientist, as well as the European scientist generally, seems more willing to do himself. In general, it may be said that scientists at all levels, from the laboratory head to the director, are more willing to involve themselves in the nonclerical aspects of administration — and specially anything which is viewed as connected with the effective conduct of the research itself.

It is not simply as a matter of prestige that the American scientist-director argues in favor of sloughing off administrative duties. Far more important in the eyes of most scientists is the opportunity to concentrate on the conduct of research without being diverted by what seem extraneous organizational and administrative responsibilities. If it is true then, as we have asserted, that the Soviet scientist is far more willing to engage in administrative tasks than his American counterpart, does he in fact spend less time on research, since presumably he has to spend more time on administration?

The answer is paradoxical indeed. Most directors of American research institutes seem to have little, if any, time for their own research. The Soviet director, on the other hand, asserts that he spends most of his day on the conduct of his research and that this is in fact his first duty. When asked for an estimate of how much time a director in the Soviet medical institute had to spend on administrative duties, he typically answered that it was an average of about an hour a day. This increased, of course, at certain times of the year when new budgets had to be in, but generally the time reported spent at the institute not devoted to research was extremely low. We then have the apparent paradox of the

[11] Published evidence for this statement is admittedly scanty. However, it was strongly supported by my own observations and interview data. In some German laboratories, for example, the Director explicitly provides "on the job training" in administrative duties for his young postdoctoral research assistants. Usually, the young man is given responsibility for "helping" with purchasing activities for a six-month period, and then may be shifted to equipment maintenance for a similar period, and so on. This is viewed, in part, as a continuation of the traditional apprenticeship pattern to ensure that the young man will have gained the experience necessary to qualify him for a more senior post ultimately. Another consequence, of course, is that the director's own total administrative load is lightened considerably by being shared with subordinates. But, significantly, the director delegates some administrative responsibility to other *scientists*, and not to professional full-time administrators. To some extent, I suspect that this pattern is less a deliberately considered policy and more an extension of the traditional patterns of the small research institutes to the much larger organization which is becoming more prevalent today. The absence of this kind of strong tradition in the U.S. is perhaps partly responsible for the greater reliance on professional administrators here.

Soviet director more willing and more likely to engage in administrative duties than his American counterpart and yet being able to spend considerably more time on his own research than his American counterpart.

Dismissing some of the more tenuous kinds of answers, we can only suggest one rather startling possibility. There is simply less administration. This is exceptional on two counts. We could expect that, given the same type of activity and the same size in comparable organizations, the administrative duties (not counting the purely routine ones, which are handled by clerks in both situations) would be roughly the same in order to meet the requirements of maintaining the organization. It might even be expected by some that, given comparable organizations, the level of administrative duties in the Soviet organization would be considerably higher because of the nature of Soviet society with its greater emphasis on centralization and its general bureaucratic tendencies.[12] But I must conclude tentatively that there is probably less administrative detail and bureaucratic red tape in the Soviet medical institute.

WHY DOES THIS DIFFERENCE EXIST?

It might be concluded that less administration and red tape would be possible in the U.S.S.R. because of the relative simplicity of the finan-

[12] The stereotype of excessive red tape and bureaucracy in the U.S.S.R. is widely supported in the literature and is generally shared by most foreigners visiting the Soviet Union. How much of this stereotype can be attributed to the facts of the case, and how much to preconceived ideas coupled with inadequate comparative analyses is difficult to determine. To our knowledge there have been no studies of bureaucratic tendencies and administrative proliferation in the research institutes of the U.S.S.R. However, medical scientists have commented on the "medical bureaucracy" in the Soviet clinical practices and in the hospitals. Cf. the comments in the U.S. Public Health Service, *The Report of the United States Public Health Mission to the Union of Soviet Socialistic Soviet Republics,* (Public Health Service Publication No. 649; Washington, 1959), especially p. 25.

Much has been written on the bureaucratic facets of Soviet industrial organization, but even here, this notion has been sharply criticized. See, for example, David Granick, *Management of the Industrial Firm in the U.S.S.R.* (New York, 1954), especially the concluding chapter in which Granick makes an explicit attempt to compare the extent of bureaucratization in Soviet and non-Soviet industrial organization. He notes, for example, "It appears an open question whether Soviet industry is not . . . less bureaucratic than are most giant firms in capitalist society" (p. 262). Granick attributes the fact that many Western observers see so much bureaucracy in the U.S.S.R. to their treatment of planned and centralized control over the economy as being synonymous with "bureaucracy." It should also be noted that there has been increasing concern with the growing bureaucratization of private business organizations in the U.S. A study by Seymour Melman of this problem over a fifty-year period in the U.S. cites an increase of 87 per cent among productive workers compared with a 244 per cent in administrative personnel in American manufacturing industries in the period 1900-1940 ("The Rise of Administrative Overhead in the Manufacturing Industries of the United States 1899-1947," *Oxford Economic Papers,* 3, N.S. [Feb. 1951], 62).

cial support structure. One of the obvious reasons for a complicated and large administrative staff in many U.S. medical institutes is the complexity of the financial structure and the necesssity to keep track of the dozens and sometimes hundreds of different grants from different agencies with differing termination dates, differing rules concerning permissible practices, differing requirements for progress reports, renewal procedures, and so on. In the Soviet medical institutes, which are under the jurisdiction of the Academy of Medical Sciences, the budget stems from that single source.

Is it very likely that this difference in the financial support structure accounts for differing administrative loads in similar medical institutes in the two societies? The answer, perhaps strangely, is that this explanation is not very likely because when we examine organizations in the U.S. essentially similar to the Soviet ones with respect to financing, we do not find this to be the case. One of the best examples of such a comparison would be one of the National Institutes of Health, which also has a single source for its budget, namely, the Department of Health, Education, and Welfare and ultimately Congress. Despite this single source, or perhaps because of the characteristic federal accounting and auditing regulations, the reporting procedures and the administrative load generally are probably not very different from that found in most other U.S. medical organizations of similar size and scope. In fact, it may be suspected that the administrative load is at least as heavy, if not heavier, in such an organization.[13] It is probably the case then that the particular kind of financial structure is not of central significance in this context, although as pointed out in the previous paper, it may influence an already existing level of administration.[14]

If it is probably not the relative simplicity of the financial structure,

[13] It must be emphasized that this comparative evaluation is purely impressionistic. It is based largely on available documentary sources and talks with scientists and administrators at the National Institutes of Health. It would certainly be desirable and worth while to check this further in a more precise quantitative fashion.

It should also be emphasized that our impressionistic comparison is between the seven institutes of the National Institute of Health and their intramural research organization with somewhat similar types of institutes in the U.S.S.R. under the central administration of the Academy of Medical Sciences. This comparison is not intended as a reflection of the effectiveness or policies of the National Institute of Health administration structure or its administrators. In fact, its administration, as a whole and at the institute level, seems to be highly regarded by the National Institute of Health as well as by other scientists and research officials who have any familiarity with it. In my own experience, these institutes, when compared with *others of the same size and scope in the United States*, are consistently highly rated in this regard. The comparison with institutes of the Academy of Medical Science, however, highlights the importance of the external environment and the demands stemming from it, which may affect administrative requirements within the organization.

[14] Kaplan, *op. cit.*, p. 32.

what other possible factors might account for the hypothesized lower level of administrative activity in the Soviet medical research institute? Perhaps the Soviet government is willing to require fewer formal controls which in turn reduces the amount of administrative activity simply because they tend to trust their scientists more than we do. This is an intriguing hypothesis because it is probably true that the average American feels that the Soviet government trusts none of its citizens at all, while the American government, industrial firm, or scientific research institute under private auspices would seem more likely to trust their scientists. Unfortunately, it was not possible to obtain any data which would either confirm or deny this hypothesis. If, however, there is less administration in otherwise comparable organizations, then a factor such as this may play an important role.

There is relatively little disagreement that the scientist is accorded considerably more prestige and is relatively better paid and rewarded in the material sense in the U.S.S.R. than he is in the U.S. Conversely, the administrator, at least in the medical research institute, enjoys far less prestige and material reward than the administrator in the U.S. To the extent that the prestige accorded, as well as the material rewards, reflect an evaluation of the relative importance of the activities carried on by scientists and administrators, we have perhaps an additional small bit of evidence in support of the hypothesis that the Soviet scientist is trusted somewhat more.

Another factor of potentially great significance is the nature of higher authority over the organization. The director of the medical institute is responsible to the Academy of Medical Sciences and specifically to the scientists who make up the Presidium of the Academy. He is thus responsible directly to other scientists and not to government administrators or "politicians." His American counterpart is typically responsible to a board composed of laymen who are not often very familiar with the nature of science. Being unfamiliar, they are much more likely to require reports, statistics, and data, which they can understand and which in turn require the services of, and enhance the importance of, the administrator.

Returning to an earlier injunction that the question must necessarily be asked both ways, namely, why does the Soviet institute seem to have "less" administration and why does the American institute have "more" administration, we are led to inquire into some of the consequences of administrative decisions and programs. Administration, in the American sense of the term as defined here, is necessary in order to accomplish a minimum of co-ordination, communication, and control in an organization. But presumably these should be the same in the U.S.S.R. and the U.S. given similarity in organization and its activity. Part of the problem, however, is co-ordination, control, communication for whom and for what purposes? At its simplest, these are necessary for the director; he must be able to exercise control functions and may need help for this. But it becomes more complicated when the director is in turn responsible to other authorities and must provide certain information to them, primarily for purposes of control. As already noted, the complex multiplicity of research budgets in many American institutes may require the exercise of control to meet the differing criteria of a large number of organizations, all of which have provided funds for part of the larger program.

The American research director's having to account for the activities and expenditures of his research organization to a board of trustees or directors — to laymen in general (at least with respect to the intricacies of scientific research) — tends to force the director to provide certain types of nontechnical reports and information. Since these board members may have little technical knowledge of the substance of the research, and since they tend to have a great deal of knowledge concerning the operation of large organizations, both they and the director of organizations responsible to them feel that certain types of reports are almost desirable to indicate proper control and reasonable progress although they may have little intrinsic value for the conduct of the research. All of these inevitably increase the administrative load and, in fact, make it very difficult for the director to spend much time on co-ordinating the research itself, let alone doing any of his own.

The additional problem of raising funds, not at all unimportant in most American research institutes, also consumes a good deal of the time and energy of a director and administrators to whom such functions can be, and frequently are, delegated. In the U.S.S.R., on the other hand, whatever the problems concerning the amounts and scope of the financial support, it is a single body of *scientists* to whom the director must go for his financial support for the following year. The men of the Academy of Medical Sciences are presumed to have a fairly intimate knowledge of the scientific character of the work and are less likely to require reports which we might consider normal for boards of trustees here.

Finally, two other far more speculative factors which may affect research administration in the two countries should be mentioned. The first has to do with the contemporary origins of the large-scale research institute in the two societies. In the U.S.S.R., it is apparently the case that the university institute, following the old European tradition, was expanded into a large-scale organization under the Academy. In the process, the high prestige and the relative autonomy of the scientist (with some notable exceptions of political incursions) was maintained. In the U.S., on the other hand, there was little tradition for the relatively autonomous institute, whether attached to the university or not, and the scientist in general enjoyed relatively little prestige or autonomy. By the time research in the U.S. was expanded in the university and outside, and the complexity of the research organization grew with this expansion, the organizational model which many felt worth imitating was the successful big business enterprise. Moreover, the business organization model was borrowed at a time when the organizational specialist — the administrator — was becoming increasingly important.[15]

The other major factor has to do with the diversity of not only our financial support structure but also the occupational structure for scientists in the U.S. Titles vary from institution to institution, salary scales vary from one institutional sphere to another (industry versus government etc.), and in general there is diversity with respect to most aspects of the employment, supervision, and evaluation of the scientist. This necessitates the collection of a good deal of information to provide some basis for the evaluation of scientists and institutes.

In the U.S.S.R., on the other hand, there is a single system, with many subdivisions to be sure, defining salary scales in different types of institutes, employment grades related primarily to educational attainment, and other more or less fixed criteria. Thus large areas open to discretion in the U.S. are fixed in the U.S.S.R. and require relatively little administrative action.[16] There are, of course, numerous formal and informal ways of by-passing this otherwise inflexible structure which need not be considered in any detail here. The point to be stressed is that having this centralized and generalized system of promotion policies, grades of employment, salary schedules, etc., may actually reduce the administrative load as well as the amount of discretion that can be exercised in any specific institute. Whether the perceived disadvantages of this centralization outweigh this particular advantage is yet another question.

In closing this section, it must be emphasized again that we are primarily concerned with exploring several significant aspects of the administration of research institutes. Obviously, neither the short period of time spent in the U.S.S.R., nor the preliminary nature of my inquiries permit anything other than a very tentative analysis. It should also be obvious that the various possibilities, theoretical and otherwise, which may account for the apparently sharp differences in the administration of medical research encountered in the U.S.S.R. and in the U.S. have hardly been exhausted. In subsequent studies of this problem, these are

[15] Some confirmation of the importance of administrative personnel in American industry may be found in Melman, *op. cit.*

[16] For a comparative study of scientific personnel systems, see: Edward McCrensky, *Scientific Manpower in Europe* (New York, 1958). Chapter vii is particularly relevant inasmuch as it contains a discussion of Soviet practices compared with others.

among the hypotheses deserving of further exploration. In the final section which follows, I turn to an examination of some of the implications of my observations and the hypotheses just noted.

SUMMARY AND CONCLUSIONS

The observations, that the character of research administration and the role of the research administrator in roughly similar types of medical research organizations in the U.S.S.R. and the U.S. are different, call for an explanation. We want to know why this is so and how these differences operate, as well as how this affects the conduct of medical research.

How this is accomplished is possibly easier to describe, and the main points previously made can be summarized briefly here. The primary difference revolves around the definition of the chief administrator. In the medical research institutes of the U.S.S.R., he is defined primarily as a chief clerk. In the U.S. there is no single clear-cut definition, but in general he tends to be defined as something much more than a chief clerk, varying from general business manager to a general manager of an organization. In the U.S., the chief administrator normally has some decision-making functions while in the U.S.S.R. he appears to have practically none. This difference in definition leads to obvious differences in recruitment patterns as well as in the rewards involved in the job.

For the Russians, there is little or no problem concerning the type of person to be recruited for this job. He does not require any advanced education. He must be a competent keeper of books and records (financial and others), and, to be a chief administrator in a fairly large institute, he must be able to supervise the activities of a number of subordinate clerks. For the American research organization, on the other hand, the character of the desirable recruit for chief administrator tends to vary. Some believe the best sort of person for this position is a man who knows how to run and manage an organization. An underlying assumption is that most large organizations, irrespective of their particular activities, are essentially alike with respect to organizational problems, and consequently the best type of man for this position is a specialist in administration who is, with respect to organizations, a generalist. That is, he can move fairly easily from running a research organization to running a soap factory. Another school of thought, however, believes that there is something fairly unique about the management of a scientific research organization and tends to favor a former scientist or at least a man with scientific background who has administrative experience or at least displays a flair for administration. Involved in such a flair is the ability to deal with people and to talk with scientists, in particular to understand their problems as well as their general antipathy toward large bureaucratic organizations.

Given the Soviet requirements and definition, the man recruited need not be paid a very high salary relative to others in the research organization. He is, in effect, a fairly low-level, white-collar worker among considerably better trained and more advanced personnel in the various scientific fields. In the U.S., on the other hand, the man recruited must be paid a fairly high salary relative to other scientists because he too has advanced training, and what is most important, his market includes other types of large organizations where he commands a high salary.

We should certainly expect that the differences built into these two conceptions of the chief administrator should manifest themselves in other ways in the research organization. As already noted, we can entertain one of the two major possibilities: Either the amount and character of administration (management control, etc.) is roughly equivalent in the Soviet and American medical institute of the same size and character, in which case we should expect that the functions of the administrator in the U.S. setting are carried out by one or more functional substitutes in the organization; or, it is possible that the amount and character of general administration is quantitatively and qualitatively different in the Soviet institutions and hence few, if any, functional substitutes may be necessary. Our tentative analysis appears to favor the latter possibility although some questions and modifications must be considered.

First, it has been suggested that there is in fact "less" administration in the Soviet institutions and that, furthermore, the scientist himself, and in particular, laboratory and department heads as well as the scientific director of the institute, appear to be more willing to carry on some so-called administrative duties, which tend to be shunned by their American counterparts. Most important, these Soviet scientists report that such duties do not infringe on their research time and, in fact, are far more likely to report that they do their own research. This suggests the hypothesis that given a reduction of administrative requirements, and an adequate division of labor with respect to the remaining requirements among the scientists, it is possible to have a more effective organization in which the primary goal of the pursuit of scientific research is not diminished significantly.

In fact, it might be argued that the apparent saving of time in delegating many management activities *bearing directly* on research is in the long run a myth. The structure becomes far more cumbersome, cleavages and antipathy may arise between the research people and the administrative people, and the administrator is forced to make decisions in situations where scientific competence and intimate knowledge of the scientific research is necessary. This results in additional mechanisms in the organization to reduce cleavage and to communicate information, which may be far more cumbersome than an ordinary division of labor among the scientists themselves. If the scientist is willing to accept some minimum amount of administrative duty as part of his job, and as part of the price he must pay for the benefits derived from working in a large complex organization, then the net results in terms of what he can accomplish scientifically may be far greater than if he delegates many of these management functions to specialists in management. Such a step would be extremely difficult in many American research organizations because, among other things, it would necessitate the reduction in status, prestige, and monetary rewards of the chief administrator as he is now defined.

It is unfortunately not possible to discuss relative differences in the effectiveness of the conduct of research in the U.S.S.R., and the U.S. medical research institutions.[17] This is so for many obvious reasons, including our lack of adequate measures, but also because of differences in emphases, relative time devoted to the attack on different sorts of

---

[17] In recent years there have been numerous reports evaluating the "quality" and other characteristics of medical research in the U.S.S.R. by American and other Western medical scientists who have visited the Soviet Union. It would obviously be presumptuous of me, a layman with respect to the medical sciences, to give my own evaluation. However, my impression from reading many of these reports and from talking with some of the medical scientists who have been there, is that Soviet medical research is generally viewed as competent, and in particular subfields, as quite outstanding. The growing program of translation of Soviet medical and scientific journals must also be viewed as evidence of the importance attached to Soviet research.

An extremely useful selected and annotated list of references has been compiled by Elizabeth Koenig of the National Institutes of Health Library: *Medical Research in the U.S.S.R.*, (Public Health Service Publication No. 710; Washington, 1960). Among the most relevant reports in terms of the institutes I visited are the following: J. R. Paul, "American Medical Mission to the Soviet Union," *Scientific Monthly*, 85 (1957), 150-156; M. B. Shimkin, "Oncology in the Soviet Union," in *Year Book of Cancer, 1957-58* (Chicago, 1958), pp. 506-510; M. B. Shimkin, and R. E. Shope, "Some Observations on Cancer Research in the Soviet Union," *Cancer Research*, 16 (1956), 915-917; J. Turkevich, "Soviet Science in the Post-Stalin Era," *Annals American Academy Political Social Sciences*, 303 (1956), 139-151; H. Hamperl, "Pathologie in UdSSR" (Pathology in the U.S.S.R.), *Deutsche Medizinische Wochenschrift*, 82 (1957), 416-419; C. W. Scull, M. Nance, F. Grant, and G. F. Roll, "Some General Observations on Medical and Pharmaceutical Research in the Soviet Union," *Journal American Medical Association*, 167 (1958), 2120-2123; *The Report of the United States Public Health Mission to the Union of Soviet Socialist Republics, Including Impressions of Medicine and Public Health in Several Soviet Republics* (Public Health Service Publication No. 649; Washington, 1959); U.S. Public Health Service, *United States-U.S.S.R. Medical Exchange Missions, 1956; Microbiology and Epidemiology* (Public Health Service Publication No. 536; Public Health Monograph No. 50; Washington, 1957).

problems, and a host of ordinary but complicated problems of assessing the effectiveness of any kind of organization. One point which has some implication for general organizational theory must, however, be stressed. In general, our observation and analysis force us to ask how much administration is necessary in a complex organization. We have tended to assume, perhaps without sufficient evidence, that the level of administrative activity in research organizations (as well as in others) is at, or very near, the minimum necessary for co-ordination, control, and communication considered adequate to maintain the organization. The findings tend to throw some doubt on the validity of this assumption, at least for medical research institutes, and in a very speculative way possibly for most other types of complex organizations as well.

In summary, it seems highly possible that the Russians really do use much less formal administration in scientific organizations than we have thought possible. I have tried to suggest some of the factors that may contribute to this and, in particular, would stress the strategic role of the larger society as well as differences in approach toward large-scale complex organizations. The nature of the financial structure, the kinds of controls exercised by higher authority external to any given organization, as well as the general prestige level of scientists relative to administrators and others seem to affect the situation. It is hoped that additional empirical research can be conducted inside the U.S.S.R., as well as further comparative research in other countries and in other types of organizations in the U.S., to test some of the assumptions and hypotheses suggested here as well as to move closer toward a theory of complex organizations.

WILLIAM A. GLASER

Hospital Administrators and Doctors

ADMINISTRATION AND ADMINISTRATIVE—
THERAPEUTIC CONFLICTS

When a sociological participant-observer enters an American hospital, he is immediately struck by the large number of administrative offices near the front entrance and by the numerous administrative employees, such as full-time or nearly full-time executives, purchasing officers, book-keepers, personnel officers, secretaries, file clerks, receptionists, messengers, and others. Many of these tasks and personnel are concentrated in central offices; others are parts of the separate medical services of the hospital. Some social scientists have made intensive studies of the administrative personnel themselves.[1] A principal theme in many sociological studies of hospitals has been conflicts between the administrative and

Reprinted with the permission of The Macmillan Company from *The Hospital in Modern Society*, Eliot Freidson, ed. © by The Free Press of Glencoe, a Division of The Macmillan Company 1963.

The chapter from which this article is taken may be identified as Publication No. A-339 of the Bureau of Applied Social Research, Columbia University. This investigation was supported by Research Grant, RG-7934, awarded by the National Institute of Health, Public Health Service.

For convenience in exposition, this chapter will contain many simplifications. I shall contrast American and "foreign" hospitals, but of course the reader must never forget that the word "foreign" embraces a great variety of forms. "Foreign hospitals" are the type of organization that originated in Continental Europe and spread to other continents; this analysis does not pertain to British hospitals, whose medical staff organization differs from both the American and Continental types. International variations in government structure, economic prosperity, skilled manpower, styles of medical practice, and other factors produce a great range of hospital types in the world. Highly developed countries with social and medical structures much like America's, such as Canada and Australia, have hospitals that are sociologically similar. Northern and Western Europe resemble America in some ways and differ in others; hospitals in the underdeveloped countries of Asia and Africa are yet more different. For the most part I shall be comparing the kinds of large general hospitals that American sociologists have usually studied, but occasionally I shall mention the smaller private and rural hospitals.

[1] For example, Edith Lentz, "Morale in a Hospital Business Office," *Human Organization*, 9 (Fall, 1950), pp. 17-21.

therapeutic personnel, arising from their different conceptions of the hospital's goals and priorities.[2]

But if the same sociological participant-observer entered a hospital in nearly any foreign country he would notice fewer administrative offices, fewer administrative personnel, and a smaller volume of administrative work. There may be fewer conflicts between the administrative and therapeutic needs of hospitals, and thus between administrators and therapists.[3] These fundamental differences have numerous causes. In many countries the nature of medical care, simpler payment methods, the expectations of patients, and the character of the society require fewer administrative tasks. In nearly all other countries certain administrative tasks performed inside the American hospital are performed on a higher level of the society. In many countries certain tasks performed in America by central administrators for the entire hospital are performed by the separate medical services within the organization. In nearly all other countries administrative work is more clearly subordinated to clinical work; it may be delegated to lay employees who clearly possess less education, lower prestige, and fewer rewards.[4]

Different Amounts of Medical Administration

Many characteristics of American medical care produce a larger volume of administrative work. For example, compared to most countries, Amer-

[2] See the many sources listed in George Reader and Mary Goss, "Medical Sociology with Particular Reference to the Study of Hospitals," *Transactions of the Fourth World Congress of Sociology* (London: International Sociological Association, 1959), Vol. II, p. 46.

[3] This is generally but not universally true. In some Asian cultures, complex administrative procedure is a cultural norm and clerical jobs are very prestigeful. Therefore, the hospitals of such countries may have more administration and more administrators than a Western sociologist might consider functional for medical and organizational success. Certainly they have more bureaucrats and more red tape than the doctors think necessary! Administrative-therapeutic conflicts may result. For example, see R. E. Rewell, "Medicine in the New India," *The Lancet* (September 13, 1958), pp. 575, 577.

[4] These differences have been noticed by other travelers, such as Frederic C. Le Rocker, "Hospitals without Administrators," *Hospitals*, 35 (January 1, 1961), pp. 47-49; and Milton I. Roemer, "General Hospitals in Europe," in J. K. Owen, ed., *Modern Concepts of Hospital Administration* (Philadelphia: W. B. Saunders Company, 1961). Detailed cross-national comparisons of administrative practice are still rare, but some exist. For an able comparison of hospital organization and procedure in America and in a developing country with typical problems, see Ahmed Kamel Mazen, "Development of the Medical Care Program of the Egyptian Region of the United Arab Republic," Stanford, Calif.: Stanford University, unpublished dissertation for the Ph.D. in Medical Care Administration, 1961. For a good comparison of American and English hospitals, see B. H. Chubb and A. Ashworth, *A Study of Staff Organization in Relation to Design of Selected Hospitals in the United States of America* (Sheffield: Sheffield Regional Hospital Board, 1962).

ican hospitals use larger amounts of new equipment and new drugs, and they perform more diagnostic tests.[5] Many administrative tasks result. Proposed equipment and drugs must be inspected and evaluated, the money raised by someone, sales and delivery negotiated and checked, special parts of the hospital building planned and adapted for the location of equipment in use or for the storage of materials and drugs, the orderly movement of materials and drugs throughout the hospital arranged, timetables prepared and checked for use of facilities, for the personnel who man the facilities, and for the patients who are diagnosed or treated by the equipment or drugs. Reports about patients' tests or treatments must be prepared and sent to the physicians who requested them, capital costs amortized in some way, and so on. Countries whose medical care is less technical — and this includes most of the world — have a smaller volume of such tasks in their hospitals and thus a smaller need for administrative specialists.

America integrates hospital practice and clinical medical research more than most other countries, and this too creates more administrative tasks than appear abroad. Since considerable prestige, professional advancement, and money are conferred upon the scientist in American medicine, more American than foreign hospital doctors perform research on their patients and write reports or journal articles. To a greater extent than in corresponding types of foreign hospitals, house staffs in larger American institutions conduct in-service educational programs that emphasize scientific lessons from the hospital's practice.[6] Even when American clinicians or administrators are not making original investigations of their own patients, more often than their foreign counterparts they may read the medical literature and check in their own hospitals whether certain new scientific findings are true. For such reasons, American hospitals have more specialized clerical personnel to file records, get information from files, aggregate facts about separate patients, type manuscripts, manage hospital libraries, and search the published literature.

Even the numerous American hospitals performing no research and no in-service staff education keep more voluminous records than their foreign counterparts. One reason is the need to protect the hospital and

[5] Foreign visitors are invariably struck by the higher technical level of American facilities and the greater use of the laboratory. For example, International Hospital Federation, *Report of Study Tour of Hospitals in the United States of America*. (London: International Hospital Federation, 1961), pp. 42-59 *passim*, and the unpublished reports by individual tour participants; Claude Huriez, "Les Hôpitaux Américains," *Techniques Hospitalières*, 12 (October, 1956), pp. 4-7.

[6] International Hospital Federation, *op. cit.*, pp. 2, 56-57, Urs Peter Haemmerli, "Principes d'organisation dans un hôpital d'enseignement Américain," *Médecine et Hygiène*, 17 (January 30, 1959), p. 39.

doctor in case of malpractice lawsuits. Such suits — very rare except in the Anglo-Saxon countries — must be defended by the hospital and doctor themselves with the aid of written evidence. Another reason for voluminous records is that they facilitate continuity of care over several hospital visits and American medicine practices such continuity more than most other countries. In a few other nations where continuity of care is attempted, such as England, the Soviet Union, and Israel, efficient patient files are kept in record rooms much like America's. Therefore, for a variety of reasons — research, in-service education, protection of the hospital, continuity of care, and American cultural habit — American hospitals keep more detailed, more voluminous, and more typewritten patient records than most foreign hospitals. American hospitals tend to keep these patient records in central and efficient files, a system that adds additional administrative tasks to the hospital.

Much of American hospital care is performed by private practitioners who visit the hospital for short periods either to treat their personal patients or to do voluntary work in clinics or on wards. In nearly every other country, hospital care is given only by permanent staff members, many of them full-time; if outside practitioners enter the hospital, they only give or receive information, and rarely do they participate in patient care. Since the "attending doctor" system produces larger and more mobile medical staffs, American hospitals have more administrative tasks. A larger number of doctors tends to work on each case than is true abroad, and the arrival of one doctor may not coincide with the time schedules of the other doctors and nurses. Thus the American doctor is more likely to communicate with other doctors and nurses by writing his findings and orders in the patient's charts and in the ward's order book; in most other countries the stable and small medical staff can more often communicate by face-to-face conversations.[7] Since a large number of private practitioners are continually entering, circulating in, and leaving American hospitals, the establishments must administer elaborate systems for taking messages, paging doctors, and sending information to private offices outside. In addition, the hospital must maintain and continually revise appointment calendars for the attending physicians' clinical work and case conferences. Finally, since the busy American private practitioner often views the hospital as a device for conserving his time and enabling him to increase the size of his practice, he may expect the hospital to perform tasks that many foreign counterparts would do themselves, such as filling out charts, making appointments, sending messages, doing diagnostic tests, and so on. Some of these delegations involve transferring administrative chores from private office practice to the

[7] Paul A. Lembcke, "Hospital Efficiency—A Lesson from Sweden," *Hospitals*, 33 (April 1, 1959), p. 38; Roemer, *op. cit.*

hospital, and in addition the very fact of delegation itself creates tasks of communication, record-keeping, and double-checking that most foreign hospitals avoid.

American hospitals must perform other administrative tasks because American patients expect more than patients in foreign public hospitals, or because American hospital executives try to please them more. In part, these tasks are designed to promote recovery, in part to maintain the favorable public images that are necessary to avoid losing public subsidies and fee-paying customers, in part to be consistent with the American cultural tradition that no products or services should displease the user. For example, many American public and voluntary hospitals — but few of their foreign counterparts — have reception staffs to give advice and specially prepared pamphlets to new patients. Many American hospitals — but few foreign ones — have elaborate catering services, often with specially trained dietitians and complex delivery services, so that patients can make choices of palatable food from varied menus. Many American — but few foreign hospitals — have special shops for ambulatory patients, such as beauty parlors, newsstands, and post offices. American hospitals usually have more elaborate libraries and recreational services. They also have more extensive public relations programs designed in part to relieve the anxieties and puzzlement of past and future patients, and to cushion the shock of admission.[8] Competition among American public and voluntary hospitals for funds and for paying patients steadily increases these public relations functions,[9] but such competition among foreign public hospitals usually takes a different form, such as political pressures within the government rather than the more laborious and expensive appeals to local constituencies and to patient clienteles. Practically the only foreign hospitals that have such comforts and public relations techniques are those with similar problems of winning patients and funds under competitive conditions, namely the small profit-making hospitals owned by doctors in the cities of Europe, Asia, and Africa.

Finally, the American hospital has a number of administrative tasks found less frequently abroad because of the administrative propensities of American society itself. More than foreigners, Americans are likely to conceive of a hospital as an organization like any other, and thus to install in the hospital administrative practices and types of administrative personnel that have established their usefulness in business or in other lay bureaucracies. For example, although the cross-national differ-

[8] These public relations services are very striking to foreign visitors. International Hospital Federation, *op. cit.*, pp. 43, 56; and unpublished reports by individual participants on the Federation's study tour.

[9] Ray Elling, "The Hospital-Support Game in Urban Center," [in Eliot Freidson, ed., *The Hospital in Modern Society* (New York: The Free Press of Glencoe, 1963), chap. 3].

ences have recently begun to diminish, American hospitals are still more likely to employ lay administrative procedures in their financial departments, in purchasing, and in intrahospital communications. Such more sophisticated and efficient procedures require more administrative effort and a larger staff that thinks in lay rather than in clinical terms. In addition, Americans generally are more likely to think of the hiring, screening, and assignment of personnel as a specialized administrative problem requiring files and a staff. Just as American organizations are more likely than their foreign counterparts to have special personnel staffs, so American hospitals have more personnel officers and more personnel procedures. Practical needs as well as cultural fashion underlie the greater American attention to personnel management; American hospitals may have higher personnel turnover than any other country's, and thus the hospital must always cope with the screening and placement of new employees and the discontent and departures of old ones.

Medical Administration Inside or Above the Hospital

American hospitals have more administration because they are more autonomous than hospitals in most foreign countries, and they must make many decisions, or perform many functions that are more often conducted on a "higher" level of the society abroad. Many such differences are financial. In most countries hospitals are owned and managed by a "higher" authority, such as local or national governments, religious orders, national trade unions, or other larger-scale organizations. Even when foreign hospitals are theoretically autonomous, they may actually be the agency of a more powerful authority that governs the hospital through regulations and subsidies. Since each voluntary and religious hospital in America must raise its own money for large capital expenses or for covering deficits, its executive (sometimes including special fund raisers) must devote time to seeking and administering charitable gifts or special grants. The greater the number of competitors for the donors' money, the greater the number of donations received by the hospital, and the more varied the sources of its funds, then the more complex the administrative task and the greater the number of specialized fund raisers and financial administrators the American hospital must employ.

American hospitals have much administrative work because most decide their own fees, many patients pay entirely from personal funds, and fees may exceed the sums guaranteed by insurance funds. Much administrative attention and many persons are involved in calculating operating costs, setting over-all fee policies, investigating each patient's ability to pay, determining each patient's daily fee, sending and collecting bills, and hearing complaints from the patient and from the patient's personal physician. But in most foreign hospitals large business offices need not exist, since the hospitals do not make their own fee decisions and since collection is simpler. Most fees are standardized on a regional or national basis according to type of treatment or according to type of patient, and fees are not determined by individual hospitals or by individual physicians. In many such countries, billing and payment are simple matters of correspondence involving long lists of patients between the hospital on the one hand and either the government treasury or insurance funds on the other. Of course, there remain some countries (although a decreasing number) where the fees of large public and voluntary hospitals are discretionary and are paid in whole or in part by the patient. One expects such hospitals to have administrative functions and administrative roles much like America's, but no comparative social research has yet been done.

American hospitals usually make their own personnel decisions. Therefore administrators must hire personnel and negotiate wages and hours according to the needs and bargaining power of the hospital. But in many countries wages and hours of nurses, auxiliaries, and sometimes even doctors are decided by higher authority — either by government statutes or by collective bargaining agreements between unions and regional or national hospital boards. In some countries the hospital directors have little voice in hiring or assigning doctors. In some, hiring is decided by competition according to statutory rules, and the hospital itself is not represented on the panel of judges. In a few countries, both the hospitals and doctors are parts of a governmental medical service, and doctors are assigned or transferred according to judgments made in the Ministry of Health, with only limited participation by the hospital.

Much of American hospital administration is devoted to planning and constructing new buildings, acquiring land, and adapting and installing new equipment. Here, too, some countries differ. In a few with government health services, the decision to build a new structure or to adapt an old one will be made by regional hospital boards or by the health ministry of the locality, region, or nation. The hospital director will participate in the new planning and decisions, but much of the administrative work will be done by the personnel of the higher agency. In a few countries new building styles and new equipment are not the subjects of extensive administrative investigation and judgment as in America, but certain standard patterns are followed throughout the hospital service.

Centralized and Decentralized Systems

Administrative tasks and personnel are less prominent in the hospitals of most foreign countries because these establishments are usually more internally decentralized than the American. Tasks are spread out among the powerful chiefs of service and need not be performed by any central administrators. For example, in the large hospitals in a few countries the chiefs hire and direct the other doctors; in some they hire and direct the nurses and auxiliaries; in many countries each service has its own laboratories, x-ray equipment, catering service, and rehabilitation service; in some countries, each surgeon has his own operating room and recovery room. There is less decentralization in the small than in the large hospitals abroad and the trend everywhere is toward more central services, but decentralization probably is greater in each type of foreign hospital than in its corresponding type in America. Throughout the United States today labs, x-ray departments, catering, rehabilitation, operating rooms, recovery rooms, and many similar facilities are financed, staffed, and managed by the central administration for the hospital as a whole. Since many of these American central services are more elaborate than the facilities scattered through foreign hospitals, they require more money and administrative effort.

Administration as a Rival to Therapy

Administrative-therapeutic conflicts seem to occur less frequently and with lower intensity in foreign hospitals. In previous pages I have suggested why administrative personnel are less important and less numerous in the hospitals of most foreign countries. In addition, the specialized administrators who exist abroad are less likely to be rivals of therapists.

In America, particularly in the large general or mental hospitals that sociologists have studied, there is an increasing tendency for administrators and clinicians to be different people. The administrators might be laymen or doctors in full-time administration. Occupying high positions in the organization and committed to the structural and financial order of the hospital, they may disagree with clinicians over the application of existing policies or the creation of new ones.

Such administrative challenges to clinical primacy are much more rare abroad. First, in most countries the administrative tasks of hospitals are usually performed by clinicians whose primary commitment is to clinical medicine. This combination of administrative and clinical tasks is possible because both are less burdensome; foreign administrative work is simpler and less time-consuming, and foreign hospital doctors may see fewer patients than their American counterparts. Foreign chiefs of service may be more willing than Americans to accept administrative duties as part of their leadership responsibilities and may be more accustomed to using their administrative positions to wield authority over younger doctors, nurses, and other personnel. (If the service chief delegates this work to anyone, he gives it not to a lay administrator but to his clinical assistant, namely, the chief resident of his service.) In contrast, the American hospital doctor may more often seek to acquire respect and power in the organization through recognized clinical skill, through research findings, and through a large and lucrative patient load.

A second reason for the possible rarity of administrative-therapeutic conflicts is that, until recently when lay administrators were incorporated into foreign hospitals, they were most always placed in unambiguously subordinate positions. They were called "secretaries," "business managers," or "engineers," but rarely anything like "directors." Their span of control was always much narrower than that of American lay administrators. They were usually subordinate to hospital directors who were clinicians.[10] Lay hospital administrators directly responsible to governing boards are now arising in England, France, Italy, Switzerland, and some other countries. Because their positions are so new, rivalry with the clinicians has not yet become general, although the visitor notices some of the beginnings of the American-type conflict. But whether they are officially subordinate to or independent of medical directors, foreign lay administrators may be more deferential to the doctors than are their American counterparts. Usually they come from class backgrounds and from educational curricula (such as commercial high schools and the business schools of universities) that give them considerably less prestige than the doctors in the eyes of both the hospital and of the larger society. In America, class consciousness is generally lower, doctors and lay administrators spring from less dissimilar class origins, lay administrators like doctors get a university education and a university degree, and administration is a job that attracts more public respect.

Therapy's Demands Upon Administration

Just as foreign administrative structures and administrators may pose fewer challenges to the therapists, so therapists may do fewer things upsetting to the hospital organization. For example, American doctors are often eager to use laboratory tests and the newest equipment. Such routine orders given by many physicians, each with only slight thoughts about costs, are one reason why American hospital administrators must cope with mounting deficits and rising patient fees. In many (and perhaps most) foreign countries, doctors routinely request fewer tests, use less diagnostic and therapeutic equipment, and may be slower in asking the hospital to employ the newest techniques. As a result, they make fewer costly demands, hospital costs rise at a slower rate than in America, and fewer administrator-therapist disputes may arise over new and excessive expenses.

Compared to the American physician, the hospital doctor in most countries seems less hurried. Few are trying to combine more than one task at the same time, such as private and hospital practices or research and hospital practice. The minority of doctors with both hospital and private practices usually are supposed to separate the two by reserving fixed morning hours for the hospital and seeing private patients else-

[10] Le Rocker, *op. cit.*; Roemer, *op. cit.*

where during the rest of the day. During comparable time spans spent in the hospital, the foreign doctor may see fewer patients than the American. For all these reasons, he may be less peremptory in giving administrative orders than his American counterpart, he may be present to guide the implementation and repercussions of his orders, and he is available for questions. Many of the tensions between administrators and clinicians in the American hospital are due to the fact that the American doctor is often hurried, peremptory, unaware of the results of his orders, and difficult to find. The administrator and nurse in the American hospital have the added irritant of knowing that many of the doctor's demands are designed to assist his lucrative private practice, rather than to assist the hospital.

Administrative-Therapeutic Conflicts

Thus, for many reasons, administrative and therapeutic structures are probably less distinct in foreign than in American hospitals, and conflicts between administrative and therapeutic roles may be less frequent and less acute. But the differences must everywhere be matters of degree, since no organization can ever be without certain functional needs that may compete with therapeutic ends. For example, every hospital in the world needs to budget its resources, and such budgeting usually conflicts with therapeutic ideals about giving maximum care to all potential patients; auxiliary personnel in every hospital in the world seem to prefer predictable work schedules, but such routine may conflict with therapists' demands for emergency action.

Certain types of administrator-therapist conflicts are different abroad, because of the different organization of public and voluntary hospitals. In many countries conflicts arise over the therapist's allocations of time between the hospital and his private practice. In theory this conflict is avoided where the senior hospital doctors are supposed to devote their mornings — usually from 8 A.M. to 2 P.M. — exclusively to the public hospital. But since these doctors earn three-quarters or more of their incomes from practice in their private offices or in their private hospitals, they often reduce their time in the public hospital by arriving late, leaving early, using some of their public hospital time for lunch, and often arranging not to be called for emergencies in their public hospital departments during afternoons or evenings. Since most countries lack the funds for salaries high enough to compensate service chiefs for loss of private practice, usually hospitals are powerless to enforce work hours on the part-time senior men. Where the system of part-time service chiefs operates in this way, there result strains for the hospital management and considerable irritation among the low-salaried full-time house staff.

Furthermore, conflicts somewhat different in character and scope from the American-style incompatibilities between organizational stability and therapeutic success within each separate hospital are likely to be found in countries where a lay public policy governs a subordinate system of hospitals. Hospital administrators implementing governmental or church orders might collide with doctors concerned only with the welfare of individual patients. For example, the Soviet Ministry of Health under Stalin obeyed the government's policy of keeping workers at their job, and hospital administrators and local party representatives responsible to the Ministry placed pressure on doctors to limit hospital admissions and accelerate discharges.[11]

MEDICAL STAFF

Structure of Authority

American sociologists have studied authority and work relations among hospital doctors. In some of the studies, superior-subordinate relations have been examined — for example, between fully qualified physicians and students, between the influential leaders of the local medical community and aspiring hospital doctors, and between the heads and members of surgical teams.[12] But one gets the impression from these studies that authority is considerably diffused within American medical staffs, and in fact some social scientists have suggested that clinicians cannot be said to have any definite organizational structure at all.[13] Medical staffs have been studied by medical sociologists much less than some other aspects of the hospital, and one reason may be the absence of the kind of structural clarity that facilitates sociological analysis elsewhere in the hospital and in other bureaucratic organizations.

But if one examines medical staffs in many foreign countries, one finds clear-cut hierarchies of the type that characteristically attracts the interest of sociologists. A number of reasons may make American medical staffs more egalitarian and more diffuse structurally.

One reason is the combination of leadership roles in certain strategic statuses, particularly the chiefs of service in the foreign hospital. These men are multifunctional experts, performing a set of roles that are often spread among many senior persons in the American hospital. The foreign "patron" or "kliniksdirektor" may be at the same time chief clinician in his service, chief administrator, and chief educator. In each role, he may share his authority less than the American counterpart. For example,

[11] Mark G. Field, *Doctor and Patient in Soviet Russia* (Cambridge, Mass.: Harvard University Press, 1957), Chaps. 9 and 11.

[12] For example, Temple Burling, Edith Lentz, and Robert Wilson, *The Give and Take in Hospitals* (New York: G. P. Putnam's Sons, 1956), Chaps. 6, 15, 16, 17, and 18; Patricia Kendall, "The Learning Environments of Hospitals," [in Freidson, ed., *The Hospital in Modern Society*, chap. 7].

[13] Amitai Etzioni, "Authority Structure and Organizational Effectiveness," *Administrative Science Quarterly*, 4 (June, 1959), pp. 52-66.

the foreign chief clinician may exercise ultimate responsibility over a larger proportion of the patients in his service; he may seek other doctors' advice less and insist more on the enforcement of his own medical judgments. As chief administrator of his service, the patron does not try to delegate the managerial and clerical chores that American doctors often avoid, since it is recognized that being a patron includes the continued exercise of organizational authority. The patron's administrative resources often exceed the American service chief's since many foreign hospitals give him control over budget, nurses, equipment, and other personnel and facilities that would often be centralized in an American hospital. As chief educator of his service (if he is a service chief in a teaching hospital), the patron would give the principal lectures in his specialty and conduct the most important and best-attended teaching rounds. Such educational duties are more widely spread in America among hospital doctors and among clinicians who are medical-school faculty members rather than hospital doctors.[14]

The clinical hierarchy is more clear-cut and authoritarian in many foreign countries because, compared to young Americans, the young hospital doctor is usually more dependent on his superiors for career advancement. At an earlier age than the American, he may be committed to a single career. By entering the hospital hierarchy he makes a lifetime commitment to specialty practice in hospitals; he would prefer not to switch into general office practice, since it is much less rewarding than a hospital career, and usually he cannot switch into a research career, since research opportunities are few and may not exist outside the hospital. Young American hospital doctors can and do find many other jobs throughout their large country; but the young foreign doctor, either because geographical mobility is unusual in his country or because good hospital jobs are few, is far more likely to stay in one hospital in the metropolis or in his home locality, if he can. Since challenging a patron may damage one's career while his favor might yield great prizes — even including designation as his successor — only a foolhardy doctor would risk displaying imprudent independence. In-

---

[14] This comprehensive role-set is true of all patrons, regardless of the amount of time they spend in the hospital. Apparently the more time the patron actually spends in the hospital, the more of this work he personally performs. Part-time service chiefs abroad delegate some paper work, the supervision of nurses, and routine care of charity patients to their full-time chief residents. But almost everywhere the chief resident thus acts as the service chief's representative and assistant, and the tasks have not been formally transferred and have not become his own autonomous responsibility. An exception is teaching in foreign university hospitals; younger staff members have their own lecture courses and their own bedside teaching rounds, on the basis of an appointment legally made by the entire faculty and by the Ministry of Education. In practice, however, most patrons dominate the teaching of their juniors, since they really decide who shall receive the junior appointments and what teaching facilities will be available for each instructor.

stead, the more important the patron, the larger the number of students at his lectures and rounds, the more numerous the applicants for his service, and the greater the deference to him.

Certain national variations in medical practice help account for the lower amount of deference by subordinates toward higher hospital doctors in America. Compared to many other countries, American medicine makes greater use of scientific and technical knowledge, and its content changes more rapidly. Among a group of doctors knowledge is more widespread, and decisions can better be made by questioning and by many contributions from among members of teams. Knowledge and skill may not always correlate with official rank, and therefore American service chiefs may be demonstrably surpassed on specific problems or in general ability by doctors junior in both rank and age. American medical culture, to a greater extent than those of many foreign countries, emphasizes the uncertainty of knowledge and judgment. Consequently decisions are often preceded by group discussions, by the critical questioning of senior men, and by citing clinical evidence, and a senior doctor addicted to *ex cathedra* assertions is suspect.

Certain national cultural differences underlie the less deferential habits of American clinical subordinates. In general, American leader-follower relations include less social distance and permit more free-and-easy fellowship than is true in most other societies.[15] Compared to most other countries, American premedical and medical education provide less rote memorization and encourage more independent critical thinking, and these habits of questioning and discussion are retained by both superiors and subordinates in clinical staffs. Possibly more than foreign patrons, American senior physicians may admire and reward the junior colleague who is an independent thinker and skilled critic.[16]

Finally, not only do the attendings in American hospitals represent a large element of instability and limited commitment, but even the regular hospital staff may not be full-time participants in their own clinical services. In most countries, doctors spend most of their hospital duty hours close to their own departments. But in American hospitals, and particularly in the large medical centers, a doctor not only sees

[15] This is obvious to any traveler. For a sociological comparison in a nonmedical field, see Stephen Richardson, "Organizational Contrasts on British and American Ships," *Administrative Science Quarterly*, 1 (September, 1956), pp. 204-207.

[16] Foreign doctors who have spent their residencies in American teaching hospitals are repeatedly struck by these intellectual and personal differences. For some typical comments, see Haemmerli, *op. cit.*, pp. 38-39; Huriez, *op. cit.*, pp. 10-11; J. F. Stokes, "A British View of an American Hospital," *New England Journal of Medicine*, 260 (January, 8, 1959), p. 69. Americans studying abroad quickly notice the same difference. For example, Frances and Donald Widmann, "London Clerkship," *Western Reserve University School of Medicine Alumni Bulletin*, 24 (First Quarter, 1960), p. 8.

patients in his own service but often is called for consultation about any patient elsewhere in the hospital who might present a problem in his specialty. For such consultations, the American hospital doctor may go to see the patient instead of waiting for him to be brought. Most foreign hospitals have considerably less movement of doctors through the corridors and across the thresholds; as a result, each clinical service is a more stable social structure.[17]

Functions of the Hospital for the Professional Community

As sociologists and others have long realized, American hospitals perform crucial functions in the community of private practitioners. The right to hospitalize and care for one's own patients in a good hospital is essential for a successful private practice. The hospital staff becomes a "club" of professional allies who provide advice and patient referrals. In most American communities there is a stratification among hospitals, so that the better one's hospital, the higher one's income and repute. The granting of hospital privileges and internal reviewing mechanisms such as Tissue Committees and rounds become methods by which the professional community regulates the clinical and personal behavior of its members.[18]

Participation by all doctors in hospitals is nearly unique to America. In most countries general practitioners cannot work in hospitals, even when their own patients are hospitalized. The separation of most private practitioners from the public and voluntary hospitals abroad results in a professional community much different from the American. Paradoxically, the integration of private and hospital practices in America produces a more diffuse medical staff structure inside the hospital and a more orderly structure in the community of private practitioners. Since the majority of doctors in most countries practice outside the public and voluntary hospitals, rank in these institutions cannot be used to arrange a hierarchy in the medical profession generally. Granting or withdrawing hospitalization privileges cannot be used to regulate professional and personal behavior; in fact, this use of hospitalization privileges

[17] Some important exceptions exist. Some English and Scandinavian teaching hospitals have long traditions of interdepartmental case conferences. In an increasing number of countries there are hospitals recently reorganized on American lines and staffed by American-trained doctors; such hospitals have more case conferences and more traffic through the corridors than the other more typical hospitals of those countries.

[18] Oswald Hall, "The Informal Organization of the Medical Profession," *Canadian Journal of Economics and Political Science*, 12 (February, 1946), pp. 30-44; Hall, "The Stages of a Medical Career," *American Journal of Sociology*, 53 (March, 1948), pp. 327-337; Hall, "Types of Medical Careers," *American Journal of Sociology*, 55 (November, 1949), pp. 243-253.

makes America one of the few countries with any controls over the quality of private practice.

Abroad, the hospital reinforces the position of the leaders of the foreign professional community, but does little more. To become a professor in the medical school and service chief in the teaching hospital seems to ensure a doctor's power and prosperity in the local medical community in all countries, and usually also in the nationwide medical profession. Since foreign cultures glorify the university professor more than America, such an appointment results in even greater rewards and power abroad. Becoming a service chief in a nonteaching hospital abroad often will make a doctor one of the recognized leaders of his specialty in the locality. The appointment is a kind of free advertising and is public certification of his competence, but his position in the medical community will also depend on the success of his private practice, either in his office or in his private hospital. The hospital staff and the leadership structure of the medical community are not always articulated; in some countries, such as parts of Greece, it is not generally assumed that leading specialists must be service chiefs in public or voluntary hospitals. Doctors can build reputations and high incomes through their own private hospitals, and they may even avoid the time-consuming and unremunerative obligations of the public hospital. However, a few countries integrate the hospital and the local medical community, sometimes going even farther than the United States. For example, in the Soviet Union the outpatient polyclinics that give all ambulatory and home care to Soviet citizens are attached to the hospital. All specialists and general practitioners in the locality hold ranks in the same medical organization, belong to the same chapter of the Medical Workers Union, and sometimes rotate between the hospital and the polyclinic. The sociological functions performed by the hospital in the medical community of such a highly integrated system would merit future research.

Norms: Rationality, Authority and Efficiency

The article by Riggs is a classic in the literature on comparative public administration. It highlights the peculiar internal characteristics of the civil service in societies somewhere between the traditional and the modern. These characteristics are not so much a mixture of the characteristics of the other two societies as a constellation all their own. They are due to the adaptation of the society to the peculiar interpenetration of changing traditional institutions such as the local community and the family with the new and old civil service.

The excerpt from Crozier's well-known The Bureaucratic Phenomenon carefully traces how patterns of behavior and attitude already built up in childhood can influence the patterns of authority and peer relationships in bureaucracies. While comparison with other countries is left implicit in the brief selection we were forced to make, the reader will have no difficulty in comparing the French pattern with the more peer-oriented culture of the United States.

Fleming's article is an excellent example of how bureaucracies, as they grow, try but only partly succeed to adapt themselves to their environment or to change it, depending on the culture. The creation of new roles within the bureaucracy and in pre-existing institutions and the reformulation of existing roles never quite solve the problem of adaptation.

10   FRED W. RIGGS

The "Sala" Model: An Ecological Approach to the Study of Comparative Administration

THE NEED FOR NEW, ECOLOGICAL MODELS

As we move toward an empirical science of public administration — as distinguished from a normative doctrine intended to guide us in administrative reform or development — we will need two kinds of knowledge: first, increasingly clear and relevant information about ad-

Reprinted by permission of the author and publisher from the *Philippine Journal of Public Administration*, 6 (January 1962), pp. 3-16. This paper was delivered at the 1961 Annual Meeting of the American Political Science Association, St. Louis, Missouri, September 6-9, 1961.

ministrative practices, organization and history in particular countries; and secondly, more testable and tested hypotheses about causal relationships among administrative variables. Both types of knowledge should be useful in the practice of administration, but in the present context they are viewed as contributing to the growth of social, and especially political, science.

A basic tool in both kinds of inquiry — area study and theory formation — is the "constructed type" or "model." Everyone uses such models, whether implicitly or explicitly, to provide a frame of reference, "criteria of relevance," in order to select from the undifferentiated universe of sense experience the data which contribute to an organized body of knowledge. They provide the outlines around which we assemble descriptive country or area information — whether American, British, Indian, Cuban or Congolese — and they suggest relationships, which we link together in our propositions, statements of causal interdependencies.

Hitherto the models upon which we have relied in political science and public administration are predominantly those derived from the study of America, Britain, and other Western countries. Because of the relative uniformity of environmental factors in all these countries, it is possible to study administrative institutions and practices as though they had an autonomous existence, apart from their environment or setting. Yet the "ecology" of public administration is as much a limiting factor as in the ecology of biological species or cities. When administration in non-Western countries is studied with the help of our non-ecological models with their implicit assumptions of institutional autonomy, or when generalizations taken from these models are applied to situations in the "underdeveloped" countries, they tend to crumble away. Hence I suggest that we need to construct alternative, ecologically based models to help us in the study of administration abroad. I make this suggestion in all modesty, quite aware that much research of value can be accomplished within the framework of the available models, especially if one makes full use of those developed by our sister disciplines, notably anthropology and sociology in which a "holistic" or ecological approach is used. However, I am persuaded of the utility of trying to supplement the existing models by attempting, consciously, to create some alternative types.

Our greatest strength lies in concepts and typologies designed for use in American and the relatively similar Western systems of government, where environmental influences are generally ignored. The social anthropologists and comparative sociologists have given us models particularly suited to the study of traditional or "folk" societies. But neither fits very well the conditions in developing countries with their mixture of tradition and industrializing-modernization. Hence I suggest our chief need is for an explicit model of transitional societies and their administrative sub-systems.

"PRISMATIC SOCIETY" AND THE "SALA MODEL"

I call one model for this purpose a "prismatic" system, not for the joy of using a new word, but because it enables me to impute to the model a limited number of characteristics, and hence to eliminate the clustering connotations that adhere to more familiar words like "underdeveloped" and "transitional."

The word itself is part of a larger system, in which polar types are used, based on definitions taken from structural-functional analysis. These terms are explained at some length elsewhere, and it would detract from this paper to repeat the discussion here.[1] Suffice it to say that the prismatic model is intermediate between a "fused" model, useful in studying traditional or primitive societies, and the "refracted" type, useful for analysis of government in advanced industrial Western societies.

Within the prismatic society one can construct sub-models for its various structures, e.g., its political, administrative, economic, social, religious. I call the administrative sub-model in a prismatic society, a "sala." The word is taken from current usage in much of Asia where a *sala* often means an office, but also a pavilion, drawing room, or place for religious meetings. I wish thereby to symbolize the resemblance of a sala to the "office" or "bureau," which may be taken as the typical locus or "ideal type" of administrative behavior in the "refracted" model. At the same time the diffuse uses to which the sala is put suggest the multi-purpose, undifferentiated character of the "home" or "court," as locus of administration in a "fused" society, where, indeed, we cannot find a separate structure for administrative as contrasted with other functions of the society.

Heterogeneity

One of the characteristics of a prismatic society is a high degree of "heterogeneity," which is to say, a mixture of traditional, "fused" characteristics, on the one hand, and modern, "refracted" traits on the other. Hence a modern city with a sophisticated, intellectual class, Western-style offices, modern gadgets of administration, is typically found in the same country with rural villages run by "chiefs," "headmen," or "elders" whose political, administrative, religious, and social roles may be quite undifferentiated and traditional in character. The significant administrative features of a prismatic society, however, would not be brought

[1] See, for example, "Prismatic Society and Financial Administration" in *Administrative Science Quarterly*, Vol. 5, June 1960, pp. 1-46, and *Ecology of Public Administration* (Bombay, Asia Publishing House, and N.Y., Taplinger, 1961.)

to our attention if we merely looked for this mixture of traditional and
modern institutions, even though we found plenty of examples of
both.

Even more significant in the mixture might be a set of new administrative structures, different from both the traditional and modern, and
a product of the mixture. This new set of administrative phenomena is
what I choose to call the "sala model." To repeat, the most characteristic administrative features of a prismatic society are to be found in the
sala, but in the heterogeneity of a prismatic system, we will find the
modern "bureau" and the traditional "court" as well as the sala. One
problem of analysis in a particular situation is to find the proportions
in which these structural features are mixed, and to explain the mixture.
I believe that only afterwards can we manipulate intelligently, i.e., re-
shape the mixture to match our goals and aspirations.

Formalism

What, then, are the essential features of the sala itself? Some are suggested by a second major feature of the prismatic model, i.e., a high
degree of "formalism." By "formalism" I refer to the degree of discrepancy or congruence between the formally prescribed and the effectively practiced, between norms and realities. The greater the congruence,
the more realistic the situation; the greater the discrepancy, the more
formalistic.

In both traditional or fused societies, and in modern industrial or
refracted societies, a relatively high degree of realism prevails. Not that
complete realism ever exists. The degree of formalism in our own society
is a measure, perhaps, of the extent to which we are not fully refracted,
to which prismatic conditions are to be found here. Indeed, one conclusion to which I have come is that the American administrative system, especially in local government and in the more "underdeveloped"
parts of the United States, is quite prismatic.

For the prevalence of formalism, to repeat, is a distinguishing mark
of the prismatic system. In other words, the laws on the statute book
are one thing, the actual behavior of the official is another. Not that
the law is irrelevant to behavior. Indeed, the official may insist on literal
performance of the law or he may disregard it utterly. What permits
formalism is the lack of pressure toward program objectives, the weakness of social power as a guide to bureaucratic performance, and hence
great permissiveness for arbitrary administration. Whether an official
chooses to enforce a law to the letter or permit its total violation depends, presumably, upon his inclinations and his advantage.

It is easy to see that administrative discretion of this type opens the
door to corruption. The client may have to pay the official to carry out

the law — as in the issuance of permits, licenses, quota allocations — or to overlook violations — as in the payment of taxes.

Some implications for administrative reform should also be evident. If reform is based on a change in the law, a reorganization, re-definition of positions and duties, etc., probably no effective change in behavior will follow the change in norms and prescriptions. In a refracted model, by contrast, where a high degree of realism prevails, clearly, acceptance of a change of law or regulation can be taken as equivalent to corresponding changes in administrative behavior. Reasoning from the refracted model, the administrative specialist may conclude that similar changes in a basically prismatic system will have similar results. Were the specialist familiar with the sala model, however, he might consider such formal changes useless, and seek first to achieve a higher degree of realism, i.e., to bring about a closer approximation of practice to prescription.

Overlapping

A third feature of the prismatic model suggests even more implications for the sala, namely the phenomenon of "overlapping." By "overlapping" I refer to the extent to which formally differentiated structures of a refracted type co-exist with undifferentiated structures of a fused type. In other words, it is typical in a prismatic situation for new structures — government offices, parliaments, elections, markets, schools — to be set up, but the effective functions of administration, politics, economics, education, continue to be performed, at least to a considerable extent, by older, undifferentiated structures, such as the family, religious bodies, caste and communal groupings. New norms or values appropriate to the differentiated structures are given lip-service, but the older values of an undifferentiated society still retain a strong hold. Thus overlapping implies a social schizophrenia of contradictory formal (conscious) and informal (unconscious) behavior patterns.

In neither the fused nor refracted models do we find substantial overlapping. In the refracted model, insofar as the structures realistically perform their "manifest functions," there is no overlapping. In the fused model, since there is only one major set of structures for all functions, there is also no occasion for overlapping. The concept is, perhaps, not an easy one to grasp in the abstract. I will try to illustrate it by several applications to the sala model.

NEPOTISM: THE SALA AND THE FAMILY

The sala is, formally, a locus for governmental administration. In a relatively refracted society, considerations of family loyalty are effectively divorced from the conduct of office. Indeed, the American administrative expert typically takes such a divorce so much for granted that he scarcely looks for it in studying or manipulating administrative behavior. In the sala, however, many administrative functions which were once performed openly under the aegis of familial or kinship institutions continue to be performed on this basis, but clandestinely. The new formal structures of an office are superimposed upon the family, and lip-service is paid to a new set of official norms.

One characteristic administrative result is the phenomenon of "nepotism." I do not think it appropriate to speak of nepotism in a fused society's administration. Here the family provides the formal basis of government. Positions are typically filled on a hereditary or "patrimonial" basis. It is scarcely appropriate to speak of nepotism when a king takes over by virtue of hereditary succession, but if an elected president or prime minister were to replace himself by a son or nephew, the epithet would be properly used. Similarly, we don't think of the inheritance of a small business by the son of the owner as nepotistic, but the appointment of close relatives to office in a large firm may be called nepotism.

My point is that in a fused society, hereditary succession to office is not nepotism; and in a refracted society, familial influence on appointments is negligible. Nepotism, however, is a characteristic mode of recruitment in the sala: characteristic because here patrimonialism is officially proscribed but actually practiced.

Overlapping of the family with the office occurs also in other aspects of sala behavior. The formal rules of the sala prescribe universalistic norms for the administration of the law, the general programs and policies of a government agency. However, family influence prevails, so that the law is applied generously to relatives, stringently against strangers. This becomes a matter of importance in law enforcement, the administration of contracts, purchase of supplies, enforcement of taxes, granting of licenses, foreign exchange control, import and export permits, etc. To the outside observer, the typical sala official appears "individualistic" or "anarchic" because he ranks his private and familial goals higher than the corporate goals of his agency, government or country.

"POLY-COMMUNALISM" AND "CLECTS"

In speaking of the family and kinship groupings I have oversimplified the basis of group solidarity. It is characteristic in a prismatic society for minority ethnic, religious or racial groups to become relatively "mobilized" for mass communications without, at the same time, becoming fully "assimilated" to the elite.[2] Such a condition produces several "communities" that live side by side in a relatively hostile inter-

[2] These concepts were developed by Karl Deutsch in *Nationalism and Social Communication* (N.Y., Wiley, 1953).

action in the same society, "differentiated" in Deutsch's terms. Furnivall calls this a "plural society," but I prefer to speak of it as "poly-communal."

The development of poly-communalism has a characteristic impact on the sala. Whereas in principle a government office administers the law impartially as between or among all citizens, the sala official discriminates in favor of his own community and against members of other communities. Such discrimination affects recruitment. In other words, perhaps more significant even than nepotism is the tendency to fill positions in a sala only with recruits drawn from a dominant community. Alternatively, different offices may be apportioned on a "quota basis" to the several communities, leading to mutual hostility, or non-cooperation between the several agencies staffed by members of rival communities. When members of the different communities are mixed in the same office, obstacles to cooperative action also arise.

This characteristic feature of the sala is, in fact, found in America, especially in local administration in the South. The relations of the white and Negro communities of the South to each other are typical of poly-communalism. In the sala of the South, as in the sala in other countries, administrative recruitment and law enforcement predictably favor the "dominant" against the "minority" communities.

A further consequence of poly-communalism occurs in the organization of "interest groups." The refracted model leads us to picture interest groups in the form of functionally specific associations, open on a universalistic basis to all who share the group's primary goals. Such associations interact with political and administrative agencies to propose and help implement public policy in diverse functional fields.

An implicit assumption of such associational patterns, however, is open participation on a universalistic basis. In a poly-communal situation, however, group membership is typically restricted to a single community. Consequently, instead of a single chamber of commerce or trade union federation, a different chamber and federation appears for each community. The result: interest group activity is designed not only to encourage a particular policy but to apply that policy "selectively" for members of the favored community, against members of disfavored groups. Or, considered from the viewpoint of the sala, administrative recruitment and policy is oriented positively toward groups based on dominant communities, negatively against groups drawn from deviant communities.

Because these interest groups exhibit characteristics different in crucial respects from the associations of a refracted society, I think it is useful to have a special term for them. They share some of the characteristics of cliques, clubs, and sects, but none of these words exactly identifies the category I have in mind. Consequently, I have coined an expression based, mnemonically, on sounds common to these three words, i.e., *clects*. A clect may be defined as an organization with relatively diffuse functions of a semi-traditional type, but organized in a modern, associational way. Sectarian oppositional political parties and revolutionary movements in a prismatic society are typically clects. They provide their members with an alternative solidarity system to replace extended family, caste, village and religious units. They stand for a total way of life, and typically demand unconditional loyalty of their members. Whereas one may belong to a variety of associations, he can belong to only one clect. Of course, not all members of a prismatic society belong to clects. Typically, only a minority do. But the clect provides a disciplined core for economic, political, religious and social action. Clects tend to be uncompromising and hostile in their relations to each other, and to the sala.

Thus we find the sala often involved in close relations with clects, or itself taking on clect-like characteristics. A particular government office or agency may be captured by a clect. Then overlapping manifests itself in unofficial orientation toward the dominant clect, despite an official mandate to serve the general public interest. An example would be an agency to regulate business conditions which favors a chamber of commerce and business men of the dominant community, at the expense of traders in "outsider" communities. Often this means that the dominant group gets special privileges, licenses, permits, foreign exchange, tax rebates. However, the recipients of these favors often do not use them, since an easier road to wealth lies in blackmarket collusion with members of the outside or "pariah" business community.

Officials in the sala also profiteer from this situation, either receiving a "rebate" or "kick-back" from the privileged clientele, or taking a "bribe" from illicit entrepreneurs in the pariah community. Thus the clect-sala relationship serves to advance the special interests of an in-group as against the interests of an out-group in the same functional field, contrary to the ideal association-bureau relationship in which policy is shaped so as to advance the interests of all members of the society who share a particular functional goal or technique.

Sometimes a particular agency in the sala becomes itself a kind of clect. Once admitted, a member is treated as though he were part of an enlarged family. It becomes impossible to discipline or discharge a member, for example, just as a family would not consider expelling a member except for the most extreme reasons. Thus clect formation within the sala contradicts the achievement and universalistic norms, typical of a refracted government bureau or office. Here again overlapping means effective behavior contradictory to the prescribed norms of the sala.

ECONOMY — THE "BAZAAR-CANTEEN"

Elsewhere I have characterized the typical features of the "bazaar-canteen" as the economic sub-model of the prismatic society.[3] The bazaar-canteen is the prismatic counterpart of the refracted "market." Here typical price mechanisms are used for the exchange of goods, but they overlap with more traditional "reciprocative" and "redistributive" institutions,[4] resulting in behavior quite different from that expected in formal economic theory.

One of these characteristics is "price indeterminacy." Although there are other important typical bazaar-canteen traits, this one will illustrate the phenomenon of overlapping. In the refracted model, market conditions are assumed. Hence such aspects of administrative behavior as budgeting, salary determination, purchasing and price decisions are based on market costs and equalitarian assumptions. By this I mean that a government service which is for sale to the public is sold at the same price without distinction of persons to all citizens. The salary of officials is based on the relative value of work performed and the market cost of labor without regard to the personal identity of the incumbent.

In the sala model the same assumption is made formally, but it does not work in practice. As we have already seen, poly-communalism is typical. Hence public services are sold at preferential rates to members of the dominant community or inside clects, but at higher rates to outside clects, to members of deviant or minority communities. Often, however, a formal price is announced, from which secret deviations are made. Victims sign a contract for purchase, but pay an under-the-table bonus. Those selling to the government may receive the official rate, have to "kick-back" an unofficial percentage.

In salary determination or appointment to office, the family considerations which I have already mentioned lead to the creation of "sinecures," i.e., an official is named to a salaried position without having to perform corresponding duties, or with only minimal duties. Again, substantial "fringe-benefits" are offered to privileged incumbents beyond the official salary. Others who lack "influence" or "pull" find themselves assigned to lowly posts, denied promotion or salary increases, unable to obtain fringe benefits.

Corruption is institutionalized in the sala model. Some officials are in advantageous positions to extort bribes and other favors from clientele groups. Part of this extra income must be passed on to superiors or influential members of the bureaucracy who protect the "rackets." Out-

[3] See "The Bazaar-Canteen Model," *Philippine Sociological Review*, Vol. VI, July-October, 1958 [1960], pp. 6-59.

[4] These concepts are based on Karl Polanyi, *et al.*, *Trade and Market in the Early Empires* (Glencoe, Ill., Free Press, 1957).

side positions as "consultants," the privilege of concurrent employment in private firms, plus other devices for augmenting income through the exercise of influence mean that the effective income and living costs of officials diverge strikingly from that officially sanctioned.

These are administrative counterparts to the economic bazaar, in which the actual price paid by a customer, after protracted bargaining, reflects not only prevailing supply-demand conditions, but also a super-imposed set of inter-personal relationships between seller and buyer. A wide fluctuation in the price of a commodity, depending upon the identity of the buyer, tends to prevail.

The canteen model refers to a situation in which uniform prices are actually charged, but prices vary widely between market-places. In some, the "subsidized canteens," prices are kept low for privileged members of an in-group; in others, the "tributary canteens," prices are raised for captive members of the out-groups.

Similarly, the sala makes its privileges available to in-group members at bargain prices, as when it seeks foreign exchange at the official rate to privileged businessmen of the dominant community. Penalized entrepreneurs of the "pariah" community are forced to buy at inflated prices in the "black-market," or obtain funds at official rates only after making informal bonus payments through extra-legal channels.

In a sense, the whole bureaucracy is privy to a subsidized canteen. Its privileges and status are a prize eagerly sought by ambitious individuals in the dominant communities. The proliferation of governmental functions, encouraged both by the first stages of industrialization and the rosy attractiveness of the "welfare state," give rise to rapid expansion of agencies, increase of offices, and conspicuous overstaffing. Yet at the same time, the economy as a whole remains poor, the national budget hopelessly unable to provide adequate salaries for all. The pitifully low salary schedule which results provides an economic incentive for capitalizing on every opportunity each incumbent encounters to augment his official salary from unofficial sources.

Whether in the bazaar or canteen form, then, price indeterminacy pervades the sala at all points where money is involved, in salaries and "fringe-benefits," contracts for purchase and supply of goods and services, in regulation of public utilities, customs and tax administration, budget making, accounting and auditing procedures, and the like.

Any analysis of the economic aspects of sala administration which accepts, at face value, the formal price structure will miss completely the effective price structure. The difficulty for analysis, of course, arises not only from the use of inappropriate models based on the assumptions of a refracted administrative bureau, but also on the formalistic discrepancy between the formally approved behavior, which is like that of the bureau, and the officially disapproved behavior, which is quite dissimilar. This consideration takes us to value systems in relation to overlapping.

POLY-NORMATIVISM AND
LACK OF CONSENSUS

The refracted bureau presupposes a set of "ground rules" or a "formula" which is generally agreed to by all participants, the officials in the bureau as well as the various clienteles served or regulated. Although there is often opposition to any particular policy or rule of government and administration, there tends to be unanimity on key rules governing adoption of norms, and on procedures to be followed to get them changed. Even those who oppose a particular rule, tax, or official procedure, generally concur in obeying the norm, even while protesting and seeking to have it changed through legal means.

In the prismatic society, however, these conditions do not exist. Here a new set of norms, political formulae and myths, based on experience in more refracted settings, are superimposed in a society which continues to adhere, in large measure, to older traditional norms, formulae and myths. The result is substantial lack of consensus.

Different individuals are involved in this lack of consensus in different ways: some adhere to traditional norms, others embrace the modern substitutes. But a substantial body of intermediate or transitional individuals are attracted ambivalently to both sets, sometimes adhering to one, sometimes to the other, sometimes to an attempted syncretism of both, and sometimes violently rejecting all norms. For these typically prismatic individuals we may speak of "poly-normative" and even of "normless" orientations.

The administrative implications of poly-normativism may be traced in the behavior of both officials and members of the public.

An official, while publicly adhering to a modern set of norms, may secretly reject them as meaningless or not binding. Hence the overlapping behavior of the sala becomes comprehensible in terms of the value system of the incumbent. For example, he can adhere publicly to the norm of objective, achievement oriented standards of recruitment, equality of status and universalistic norms, but privately subscribe to more subjective, ascription oriented standards, to a rigid hierarchy of status and particularistic norms. He can publicly castigate bribery and corruption, but secretly encourage it. He can insist, one moment on a strict and literal enforcement of regulations, but the next moment work at their open violation.

Another contrast between the formal and effective norms in the sala model may be discerned in the "status-contract" distinction. The formally prescribed norm of the sala is based on contractual assumption: obligations and rights are voluntarily undertaken by the public servant in an agreement between himself and the "government." But in the overlapping status system, officials have privileges and duties which stem from their personal identity, their family and social position, their station in life.

The sala bureaucrat seeks to maximize the advantages to himself to be gained from both the contract and status systems: to minimize the disadvantages. The typical manifestation of this status/contract mix is heavy stress on "rank." Rank differs from ascribed status in that it is not inherited or claimed as a matter of right but must be "attained." Typically, a school or university degree or an examination, lays the basis for a claim to rank. But unlike the achieved position of the bureau model, in which performance validates official rewards, in the sala model attained rank becomes its own justification. Thus one who has been granted a particular rank on a semi-achievement basis can thereafter claim its corresponding perquisites on a semi-ascribed basis. In other words, he seeks entry to rank by contract, but then rests on his laurels by status.

Another manifestation of the overlapping between refracted and fused norms may be discovered if we reflect on the relationship between ends and means. In the refracted model a "scientific" or "rational" orientation is stressed, by which I mean careful study and testing of the adequacy of any given means to accomplish specified ends. Administratively, the ends are prescribed by political processes, and the bureaucrat takes them as given. Within limits, therefore, he strives for optimum utilization of scarce resources to achieve these specified goals. His goal is "efficiency"; his approach "rational."

By contrast, the official in a fused society focuses on ends as intrinsically important. He cannot test the efficacy of the means. This basic orientation is "ritual." Not that his ultimate ends are philosophically any less justifiable than those of refracted man. Moreover, he is also quite aware that his chosen means are not in themselves ends. A rain-making ceremony, for example, is clearly intended to bring rain, but its efficacy for this purpose cannot be demonstrated.

In the sala, the intrusion of rationalism has sufficiently discredited old rituals to throw doubt upon their effectiveness, but it has been insufficiently assimilated to provide satisfactory proof of alternative procedures. Hence the sala bureaucrat resorts to methods which are neither truly rational nor ritual. On the one hand, he may try to discover and revive ancient and presumably corrupted rituals — a procedure we can call "ritualistic." Alternatively, he may borrow techniques from the administrative repertoire of a refracted society without knowing how they can really help him solve his problems — a procedure we may call "rationalistic." The two approaches, looking to the historic past and the external present, the ritualistic and rationalistic, both imply an element of copying or imitation which we can term "mimetic." Hence another example of the characteristic overlapping in the sala model is a high degree of mimesis. This, incidentally, may help to explain a relatively high degree of receptivity to largely irrelevant technical advice from abroad in many countries today.

The same ambivalence of orientation characterizes the public in its dealings with the sala. On the one hand, the enraged citizen makes unreasonable demands and censures the administration for its failure to abide by modern, refracted norms. But the next moment, without any sense of contradiction, he busily works to undermine these norms by collaborating with corruption to secure special privileges for himself. Indeed, he lacks any strict sense of principle and the implications of a "rule of law." Rather, he takes advantage of opportunities to "break the law" when that serves his interest, but demands rigid "law enforcement" when that happens to fit his convenience. Ultimately, the public is cynical about law and administration. The official is viewed as a leech, and the accepted attitude toward government is normless. One abandons attempts to reform and seeks rather to "cope" with situations as they arise, pulling wires, paying what must be paid, hoping somehow to survive and, if possible, gain entré to some of the spoils of the system. Objectivity and truth as criteria of information tend to dissolve, and the victim is left with no option but to judge information by the status of its source, its usefulness as a means.

POWER DISTRIBUTION:
AUTHORITY VS. CONTROL

In closing this discussion of the sala model, I wish to note the phenomenon of overlapping in the power distribution system. A widespread observation of experts visiting "underdeveloped" countries is the tendency to extreme "over-centralization," inability to delegate authority, to decentralize. One of the most frequent recommendations made is to strengthen field offices, to train intermediate and subordinate personnel so they can take over more powers, induce superiors to delegate functions to others, in general to loosen up the bottleneck at the center which keeps the administration in a perpetual state of crisis.

Unfortunately, these recommendations mistake the formal aspects of sala behavior for the effective. If we bear in mind the concept of overlapping, we may see that other institutions than the prescribed office actually govern, to a greater extent, effective administrative behavior. Indeed, our whole discussion of corruption, nepotism, poly-normativism, clect influence, etc., suggests that effective power is widely dispersed in the sala model. If the central authorities had the highly over-centralized power attributed to them, all these deviations from the rules could scarcely be permitted.

The reality, as I see it, can only be understood if we distinguish clearly between officially sanctioned or legitimate power, i.e., "authority," and unofficially permitted or illegitimate power, i.e., "control." In both the fused and refracted model power includes both the elements of authority and control. Indeed, this linkage is so much a part of our thinking that we have difficulty making this distinction, or describing a situation in which the two are divorced. Yet one of the salient characteristics of the prismatic model, as noted above, is a high degree of formalism. Translated in terms of power structure, this means a separation of authority and control.

Or, in terms of overlapping, it means that the authority structure of the sala overlaps with a different kind of control structure. I have already pointed to the roots of the control structure in the prevalence of poly-communalism, the rise of clects, the pervasiveness of poly-normativism and normlessness. I suggest that in practice control in a prismatic society is highly dispersed. Traditionally-oriented groups in the hinterland resist central government control. Deviant communities and their clects also cannot be brought within the control system of the official government. Normlessness makes many, even members of the elite, surprisingly unresponsive to official norms, as reflected in widespread violation of tax and other laws. Even members of the bureaucracy itself, as our argument has shown, are singularly unwilling to subject themselves to effective regulation by the agencies of which they are nominally a part, at least in their formal requirements.

Viewed from this perspective, centralization of authority can be understood as a desperate attempt to bring the government and society under control. Indeed, when effective control weapons are so notably lacking, the cheapest and most apparent remaining weapon is the power of formal authority. Unfortunately, this nominal power turns out to be without potency, resulting, often enough, in a final resort to violence.

Centralized authority is largely formalistic. Hence recommendations to decentralize are greeted with fear as a threat to that limited power base which remains to the central authorities; or as irrelevant, since those on the inside already know how limited is their effective control.

The power structure of the sala model, then, may be said to consist of a highly centralized and concentrated authority structure overlapping a control system that is highly localized and dispersed. Here again, unless one has this model in mind, he is likely to rely on the refracted bureau as a model, and hence to look upon the formal authority system as a sound clue to understanding the effective power structure.

The paradox of overlapping may be viewed from another point of view, the relationship of bureaucratic to non-bureaucratic power. The formal administrative bureau in a refracted society is regarded as a purely instrumental "apparatus" for the execution of policies formulated by a separate political system, as institutionalized in legislative bodies and elected executives. Hence the formal model, in terms of which public administration in a prismatic society is both understood and evaluated, presumes that power is concentrated in directing centers outside the bureaucracy.

But the traditional locus of power in relatively fused systems is in the hands of officials working with an hereditary ruler. Here any distinction between "administrative" and "political" structures is quite arbitrary, since the same men and offices perform both types of function without even being aware of the distinction.

In the sala, the official continues to exercise the undifferentiated political-administrative functions of the fused model, but behind a façade of administrative institutionalism borrowed from industrial, relatively refracted societies. Hence he can scarcely admit to the public, or even to himself, that much of his actual behavior is essentially political, involving a struggle for power and participation in the making of whatever decisions are made for the society. The Western-trained observer who tries to identify the locus of decision-making in such a system comes away baffled, convinced that decisions are made surreptitiously, conspiratorially, clandestinely.

Thus the sala official who exercises control often lacks authority, first because it has not been formally delegated to him by his status superiors, and secondly because, as a bureaucrat, he is not supposed to make decisions according to the formally announced constitutional system. There are two characteristic responses for the sala official caught in this paradoxical situation. We may view these responses as polar opposites on a scale, typical behavior involving some combination of both, though in varying proportions.

At one extreme, the official takes the initiative and assumes the mantle of "tutelage." He announces that, in the long run, he will serve as an "instrument of the people," but in view of their present lack of education and political sophistication, he will teach them, help them prepare to assume real political power. Thus he openly admits the exercise of power, but at the same time he gives lip-service to the view that his ultimate role, as a bureaucrat, should be instrumental.

The other extreme is suggested by the word, "sinecure." This is the posture of officials who give up the attempt to make decisions. The formal power holders — the people and the "politicians" — cannot guide or control him, and he abandons the attempt to seize the initiative himself. Rather, he accepts and clings to the privileges of office, but rejects any serious attempt to exercise the duties of office. While refusing to delegate responsibility, he is unable to exercise it effectively himself.

This posture, of course, is not one to be rationalized but rather to be concealed, and so the sinecurist makes a pretense of busy-work, while in essence abandoning the tasks of government.

The extent to which officials in a sala make policy or reject responsibility may be disguised by the extent to which such policy is weakly oriented toward an agency's program goals. Where nonbureaucratic power is substantial, bureaucrats are provided with a strong incentive to promote program goals since success is well rewarded. Often, indeed, they "identify" to a great extent with these goals. When this happens, efforts by public servants to promote policy decisions are directed toward the realization of "principled interests," the manifest ends of the agency concerned.

However, when non-bureaucratic power is weak, bureaucratic achievement is poorly rewarded. Indeed, an official who "identified" with a public goal and sought its achievement would court punishment by his colleagues as a "rate buster." Familiar "feather-bedding" techniques come into play. Hence bureaucratic influence in policy is directed rather more to safeguard strictly bureaucratic interests — such matters as security of tenure, recognition of seniority, fringe benefits, enhancement of status and prestige, toleration for violation of formal norms. In other words, bureaucratic policy-making is oriented chiefly toward "expediency interests" in the sala.

The observer who sees in every bureaucrat a man carrying out politically framed policy can only choke with indignation when he discovers officials who either arrogate to themselves the policy-making role, or meekly refuse to carry out any policy. Yet, if he were to analyze the situation in terms of the sala model, he might come closer to understanding the reasons for what he saw and perhaps even to discovering a way to stimulate the kinds of change he wanted to induce.

CONCLUSION

In closing, I should like to repeat the statement made in opening this paper that a model, like that of the sala, is not intended to serve as a description of any particular society or system of government. Rather, it serves an heuristic purpose. It gives us a tool by which we can better describe and, hopefully, understand, situations in real life. It seeks to relate administrative behavior to ecological factors typical of transitional societies.

In other words, with this tool one should be able to go into a particular country and study its administrative system more illuminatingly. The model suggests possible ecological relationships to look for, relationships which would not be suggested by the more familiar, non-ecological administrative bureau models based on the relatively refracted situation in the United States. One might also be able to describe the country or governmental system studied as being highly prismatic, semi-prismatic, relatively refracted, etc. Indeed, one consequence of this exercise might be to enable students of American administration to recognize in a more systematic way the "prismatic" elements of our own government. I am convinced, for example, that we will understand much of our system of county and township administration better in terms of the sala rather than the bureau.

Finally, the analysis of relationships suggested in the sala model may enable us to formulate hypotheses or propositions about possible relationships between variables in administration. Such hypotheses, growing out of observation in a variety of settings and linked to the elements of the sala model, can be further tested by looking at new settings, or re-examining those first studied at a later date. In so doing, of course, the concepts could be refined and made more operational. As the hypotheses become stronger, they should give us a better basis for explaining and predicting actual administrative behavior. This, in turn, will provide us with a more powerful weapon for administrative action, since it will help us to establish demonstrable cause-effect relationships, and hence to change phenomena by modifying their causes rather than by attacking only the symptoms or manifestations of administrative pathology. In this sense, I submit the sala model primarily as a contribution to the development of empirical, ecologically-oriented research in comparative administration, but also as a potentially useful weapon for those more particularly concerned with administrative development.[5]

[5] The relationship of the approach outlined in this paper to the general development of research in comparative public administration is discussed in my paper "Trends in the Comparative Study of Public Administration," prepared for the American Society for Public Administration conference, April 1961.

11   MICHAEL CROZIER

The French Bureaucratic
System of Organization

The model of a bureaucratic vicious circle and its four basic elements
— the impersonality of the rules, the centralization of decisions, the
strata isolation, and the development of parallel power relationships —
may appear to have a universal application. And we have tried to work
out the most general and abstract schemes from our case studies.

However, could not another interpretation be made that would explain what we observed and described? The many parallels that can be
drawn enable us to think that the behavioral traits and the patterns of
human relations that we have relied upon to elaborate our bureaucratic model correspond to a number of traits typical of French
society.

If this is so, we shall have to ask to what extent our model is exclusively a French model, and whether other kinds of models can be
worked out for different cultural systems. In any case, it will be necessary to have a new and broader perspective in order to judge the relevance
and the limits of usefulness of one model. . . .

THE PROBLEM OF INTERPERSONAL
AND INTERGROUP RELATIONSHIPS

Interpersonal and intergroup relationships present some characteristic,
and rather similar, traits in the Clerical Agency and in the Industrial
Monopoly.* These traits — the isolation of the individual, the predominance of formal over informal activities, the isolation of the strata,
and their struggles for privileges — play an important role in our model
of a bureaucratic system of organization. Strata isolation, especially, is
a key point for the development of the vicious circle which is the basis
of our scheme of interpretation. Yet all these traits may also be considered as permanent French cultural traits.

Let us examine our data carefully. We noticed how few informal

Reprinted by permission of author and publisher from Michael Crozier, *The
Bureaucratic Phenomenon* (Chicago: Phoenix Books, 1963), pp. 213-227, 231-236.

* [The terms Clerical Agency and Industrial Monopoly refer to previous chapters
of *The Bureaucratic Phenomenon.*—Ed.]

relationships there were among the employees of the Clerical Agency. Girls remained isolated, although this entailed hardship for many of them who were strangers in the city and had been abruptly severed from families and friendship ties. They reported that they very rarely had friends in the agency. They reiterated that they preferred having their friends outside. Even among those who had friends, the friendships seemed never to develop into articulate groups. There were very few associations of any sort — no cultural, educational, or leisure joint activities worth mentioning. Trade unions were more active; but for the average girl, whether or not she belonged to one, they remained rather formal affairs in which she did not participate. On the whole, we were left with the impression of a significant lack of informal groups. No clans or cliques of any sort were able to exist for long, and none of them was ever able to cut across different categories.

More friendships were reported in the Industrial Monopoly, but they did not develop into cliques or even into stable informal groups. Cliques were viewed with great disfavor, and groups that could cut across several categories were inconceivable.

These patterns contrast strongly with the usual picture of the American industrial shop climate as it has been portrayed since the first experiences of the Hawthorne testroom. They contrast also with reports on American public agencies,[1] such as those of Peter Blau, and of Roy Francis and R. C. Stone.[2]

These pecularities fit very well with the rationale of the strata system that we have analyzed. In a bureaucratic system of organization, the individual is adequately protected by the abstract formal group[3] — i.e., the stratum or ranking category — to which he belongs. The rules of seniority prevent interference by outside authorities and impose a strict equality among all the members of the group. As a consequence, the individual does not need the protection of an informal group. In addition, he knows that separate informal activities are likely to threaten the cohesion of the formal category to which he is bound, and he is vulnerable to the pressure of this whole formal category against such activities. Cliques that cut across categories are especially objectionable, since they inevitably foster *favoritism*, the system's cardinal sin.

---

[1] Peter Blau, *The Dynamics of Bureaucracy* (Chicago: University of Chicago Press, 1955); Roy G. Francis and Robert C. Stone, *Service and Procedure in Bureaucracy* (Minneapolis: University of Minnesota Press, 1956).

[2] One can contend that the French industrial shop climate is also characterized by many informal group activities, but the evidence for this is not so conclusive as it at first appears. We have shied away from such discussion for lack of relevant empirical data. See Jacques Barbichon, "Etats d'insatisfaction, la vie parallèle dans l'entreprise et dans les loisirs," *Peuple et Culture, XIIème Congrès National*, 1956.

[3] It is abstract, in the true sense, for the technical engineer who never sees his own colleagues.

Thus, in a world where conformity is achieved through the joint influence of impersonal rules that apply to all, and of group pressure that polices behavior within each category, the formal group takes precedence over the informal, and the individual remains isolated. This mechanism, which was especially obvious in the industrial Monopoly,[4] is directly linked with the disappearance of formal and informal hierarchical pressure. Instead of the usual pattern of subordinates' developing informal groups to resist the pressure of the superordinate system, we have a very different pattern. Here, the superordinate system has been stripped of its potential of discrimination by being too well formalized, and isolated individuals control and check each other in order to maintain the formalism that protects them.

The precedence of the formal group over the informal, the tight control of each stratum over its members — these are associated with the isolation of the strata, the difficulty of promotion from one stratum to another, the difficulty of communicating across strata, and the development of ritualism. We have analyzed the importance of the formal peer group as a direct consequence of strata isolation and an indirect consequence of the pressure to impose impersonal rules, in order to eliminate the discretionary will of any individual.

But it can also work the other way around. If they already exist as distinct cultural patterns, such traits as the isolation of the individual and the lack of informal activities may act as powerful incentives for the development of this kind of bureaucratic system of organization. In any case, they will be important elements for understanding the success of certain patterns of organization within a given cultural context.

These traits indeed appear, to a large extent at least, to be rather well-established French cultural traits. We cannot rely, unfortunately, upon neat comparative tests, since empirical comparative studies remain to be made. But most observers have pointed out the low state of free group activities in France and the difficulty that Frenchmen experience in co-operating on a formal basis.

The few serious anthropological studies made provide significant and concordant details in the same direction. Lucien Bernot and René Blancard, in their thorough study of a village near Paris, note, for example: "Already, among children, one discovers one of the characteristic features of Nouville's life, the absence of groups. One does not find among the children any gang or clique within the village."[5] The

---

[4] . . . Production workers and maintenance men conformed rigorously to the norms of their group in all strategic areas and . . . the official line took precedence in a public encounter over individual personal opinions. [See p. 104 of Crozier, *op. cit.* — Ed.]

[5] *Nouville, un village français* (Paris: Institut d'Ethnologie, 1953), p. 148.

same thing, they tell us, prevails among adults, and even among the industrial workers of the nearby factory, who do not develop lasting ties although, or perhaps because, they live in the same close community. The only group that exists in the village is a group of youngsters who have a significantly higher status than the rest of their peers; but their group, which has no leader, is not very successful. If the Catholic priest and the schoolteachers were to leave, "the very small amount of collective life or organized leisure would disappear because of the apathy of a youth group that does not dare to take the risks of responsibility."[6] The political field is the exact image of this apathy, although a good part of the votes will go to the extreme left in a general election.

There is rather more activity in the sunny village in the Vaucluse that Lawrence Wylie discusses.[7] However, the insightful remarks of the author indicate that the situation is basically the same. People tend to remain aloof; they have the same difficulties in co-operating. No organized activities are allowed to disrupt the theoretical equality between the villagers. Anyone who shows initiative is likely to be accused of trying to boss the others.

In a study of a rural community under the impact of drastic change (flooding of the area for the erection of a big dam), Jean Dubost[8] documents the same amazing lack of constructive organized activities. Leadership emerged only in the last extremity — and then on a temporary basis and for a negative purpose.

In the past history of France, there is abundant testimony to the persistence of these patterns over long periods of time. None is more eloquent than this short statement of Turgot, the most famous reform minister of the late Monarchy, as quoted by De Tocqueville: "A French parish is a congeries of huts and countryfolk as inert as their huts."[9]

The most penetrating analyst of these traits is De Tocqueville himself. He explains at length how the municipal policy, and especially the fiscal policy, of the kings in the seventeenth and eighteenth centuries had quelled all possibility of spontaneous organized activities, especially at the lower levels:

> Such was the system of taxation that every taxpayer had an urgent and unfailing motive for spying on his neighbours and promptly notifying the Collector of any increase in their means.[10]

He sees clearly the link between the isolation of the individual and

---

[6] *Ibid.*, p. 169.
[7] *Village in the Vaucluse* (Cambridge, Mass.: Harvard University Press, 1958).
[8] Jean Dubost, "Commissariat General du Plan, Paris" (unpublished paper).
[9] Alexis de Tocqueville, *The Old Régime and the French Revolution* (New York: Doubleday, 1955), Book II, chap. 3, p. 121.
[10] *Ibid.*, Book II, chap. 12, p. 183.

the lack of collective spirit, on the one side, and the isolation of the different strata and their perennial fight for rank and status, on the other:

> Each group was differentiated from the rest by its right to petty privileges of one kind or another, even the least of which was regarded as a token of its exalted status. Thus they were constantly wrangling over questions of precedence, so much so that the Intendant and the courts were often at a loss for a solution of their differences. "At last an order has been passed that the holy water is to be given to the judges of the presidial court before being given to members of the town corporation. The parlement had been unable to come to a decision, so the King took the matter up in Council and had decided it himself. It was high time, too, as the whole town was in a ferment." When a group was not given the precedence its claimed in the general assembly of notables, it ceased to attend, preferring to withdraw from public affairs altogether rather than to stomach such an affront to its dignity.[11]

Leadership and constructive activities could have merged only if groups cutting across ranks had developed. However, their development was prevented by the continuous policy of the royal administration, which preferred failure to the risk of competition:

> Any independent group, however small, which seemed desirous of taking action otherwise than under the aegis of the administration filled it with alarm, and the tiniest free association of citizens, however harmless its aims, was regarded as a nuisance. The only corporate bodies tolerated were those whose members had been hand-picked by the administration and which were under its control. Even big industrial concerns were frowned upon. In a word, our administration resented the idea of private citizens' having any say in the control of their own enterprises, and preferred sterility to competition.[12]

The privileges and particularisms of the *ancien régime* have gone. But the same patterns — individual isolation and lack of constructive cooperative activities on the one side, strata isolation and lack of communication between people of different rank on the other — have persisted.

The persistence of strata isolation was especially well analyzed in the 1920's by a shrewd observer of the French bourgeois pattern of living, the philosopher Edmond Goblot. According to Goblot, bourgeois society in France was ruled by two great principles, which he called "the barrier" and "levelling."[13] "The barrier" refers to all the kinds of obstacles raised by the bourgeoisie to prevent people from achieving bourgeois

[11] *Ibid.*, Book II, chap. 9, p. 157.

[12] *Ibid.*, Book II, chap. 6, p. 132. For an analysis of the persistence of this spirit in contemporary France see Arnold Rose, "Voluntary Associations in France," in *Theory and Method in the Social Sciences* (Minneapolis, Minn.: University of Minnesota Press, 1954).

[13] Edmond Goblot, *La Barrière et le Niveau, étude sociologique de la bourgeoisie française moderne* (Paris: Alcan, 1925), pp. 126-27.

status. "Levelling" refers to the theoretical equality conferred to each person once he has crossed over. Goblot's study consists mainly of analyses of all the different and indirect kinds of obstacles and the rationalizations used to justify them. Classical culture as sanctioned by the baccalaureate, professional ethics, fashion, and art have provided ways of isolating the bourgeoisie from the common man. But whatever the obstacles, they are conceived as restrictive for those who are outside and in an equalitarian way for those inside. Here again, we see the link, emphasized several times already, between equalitarianism and stratification.

Finally, echoing De Tocqueville, Goblot insists on the social and collective aspect of the barrier. It does not vanish because individuals can cross it. On the contrary, it becomes even more humiliating.[14]

Individual isolation and lack of constructive activities have been studied more recently by an American sociologist, Jesse R. Pitts. Pitts has presented a new and interesting interpretation of this pattern of action.

According to Pitts, informal activities are not absent in the French way of life. However, they are negative, instable, and never expressed openly. To characterize them, Pitts has coined the suggestive term, the "delinquent community," which he used first in an analysis of the children's activities at school.[15] It suggests a kind of implicit solidarity among all members of the same rank, which can be tapped when necessary but can never appear in the open. This is a negative kind of solidarity, directed against superiors and against other groups. It is extremely successful in preventing any attempt at leadership within the group. For Frenchmen, the delinquent community is the model of all collective activities in which they participate.[16] In a recent paper, Pitts summarizes its importance as follows:

> The school peer group is the prototype of the solidarity groups which exist in France beyond the nuclear family and the extended family. They are characterized by jealous equalitarianism among the members . . . conspiracy of silence against superior authority, incapacity to take any initiative outside of the interpretations and accommodations with the directives of superior authority, in an effort to create for each member a zone of autonomy, of caprice, of creativity.[17]

[14] De Tocqueville himself said about the French nobility: "But the barriers between the French nobility and the other classes, though quite easily traversed, were always fixed and plain to see; so conspicuous, indeed, as to exasperate those against whom they were erected. For once a man had crossed them he was cut off from all outside the pale by privileges injurious both to their pockets and their pride." (De Tocqueville, *op. cit.*, Book II, chap. 9, p. 152).

[15] Jesse R. Pitts, "The Bourgeois Family and French Economic Retardation" (Ph.D. diss., Harvard University, 1957), pp. 329-31.

[16] *Ibid.*, pp. 338-43.

[17] Jesse R. Pitts, in *In Search of France* (Cambridge, Mass.: Harvard University Press, 1963).

This analysis of the "finishing school of the French citizen" fits very well with our own observations of the girls and their supervisors in the Clerical Agency, and of the production and maintenance workers in the Industrial Monopoly. The delinquent community, in those cases, is the implicit pact of defense of all the members of the formal group, and its meaning is narrow but clear. If and when a member asks for help from another member of his formal peer group, for the protection of his zone of independence and free activity, any other member is required to assist him, whatever the former's feelings toward him may be.

THE PROBLEMS OF AUTHORITY AND THE AVOIDANCE OF FACE-TO-FACE RELATIONSHIPS

The specific patterns of action of the French peer group as described by Pitts, the isolation and lack of initiative of the individual as described in the remarks of Bernot, Blancard, and Wylie, the protective role of the strata which Goblot analyzed, and the long tradition of apathy in public affairs that De Tocqueville and Taine emphasized, correspond to the patterns of interpersonal and intergroup relations that we observed in our case studies. At the same time, it seems quite clear that all these traits finally revolve around the basic difficulty of facing conflict and developing acceptable leadership at the level of the primary group. They directly raise the problem of the cultural aspect of basic authority relationships.

This is apparent in each case. The "delinquent community" is a protective device against external authority — whether that of the teacher, that of the state, or that of the boss — and at the same time an indirect but extremely efficient way of making it impossible for an individual member of the group to become its leader. Groups described by Bernot, Blancard, and Wylie are extremely anxious to prevent any one of their members from raising himself above the others. If a group member shows initiative, he risks being deserted by his fellows and being deeply humiliated. Apathy, the refusal to participate, as we have argued in the preceding chapter, is a rational response if people want, above all, to evade conflict situations and to escape dependence relationships. Strata isolation, focusing on rank and status, and the impossibility of informal grouping across strata, all stem from the same difficulties. All these traits ultimately refer to the basic cultural conditions predetermining the possible scope of authority relationships.

We should like, at this point, to review the data, remarks, and analyses of other social scientists and writers who have studied this central relationship. Unfortunately, authority has been a neglected field — at least, authority as a modern cultural pattern. We have little reliable information about it, and nothing comparable to the greater amount of material on interpersonal and intergroup relationships. The works of philosophers and essayists who have studied the peculiarities of French rationalism and Cartesianism as a basis of French culture cannot be too helpful.[18] The work of the study group on contemporary cultures inspired by Margaret Mead,[19] and the cultural analyses of the characteristic plays and movies of a period as performed by Wolfenstein and Leites,[20] may be more interesting, but much consists of anecdotes and is often debatable. We can point out, however, that the descriptions of the classroom by Wylie, and to some extent by Bernot and Blancard, confirm the scheme Rhoda Métraux and Margaret Mead propose in *Themes in French Culture*.[21] Furthermore, there is no contradiction between this scheme and our model. But the field is still so unexplored that one cannot make too much of these correspondences.

We shall thus have to be content with a more modest endeavor. We shall elaborate a working hypothesis, starting with our observations in our two case studies, and discuss the extent to which it fits with the recorded experiences of the functioning of other organizations.[22]

In both cases we analyzed, there is a central and recurrent pattern. Direct face-to-face authority relationships are avoided as much as possible. Open conflicts appear only between groups that do not directly confront each other. Partners appear just like the children described by Wylie, or the famous characters of the Pagnol folk plays, who shout insults at each other only in situations where they do not run any physical risk. Authority is converted, as much as possible, into impersonal rules. The whole structure is so devised that whatever authority cannot be eliminated is allocated so that it is at a safe distance from the people who are affected.

---

[18] One may, however, propose some subtle indirect analogies in the works of such astute observers as Ernst Robert Curtius, *Essai sur la France* (Paris: Grasset, 1941); Paul Distelbarth, *La personne France* (Paris: Alsatia, 1942); and Salvador de Madariaga, *Anglais, Français, Espagnols* (Paris: Gallimard, 1930).

[19] Rhoda Métraux and Margaret Mead, *Themes in French Culture* (Stanford, Calif.: Stanford University Press, 1954); Margaret Mead and Martha Wolfenstein (eds.), *Childhood in Contemporary Cultures* (Chicago: University of Chicago Press, 1955); see also the valuable study of Erik Erikson on Germany, in his *Childhood and Society* (New York: Norton, 1950).

[20] Martha Wolfenstein and Nathan Leites, *Movies: A Psychological Study* (Glencoe, Ill.: Free Press, 1950). Recently, Nathan Leites has moved forward again in that direction, discussing, in a very brilliant although still anecdotal manner, the basic cultural traits of French society and of its elite. See Nathan Leites, "Le Règle du jeu" and "L'Obsession du mal" (mimeographed reports; Paris: Ecole Pratique des Hautes Etudes, 1960 and 1961).

[21] According to these authors, it will be remembered, French education "is characterized by a tight control and a repression of movement and physical aggression, a great pressure of the outside world with socialization achieved by shaming and nagging and a reliance on oral aggression as a way of relief."

[22] In [chapter 9 of Crozier, *The Bureaucratic Phenomenon*] we shall use this hypothesis as a scheme for analyzing a number of characteristic patterns of action in other walks of life — thus putting the model to a kind of test.

We wish to suggest the following hypothesis. This pattern of human relations may provide an adequate answer to the problems raised by the functioning of modern organizations. It is its "bureaucratic," or one of its "bureaucratic," answers. But at the same time it is also specifically French. Face-to-face dependence relationships are, indeed, perceived as difficult to bear in the French cultural setting. Yet the prevailing view of authority is still that of univeralism and absolutism; it continues to retain something of the seventeenth century's political theory, with its mixture of rationality and *bon plaisir*.[23] The two attitudes are contradictory. However, they can be reconciled within a bureaucratic system, since impersonal rules and centralization make it possible to reconcile an absolutist conception of authority and the elimination of most direct dependence relationships. In other words, the French bureaucratic system of organization is the perfect solution to the basic dilemma of Frenchmen about authority. They cannot bear the omnipotent authority which they feel is indispensable if any kind of co-operative activity is to succeed. It can even be argued that this dilemma has been perpetuated by the long tradition of the French bureaucratic patterns, whose strength comes from their meeting two contradictory and equally potent aims, preserving the independence of the individual and insuring the rationality of collective action.

Bon plaisir is the law of formal apparatus. Authority at each echelon is conceived of as absolute. There are no checks and balances. There is not so much respect for due process as in Anglo-Saxon countries.[24] But although subordinates are not protected by law and are thus more vulnerable to arbitrary procedures, they benefit from another and equally strong protection — the counter-pressure of the peer group.[25] *Bon plaisir*, however, is not completely imaginary. It is expressed in the symbols and paraphernalia of the ranking system. It bears on the status rewards received from membership in each of the strata. Finally, it may

[23] *Bon plaisir* ("good pleasure," i.e., the arbitrary will of the ruler) was the official term for legitimating the king's order at the time of absolutism. In Parsonian categories, the French conception of authority should be considered as diffuse, in contrast to a more modern "specific" conception. In this perspective, the main contradiction of French society, made possible by the permanence of a bureaucratic system of organization, is the coexistence of universalistic traits with diffuse, non-specific ones.

[24] This analysis, of course, would have to be qualified in many ways. Good observers have contended that in no other country were subordinates as well protected against arbitrary action as in the French public service. Yet the government public administration theoretically disposes of a great number of discretionary powers and only administrative courts can review their acts. See Brian Chapman, *The Prefects and Provincial France* (London: Allen & Unwin, 1955).

[25] This relative helplessness of central authority enables us to understand why it is so desperately attached to maintaining arbitrariness when applying the rules. This is the only way for it to retain some influence over subordinates otherwise impossible to cope with.

become operative during a crisis, when people must overcome their *amour-propre* and co-operate to achieve common ends.[26]

Individual isolation and strata isolation, on the other hand, allow some part of *bon plaisir* to everyone, although largely in a negative sense. People are protected against interference from above. They do not have to yield to someone's pressure; what they do, they do of their own accord. Work tends to be done without any obligation or pressure. People do not work because they have to, but because they want to.[27] This freedom from interference — this independence — is, therefore, another form of the absolutist conception of authority. To compromise, to make deals, to adjust to other people's claims is frowned upon; it is considered better to restrict oneself and to remain free within the narrower limits one has fixed or even those one has had to accept.

This insistence on personal autonomy and this pattern of restriction are old in France. They were, and to some extent remain, one of the main elements of the value system of traditional French peasantry. The terms in which De Tocqueville, among others, has characterized these feelings are meaningful: "On the other hand the small landowner's motive for action comes from himself alone; within his narrow sphere he moves freely." This is to be understood in contrast to "la petite fortune mobilière" despised by the French, with which "one is dependent almost always, more or less, on the whims and fancies of someone else. One must bow before the rules of an association or the will of another man."[28]

A bureaucratic system of organization of the French type makes it possible to retain something of the independence of another time within the framework of modern organization. One always obeys the rules, but one need not submit to other men's whims. This is, however, a negative advantage; on the positive side, one does not gain so much. Each member of a superordinate group is given a judicial function over some members of the subordinate strata. It is still an absolute and awe-inspiring function, and he may enjoy it if he does not care too much for actual power.

Privileges, strategic individual and group influences working everywhere within the organization, only reflect the impossibility of isolation from the outside world. They are the dark spots in an otherwise perfect rationalistic system of organization. But they, as we noted earlier,

---

[26] This may be one of the reasons why people are so fascinated by crises and why crises are so frequent.

[27] This is, of course, in many cases a figure of speech; yet there are frequent instances of careers completely divorced from achievement at work, and situations in which people are rather free to choose whether to give or to refuse their personal co-operation at work.

[28] Freely translated from De Tocqueville, *L'ancien régime et la Révolution* (Paris: Gallimard, 1952), p. 52.

actually reinforce it. They give the system its short-run dynamism. The issue of equality and resistance to favoritism is kept alive by the persistence and constant reappearance of privileges. From this viewpoint, French public administration must not be considered as a static organization. It is always in the process of rationalizing, eliminating abnormal situations, undue interference, and undue competition, and, above all, it is constantly chasing privileges.[29]

To conclude: To the French, a bureaucratic system of organization seems the best way to afford some participation in *bon plaisir* to the greatest number of persons. Its development may be analyzed as a process of granting new strata adequate status and the concomitant guarantees of participation in the game. Certain of the lowest subordinate groups do not participate very much as yet, as e.g., the girls of the Clerical Agency. But even these employees have some leeway, and, in any case, they are supposed to be there only for a few years and may accept their lot because they have the prospect of future rewards.

THE PROBLEM OF CHANGE AND THE PARADOXICAL WEAKNESS OF POWER

. . . we analyzed the problem of change in a bureaucratic system of organization from a rather formal point of view, for the sake of the mechanism. There was some universal validity in the general model of change we presented, since the main problem of such a system of organization is its lack of flexibility in the face of a constantly changing environment. But the specific mechanism of the alternation of routine and crisis that we have shown operating must be considered as a distinctively French feature, inasmuch as it relies on the complex model of individual isolation, lack of communication between strata, and avoidance of face-to-face relationships that we have described. We have shown that, if authority is conceived of as diffuse and absolute, if it cannot be shared or compromised, and if dependence relationships, at the same time, are not easily accepted, then impersonal rules and centralization offer the only way out of the inevitable contradictions. As a consequence, however, power will tend to recede further and further away, and the kind of rigidity that will develop will make it impossible to adjust gradually to the transformations of the environment. No real change will be accepted without a formal rewriting of the rules, and this will be considered a great crisis by all the people who may be affected.

---

[29] One can see a paradox in the contrast between the relentless egalitarian claims one always hears in all French bureaucratic organizations, and the relative lack of favoritism that really occurs compared to other countries' patterns of action. From this point of view, the difference between private and public organization may be smaller than is usually expected.

One can now understand the paradox of the weakness of the ostensibly omnipotent central power that has been frequently emphasized by many observers of French administrative practices, as well as French traditional political life.

People on top theoretically have a great deal of power and often much more power than they would have in other, more authoritarian societies. But these powers are not very useful, since people on top can act only in an impersonal way and can in no way interfere with the subordinate strata. They cannot, therefore, provide real leadership on a daily basis. If they want to introduce change, they must go through the long and difficult ordeal of a crisis. Thus, although they are all-powerful because they are at the apex of the whole centralized system, they are made so weak by the pattern of resistance of the different isolated strata that they can use their power only in truly exceptional circumstances.

This is what we observed in both the Clerical Agency and the Industrial Monopoly. In the Clerical Agency, the whole militaristic structure converged on a weak and divided management whose only function was to maintain the system in its present stable steady state. This management, unable to discriminate between its supervisors, could not even try to propose change. Change could come only from further up, i.e., from the all-powerful Ministry. However, the Ministry's services were so far removed that their possibilities of action were extremely reduced and their grand schemes very rarely put into practice.

In the Industrial Monopoly, only the director and his assistant were able to make changes in the factory. But their power, which was theoretically great, was held completely in check by the inadequacy of the communications system that was the consequence of the power structure we have analyzed. The general management, which had always been careful to preserve all its rights and privileges of absolute power, was completely the prisoner of the tight impersonal system it had built to maintain these prerogatives.

Such stalemates can be broken only through crises. Indeed, serious crises attended the source of the main developments of the two organizations. These situations are, of course, characteristic of well-protected areas, where bureaucratic tendencies can develop easily. But similar patterns are recurrent in France's organizational life in the political as well as in the economic field. This is well known in the over-centralized polity, where, as we shall see later, there has been a regular rhythm of small crises, whose problem-solving functions were preponderant, deeply felt regime crises, and revolutions corresponding to major readjustments.[30] Even in the social and economic field the resistance to change of a rigid structure seems to have led also to successive crises of readjustment.

---

[30] Wars have often performed the function of revolutions.

A Parsonian interpretation of the whole system may easily be made by emphasizing this extremely important end product. Or one may simply say that, basically, French society did not accept change as a value or did not accept it so much as Anglo-Saxon societies, especially American society. Upon careful study, however, it does not seem that the French record is too bad, compared to its neighbors'. In terms of the rate of increase of the whole national product, France has lagged behind at certain periods but made up for it later. In the long run, all Western European countries have ended up with 2 or 3 per cent annual increases,[31] and the slight differences which can be observed cannot rationally be considered to correspond to such deep differences in values.

In our view, the pattern of change, and not the amount of change itself, must be considered as the basic variable. Certain values condition the prevailing patterns — the values of harmony, security, and independence, the difficulty of assuming face-to-face conflicts and face-to-face dependence relationships and of tolerating ambiguous situations; ultimately, the value of *bon plaisir*, the primacy given to rational well-ordered mastery over the environment. Frenchmen do not dislike change; they dislike disorder, conflict, everything that may bring uncontrolled relationships; they cannot move in ambiguous, potentially disruptive situations. Like players in stalemate (or adversaries in a war of position), they wait for an opening; and when it comes, most probably from the outside, they move in, all at once, thus reconstructing a new stalemate. What they fear is not change itself, but the risks they may encounter if the stalemate that protects them (and restricts them at the same time) were to disappear.

One may argue that the prevalence of these values in a given society is certain to prevent progress, but this is only partially true. The French model of change also presents certain advantages. It does not prevent, and may even stimulate, individual pioneering; and it is especially successful in establishing rational and coherent impersonal systems.[32] As we shall see later, French successes have always been most conspicuous at the two ends of the scale — individual explorations in science and adventures where man is complete master of his own endeavor; and

---

[31] See e.g., Charles Kindleberger, "The Postwar Resurgence of the French Economy," in *In Search of France* (Cambridge Mass.: Harvard University Press, 1963), pp. 118-58.

[32] Frenchmen have been known throughout modern history both for adventurous explorations and for bureaucratic achievements. The comparison of French and British colonization in the New World is a good example. On the one side, a centralized and well-controlled society and a multitude of lone adventurers, the *coureurs de bois*; on the other, more diversified and richer self-governing communities, but much fewer daring explorations by lone adventurers. See [Crozier, *The Bureaucratic Phenomenon*, pp. 263-69].

large-scale routine operations where a bureaucratic system of organization that protects the individual completely from human interference is more efficient than more flexible competitive systems.[33]

12   WILLIAM G. FLEMING

Authority, Efficiency, and Role Stress:
Problems in the Development
of East African Bureaucracies

This analysis is concerned with the problems of endowing developing political bureaucracies with authority and efficiency. By authority is meant the ability of members of the bureaucracy to have their orders obeyed by their clientele. Efficiency is defined as the normal characteristics of a bureaucracy—hierarchical control, ability to maintain records, routinized action patterns for dealing with specified problems, and so forth. Thus, "authority" is a concept which describes the external relations between the political control agency and the people it governs, while "efficiency" is concerned with the internal standards of the bureaucracy. The following examination is focused on the critical relationship between two administrative roles during the period of colonial rule in East Africa — the British district commissioner and the African civil service chiefs — and on the bureaucratic roles and new authority systems that have emerged since independence.

COLONIAL AND AFRICAN AUTHORITY ROLES

District Commissioner

The former British Empire was administered by a civil service which extended from London to the various territorial capitals and outlying areas within the colony. The officer in the lowest level of the organization

---

[33] The railroads and the postal services are two conspicuous cases of such outstanding successes.

Reprinted by permission of the author and publisher from the *Administrative Science Quarterly*, 11 (December 1966), pp. 386-401, 404.

went by various titles — collector, resident, agent — but more often he was called "district officer" or "district commissioner." The power and duties of this official varied greatly over time and across colonies.

The district commissioner occupied a particular "status" in the colonial bureaucracy which governed the former Uganda Protectorate, Kenya Colony, and Tanganyika Territory. As a field officer he was the lowest administrative official in the Colonial Service. Below him were his assistants, police and technical officers in the district, his agents, the civil service chiefs, and his clientele, the people. The relationship between the "district commissioner" and these others defines the "role set" associated with the office.[1] The concept of role set describes the expected forms of behavior between role mates. In other words, the norms which governed the behavior between a district commissioner and the provincial commissioner were different from those which defined the relationship between district commissioner and African headmen.

The Colonial Service bureaucracy (later called H.M. Overseas Service), which administered the East African territories, had a highly elaborate and hierarchical structure of roles. Procedures for dealing with clientele (tribes and people) and with members of other roles were specified, and the processes of recruitment and promotion at first of British and later of Africans as well were prescribed on a basis of merit. The rational goals of the bureaucracy were originally to maintain law and order, and later to develop the colony politically and economically. This entailed many instrumental goals, some of which conflicted with each other and with the ultimate goals. Inadequate procedures for goal definition; that is, policy formation and execution, were often causes of conflict in instrumental goals. For example, the lack of a clearly defined policy on Kenya — the competing ultimate goals of developing the country for eventual African rule, multiracial rule, or settler rule — led to confusion in defining instrumental goals and resulted in conflict in administrative practices.

Relation to African Chief

The elements of the district commissioner's role set that describe his relations with other roles in the colonial bureaucracy are more readily ascertainable than those concerned with the chiefs, and his clientele, local councils, tribal groups, and the people generally. In the early days of administration, the role set was fairly simple. Such administrators as Ainsworth in the Machakos district of Kenya or Weatherhead in the West Nile district of Uganda, were concerned with the establishment of

[1] Robert K. Merton, *Social Theory and Social Structure* (Glencoe, Ill.: Free Press, 1957), pp. 368-384.

effective rule in the years before World War I. They were often alone serving on the outposts of empire, miles and days away from their superiors in the bureaucracy and their main official relations were with the Indian soldiers and perhaps one European assistant. Their duties often forced them to engage in semimilitary campaigns to establish their authority. These early activities helped to set the expected pattern of behavior between the district commissioner and the people. Their exploits became proverbial and they were often absorbed into the folklore and myths of the tribes.[2]

One of the first tasks of the new colonial officials was to discover and adapt or create roles in the African tribal system which could be invested with authority. This policy was necessitated by a lack of European personnel available for field service, and the impracticality of maintaining a large military force at the district level. The system of "indirect rule" was devised, not so much out of philosophical concern for the maintenance of African tribal structure as out of practical necessity.[3]

The various types of tribes which the first administrators encountered set conditions on the development of authority roles, and consequently on the district commissioner's role set. The East African interlacustrine kingdoms and chiefly societies possessed a political structure with well-articulated authority roles with varying degrees of differentiation from the kinship system. There is some evidence which suggests that in at least two of the Uganda kingdoms (Buganda and Bunyoro), a type of civil service had existed before British intervention. By contrast, in the acephalous tribes, political authority was often dispersed, and there were few positions which had power to make binding decisions for the entire society. What political power did exist in these tribes was neither concentrated nor highly visible, and limited powers of decision were variously distributed between lineage and clan heads, village elders, and religious leaders. Even in the kingdoms and chiefdoms, the legitimate scope of political decision making was often overestimated by the colonial administrators.

When a district commissioner had to deal with indigenous kings and

[2] See W. G. Fleming, *The District Commissioner and Tribal Administration in Uganda*, Ph.D. dissertation, Northwestern University, 1964; J. Middleton, *Lugbara Religion* (New York: Oxford University, 1960). The present paper is based on research in East Africa supported by the Comparative Politics program and the Program of African Studies, Northwestern University.

[3] For a discussion of the controversy regarding direct rule and indirect rule see L. P. Mair, *Native Policies in Africa* (London: George Routledge, 1936); Lucy Mair, *New Nations* (Chicago: University of Chicago, 1963); for an East African example of indirect rule in practice see R. Young and H. Fosbrooke, *Smoke in the Hills* (Evanston: Northwestern University, 1960).

chiefs he had to adapt and modify existing roles to the needs of the colonial bureaucracy; when he had to administer acephalous societies he had to create political roles. The relations between the district commissioner in Toro district or Bunyoro district and the traditional kings of those Uganda tribes, were different from the relations between the district commissioner of Machakos district in Kenya or Morogoro district in Tanganyika and the externally imposed chiefs of the acephalous Akamba and Luguru respectively. To deal with these different political structures, the colonial bureaucracy evolved distinctive patterns of administration and policy.[4]

Role Stress of African Chief

In all three territories, therefore, the first instrumental goal was the establishment of "local native authorities," who could act as an extension of the colonial service bureaucracy. This was accomplished by the enactment of various ordinances and regulations, which established the new roles and provided for lines of responsibility and scope of authority.[5] These authorities, or chiefs, eventually became organized systematically and could be identified by some of the characteristics usually associated with Western bureaucracies — hierarchical structure of control and responsibility, merit criteria for recruitment and promotion, and so on. Role stress developed because of different patterns of behavior expected by the district commissioner and the people.

The chief was caught between conflicting elements in his own role set. Each chief or headman endowed with "legal" power by the colonial administration was frequently faced with a difficult dilemma. In any given task — collecting taxes, growing cash crops, repairing roads, enforcing local laws, and others — the African leader was often forced to choose between distasteful and incompatible courses of action. He could enforce the directives of the local district officer, regardless of its basis in tribal tradition, and thereby lose the respect of his tribesmen and diminish his own customary authority. Or he could refuse to enforce such a measure, either through subterfuge or outright insubordination, and thus earn a reputation as being inefficient and unreliable — which could bring eventual dismissal from the service. It was not unusual for a chief to say,

[4] See Lord Wm. Hailey, *Native Administration in the British African Territories, Part I, East Africa* (London: H. M. Stationery Office, 1950); A. Richards (ed.), *East African Chiefs* (London: Faber and Faber, 1960).

[5] Kenya Government Archives: *Native Courts Regulations, 1897; Village Headman Ordinance, 1902; Native Authority Ordinance, 1912* (Nairobi, Government Printer). Uganda Government Archives: *The Uganda Agreement, 1900; The Toro Agreement, 1900; Ankole Agreement, 1901; Bunyoro Agreement, 1933, Laws of Uganda Vol. VI (Revised)* (Entebbe: The Government Printer, 1936). Tanganyika Government Archives: *Native Authority Ordinance No. 25, 1923; Native Authority Ordinance, 1926* (Dar es Salaam: Government Printer).

"Why don't you enforce the soil erosion measures since you think them necessary? Then the people will not hate me."[6]

The methods used by chiefs to resolve this stress varied. The author would hypothesize that the older chiefs, those tied more closely to their tribal systems and who derived part of their legitimacy from that system, tended to resolve the problem in favor of the people, i.e., in favor of their tribal status. The newer chiefs, however, who did not come from traditional chiefly clans and who owed little of their authority to the tribal system, tended to resolve conflict in favor of the administration, i.e., in favor of their bureaucratic status.

Lloyd Fallers has shown in his interesting study of chieftainship in Uganda how the colonial system was maintained through the internalization of stress in the personality of the chief. With the increase in number and complexity of authority systems, however, it became almost impossible for the chief to resolve the conflict.[7]

The development of an indigenous African bureaucracy, which mediated between the colonial rulers and the people, was one of the most significant developments in British colonial rule in Africa. Because of this bureaucracy the district officer was often insulated from direct contact with the people. The local civil service chiefs were, at the same time, channels of communication important in policy formation and agents of policy execution. The intermediate position of chief was of tremendous importance for the maintenance of the colonial system of political control. While the colonial officer could use the chief for implementing unpopular policy, he was himself shielded from the opposition which might be aroused. Although chiefs sometimes became wealthy and powerful men, they also became the targets of popular attack. Their positions were almost untenable in the last days of colonialism, when they often became a focus for nationalist hostility.

BUREAUCRATIC DEVELOPMENT IN THE COLONIAL PERIOD

Administrative practice differed considerably in the three former East African territories. The relations between district commissioners and chiefs and people varied even from district to district within a colony. Some major administrative differences can probably be attributed to the differences in general social and geographical factors — Uganda Protectorate with its multiplicity of kingdoms and structured tribes, Kenya Colony with many acephalous societies and a large European settler

---

[6] A. Richards, *op. cit.*, p. 364; for an interesting account of this phenomenon see also Lloyd Fallers, "The Predicament of the Modern African Chief: An Instance from Uganda," reprinted in William Hanna (ed.), *Independent Black Africa* (Chicago: Rand McNally, 1964), pp. 278-296.

[7] Lloyd Fallers, *op. cit.*

population, and Tanganyika Territory with its large land mass and many types of tribes exposed to the conscious application of indirect-rule principles.

Uganda

Because of the relatively small geographical area to be administered and because of the social structure of the tribes, Uganda had fewer officers than either Kenya or Tanganyika. Special agreements were made with all of the kingdoms. Buganda was given a pre-eminent position within the administrative framework of the Protectorate; it acquired extra land in compensation for the assistance given the British in the war against Bunyoro. It was treated as a separate province, while the other kingdoms (Ankole, Toro, Bunyoro) were only districts.

The British mistakenly believed that all of the tribes in Uganda had chiefs, so at first organized administration throughout the Protectorate on the pattern of Buganda. This practice had deleterious consequences in the northern and eastern part of the country where few of the indigenous societies possessed clearly articulated political systems.

Uganda was divided into provinces, as were all of the East African dependencies (the Eastern, Western, Northern, and Buganda), under the supervision of a provincial commissioner. Each province was further divided into districts under the direction of a district commissioner and a staff of assistant district commissioners and clerical workers. The number of district officers, i.e., district commissioners and assistant district commissioners, in each district varied according to the size of the area and the period. Each district was divided into county and subcounty units under the control of African civil service chiefs.

In Uganda it was the custom for each of the district officers to live at the "boma," the district headquarters. The assistant district commissioners and the district commissioner himself would make regular tours through the counties attending "barazas" (meetings) of the chiefs and people. These tours were carried out as often as time and personnel would allow and were a characteristic practice of colonial administration in Uganda. The main functions of touring were to inspect judicial and financial books of the county chiefs and subchiefs, to meet with the people directly, to explain and cajole, to execute policy and gather information. Assistant district commissioners were provided with regular schedules of duties, among which would be the counties for which they were administratively responsible. Of course, this was the ideal situation; actually all officers were called upon to tour any area of the district and to undertake any administrative duty.[8]

[8] For a fuller discussion of the role of the district officer in Uganda, see Fleming, *op. cit.*, ch. 3 and 4; for the development of local government see F. Burke, *Local Government and Politics in Uganda* (Syracuse: Syracuse University, 1964).

Kenya

In Kenya the proliferation of acephalous societies made it very difficult to imitate the administrative practice of Uganda. There were few large tribes with centralized authority systems that could be adapted by the colonial rulers. Consequently the government was forced to appoint many location chiefs or headmen and attempted to define their area of jurisdiction according to clan or lineage boundaries. These latter criteria were not universally applied, and many locations were delimited purely for administrative convenience. Divisional chiefs were later created to oversee headmen, and an attempt was made to build a bureaucracy. Colonial administrative officers would often try to ascertain local opinion before appointing a chief or headman; nevertheless, conflict between the traditional tribal elders and the appointed headmen and chiefs could not be prevented. As in Uganda, chiefs became powerful and wealthy through support of the colonial government, but their roles had little sanction in the traditional system. The aura of traditional legitimacy which surrounded the chief in certain Uganda societies was rarely found in Kenya, and chiefs became a central focus for Mau Mau attack during the Emergency in the 1950's.

This difference in the role of the chief had a strong influence on the role set of the district commissioner in Kenya. Since the chief had no basis for his authority in the tribal system, he was ultimately dependent upon the district commissioner for the execution of his orders. Good relations with the administration were of critical importance in maintaining his office. On the other hand, this lack of independence meant that district officers had to keep a closer surveillance over the headmen than was necessary in Uganda. In order to accomplish this, the practice developed of having district officers live out among the sections under administration. Location headmen were thus subjected to closer supervision than their counterparts in the Uganda Protectorate. Only the district commissioner and maybe one or two assistants and clerical staff would live at the boma; other officers lived out on location.[9] Thus colonial rule in Kenya approximated the "direct rule" ideal.

Tanganyika

Tanganyika Territory was administered between 1920 and 1946 as a mandate of the League of Nations and thereafter until its independence

---

[9] These generalizations only approximate real conditions. For example in the northern areas of Uganda, the development of a chiefly bureaucracy had little basis in indigenous systems and the British used Buganda African agents as rulers there in the early days. In the North Nyanza District of Kenya, tribes could be found that had recognizable political roles. See Hailey, *op. cit.*, sect. 5; Burke, *op. cit.*, ch. 5; Fleming, *op cit.*, ch. 4 and 5; L. P. Mair, *Primitive Government* (Baltimore: Penguin Books, 1964), ch. 11.

in December 1961 as a Trust of the United Nations. It is important to note here that the colonial government made a deliberate attempt to apply principles of "indirect rule" which had been previously tested in Northern Nigeria. Moreover, before the British administration, Tanganyika had been governed under a system of "direct rule" by Germany from 1890 to 1916.[10]

The introduction of indirect rule, specifically encouraged by Sir Donald Cameron, the second governor, required that district officers discover the tribal authority structures and endow them with legal powers as local "native authorities." The territory had so many different kinds of indigenous political systems that the native authorities resulting from this policy were widely disparate in powers and composition. A few tribes, such as the Haya, did possess chiefs, but many more were acephalous. In 1927 the government published a list of recognized tribal leaders; the list had over 650 names on it! Eventually the authorities were combined to form more manageable units.

Thus the role relations between a district commissioner and chief in Tanganyika took on aspects of corresponding situations in the other two possessions. An officer in one district might be able to depend fully on his chiefs to act in a responsible and efficient manner, whereas in other districts the native authority would be ineffectual; the district commissioner himself would be required to direct affairs.[11]

Pattern of Bureaucratic Development

In all three territories the patterns of bureaucratic development took unexpected turns. In Uganda the traditional criterion for the recruitment of chiefs became somewhat attenuated. In the later days much of the personnel were not selected by the tribal king nor from a traditional "noble" or "royal" class, but from the educated elite who could maintain and meet some external standard of merit. In Kenya and some parts of Tanganyika, however, other criteria of recruitment were used. The chiefly roles which were created by the colonial administration and which were originally filled by an external selection process (the district commissioner) eventually came to be filled through neohereditary principles of recruitment. Thus, many appointed chiefs attempted and succeeded in establishing the rights of their families to inherit positions of power within the bureaucracy, and popular elections often confirmed the positions.

[10] Hailey, op. cit., pp. 211-13; Young and Fosbrooke, op. cit., ch. 1; M. Bates, "Tanganyika," in G. Carter, African One-Party States (Ithaca, N. Y.: Cornell University, 1962), pp. 403-412; for a useful comparison with Uganda see A. Richards, op. cit.

[11] Ibid. M. Bates says that by the late 1930's at least five major categories of native authorities could be found while Lord Hailey was able to distinguish three classes ten years later.

For the most efficient functioning (i.e., bureaucratic goal attainment) the role of district commissioner required role mates who could effectively execute orders, i.e., play the role of agent. This necessitated that the chiefly role be filled by someone who was educated enough to understand bureaucratic behavior and who also had some basis of support among the people. In Uganda, although the first chiefs might have possessed authority based on the legitimacy of their role within the traditional system, they were neither educated nor socialized in bureaucratic norms. The tendency was, thus, to replace some traditional chiefs with educated individuals. However, the same bureaucratic requirements produced different results in Kenya and Tanganyika. There the problem was to gain support for chiefs whose roles had no traditional legitimacy. This was accomplished, in part, by selecting individuals who gained popular approval through the newer source of legitimacy. The legitimacy was further enhanced by the facility with which later chiefs could afford to send their sons to school and so equip them to meet the bureaucratic standards of recruitment. This elite tended to perpetuate themselves.

The role-set relations between the district commissioner and chiefs differed, then, according to how the indigenous system met the initial needs of the bureaucracy — efficiency and authority. In some districts authority was obtained by adapting the traditional roles, and efficiency was maintained by recruiting "modernized" local elites to fill these roles. In the other areas, efficiency was gained through the creation of bureaucratic roles, and by recruiting individuals to these roles who had some popular support, and authority was maintained through the external generation of legitimacy. Thus the vitiation of "traditional" principles in some districts of the Protectorate worked in favor of the bureaucratic need for efficiency, while the development of efficiency elsewhere worked to fulfill the need for authority.[12]

Since the civil service chiefs mediated between the district commis-

FIGURE 1. CIVIL SERVICE CHIEFS' ROLES IN EAST AFRICA

		Authority	
		+	−
Bureaucratic Efficiency Values	+	A	B
	−	C	D

[12] Again the *caveat* must be entered that these generalizations may be inaccurate in specific cases. A good short discussion of the problem may be found in Mair, *Primitive Government, op. cit.*, pp. 250-279.

sioner and the people, the ability of the administration to achieve any given goal depended upon the efficiency and authority of those chiefs. In districts where the chiefs had low authority and high efficiency, the district commissioner's tasks approached the pole of "direct rule." He might have to engage in many safaris in the district, hold many "barazas" and attempt to administer rules himself. District officers might be required to live out on location near the chiefs and people. Part of the job would be to discover procedures for bolstering the authority of the chiefs. Thus the administration would attempt to find individuals who met requirements for bureaucratic efficiency and who might also enjoy some popularity among the people and would not antagonize the tribal elders.

In the districts with tribes having traditional chiefs, the problem was to increase the bureaucratic efficiency of the role and yet retain its traditional authority. In such areas the district officer's task approached the "indirect rule" ideal. He would be concerned with a close supervision of the chief's work, with his poll tax receipts, and with his judicial records, i.e., with improving his efficiency as a bureaucratic administrator.

It is possible to represent these relationships as in Figure 1. Acephalous societies tended to fall initially into cell D and chiefly tribes into cell C. It is assumed that the ideal role mate (chief) for the district commissioner, and the main instrumental goal to be achieved, was the position of cell A. The officers administering tribes C tried to increase efficiency by filling the chiefs' roles with individuals who were not necessarily from "noble" clans or families or were sanctioned by the traditional king. This tended to undermine the legitimacy of the roles and so to decrease authority. Officers in such districts often found themselves embroiled in arguments between lineages or sections over the "rightful heir" to the position, as was often the case in northern Uganda. The ideal relationship, of course, was when a legitimate heir was also educated, and could be expected to perform well as a bureaucrat. In Uganda this process of replacement for the sake of efficiency went so far that two experts have termed it "Government by imitation rather than adaptation" and "indirect rule indirectly applied."[13]

Administrative officers who were faced by the situation described in cell D believed they had two possible alternatives. Ideally they would attempt to maximize both values; in reality their programs had to be organized according to priorities. They could attempt to increase efficiency at the expense of authority, or vice versa.

In Kenya, the policy was to attempt a first move from D to B. Efficiency was achieved through the creation of headmen and local chiefs who had little authority within the tribal system. The next step

[13] Mair, *Native Policies in Africa, op. cit.*; Burke, *Local Government and Politics in Uganda, op. cit.*, ch. 5.

was to generate support for the roles created. This was accomplished by consulting with opinion leaders in the tribe — sometimes even holding rudimentary elections — and by allowing a new "tradition" of inheritance to develop.

In Tanganyika, the conscious effort to apply principles of indirect rule resulted in an initial move from D to C. The administration hoped to adapt the many forms of indigenous authority structures to the purposes of colonial rule. Much administrative time and resources were expended on discovering the "legitimate" rulers and investing them with "legal" power; then, more time was spent in combining the original jurisdictions into more wieldy units. But this second step was already an admission that an attempted maximization of authority values decreased bureaucratic standards of efficiency.

Increase in Complexity of Chief's Role

By the time independence came to the East African dependencies, ambiguity about the powers and position of the chiefs had increased in part, because of the addition of new role mates in the district commissioner's set. Local government bodies and technical roles had evolved which complicated the original simple relations between the district commissioner and the chief, and the increasing complexity led to increasing role confusion. The distribution of powers and responsibility of the chief were not clearly defined. He was called upon to undertake many new tasks and to follow the advice of many new technical officers. He might be required to enforce the marriage by-laws of the local councils, build or maintain roads according to specifications of the Public Works Department, and follow the instructions of the agricultural officer on planting and harvesting procedures. For all of these he was ultimately responsible to the district commissioner. These new intervening roles created multifarious and often conflicting demands upon him. The chief now had to be concerned not only with the vitiation of his authority by carrying out unpopular orders, but also by a decrease in efficiency caused by the more complex technical and administrative organization of colonial control.

Adaptation to Role Stress

The increase in size and complexity of the district commissioner's role set was accompanied by a comparable change in the chief's set. The district commissioner was able to adapt to this situation by becoming less involved in day-to-day administration, acting more as an executive officer and policy coordinator. He was still legally responsible for the success of all government policies in the district. Various mechanisms evolved to assist the district commissioner in overcoming the role stress which developed as he had to deal with more and more roles. The most important of these was the "district team." This was an organization whose membership consisted of all the various technical officers in the district as well as representatives of the African local government. The district commissioner was chairman of this committee, and through it coordinated the various activities of the central government and maintained control.

FIGURE 2.   AUTHORITY SYSTEMS IN COLONIAL EAST AFRICA

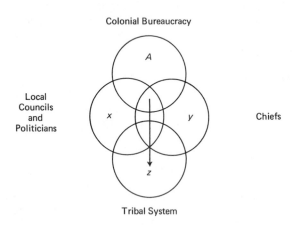

Unfortunately, no comparable stress-resolving mechanisms evolved for the role of chief. He remained beset by multiple demands and orders. One of his worst problems was learning to deal effectively with the local African councils and the new politicians. To these nationalists, especially, the chief was the lackey of imperialism. Although the early councils were little more than a committee of chiefs, the later ones were often composed of educated local elites recruited by election. The elected councillors had to attend to only one base of support — the people. The chief, on the other hand, had to be concerned not only with maintaining rapport with the people, but also with the colonial administration in all of its aspects.

It is possible to conceptualize this problem in role stress in terms of the overlapping and sometimes competing systems of authority which developed under colonial hegemony (see Figure 2). The original linkage between the people and the district commissioner was the chief. The overlap between y and z shows the extent to which the appointment of chiefs articulated with the tribal system. The overlap between y and x indicates the extent to which chiefs dominated the councils, and that between A and x the control of the district commissioner exerted over the council. In some areas x and y together constituted the "native authority." The arrow between A and z is the direct contact between colonial administrators and the people. In the early days this might be the district commissioner leading campaigns against revolts, or day-to-day administration as in Kenya; in the later days, most direct contact was between the people and various agents of the technical departments.

At first, the control linkages were more effectively maintained between the colonial bureaucracy and the chiefs in the acephalous tribes, and between chiefs and people in districts where the traditional policy was characterized by a more articulated system of political roles. In both areas, however, an unintended consequence of the policy of increasing efficiency was a decrease in authority. Later efficiency itself was endangered by the increasing number and complexity of bureaucratic role relationships. An eventually chiefly authority was vitiated by the growth of competing control systems — councils, local government agencies, and political parties. The people were exposed to a multiplicity of overlapping and sometimes conflicting authority patterns. New sources of loyalty and legitimacy developed outside the traditional tribal-colonial arena. In this welter of new systems the role of chief became less and less effectual as an agent of control. His authority was challenged and efficiency diminished. . . .

CONCLUSIONS

It has been shown in this study how the social environment that existed at the time of British intervention in East Africa placed conditions upon the development of bureaucracies and forced colonial administrators into different approaches in their attempts to achieve maximum efficiency and authority. The new independent governments are apparently pursuing policies that make less use of the traditional political systems, although there are marked differences between Tanzania and Uganda in this regard. The role stress which civil service chiefs experienced has been alleviated in Tanzania to some extent by the elimination of the role and by heavy emphasis on modernizing the national political structure. It remains to be seen whether such rapid modernization, i.e., pursuing efficiency values at the expense of authority, can be successfully achieved with little regard for traditional sources of legitimacy. In Uganda a more conservative approach has been taken although there is some indication of a move toward the Tanzania pattern.

Outputs

The Organization's Formal Product

In the first article devoted to the determinants of organizational output, Ben-David makes an unusual but crucial point, perhaps comparable to that made by Baron and Tropp. In addition to totally different institutions — the family, for example — in the environment of the organization that may be important, the way similiar organizations are structured into a system or sector affects each of them. In particular, Ben-David sees the competition of institutes of scientific research with each other, and the consequent creation of certain career lines and advancement possibilities, as critical stimulants to research productivity.

Scientific Productivity and Academic Organization in Nineteenth-Century Medicine

The purpose of this paper is to describe and explain differences as well as fluctuations in the productivity of the medical sciences in Germany, France, Britain, and the United States, from 1800 to about the time of World War I. Scientific productivity as defined here does not comprise any evaluation of the greatness or depth of various scientific ideas, or of the "efficiency" of scientific production as measured by some input-output ratio. It refers only to two gross quantities: the number of scientific discoveries (including scientifically important technical inventions), and the numbers of people making such discoveries. Provided that these numbers are not a fixed proportion of the general population or some other general quantity, they are a measure of the active interest in science existing in a society at a certain point of time.

The two suggested indexes of productivity — the numbers of discoveries and of discoverers — have not precisely the same meaning and there are obvious objections to both. It can be argued that since scientific discoveries are disparate units of unequal significance, it is meaningless to count them.[1] The first part of the claim is true, but not the deduc-

Reprinted by permission of the author and the American Sociological Association from the *American Sociological Review*, 25 (December 1960), pp. 828-840, 842. A section concerning Britain and the United States has been deleted.

A preliminary draft of this paper was written while the author was a fellow at the Center for Advanced Study in the Behavioral Sciences, Stanford, California. He is indebted to Harry Alpert, S. N. Eisenstadt, Jacob Katz, Morris Janowitz, Robert K. Merton, D. Patinkin, Dr. George G. Reader, and the late Dr. J. Seide for comments on the manuscript or discussion of its subject matter, and to A. Zloczower for his help with the research.

[1] The method is applied and discussed by T. J. Rainoff, "Wave-like Fluctuations of Creative Productivity in the Development of West-European Physics in the Eighteenth and Nineteenth Centuries," *Isis*, 12 (1929), pp. 291-292. See also S. C. Gilfillan, *The Sociology of Invention*, Chicago: Follet, 1935, pp. 29-32; Joseph Schneider, "The Cultural Situation as a Condition for the Achievement of Fame," *American Sociological Review*, 2 (August, 1937), pp. 480-491; Frank R. Cowell, *History, Civilization and Culture: An introduction to the Historical and Social Philosophy of Pitirim A. Sorokin*, London: Black, 1952, pp. 90-106; and especially the methodological comments of Robert K. Merton, "Fluctuations in the

tion from it. It has been shown time and again that "great" discoveries had been preceded by intensive activity manifested in numerous "small" discoveries, often leading to the simultaneous finding of the final solution by more than one person.[2] Similarly, one of the signs of a great discovery is that it leads to a greater number of smaller discoveries based on the newly discovered principle.[3] Therefore, viewing science as a flow of constant activity, great discoveries appear as waves built up gradually by the ant-like work of predecessors, leading first to an upsurge of activity by followers and disciples and then diminishing into routine when the potentialities of the great idea have been (or seem to be) exhausted. Thus there is no need to weight the individual discoveries. The weighting is done automatically by the clustering of discoveries around the significant event. This is not to deny that there are lone discoveries, neither expected beforehand nor understood after they are made. For the historian who sits in judgment of individual greatness and stupidity, these are important events that prove the absurdity of our method of counting. But if one's purpose is to gauge the extent to which various social systems induce people to scientific productivity, then the relatively negligible weight accorded to the lone discovery is a good index of the relative lack of inducement to engage in research in that society.

The use of the number of discoverers (not students or graduates) as an index of scientific activity can be justified by similar reasoning. Such men as Newton, Lavoisier, and Einstein did not spring up in scientific deserts but in environments of intensive scientific interest, and their work inspired disciples and followers. So we can expect a general correspondence between this index and the previous one. Yet, there are numerous problems involved in the use of this index. In principle, the same numbers of discoveries can be made by quite different numbers of people, so that there may be no relationship between the two counts. In fact, however, the variation is quite limited, because the accomplishment of even a single scientific discovery demands as a rule considerable investment of time and training: one can assume that discoveries will be made by persons with special characteristics ("discoverers") and not randomly either by them or others. Thus we take this figure too as a good index of the social inducement to engage in research. No more than general correspondence between the two sets of data is expected, however, because, first, there may be variations due to institutional circumstances in the length of the creative period of discoverers, and in the

---

Rate of Industrial Invention," *The Quarterly Journal of Economics*, 59 (May, 1935), p. 456.

[2] *Cf.* William F. Ogburn, *Social Change*, New York: Huebsch, 1922, pp. 90-122; Bernhard J. Stern, *Society and Medical Progress*, Princeton: Princeton University Press, 1941, pp. 41-44.

[3] Merton, *op. cit.*, pp. 464-465.

chances of "outsiders" for making discoveries; and, second, even if these things were constant, the shape of the two curves would still differ because each discovery is a single event counted only once, at the time of its occurrence, while discoverers must be counted over a period of time or at an arbitrarily fixed point of time (such as their age at the beginning of the professional career). For these reasons we expect this second index to correspond with the first only in registering relatively long-term and gross changes. But in such details as the exact time of the changes and short term fluctuations no correspondence between the two indices can be expected.

A second problem requiring preliminary clarification is the definition of medical sciences. We have adopted the criteria of our sources, which include all discoveries that eventually became part of the medical tradition. Undoubtedly this implies the inclusion of some non-medical discoveries and discoverers; therefore, from the viewpoint of the history of scientific ideas, this may not be too meaningful a category. However, in a study of scientific activity one needs data reflecting activity in more or less homogeneous institutional frameworks, irrespective of whether they do or do not relate to a logically coherent system of ideas. On this score, medicine in the nineteenth century seems to be a good choice. Through most of the century it was closely interwoven with the natural sciences. It had been the first profession based on the study of natural sciences, and medical faculties were the first university departments to teach them. For many years the only large-scale and permanent organizations where research was systematically conducted were the teaching hospitals. Also, the art of the apothecary and the science of chemistry were often connected until the early nineteenth century. Thus the sciences associated with medicine have formed a complex of scientific activity which has been related to well defined social structures since the eighteenth century, whereas most of the basic sciences were the professional concern of only a few individuals in any country well into the second half of the nineteenth century. The medical sciences, therefore, appear to be well suited for discerning the effect of structural changes upon scientific creativity during the period under consideration.

THE QUESTIONS TO BE EXPLAINED

Table 1 is based on a count of medical discoveries made in the countries here surveyed from 1800 to 1926, according to a "Chronology of Medicine and Public Hygiene."[4] The data reveal two different trends.

First, between 1810 and 1819 a rise in the number of discoveries in France and Britain begins, followed in Germany in the next decade. By 1840, the rise has passed its peak in France and Britain and a decline

[4] Published in F. H. Garrison, *An Introduction to the History of Medicine*, 4th edition, Philadelphia and London: Saunders, 1929.

TABLE 1. NUMBER OF DISCOVERIES IN THE
MEDICAL SCIENCES BY NATIONS, 1800-1926

Year	U.S.A.	England	France	Germany	Other	Unknown	Total
1800—09	2	8	9	5	2	1	27
1810—19	3	14	19	6	2	3	47
1820—29	1	12	26	12	5	1	57
1830—39	4	20	18	25	3	1	71
1840—49	6	14	13	28	7	—	68
1850—59	7	12	11	32	4	3	69
1860—69	5	5	10	33	7	2	62
1870—79	5	7	7	37	6	1	63
1880—89	18	12	19	74	19	5	147
1890—99	26	13	18	44	24	11	136
1900—09	28	18	13	61	20	8	148
1910—19	40	13	8	20	11	7	99
1920—26	27	3	3	7	2	2	44

Source: see footnote 4.

sets in lasting until the 1870s. Second, an upsurge starts simultaneously in all these three nations and in the United States in 1880. These parallel movements reflect the story of the convergence of chemical, anatomical, physiological, and pathological discoveries in the first half of the nineteenth century, and the spate of bacteriological and surgical innovations which followed the work of Pasteur, Lister, and Koch in the last quarter of the century. Both waves shows only that certain fruitful ideas had been simultaneously, or nearly simultaneously, exploited in Western European countries beginning from the early nineteenth century, and in the United States as well from the end of the century. Apart from indicating that scientific communication among these countries was well established by that time and that therefore the phenomena reflect the course of scientific ideas, they call for no sociological explanation. What needs to be explained is the conspicuous change in the relative shares of the countries during this period. French supremacy in the beginning of the century with Britain a close second gave way to an overwhelming preponderance of German discoveries through the second half of the last century. The American share was rapidly increasing from the 1880s and became the largest by 1910-1919. Since this was the time of World War I, comparison with the European countries may seem of doubtful validity; but the relative decline of the European countries started prior to the war and lasted well into the twenties, so that it should not be attributed entirely to the war. Figure 1 shows the proportion of the total discoveries made in each nation during each period as a proportion of the country's relative share over the whole period:

$$\left(y = 100 \frac{\text{country's share in decade } (\%)}{\text{country's share over whole period } (\%)}\right).$$

A significant aspect of this change of relative positions is that it is

FIGURE 1.   CHANGES IN THE RELATIVE SHARE OF MEDICAL
DISCOVERIES IN SELECTED COUNTRIES, 1800-1926

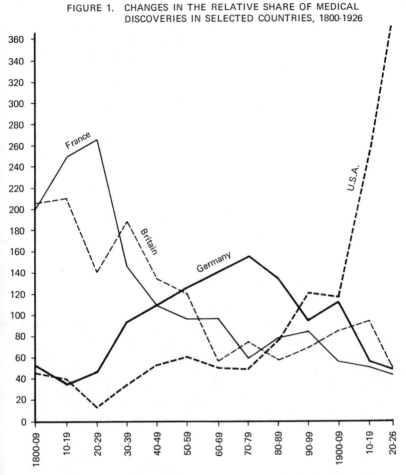

connected with an atypical growth in the curve of discoveries in the
country which is gaining the largest share. Thus the number of German
discoveries continually increases through the middle of the nineteenth
century in a period of decline in France and Britain. A similar deviation
marks the change in the relative position of the United States at the
beginning of the twentieth century.

A similar pattern marks the number of discoverers. Table 2 shows the
"productivity" of the various countries in terms of scientists.[5] France
and Britain, with the largest numbers at the beginning of the century,

[5] Based on W. A. Newman Dorland, *The American Illustrated Medical Dictionary*, 20th edition, Philadelphia and London: Saunders, 1946.

TABLE 2. DISCOVERERS IN THE MEDICAL SCIENCES AT THE
AGE OF ENTERING THEIR PROFESSIONS (AGE 25)
IN VARIOUS COUNTRIES, 1800-1910

Year	U.S.A.	England	France	Germany	Other
1800	1	7	8	7	4
1805	1	8	5	8	2
1810	3	11	6	6	2
1815	2	12	12	7	3
1820	3	11	23	18	2
1825	2	17	15	18	6
1830	8	12	25	10	6
1835	11	13	26	29	7
1840	5	24	22	35	12
1845	5	14	13	33	5
1850	10	18	21	37	10
1855	15	16	20	49	27
1860	16	23	13	61	23
1865	25	15	36	71	26
1870	25	15	31	83	41
1875	40	31	23	84	46
1880	48	17	40	75	50
1885	52	16	34	97	52
1890	43	11	23	74	41
1895	47	9	27	78	29
1900	32	9	17	53	30
1905	28	4	4	34	25
1910	23	6	7	23	18

Source: Dorland's Medical Dictionary (20th ed.).

fall behind Germany starting about 1835. While the number of German
scientists entering upon their careers increases regularly, with only one
considerable drop until 1885-1890, there are fluctuations and a generally
downward slope in France and England through the middle of the
century. The American trend, like the German, shows much less fluctuation. Thus, with respect to major trends, the two indexes validate
each other.[6]

[6] The pattern which emerges from these indexes parallels the qualitative descriptions of up-to-date histories of medicine and science. See, e.g., Arturo Castiglioni,
A History of Medicine, New York: Knopf, 1947; Richard H. Shryock, The Development of Modern Medicine, New York: Knopf, 1947; H. T. Pledge, Science Since
1500, London: Philosophical Library, 1940. Rather than simply referring to such
sources, I prefer to present the numerical indexes in detail for two reasons: (1) They
contain some information not sufficiently emphasized — or even blurred — in those
sources. Thus the small amount of medical research in Britain is blurred in the
qualitative descriptions by the dazzling brilliance of England's few scientist-intellec-
tuals and by the glamor of the British medical profession. Also, the different patterns of growth of scientific personnel (discoverers) is a subject not sufficiently
emphasized in the histories of medical science. (2) What is called here scientific
productivity is only one aspect of the development of science; in terms of the inter-
relationships of scientific ideas it is perhaps a peripheral one. Since traditionally the
history of science is an history of ideas, even the few historians interested in such

Two questions emerge: What explains the change of scientific leadership from France to Germany to the United States? And what explains the "deviant" nature of the development in Germany during the middle and in the United States toward the end of the nineteenth century, as manifested in (1) the continuous rise in the number of discoveries during periods of relatively low creativity in the other countries; and (2) the relatively smaller fluctuations in the number of people embarking upon scientific careers in these two countries compared with the others?

HYPOTHESIS: THE ORGANIZATIONAL FACTOR

Neither the changes in scientific leadership nor the deviant nature of the German and American developments can be manifestations of differences in the scientific ideas in the various countries. This could be the case only if international communication had been deficient, so that new ideas in one country would have no effect upon the work of scientists in the others. This was by no means the case, as demonstrated by the parallel upward movements of the curves of discoveries in all the countries in periods of crucial scientific advance. Independently from this fact, whatever barriers to scientific communication had existed between France and Germany during the first decades of the nineteenth century had disappeared by the beginning of the fourth decade. By about the same time, the British too established contacts with continental science, from which they had become isolated with decreasing splendor during the eighteenth century, as did the Americans.[7] Therefore nothing immanent to science as a body of ideas explains the observed differences and changes. The explanation has to be sought in external circumstances.

Among the possible external causes there are some general and obvious ones, such as population growth and the growth of national income. A few unrefined attempts to assess the population factor suggested that this is not a promising line of approach. The introduction of this factor does flatten out the curves somewhat, but does not eliminate the characteristic waves of development, and it hardly affects the changes in the relative position of the nations.[8]

---

sociological phenomena as differences in the scientific development of various countries are not very explicit about the bases of their judgments, nor do they sufficiently differentiate between the various aspects of science as a social activity. It is important, therefore, to present explicitly the quantitative basis of the historians' judgment and clearly delimit the particular aspect of scientific activity dealt with here from others.

[7] *Cf.* Shryock, *op. cit.*, pp. 193-196; Paul Diepgen, *Geschichte der Medizin*, Berlin: Gruyter, 1955, Vol. II/1, pp. 204-207; Charles Newman, *The Evolution of Medical Education in the Nineteenth Century*, London: Oxford University Press, 1957, pp. 265-269.

[8] The sources used for population data were *La Population Française: Rapport*

Nor do differences in national or personal income seem to be relevant. The indexes of national income in all the countries here surveyed show a fairly gradual and constant rise through the whole period without such ups and downs and such extensive changes in the relative positions of the countries as indicated by our data. Moreover, the United States and Britain were the richest of these countries, at least since the middle of the nineteenth century (and no doubt earlier in the case of Britain). Yet, as to medical discoveries, these countries were relatively backward during much of the period.[9] None of these factors, therefore, seems to be directly and consistently related to the differences in the growth of discoveries in the various nations.

Thus, it is assumed that the conditions determining the differences are to be sought in the *organization* of science. But this is a complex phenomenon: we still must seek the particular organizational factor which reasonably answers our questions. It is proposed to isolate this factor by comparing the main aspects of the organization of science in France and Germany during the first half and the middle of the nineteenth century and those same aspects in Britain and the United States during the three decades preceding World War I. This particular pairing is selected because France and Germany maintained a publicly supported network of scientific instruction and research from the early nineteenth century, while Britain and the United States did not begin to develop their systems until the second half of the century. There were short-lived experiments in Britain during the first half of the century, but these were overshadowed by the archaic nature of the most important universities. If it is possible to isolate a theoretically relevant condition common to the organization of science in Germany and the United States, but absent in France and Britain, that condition may reasonably be taken as the cause of the observed differences.

FRANCE AND GERMANY

Three conditions are mentioned in the literature in explanation of German scientific superiority in the nineteenth century: (1) the relative excellence of laboratory and hospital facilities for research and the faster recognition of the importance of new fields of research, especially physiology; (2) the clear recognition of the aim of the university as a seat of

du Haut Comité Consultatif de la Population et de la Famille, Paris: Presses Universitaires de France, 1955, p. 19; Michel Huber, Henri Bunle, et Fernand Boverat; *La Population de la France*, Paris; Librairie Hachette, 1943, p. 19; W. S. and E. S. Woytinsky, *World Population and Production*, New York: Twentieth Century Fund, 1953.

[9] For national income data, see, e.g., Colin Clark, *The Conditions of Economic Progress*, 2nd edition, London: Macmillan, 1951.

original research, and efficient organizational devices to achieve that aim, such as far-reaching academic self government, the freedom of the teacher regarding the content of his courses, the freedom of the student in the choice of his courses and his teachers (including easy transfer from one university to another), the requirement of submitting theses based on research for attainment of academic degrees, and, above all, the institution of *Habilitation,* that is, the submission of a high level scientific work based on original research as a precondition of academic appointment; (3) the existence of a large number of academic institutions which made possible the mobility of teachers and students, and resulted in an atmosphere of scientific competition that did not exist elsewhere.[10] The superiority of the German scientific facilities from about the middle of the century is an undeniable fact. But instead of explaining the differences in creativity, it is itself a phenomenon that needs explanation.

The pioneering country in the establishment of modern scientific facilities was France. Founded in 1794, the Polytechnique had been the model academic organization in the natural sciences. Among other new features, it possessed the first academic research laboratories (in chemistry). The physiological laboratory at the Collège de France, where Magendie and Claude Bernard conducted their studies, was considered most inadequate by the middle of the nineteenth century. Yet it was there that modern experimental physiology began. The idea of studying illness as a natural phenomenon, not necessarily for the sake of cure, was first conceived in Paris, and the beginnings of systematic clinical research in medicine were made in the hospitals of that city.[11]

Until the 1830s German medical research and natural science research in general was backward compared with the French, and probably with the British too. The famous network of modern German universities already existed from the time when, following tentative beginnings at Halle, Goettingen and Jena, the University of Berlin was established in 1809.[12] But the universities, rather than promoting, retarded the development of empirical science. They regarded philosophy as the queen of sciences, and usually disparaged empirical research. The biological

[10] *Cf.* Abraham Flexner, *Universities: American, English, German,* Oxford: Oxford University Press, 1930, pp. 317-327; Donald S. L. Cardwell, *The Organization of Science in England,* London: Heinemann, 1957, pp. 22-25; H. E. Guerlac, "Science and French National Strength" in E. M. Earle, editor, *Modern France,* Princeton: Princeton University Press, 1951, pp. 85-88.

[11] *Cf.* Shryock, *op. cit.,* pp. 70-71, 151-169; Newman, *op. cit.,* p. 48; Guerlac, *op. cit.,* pp. 81-105.

[12] *Cf.* Flexner, *op. cit.,* pp. 311-315; R. H. Samuel and R. Hinton Thomas, *Education and Society in Modern Germany,* London: Routledge & Kegan Paul, 1949, pp. 111-113; Jacob Barion, *Universitas und Universitaet,* Bonn: Rörscheid, 1954, pp. 14-20.

sciences in particular were under the sway of *Naturphilosophie*, which stimulated much imaginative writing but little research.[13]

Only around 1830 did this atmosphere change under foreign influence. Liebig, who had studied in Paris, established in 1825 the first chemical laboratory at the small university of Giessen. A few years later Johannes Mueller, the central figure of German physiology, abandoned his early attachment to *Naturphilosophie* and became converted to the empirical method by studying the works of the Swedish chemist, Berzelius. About the same time the Vienna school of clinicians adopted the methods of investigation initiated by the Paris clinicians, and various learned journals began to propagate the new scientific approach in the medical sciences.[14]

Thus the French showed at least as much understanding of the value and the needs of scientific research as the Germans. It should not be assumed that this understanding suddenly declined around the middle of the century. The influentials of French science at that time, such as Dumas, and later Pasteur, Claude Bernard, and Victor Duruy, were certainly not less enlightened and brilliant than their German counterparts. In fact, they may have been more sympathetic to the needs of scientific research than German academic policy makers, since obscurantism was rather prevalent within both the faculties of the German universities and the governmental offices in charge of higher education.[15] The greater expansion of German scientific facilities and the prompter recognition of new fields are therefore as much in need of explanation as the continuous growth in German discoveries.

The second condition — the presumably peculiar values and organization of the German university — is also a very doubtful explanation. The idea of academic freedom notwithstanding, atheists, Jews, and socialists were often kept out of academic careers in Germany. Academic self-government was not necessarily enlightened: liberal scientists in the 1840s regarded it as an essentially retrograde arrangement. In fact, some of the most beneficial academic decisions — with relation to the growth of science — were taken by civil servants, most notably Friedrich Althoff, who interfered with academic self-government. Even the *Habilitationsschriften* were often rather mediocre pieces of research, and there was

[13] Cf. Shryock, *op. cit.*, pp. 192-201; Diepgen, *op. cit.*, Vol. II/1, pp. 23-28.

[14] *Cf.* Cardwell, *op. cit.*, pp. 22-25; Shryock, *op. cit.*, pp. 188, 195; Garrison, *op. cit.*, pp. 451-452.

[15] See Guerlac, *op. cit.*, pp. 85-88 on France. On the relative backwardness of German academic administration, see Ervin H. Ackerknecht, *Rudolf Virchow: Doctor, Statesman, Anthropologist,* Madison: University of Wisconsin Press, 1953, pp. 139-140; Samuel and Thomas, *op. cit.*, pp. 114-130; Max Weber, *Jugendbriefe,* Tübingen: Mohr, n.d., pp. 151-152. In order to realize the amount of obscurantism and intolerance in German universities at the time it is useful to read the otherwise shallow work of Richard Graf du Moulin Eckart, *Geschichte der deutschen Universitaeten,* Stuttgart: Enke, 1929.

nothing in the constitution of the universities efficiently to prevent mediocre professors from confirming inferior theses.[16]

At the same time, the ideas as well as some of the arrangements said to be characteristic of the German universities also existed in France. Freedom of teaching already formed the core of the tradition at the Collège de France before the Revolution and was carried further than in the German universities. The ideals of pure research were formulated in French scientific ideology at least as clearly as in German and they were practiced and encouraged in a great many ways.[17] There is no proof that the lack of the paraphernalia of academic self-government interfered with the research of French scientists more than in Germany. It is true that, compared with the *Habilitation*, the French *aggrégation* and the system of open examinations seem to be inefficient ways of selecting people for academic careers. But there is little evidence that this irrelevant hurdle actually prevented potentially creative people from entering scientific careers. Moreover, there were other means, such as numerous prizes and public honors, which encouraged original research in France.[18]

Decentralization has been written about much less than the first two conditions, partly because it was an unintended circumstance, and partly because its effect upon research is less immediately evident. The decentralization of the German academic system was the result of the political dismemberment of the German-speaking people. There were 19 independent universities in Germany proper, maintained by the princes of the numerous small states constituting Germany in the eighteenth and early nineteenth centuries, as well as German language universities in Switzerland, Austria (including the Czech provinces), and Dorpat in the Baltic Sea Provinces of Russia.[19] At the same time the

[16] *Cf.* Flexner, *op. cit.*, pp. 317-327; Samuel and Thomas, *loc. cit.*

[17] See Claude Bernard, *Morceaux Choisis*, dirigé et préfacé par Jean Rostand, Paris: Gallimard, 1938, pp. 16-18, for one of the most beautiful descriptions of the traditions of the freedom of teaching and research as it was practiced at the Collège de France. See also Ernest Lavissé, *Histoire de France*, Paris: Librairie Hachette, n.d., Vol. IX/1, p. 301, on the pioneering beginnings of the teaching of pure sciences in the same institution in the 1770s and 1780s.

[18] For a good description of how the French system of examinations actually worked, see René Leriche, *Am Ende meines Lebens*, Bern und Stuttgart: Huber, 1957, pp. 53-55. Leriche, like others, attributes the lack of originality of French medicine to the examinations. But his own account shows that the problem was rather the lack of career opportunities for young medical scientists (*ibid.*, p. 34).

[19] With the addition of Strassburg in 1872 there were 20 universities in Germany. *Cf.* Christian v. Ferber, *Die Entwicklung des Lehrkörpers der deutschen Universitaeten und Hochschulen 1864-1954*, Vol. III of Helmuth Plessner, editor, *Untersuchungen zur Lage der deutschen Hochschullehrer*, Göttingen: Vandenhoeck & Ruprecht, 1956, pp. 37-38. The German-language universities of Switzerland were Zürich, Bern, and Basel; and of Austria, Vienna, Prague, Graz, and Innsbruck.

French boasted a unified academic system, most of it situated in Paris. Although some of the features of this centralization introduced by Napoleon were deplored, the central administration of science and academic institutions generally was considered to be desirable by French politicians of science.[20]

Nevertheless, decentralization seems to have been the decisive factor in determining the differences in the scientific creativity of the two countries. It gave rise to academic competition, and competition forced upon the individual institutions decisions which would not have been made otherwise, or at least not made at that time. In all areas crucial to the development of the medical sciences German policies turned out to be in the long run more farsighted and bold than French policies, although the first initiative was often taken by the French. — What, then, was the actual competition and how did it influence the decisions about the crucial problems of academic policy?

THE CRUCIAL DECISIONS

Given the situation of the medical sciences (and perhaps of the sciences in general) at the beginning of the last century, the problem faced by the French and the German systems (and not confronted by Britain and the United States until later) was to find adequate criteria for the evaluation and support of science. The governments, and increasingly the people too (especially in France), believed in the value and usefulness of science. Academies, universities, and other institutions were set up everywhere, or rejuvenated where they existed before, in order to promote research and to disseminate knowledge. One of the aims of these institutions was to enable a selected few scientists, who had already proved their greatness, to devote all of their time to financially supported scientific research. But it was not intended to create in these institutions academic careers which one entered as in any other profession. The large majority of the scientists had independent means or a lucrative profession (very often medical practice, even in sciences not connected with medicine), and pursued their scientific interests in their free time, often at a considerable personal cost. This idealistic pattern seemed to fit perfectly that sacred pursuit of truth which was science. Academic appointments therefore were regarded as honors rather than careers, and turning science into an occupation would have seemed something like a sacrilege.

A corollary, in this amateur stage of science, was the absence of specialization. The great names of the early nineteenth century were those of generalists who were creative in more than one field. And the new scientific disciplines developed from their work. While it was increasingly believed that the new disciplines required specialists, the fact

[20] *Cf.* Guerlac, *op. cit.*, pp. 87-88.

that they were opened up by generalists seemed to indicate that specialization was not really necessary. Moreover, there persisted the reluctance to abandon the conception of general science which explains to the adept all the secrets of nature. Thus there was considerable disinclination to substitute for the *savant* such narrow specialists as chemists, physiologists, and the like. And there was even more reluctance to redefine such a traditionally unified field as medicine into a number of subspecialties.

The second problem was the development of criteria for the support of research. Today it is still difficult of course to decide what constitutes adequate and sufficient support of research, but at least budgets can be drawn for determined purposes. At that time even this was impossible, since research was an unpredictable, erratic process, and important discoveries were made as often outside as inside the laboratories.

Finally, there was the question of training scientists. Until the second half and particularly the last quarter of the nineteenth century, science had few practical applications. Most of it was pure science benefitting no practice. Under these circumstances, to train every medical student, would-be chemist, and engineer in scientific research was about as justified as it would be today to teach every concertgoer advanced musical composition.[21]

These problems existed in both countries and were approached in France and Germany with the same concepts. Yet, to repeat, the long-term decisions made in France concerning all three problems were the opposite of those made in Germany.

Scientific Careers and Specialization

The creation of regular careers in science and the recognition of specialized disciplines were closely connected problems. Both may be illustrated with the case of physiology, the most decisive science for the development of medicine in the nineteenth century.

As a systematic discipline, physiology emerged at the beginning of that century. François Magendie, considered to be the founder of experimental physiology, was professor of medicine. He established the new specialty and could follow it undisturbed (though practically unsupported) at the Collège de France, because of the full degree of academic freedom prevailing in that institution. But his disciple, Claude Bernard, who became the most outstanding representative of the new field around the middle of the century, for many years had to use his private laboratory and private

[21] On the state of science in the early nineteenth century, see Pledge, *op. cit.*, pp. 115-151. On scientists in the same period, see Elie Halévy, *History of England in 1815*, London: Pelican, 1938, Vol. 2, pp. 187-200; René J. Dubos, *Louis Pasteur: Franctireur de la science*, Paris: Presses Universitaires de France, 1955, pp. 3-4; and Diepgen, *op. cit.*, Vol. II/1, pp. 2-5, 66-69, 152-153.

means to pursue his research. At last, against the opposition of those who regarded the new discipline as merely a branch of anatomy, a special chair was created for Bernard at the Sorbonne in 1854. Soon thereafter he also fell heir to Magendie's chair at the Collège de France and held both appointments until 1868; he then transferred his work to the Museum of Natural History, relinquishing the post at the Sorbonne to his disciple, Paul Bert.

The recognition of the discipline of physiology, however, did not create opportunities for purely scientific careers in the traditional field of medicine. In this connection, the only change was that after the retirement of the chair's incumbent a single successor would have to be found. This was not a prospect on the basis of which one could realistically take up research as a career. Therefore, potential scientists first had to build up a practice, and engaged in research as a part-time activity.[22]

Thus, the academic career changed very little in France through the nineteenth century. Appointments were made from an undifferentiated group of practitioners — amateur scientists — and usually at a fairly advanced age. Even academically successful persons did not become full-time scientists before they reached their forties or fifties, and since the chair to be vacated was not known they had to maintain as broad interests and activities as possible. But in the second half of the century there was increasingly less chance for non-specialists to make important discoveries. French scientific productivity therefore declined even in fields pioneered by Frenchmen. Whenever a discipline reached the stage of development where its efficient pursuit required specialists, there was little chance that the French system would produce such scientists.[23]

Physiology as a science was received with more sympathy in Germany than in France, but its recognition as an academic specialty there also ran into difficulties. The man who did most for the introduction of the discipline to Germany, Johannes Mueller, was a generalist who taught, in addition to physiology, anatomy, ophthalmology, and surgery.[24] His eventual successor in Berlin, Du Bois-Reymond, had been refused one professorial chair after another because he was considered a mere

[22] Cf. Bernard, op. cit., pp. 154-157, 263-285; J. M. D. Olmsted, Claude Bernard: Physiologist, New York: Harper, 1938, pp. 51-89. For the situation at the beginning of the twentieth century, see Edouard Rist, 25 Portraits des médicins français, 1900-1950, Paris: Masson, 1955, pp. 29-40.

[23] See Rist, op. cit., pp. 97-104, on the career of S. A. Sicard, who seems to have been a relatively lucky and successful scientist. When at the age of 51 he was appointed as professor he had to abandon his life-long interest and research in neurology because the vacant chair was designated for internal pathology, and course preparation in the new field required a great effort.

[24] Cf. K. E. Rothschuh, Geschichte der Physiologie, Berlin-Göttingen-Heidelberg: Springer, 1953, pp. 93, 112-118.

specialist.[25] The early creation of a separate chair in physiology (for Purkinje in Breslau, 1839) had no general effect, and for some years physiology and anatomy continued to be taught by the same person in all other German universities. But pressure for the separation of the disciplines by the younger generation of scientists continued, and those with some bargaining power raised the demand when they were offered university chairs. Thus, when Carl Ludwig was offered a professorship at Zürich in 1849, he accepted it only on the condition that a separate teacher be appointed for anatomy;[26] thereafter the recognition of the new discipline proceeded rapidly. No university could afford to neglect the new field, so that by 1864 there were already 15 full professors of physiology in Germany and several others in the wider system of German-language universities.[27] The separation of physiology from anatomy at this stage became the official policy of university administration. In some cases, where traditionally-minded incumbents were reluctant to abandon one of the disciplines, the separation was forced upon them by administrative pressure.[28]

All of this led to a complete transformation of the scientific career in Germany. In spite of the strictures against narrowness and of the continuing lip-service paid to the image of the scientist who works because of devotion, science became a specialized and regularized occupation. As we have seen, success, fame, or even sheer enterprise had a good chance for reward. Once a new and fruitful field was recognized in one university, strong pressures led other universities to follow suit, thereby creating more opportunities for those willing to work in the new field. Therefore, it was possible — and for the very able also worthwhile — to concentrate after graduation on one well defined and promising field of research with the definite aim of a scientific career. Not only was it unnecessary

[25] George Rosen and Beate Caspari-Rosen, *400 Years of a Doctor's Life,* New York: Schuman, 1947, pp. 248-150; Ernst Gagliardi, Hans Nabholz and Jean Strohl, *Die Universitaet Zürich und ihre Vorlaeufer 1833-1933,* Zürich: Erziehungsdirektion, 1938, pp. 548-549.

[26] *Ibid.,* pp. 539-548. Virchow, who was also offered the chair, refused to accept it on the ground that he wished a chair for pathological anatomy exclusively (without teaching responsibilities in either surgical anatomy or physiology). In Ludwig's time the nominal unity of physiology and anatomy was still maintained; the separate teacher in anatomy was only an extraordinary professor. But when Ludwig left Zürich in 1855 and the position was offered to Koelliker, the chairs were finally separated upon the latter's suggestion (although Koelliker himself refused the job). For similar instances of creating new specialties at the same university in order to attract or retain teachers, see *ibid.,* pp. 562, 879.

[27] *Cf.* Von Ferber, *op. cit.,* p. 204.

[28] For example, Valentin in Bern, in 1865; see Bruno Kisch, *Forgotten Leaders in Modern Medicine,* Philadelphia: American Philosophical Society, 1954, pp. 174-175.

first to build up a practice and to retain as general interest as possible, but if one had taken such a course his academic prospects would have been negligible in competition with the full-time specialists. Thus specialized science became a career, and the amateur general scientist disappeared in Germany.[29] This difference in career possibilities, not the distinction between *Habilitation* and *aggrégation*, explains the greater research orientation of German than of French science.

The same mechanisms which explain the development of scientific roles also explain the development of facilities for research, and the introduction of scientific methods into the training of physicians. The creation of new facilities was part and parcel of the bargaining between universities and scientists. Facilities (laboratories, assistants, and so on) were offered to attract desirable candidates or to prevent scientists from moving elsewhere. The extension of facilities made possible, and to some extent made necessary, the training of a growing number of persons capable of doing research. Since not all such individuals could be given academic appointments in the basic medical sciences or otherwise, they used their research skills and interests to transform clinical medicine into an exact science. These processes and their results may be briefly illustrated.

Research Facilities

As has been pointed out, the French were the first to establish modern institutions for scientific training and research. But the facilities and arrangements established in France about 1800, considered to be ideal for their time, were hardly extended or changed until World War I or later. The Pasteur Institute, established in 1888, was the first independent research institute of the world. Again, it remained the only one in its field in France at least until World War I.[30]

Thus in France a new type of organization was apt to remain a single

[29] Max Weber, writing in 1918, regarded science as a most risky career; see his "Science as a Vocation," in H. H. Gerth and C. Wright Mills, *From Max Weber: Essays in Sociology*, London: Oxford University Press, 1947, pp. 132-134. But, it should be realized that Weber was referring to a crisis situation in an already established discipline; the circumstances were much more hopeful in the middle of the nineteenth century. Of those who took their *Habilitation* between 1850 and 1859, 85 per cent received full-time academic appointments, while for those who received their *Habilitation* between 1900 and 1909 only 62 per cent received such posts. The corresponding proportions in medicine are 84 and 48 per cent, respectively. (This does not necessarily mean a relatively greater decline of research opportunities in medicine, because there were good research opportunities outside the universities in public hospitals.) See Von Ferber, *op. cit.*, pp. 81-82, for the statistical data; and Adolf Struempell, *Aus dem Leben eines deutschen Klinikers*, Leipzig: Vogel, 1925, on the *Habilitation* as a preparation for a hospital career.

[30] The ideal arrangements of French medical schools in 1798 are noted in Newman, *op. cit.*, p. 48. Concerning the quite different picture presented by French academic medicine early in this century, see Abraham Flexner, *Medical Education*

show-piece for 50 years, while in Germany such novelties became routine features of the organization of research in a much shorter time. By the 1840s there were apparently more and better chemical laboratories in Germany than in France, and by the sixties the contrast was extreme. At a time when it was an achievement for Pasteur to obtain any (and most inadequate) laboratory facilities, the Prussian government built new laboratories at Bonn and Berlin (the Bonn laboratory, for example, could accommodate more than 60 students) equipped with the most up-to-date facilities, and the older ones probably were also more adequate than anything that existed elsewhere. And there were good laboratories at other universities in Germany.[31]

There were similar differences between Germany and France in the development of facilities for medical research and of specialized research institutions. The New Vienna School of clinical research began in the thirties, and its facilities seem to have been modest even until midcentury. But there were gradual improvements in one place after another, and by the sixties there evolved fairly uniform standards which made it possible to conduct clinical research with the aid of adequate laboratory facilities in a number of places.[32] Finally, the establishment of specialized research institutions became a matter of routine in Germany soon after the beginnings made in France. They became a tool regularly used by the universities' administrations, the governments, and local bodies to encourage and develop the work of famous scientists.[33]

Scientific Training

The differences in the development of medical training were no less conspicuous. The fact that until about the 1880s all the great advances in the basic medical sciences contributed little to the cure of illness largely explains the persistent and overwhelming emphasis on the practical art of medicine rather than on its few scientific bases in the training of the student-physician. Indeed, apprenticeship and bedside demonstrations were the most important parts of medical training in France, England, and the United States.[34]

---

in Europe, New York: The Carnegie Foundation for the Advancement of Teaching, 1912, pp. 221-223; and Leriche, *op. cit.*, p. 34. On the Pasteur Institute, see Guerlac, *op. cit.*, p. 88.

[31] *Cf.* Cardwell, *op. cit.*, p. 80; and Dubos, *op. cit.*, pp. 34, 78-79.

[32] *Cf.* Diepgen, *op. cit.*, Vol. II/1, pp. 207-209; on the situation in the 1860s, see Theodor Billroth, *The Medical Sciences in the German Universities*, New York: Macmillan, 1924, p. 27; and at the turn of the century, Flexner, *op. cit.*, pp. 145-166.

[33] *Cf.* Flexner, *op. cit.*, 1930, pp. 31-35.

[34] *Cf.* Diepgen, *op. cit.*, Vol. II/1, pp. 212-214; Vol. II/2, pp. 154-155, 286-288; Abraham Flexner, *Medical Education: A Comparative Study*, New York: Macmillan, 1925, pp. 211-212, 241, 248.

Only in Germany did the training of the doctor become a privilege of scientists. By the 1860s even clinical chairs were given exclusively to people with attainment in research rather than to outstanding practitioners. And from the middle of the century, even public hospitals were increasingly staffed by doctors both interested and trained in research. Thus much earlier than elsewhere (possibly prematurely), medicine in Germany became an applied science.[35] As a result, when the great opportunities for clinical research arose, following the discovery of the bacteriological causation of illness and the perfection of anesthesia and aseptic surgery, there were in Germany enough doctors trained in research to take full advantage of the opportunity, and to transform public (even non-teaching) hospitals into veritable institutions of applied medical science.[36]

DECENTRALIZATION AND COMPETITION

Thus, regarding all three crucial decisions — developing scientific facilities, creating scientific roles, and training larger numbers of research personnel than were justified by existing practical needs — the German system "behaved" with uncanny foresight. It has been shown that this foresight was not the result of greater individual wisdom. It was the result of competition due to the unintended decentralization of the German system.

"Competition" in this paper refers to the general condition underlying all the processes described above: it is a situation in which no single institution is able to lay down standards for the system of institutions within which people (in this case students and teachers) are relatively free to move from one place to another. Under such circumstances, university administrators required neither exceptional boldness nor foresight for continually expanding facilities and training, and for creating new scientific jobs. There was little if any need for fateful individual decisions. Improvements and innovations had to be made from time to time in order to attract famous men or keep them from leaving. In this way, laboratories and institutions were founded, assistantships provided, new disciplines recognized, and scientific jobs created. These innovations were repeated throughout the system because of pressure from scientists and students in general, irrespective of practical needs and of what a few scientific influentials thought.

[35] Diepgen, *op. cit.*, Vol. II/1, pp. 152-153. See also Theodor Billroth, *loc. cit.*; Bernhard Naunyn, *Erinnerungen, Gedanken und Meinungen*, Munich: Bergmann, 1925, pp. 375-376.

[36] There was a parallel development in chemistry. There too the availability of relatively large numbers of trained chemists afforded Germany the opportunity to build up within a short time a chemical industry based on applied science, after the discovery of the aniline dyes made the practical application of science a permanent possibility; *cf.* Cardwell, *op. cit.*, pp. 134-137, 186-187.

If competition inevitably brought about the adoption of fruitful innovations in the universities, it also forced them to correct mistakes and to eliminate traditions which retarded scientific development. This process has been shown in the case of the separation of physiology from anatomy and the introduction of scientific criteria in clinical training in Germany. . . .

CONCLUSION

The continuous growth in the curves of German discoveries during the middle decades of the nineteenth century and in the American curves starting from the 1880s is thus attributed to the extent to which these societies exploited, through enterprise and organizational measures, the possibilities inherent in the state of science. They were quicker than France and Britain in the recognition of new disciplines, the creation of specialized scientific jobs and facilities for research, and the introduction of large-scale systematic training for research. They were also quicker to abandon traditional notions which had lost their usefulness. None of these conditions alone could have sustained scientific growth for a long period of time. It was no coincidence, however, that they went together, since a common underlying factor, competition, determined the crucial decisions concerning all of these conditions in the two decentralized systems. Successful scientists were rewarded with university chairs and facilities. Their success encouraged others to take up science and, incidentally, transformed the pursuit of science into a regular professional career; it created pressure for further expansion of facilities and training, and exposed the inadequacies of out-of-date traditions.

This interpretation of the curve of scientific discoveries, according to which their growth was due to increased opportunities for entering research careers (and not, for example, to better selection of scientists), is also consistent with the differences between the countries shown in the second index based on the numbers of discoverers. As pointed out earlier, beginning in 1835 in Germany and in 1860 in the United States, the growth in the numbers of those entering upon scientific careers became continuous, while in France and Britain there were fluctuations over the whole period. Continuous growth represents a situation in which research becomes a regular career; fluctuations, a situation in which research to a large extent is a spontaneous activity engaged in by people as the spirit moves them.

In conclusion, some of the implications and problems raised by the existence of a positive relationship between scientific productivity and academic competition may be noted. According to the present explanation, this relationship is due to the impetus provided by competition for entering promising but undeveloped fields of research. This, however, suggests that the growth of discoveries in any field may be limited by the capacity for expansion of the institutional framework (jobs and facilities), a suggestion which seems to be worth further exploration.[37]

Another question concerns the *quality* of the impetus given to science by competition. The present hypothesis suggests that competition increases the gross amount of discoveries of all kinds through the thorough exploitation of potentially fruitful fields of research. It says nothing about the conditions conducive to the creation of fundamentally new ideas, and it is quite possible that the social conditions that stimulate basic innovations differ from those that facilitate the exploitation of fruitful ideas already discovered.[38]

Finally, nothing has been said about the conditions that maintain scientific competition. Political decentralization gave rise to competition in Germany, and political decentralization enhanced by private financing and administration of higher education led to competition in the United States. It is not argued, however, that competition is the only possible outcome of any state of decentralization, or that competition, once established, is self-maintaining. Decentralization may lead to collusion or mutual isolation as well as to competition; and competition may be replaced by either of these alternatives. Determination of the general conditions that ensure competition, therefore, is another problem which needs further study.

The Organization's Power

Eisenstadt's article, dealing with power as a form of organizational output, is in part a case of non-performance. After a survey of the very different historical origins of public bureaucracies in various kinds of developing countries, Eisenstadt concludes that cultural traits as well as economic and political problems common to all of them are likely to cause

---

[37] This is the subject matter of A. Zloczower, "Career Opportunities and Scientific Growth in 19th Century Germany with Special Reference to the Development of Physiology," unpublished M.A. thesis, Hebrew University, Jerusalem, Israel, 1960.

[38] *Cf.* Joseph Ben-David, "Roles and Innovations in Medicine," *American Journal of Sociology*, 65 (May, 1960), pp. 557-568.

the new civil services to operate unsatisfactorily, yet to wield a good deal of power. Similarity rather than contrast is his theme.

Janowitz considers the military, and his article covers all elements of our framework from the kinds of environmental inputs that determine the internal structure of the military to its goals. This selection is of particular interest to us because it treats the military as an organization, and because it views power and domination as output variables. From a methodological point of view, the article is of interest because it compares the relative scientific fruitfulness of an approach to organizations via statistical indexes of economic development with an approach using culture area and history. Finding relatively unstable results by both methods, Janowitz proposes a third: a broader contrast between developed and underdeveloped countries as a whole.

14   S. N. EISENSTADT

Problems of Emerging Bureaucracies in Developing Areas and New States

I

In all developing countries, bureaucracies very rapidly tend to develop and extend their scope. As the post-colonial new states attained independence, and as some of the older states (e.g., Latin America or the Middle East) surged toward modernization and expanded the range of state activities, they took over many organs of public administration remaining from the former period; the scope of their activities greatly expanded, and new organs were created. Each became a very important part of the political framework in these countries. Since, in most of

Reprinted by permission of the author, the editors, and the United Nations Educational, Scientific, and Cultural Organization from Bert F. Hoselitz and Wilbert E. Moore, eds., *Industrialization and Society* (Paris: UNESCO, 1963), pp. 159-174.

these countries, the government plays a great role in economic development, the bureaucracies also began to engage significantly in the activities
of the economic sphere. The bureaucracy's activities could then have
great influence on the direction and tempo of the country's economic
development.

What will this influence be? What part will the bureaucracies play
in the political life of these nations? Will they help in the establishment of viable modern political systems? Or will they contribute mostly
to the development of unstable, tension-ridden, and inefficient political
structures? And what is the structure of the bureaucracies? How is it
related to their functioning in these societies? To what extent is it similar
to the major bureaucratic organizations that can be found in the West,
and how does it differ from them? To what degree are the bureaucracies
capable of efficiently implementing various social, political, and economic
policies? Finally, how will they affect the process of economic development — will they facilitate or hinder it?

II

One of the striking facts about the bureaucracies of the developing
areas is that, in most of these areas there exist not one but usually two
or three, bureaucracies — or, at least, different layers of bureaucratic
organization and structure. First, there is what may be called the "pre-
modern" or "pre-development" layer, which had developed before the
attainment of independence or the introduction of modernization. The
second stratum has, as a rule, developed since World War II. It was
engendered by the dual impacts of the attainment of independence and
of modernization and of establishing new social, political, and economic
goals.

In the post-colonial new states, the "old" colonial civil service still
survives in remaining personnel, organizational structure, and tradition.
The structure and organization of the old civil service provided the
basic framework for the extension and development of bureaucratic
administration after the attainment of independence.

Within these societies, the initial emergence of bureaucracies had
been rooted in the need of the colonial powers for various resources
and for the maintenance of law and order. The bureaucracy was based
on over-all political control by the metropolitan powers; the administration participated minimally in the indigenous political and social life
of the community. This necessarily limited its activities, confining them
to the basic administrative services. It also dictated some of the bureaucracy's structural characteristics, such as the high degree of centralization,
the great adherence to legal precepts and rules, and the relatively small
internal differentiation. Thus the pre-independence bureaucracies helped
establish the framework of modern, universalistic legal and administra-

tive practices and organizations. On the other hand, they were highly apolitical. They did not meddle in politics, and they kept up the ideal of a politically neutral civil service. They were also apolitical in that they never really participated in the indigenous political life of the countries in which they served. Their very limited goals were prescribed by the colonial powers, who were not responsible to the political groups and opinions of the countries which they ruled. They did not perform any important functions in the regulation of internal political interests and activities among the "colonial" population, or in the articulation and aggregation of the political interests of that population.[1] Whatever "internal" political activities they undertook were perceived mostly in terms of administrative injunctions and enforcement of law. It is significant that the scope and impact of the activities of the colonial civil service were much greater in countries, such as India, in which "direct rule" was applied, than in countries governed according to precepts of "indirect rule," where the native population was left more or less alone to manage its own affairs, especially on the local level.

The second main layer of the bureaucracies in the new states consists of those departments and echelons which were developed after the attainment of independence. Here a new civil service — "new" in personnel, goals, departments, and activities — evolved. This stratum had to be staffed with new recruits — frequently with inadequately trained recruits whose chief claim to or qualification for office was their former participation in the nationalistic political movements. These new bureaucratic organs have had new types of goals, like economic development, social betterment, educational advancement, or community development.

Unlike members of the "colonial" civil service, most of the recruits to the new have usually had a clear and articulated political orientation and sense of political responsibility. They have very often perceived themselves as representatives of their respective movements, parties, or sectors. Moreover, they frequently have seen themselves as fulfilling chiefly political functions — either as implementing political goals, or as representing, articulating, and regulating the political interests and activities of different groups and social strata.

The relations between the older bureaucracy and the new echelons have not always been easy. In the first period after independence, particularly, the nationalist leaders' prevailing attitude toward the remnants of the older colonial services was distrust. In some cases, this led to the almost complete destruction of the older structure. In most instances, however, some sort of *modus vivendi* has been evolved between

---

[1] For the terms used here, see G. A. Almond, "A Functional Approach to Comparative Politics," in G. A. Almond and J. S. Coleman (eds.), *The Politics of the Developing Areas* (Princeton, N.J., 1960), pp. 26-58.

the older and newer echelon. One or the other is usually predominant; but necessarily the implementation of new social, political, and economic goals has been strongly emphasized, and the involvement in the political process has been much greater than before.

An even more explicitly politically oriented type of bureaucracy has tended to emerge in most of the new states. This type consists of the different "party" bureaucracies which grew out of the leading nationalistic movements which became dominant parties — e.g., the Congress of India, the CPP in Ghana or the Neo-Destour in Tunisia. These party bureaucracies have been oriented more to the political manipulation of groups of population and to the provision of political support and loyalty to the new regime than to the upholding of universalistic legal norms, the development of public services, or the creation of new public administrative services. In personnel or over-all political supervision, the party bureaucracy has often been very similar to the new echelons of the governmental bureaucracy, and has sometimes also been closely related to it, especially through the activities of prime ministers and cabinet ministers. However, the basic patterns of activities and orientations of the members of the party bureaucracy have frequently differed to a very great extent from those of the governmental bureaucracy, and have clashed.[2]

III

The bureaucracies in developing countries which have not been under colonial rule exhibit a somewhat different, although not entirely dissimilar, pattern. Within each there existed, first, a traditional bureaucracy — whether "royal" (as in the Middle Eastern countries) or "oligarchical-republican" (as in most Latin American countries). These bureaucracies usually dominated the political scene until the end of World War II. Within them, some traditional elements were mixed with more modern ones. Frequently, the modern elements were copied from some European country — for example, the French pattern had strong influence in most Latin American countries.

These administrations were usually concerned with supporting the interests of the ruling oligarchies, and with implementing rather limited social and economic objectives. Whatever tendency to modernization they may have exhibited — e.g., in the fields of military affairs or education — their major political aim was to restrict modernization to those minimal spheres in which it was necessary to maintain the viability of the then existing system.

[2] See D. Apter and R. A. Lystad, "Bureaucracy, Party and Constitutional Democracy," in G. M. Carter and W. O. Brown (eds.), *Transition in Africa* (Boston, 1958).

With increasing modernization, with the growing impact of internal democratization, and with the development of new social, political, and economic goals, these bureaucracies had to extend the scope of their activities and to recruit new personnel. However, the older pattern usually continued to leave its imprint on the new echelons and departments, in administrative training, organization, and to some extent also in social and political orientation.[3] Only in a few older countries, like Mexico, widespread, well-organized semi-revolutionary parties succeeded in upsetting the oligarchy and established a stable and viable modern political framework. There, a somewhat new pattern of bureaucratic organization was established, not dissimilar from those of new states.

In most of these older countries, the party bureaucracies were usually less important than in the new states. This was mainly because the oligarchical or monarchical elements were much stronger in the political structure, and because several major institutional interest groups, especially the armed forces, developed as important channels of political struggle and often constituted hotbeds of politics and influential pressure groups.

Both within the formerly colonial societies and in the states with longer traditions of independence, another distinct type of new bureaucratic organization has also emerged — the big economic or business corporation. Within the older countries, these corporations are usually more concentrated in the private sector; in the new states, more in the public or mixed sectors. In all these societies, however, the corporations play an important role in the economic and political life of the country.

IV

We see thus that, in each emerging country, the pattern of development of bureaucracies has been very mixed and heterogeneous. Each part of the bureaucracy developed under somewhat different conditions and in response to different types of needs and pressures. It was only after the attainment of independence, and/or the development of goals and programs of modernization, that these parts were brought together into a common framework and confronted with the need to find some *modus vivendi* in order to deal with the new tasks which they faced.

Perhaps the most important general problem which faced all the bureaucracies was the necessity to adapt themselves to the goals, new spheres of activity, and new social needs that arose from the growing

[3] See the papers by G. Blanksten and D. Rustow in Almond and Coleman, *op. cit.* See also the papers by W. R. Sharp (on Egypt), A. Lepawsky (on Bolivia), F. Heady (on the Philippines), and J. N. More (on Thailand), in W. J. Siffin (ed.), *Toward the Comparative Study of Public Administration* (Bloomington, Ind., 1957).

differentiation and diversification of the social structures, the extension of the scope of social and political participation of many groups in the society, and the development of new social and political goals. In trying to adapt themselves, the merging bureaucracies developed several characteristics which were greatly influenced by their heterogeneous origins and by the conditions in which they found themselves.

In almost none of these countries has the bureaucracy evolved into the "classical" Weberian type of legal-rational organization or an entirely neutral civil service. True, in several of the post-colonial countries — notably in India and Ghana, and, to a lesser extent in the countries which were or are under French colonial rule — the ideal of such a service was transmitted and still has a strong hold on the developing civil service. But even in these countries, events have occurred that have greatly changed the major political orientation of the bureaucracy. Similarly, the structural characteristics and the patterns of activities of these bureaucracies differ in varying degrees, from those of the usual Western pattern.

The first and most important development in the social and political orientations of these bureaucracies is their high involvement in the political process in their respective countries. This is manifested in several ways.

In many of these countries, for example, the bureaucracy becomes not only the administrative arm of an executive, supervised by the legislature; it also constitutes itself as an effective executive or a component thereof, and plays a basic part in establishing, determining, and implementing political goals and major policy directives. In many nations, the bureaucracy may be the main or the only body which, apart from the head of the executive, is capable of formulating clear political and administrative goals and objectives.

The second major aspect of the bureaucracy's involvement in the political process is grounded in the fact that it tends to evolve as one of the principal instruments of political regulation — one of the main channels of political struggle in which and through which different interests are regulated and "aggregated" — and it tends to be very important, even predominant, in this facet of the political process. In some cases, e.g., in some Latin American countries, the bureaucracy also becomes a powerful pressure and interest group in its own right, strongly allied to other oligarchical groups.

Thus, in all these countries, the bureaucracy may tend to fulfill different types of political functions and — like parties, legislatures, and executives — become a center of various kinds of political activity. Although, through such activities, it may establish some of the basic frameworks of modern politics, it may also minimize the extent of differentiation of divers types of political roles and activities. In the latter case, it would greatly impede the development of autonomous and differentiated political activities, organizations, and orientations.

The second basic characteristic of the social orientations of emergent bureaucracies is that they are also major instruments of social change and of political socialization in their respective countries.

These bureaucratic organizations are (at least initially) based on universalistic and functionally specific definitions of the role of the official and the role of the client. The majority of the population of these countries, however, have a different orientation. In social life, their traditional orientations and structures, such as the extended family, are predominant. In these societies, most of a person's role relations are set within traditional groups; and rights and duties are defined in terms of personal relationships. Previous experience with bureaucratic organizations was restricted, and was rarely of any great significance.

Thus, the contacts of the public with governmental organizations provided a framework for a wider process of political socialization. The public's accommodation to the new political structure became, to a considerable extent, dependent upon its successful learning in these situations of contact. This has very often forced the bureaucracies to go beyond their proper specialized roles and to assume various roles of social and political leadership and tutelage — without which they could not have effected the necessary changes in the behavior of the population at large. This need to foster change often extended the scope of the activities of bureaucrats beyond their specific goals, and made them reach also into the realm of family, kinship, and community life of wide strata of the population.

V

What are the causes of these developments in the structure of bureaucracies? And what can be their possible impact on the processes of political modernization and economic development?

Generally, two types of causes can be discerned. One basic cause, often mentioned in the literature, is the difference between the general cultural values and social setting of the developing areas and those of Western countries where "modern" bureaucratic organizations originated. Presthus has illustrated these problems:

> In sum, the dominant educational philosophy tends to devalue practical training and this constitutes a barrier to bureaucratic evolution. Middle East youth prefer to become white-collar rather than blue-collar workers. This inapposite value has an immediate impact on technical and economic development, since it becomes difficult to build up the required force of skilled technicians. In the universities, subjects like statistics and research methods are resisted since they, too, tend to undercut the existing theoretical and subjective conception of learning.

Such beliefs deny the demands of modern bureaucratic organizations for precision, specialization, and scientific method.[4]

For our purposes, the relevant point is that subjective, political values outweigh objective, bureaucratic demands of skill and experience.

In so far as recruitment and the locus of bureaucratic loyalties are concerned, it is well known in Middle Eastern countries that subjective, "particularistic" considerations compete strongly with objective standards in appointment and in policy determination. Western "universalistic" concepts of impersonality, technical supremacy, and loyalty to some abstraction, such as the "public interest," remain alien in societies in which primary loyalties are directed to members of one's family and to personal friends. A recent observer of the Egyptian civil service concluded that people in the Near East are not yet accustomed to looking upon others impersonally in any situation. They tend to regard others as individuals, with families, friends, and communities behind them; this trend is carried into realms where recent changes have established different formal requirements.

These general cultural values and social settings undoubtedy influence the nature of administrative structure and behavior in the new countries, and must be taken into account in their analysis. The cultural traits may explain many of the different patterns of bureaucratic behavior which have been mentioned above. However, in themselves, they cannot explain the basic common political problems of these bureaucracies, nor the great variety of administrative structures and behavior that can be found in these societies.

It seems that consideration of these general cultural traditions and social orientations is not enough. It is necessary also to analyze some basic social aspects of the processes of political development and modernization in these societies.

VI

What are these processes? Perhaps the common central facets of the problem are the crucial role, in the process of modernization, of the state or of political leaders, and the internal contradictions which have necessarily developed in their activities in this context.

The first important fact in this respect is that — although the new ruling elites have attempted to establish frameworks of modern polities, have developed new political goals, and have tried to find the instruments for their implementation — the extent of general participation in the political process has been relatively small. There have existed few groups and strata capable of engaging in the process of modernization

[4] Robert V. Presthus, "The Social Bases of Bureaucratic Organization," *Social Forces*, XXXVIII, No. 2 (December, 1959), 103-09.

on their own, and able to articulate their political interests in a modern, differentiated way.

Many ascriptive (communal, tribal, and caste) groups existed. Their chief political orientations were traditional and restricted either to passive supplication and petition or to the old kind of court politics.

On the other hand, there were many small, splintered interests, such as divers small business groups, that were not able to articulate and aggregate their political interests. In some countries, especially in Latin America and the Middle East, there were also major institutional interest groups (churches, army groups) which monopolized most of the political positions and impeded the growth of modern independent political forces.

In general, in all of these societies, there developed only few and weak functionally differentiated groups and general responsible public opinion capable of generating an independent and diversified political leadership and organization.

Thus, the articulation, aggregation, and regulation of political activities and interests became mostly concentrated in the hands of the ruling elite — the leaders of the old nationalist (and military) movements. At best, they became concentrated in one major party which was able to establish a unified framework of modern polity. In other cases, they were splintered among different small parties and did not crystallize into more stable patterns.

With the attainment of independence, or with growing modernization, the elites faced several tasks in the area of political organization. They could not confine political participation to its former level; they had to extend it to the politically more passive or inarticulate groups from whom new types of allegiance, political involvement, and loyalties were being demanded. The new regimes could not maintain themselves entirely on the passive allegiance that had predominated in colonial times, since they themselves had undermined this allegiance. Through their emphasis on governmental activities in many spheres of society, they penetrated more and more into various social layers. Somehow, they had to foster the development of new social and political motivations and participation. Schemes for community development, for new industrial and agrarian organizations, and for agrarian reforms whenever these were undertaken — all implied the necessity for new orientations, incentives and the development of many new motivational patterns.

By engaging in these, however, the new political rulers found themselves in a series of new dilemmas.

In most countries under discussion, a double contradiction developed in the activities of the ruling elites, and in their efforts to activate the various strata of the population toward participation in the common collective goals. First, there was the contradiction between the traditional forces and the development of relatively modern, "free-floating" resources and divers professional, economic, and cultural groups. Second, there was the contradiction between the tendencies of the more modern forces to coalesce in relatively independent and autonomous centers of power, and the aims of the ruling elites to control as many of these forces and centers of power as possible.

Simultaneously, the elites confronted another problem or contradiction. The new goals which they proclaimed often contained various implicit or explicit promises to the population, particularly in the economic field. Many social groups were ready to present this bill to the elite for payment, especially when their support was demanded. In this way, the government could, through the distribution of various goods and services — which it controlled — to its own supporters, maintain its position and attempt to control other social forces. However, the elite could thus arrive at an impasse, in which the implementation of the various societal goals, and its own ultimate claims to legitimation, would become seriously impeded by the necessity to spend many of its resources as emoluments for its supporters. The very need of the elite to control the traditional and, especially, the modern forces, and its ambivalent attitude toward many of them, can aggravate this problem.

VII

One of the main consequences of these contradictions — an outcome in which the political elites and the bureaucracies both co-operated — was the intensification of the inherent tendency of the political elite and bureaucracy to enhance their monopolization of power and prestige. This tendency is closely related to the social transformations attendant on the attainment of independence. It has manifested itself in: (a) attempts to create a strong hierarchy of status in terms of political power; (b) efforts to subject most processes of social mobility to the control of the political elites; and (c) efforts to subject a large number of economic, professional, and cultural activities to political control.

The political elite and the bureaucracy were inclined to belittle the importance and efficiency of purely economic activities and the claims of economic groups toward social autonomy. It tended to superimpose extraeconomic criteria on economic activities and on their bearers — not only by stipulating broad, general "social goals," but also by the daily regulation and direction of activity. Moreover, the political elites sometimes attempted to undermine the autonomous development of the middle and working classes, and of cultural and professional elites, and link their positions entirely to directives.

The efforts of the political elite and bureaucracy to direct and control all the main avenues of local mobility are closely associated to these developments. Through such efforts, they tend to maintain their hold on potential centers of power and to control their evolution. But these attempts are often self-contradictory; the close control exercised by the bureaucracy undermines efforts for economic development. More aspirants are created for new posts than there are posts available, and thus the bureaucracy itself is put in an insecure position.

This process took a somewhat different direction in the noncolonial countries. While the extent of political articulation and organization of wider groups and strata was relatively small and weak, the picture was different. In these countries, a much stronger competition between the older oligarchy and some of the new groups and parties usually emerged.

However, some modern political frameworks — even though born by a relatively restricted oligarchy — already existed. They were the main organs of political activity and regulation, and their very existence impeded both the "political" articulation of new social groups and, often, also any further political modernization. Hence the social and political predominance of these groups, which frequently also impeded the efficiency and rationalization of the structure of the bureaucracy.

VIII

These characteristics of the process of modernization were most influential in the development of bureaucracies in emerging countries. The most crucial facts are that this process was greatly fostered by the political elites; that political movements, and later the state, played such an important role in the breaking up of the framework of traditional society and in advancing growing social and economic differentiation; and that there were only a few other groups which participated autonomously in this process and were able to help in the implementation of new goals. These factors necessarily gave the bureaucracy a vital place in the political process and social structure of these societies: it had to become one of the major agents of change in all spheres of social life. But, just because it became such an agent of change, it had also to generate new types of interests and activities and to undertake many functions of political aggregation and articulation.

As a result, the bureaucracy in these countries was involved in dilemmas similar to those faced by the new rulers. Efficient implementation of goals and the establishment of viable frameworks of modern political institutions depended greatly on political stability and on the development of new political and administrative attitudes and activities. However, these same conditions could create pressure for certain kinds of activities on behalf of the bureaucracy that could easily undermine its efficiency and its ability to implement goals and services while withstanding the demands of many potential political supporters.

In this context, we also must analyze the relation between certain economic processes in these countries and their developing bureaucracies. The most important aspect is that, in these countries, the bureaucracies constitute one of the principal channels of economic and social mobility and advancement. Several factors account for this. One is the central place of the government in the sphere of economic development. Another is the great prestige of white-collar work that is widespread in most of these countries — a prestige which was only enhanced by political developments and the growing social importance of the political elites. The third factor comprises the growing aspirations to mobility that emerged under the impacts both of political and economic modernization and of the need of the rulers to satisfy the aspirations to mobility and to minimize their political explosiveness. The fourth factor is the structure of the educational system, with its strong emphasis on literary, as distinct from technical, education, and its influence on the structure of the labor force and occupational choice. For all these reasons, great pressure developed on governmental and civil service jobs. These pressures, obviously, potentially could have grave repercussions on the economic and the political developments. From the economic point of view, the demands and aspirations could easily create a lack of adequate manpower for technical jobs and widespread white-collar unemployment and underemployment. Politically, these tendencies created many potential pressures and tensions. Moreover, they could weaken the efficiency of the bureaucracy, by making it into a sort of system of sinecures in which there was little relation between job security and performance, and in which extraneous (political and personal) criteria could become the main determinants of recruitment and advancement. In these combined economic and political pressures, one can find the roots of the widespread tendency to corruption that has emerged in these bureaucracies.

IX

All these forces — the cultural orientations prevalent in these societies, the political and economic processes and pressures — necessarily have their repercussion on the structure of the bureaucracies and on their ability to implement major political and social goals and to provide continuous services to the population.

Among the most important of such structural problems, the following have often been noted:[5] (a) the low density of administrative structure, i.e., the relatively small ratio of officials to population and tasks;

[5] See, for instance, J. L. Quermonne, "La sous-administration et les politiques d'équipment administratif," *Revue française de science politique*, IX, No. 3 (September, 1959), 629-67.

(b) the lack of fully qualified and adequate personnel; (c) the small extent of diversification of functions, and consequent overlapping between different echelons and departments; and (d) overcentralization, poor co-ordination, and lack of autonomy and initiative of the linestaff.

Riggs has aptly summarized some of these problems, especially as they apply to older independent countries:

> Obstacles to identification of personal with program goals are especially conspicuous in the way the work load and responsibilities of different officials are allocated, that is, in "organization and management." These often make it impossible for anyone to carry out a constructive project without waiting for the concurrence of many others, whereby many people have the power to block action. One result is often to elevate the level of settlement of even minor disputes to ministerial, cabinet, and chief executive levels. Top administrators become embroiled in continual interagency conflicts while subordinates piddle away their energies waiting for requisite approvals. Moreover, because many persons far from the scene of action become involved in decision making, questions are often referred to persons with only remote interest in them, it becomes difficult to assign responsibility for action, and final decisions hinge on the outcome of power struggles among individuals only indirectly concerned.[6]

In some countries, elaborate ministerial secretariats, staffed by generalists, who rotate frequently between headquarters and district assignments, have been placed in the line of communication and command between ministers and executive or administrative departments and divisions. Invariably, great delay ensues while secretariat officials review more and more of the work nominally assigned to and originating in the departments. We may quote the words of a distinguished former civil servant in India about the result:

> The head of the department is deprived of all initiative and instead of being allowed to attend to and make progress with his own work, has to spend a great deal of time submitting unnecessary reports, explaining the position in individual matters to the Ministry and getting its orders on points which lie well within his own sphere of authority.
>
> Because of overcentralization and lack of delegation, those close to the goals of action cannot easily cooperate with their colleagues in other agencies whose work directly affects the success of their own efforts. Characteristically, to overcome this stagnation, new agencies are often set up in the hope that, outside the bog of established structures, action may be possible. But the new agencies simply add to the

[6] F. W. Riggs, "Public Administration — A Neglected Factor in Economic Development," *Annals of the American Academy of Political and Social Science* (May, 1956), pp. 70-81.

228 S. N. Eisenstadt

intra-bureaucratic conflict and competition, increasing the burden on the top of the hierarchy to impose coordination.[7]

The relative importance of these problems naturally varies in different countries. In the post-colonial countries, the most critical problems seem to be lack of adequate staff, overcentralization, and too little diversification. In the independent countries, the most vital problems are the excessive control, rigidity, and lack of initiative of the officials, and their regarding their offices as sinecures. However, there is much overlapping between these different structural aspects. And beyond all these, there always hovers the double specter of corruption and growing inefficiency of the bureaucracy.

X

The patterns of activities, organization, and political and social orientations of the bureaucracies in developing areas differ greatly from those of Western countries. However, it does not suffice to stress the differences between the new emerging bureaucracies and the older bureaucracies of Western countries or to point out the former's structural deficiencies and problems. Except for their common characteristics, outlined above, the exact ways in which they will develop differ greatly between countries. These differences may be of crucial importance in their implications for political and economic development.

In evaluating the effect of these bureaucracies on political modernization and economic development, we must again stress the fact that they have become major agents of social and political change, and examine what influence they may have on such change. Generally, there are two major, and sometimes overlapping, possible influences the bureaucracies can have on processes of change and development in the developing areas.

The first major possibility is the development of relatively efficient frameworks of modern administration; the upholding of legal norms and rules and the maintenance of basic services, even if this is effected through the bureaucracy's extension of its scope of activities; and the assumption, by its officials, of many social, political, and leadership roles. These bureaucracies may generate through the establishment of new political frameworks and through the development of such activities, many new social organizations and activities on both the central and local level, and may contribute both to the establishment of viable political frameworks and to conditions conducive to economic development.

The evolution of this type of orientation and activities of the bu-

[7] A. D. Gorwala, *Report on Public Administration* (New Delhi, 1951), p. 39. See also Paul H. Appleby, *Public Administration in India; Report of a Survey* (New Delhi, 1953), Sec. II, especially p. 21.

reaucracy depends greatly on two conditions. (1) Some basic, unitary political framework, a relatively unified political elite, and a degree of political consensus must exist. (2) Purely institutional interest groups (e.g., army, churches, etc.) must be relatively weak in comparison to ecological strata and certain functional groups.

The main issues facing the elites are the extent to which they can overcome the pressures for a higher level of consumption, and the degree to which they can advance wider educational schemes capable of providing adequate training for personnel in technical fields and thus alleviating the pressures on the white-collar jobs.

The structure and patterns of activities of the bureaucracies which develop under these conditions differ greatly from those of "classical" bureaucratic organizations. However, the very fact that the scope of their activities is relatively wide, combined with a firm political orientation and a high measure of political consensus, may facilitate the maintenance of relative stability and continuity, induce and generate new types of economic entrepreneurship, and generate professional activities and political leadership on the local and even on the central level. Furthermore, the bureaucracy also may gradually generate diversification of functionally specific groups and independent public opinion and leadership. It is interesting to note that, in these cases, there usually exist also rather strong party bureaucracies. While, initially, there may be conflicts between them and the civil service, the very fact that there is some initial diversification of functions within a relatively unified political framework may help generate change and economic development.

The second important kind of possible bureaucratic development is characterized by the bureaucracy's contributions mainly to what Riggs has called "negative development."[8] Here the bureaucracy tends to monopolize some central political functions; in addition, it tends to become a major interest group, usually closely allied with some institutional interest groups and with various oligarchical strata. Because of this alliance, the bureaucracy is inclined to become a center of attraction for various "white-collar" aspirants, and thus overstaffed. On the other hand, it necessarily becomes a "narrow" interest group, which tends to stifle any development of independent political action. It may easily obstruct schemes of economic development that threaten its level of relative income and other vested interests. In such cases, the bureaucracy usually becomes an active participant in the narrow political and economic struggle. Corruption usually becomes rampant; the stability of the basic administrative services, universalistic legal framework, and economic activities may be broken down. Such processes are facilitated when there is no unified political framework and consensus; when the

[8] F. W. Riggs, "Economic Development and Local Administration," *The Philippine Journal of Public Administration*, III, No. 1 (January, 1959), 86-146.

rift between traditional and modern elites, or the lack of consensus within the modern elite, is very great; and when institutional interest groups, like a church, army, and other narrow oligarchical groups, predominate in the social and economic structure.

As indicated above, both possible developments within the bureaucracies are inherent in the basic conditions of economic and political evolution in the developing areas. In any concrete case, these tendencies can overlap, but the bureaucracy itself often influences, to some degree at least, the concrete outcome of these developments, through its own adherence to common political goals or through educational policies.

15   MORRIS JANOWITZ

The Military in the Old and the New Nations

In the comparative study of new nations, two different questions can be asked about the role of the military in political change. First, what characteristics of the military establishment of a new nation facilitate its involvement in domestic politics? Second, what are the capacities of the military to supply effective political leadership for a new nation striving for rapid economic development and social modernization?

These two questions seem to generate very similar answers. Those organizational and professional qualities which make it possible for the military of a new nation to accumulate political power, and even to take over political power, are the same as those which limit its ability to rule effectively. Thus, once political power has been achieved, the military must develop mass political organizations of a civilian type, or it must work out viable relations with civilian political groups. In short, while it is relatively easy for the military to seize power in a new nation, it is much more difficult for it to govern.

Social science literature is rich in its analysis of the social, economic,

Reprinted by permission of the author and publisher from Morris Janowitz, *The Military in the Political Development of New Nations* (Chicago: Phoenix Books, 1964), pp. 1-29.

and political conditions of new nations which weaken parliamentary institutions and civilian political organizations and thereby increase the possibility of military intervention. It is the purpose of this essay, however, to explore civil-military relations from the point of view of the internal social organization of the military, which conditions its political capacities. This includes the dimensions of organizational format, skill structure and career lines, social recruitment and education, and professional and political ideology, as well as cohesion and cleavage.

The focus of this study can be stated alternatively in comparative terms. First, there is the comparative analysis of the military profession in old nations and new ones. Why are military officers of new nations, as compared with those in Western industrialized societies, more influential in domestic politics? Clearly, the social structure of their countries predisposes them to political activism. But, to what extent can this greater involvement be accounted for by particular sociological characteristics of the military profession? Second, comparative analysis deals with variations in the extent and form of military involvement in domestic politics from country to country. The capacity to act in politics is hardly a constant. What characteristics of the military profession help account for differences in civil-military relations in different new nations?

CIVIL-MILITARY RELATIONS: OLD NATIONS AND NEW

Experience in civil-military relations in different Western nation-states has hardly been uniform. But where mass democracy has emerged, the intervention of the military establishment in domestic politics has become limited, and its influence is felt mainly in the conduct of foreign affairs and defense policies. Similarly, in one-party Communist regimes, the military has been neutralized in its internal political power, although, as in mass democratic states, it remains an important agent in influencing foreign affairs.

As a basis for comparing industrialized states with new nations, it is possible to identify three models of political-military or civilian-military relations — aristocratic, democratic, and totalitarian.[1] It seems appropriate to speak of the aristocratic model of political-military elite structure as a composite pattern of Western European powers before industrialism began to have its full impact.[2] There is a comprehensive hierarchy in the aristocratic model which delineates both the source of authority and the prestige of any member of the military elite. The low specialization of the military profession makes it possible for the political elite to supply the bulk of necessary leadership for the military establishment.

[1] For a fuller exposition of these models, see Appendix [of Janowitz, *The Military in the Political Development of New Nations.*]
[2] Alfred Vagts, *The History of Militarism* (New York: W. W. Norton, 1937).

The classic pattern is exemplified by the aristocratic family which supplies one son to politics and one to the military. Birth, family connections, and common ideology insure that the military will embody the ideology of dominant groups in society. Political control is civilian control, because there is an identity of interest between aristocratic and military groups. The military is responsible because it is a part of the government and, as such, develops a conservative political outlook.

In contrast to the aristocratic model stands the democratic one. Under the democratic model, civilian and military elites are sharply differentiated. Civilian-political elites exercise control over the military through a formal set of rules, which specify the functions of the military and the conditions under which the military may exercise its power. In particular, these rules exclude the military from involvement in domestic partisan politics. Military personnel are professionals in the employ of the state, and their careers are distinct from civilian careers. In fact, being a professional soldier is incompatible with holding any other significant social or political role. Military leaders obey the government because they accept the basic national and political goals of a democracy, and because it is their duty and their profession to fight. Professional ethics, as well as democratic parliamentary institutions, guarantee civilian political supremacy.

The democratic model is not a historical reality but an objective of political policy. Elements of the democratic model have been achieved only in certain Western industrialized countries, since it requires viable parliamentary institutions and broad social consensus about the ends of government. The democratic model assumes that military leaders can be strongly motivated by professional ethics, and this objective is most difficult to achieve during periods of sustained conflict.

In the absence of a development toward the democratic model, historical change tends to replace the aristocratic model with a totalitarian one.[3] The totalitarian model, as it developed in Germany, in Russia, and, to a lesser degree, in Italy, rests on political control of the military by a centralized and authoritarian one-party political system. In part, the military supports the political elite because the totalitarian party places extensive resources at its control. The revolutionary elite, bedecked with paramilitary symbols, is dedicated to revitalizing the military. The expanded military profession is given an area of professional competence within the strategic goals of the totalitarian party. Political control of the totalitarian variety is enforced by the secret police, by infiltration of party members into the military hierarchy, by the party's arming its own military units, and by control of the system of officer selection. While he helps fashion defense policy, the organizational inde-

[3] Hans Speier, *War and the Social Order: Papers in Political Sociology* (New York: G. W. Stewart, 1952.)

pendence of the professional officer is weakened and he is eliminated from domestic politics.

But neither the democratic nor the totalitarian model adequately serves to describe civil-military relations in the "typical" new nation. These models are not applicable because the military has wider involvement in domestic economic, social, and political change.[4] Fundamentally, this derives from the weakness of civilian political institutions, as described by Edward Shils[5] and others. It is the result of the sheer quantity of resources that the military establishment, in comparison with other bureaucratic institutions and professional groups, has been able to accumulate.

In the second half of the twentieth century, the processes of government are so complex, even in the new nations, and the pressures of mass political movements are so intense, that personal military dictators are outmoded, or at best transitional devices. Therefore, models for describing the political activities of the military in new nations during the last fifteen years range from performing the minimal governmental functions essential for any nation-state to that of constituting themselves as the exclusive governing political group. For the purposes of analyzing the military in the political development of new nations, five types of civil-military relations can be identified: (1) authoritarian-personal control, (2) authoritarian-mass party, (3) democratic competitive and semi-competitive systems, (4) civil-military coalition, and (5) military oligarchy. (See Table 1, where the new nations of this study are classified into these categories as of January, 1963.)

Although the first three differ markedly in the form of internal political control, they have the common feature that the military's involvement in domestic politics is at the minimal level; it is therefore possible to describe its activities as limited to the mark of sovereignity.

[4] Harold Lasswell's concept of the "garrison state" is more applicable (see "The Garrison State and Specialist on Violence," *American Journal of Sociology*, XLVI [January, 1941], 455-68). The garrison state is a model for describing the weakening of civil supremacy, especially in democratic states, because of the "permanent" threat of mass warfare. While the end result of the garrison state approximates aspects of the totalitarian state, the garrison state has a different natural history. It is, however, not the direct domination of politics by the military. Since modern industrial nations cannot be ruled merely by the political domination of a single small leadership bloc, the garrison state is not a throwback to a military dictatorship. It is the end result of the growth of power by the military elite under conditions of prolonged international tension. The garrison state is a new pattern of coalition in which military groups, directly and indirectly, wield unprecedented amounts of political and administrative power. The military retains its organizational independence provided that it makes appropriate alliances with civil political factions. Since the garrison state requires a highly developed industrial base, the concept is not directly applicable to the new nations.

[5] Edward A. Shils, *Political Development in the New States* (The Hague: Mouton & Co., 1962).

As such, the officer corps is not involved in domestic partisan politics but functions as an institution symbolizing the independent and legitimate sovereignity of the new nation, both at home and abroad. The mark of sovereignty includes the military's contribution to internal law and order and to the policing of the nation's borders. Since new nations are immediately involved in international relations, the military is required as a token force for United Nations operations and regional security affairs.

There are alternative political formats by which the military may be limited to the role of a mark of sovereignty. The first is an authoritarian regime, which may be based on personal and traditional power, as in Ethiopia, or it may be a newly developed personal autocracy, as in South Vietnam.* This is the (1) *authoritarian-personal* type of civil-military control and is likely to be found in nations just beginning the process of modernization (see Table 1). In a few countries, the military is no more than a mark of sovereignty and is excluded from domestic politics by the power of civilian authoritarian political power; for example, in Ghana, Mali, and Guinea. Such authoritarian power may be rooted in a one-party state, under strong personal leadership, without parliamentary institutions. This type of civil-military relations can be labeled (2) *authoritarian-mass party* control. In these states, both the civilian police and paramilitary institutions operate as counterweights to the military, which is small and not yet fully expanded. Elsewhere the military has a limited role because it is organizationally undeveloped, or, as in the case of some ex-French West African countries, the Africanization of the officer corps is not yet completed. On the other hand, in a few nations, e.g., in Nigeria, Malaya, and India, the military is limited to these functions because of the strength of competitive democratic institutions, and the pattern of civil-military relations which is based on civilian control can be called (3) *democratic-competitive*. In the democratic-competitive system, which must be defined to include semicompetitive systems, as in Tunisia and Morocco, civilian supremacy operates to limit the role of the military in part because colonial traditions implanted a strong sense of self-restraint on the military. In these countries, there are competing civilian institutions and power groups, as well as a mass political party which dominates domestic politics but permits a measure of political competition.

When the military expands its political activity and becomes a political bloc, the civilian leadership remains in power only because of the military's passive assent or active assistance. The extent of political competi-

* [This was written during the regime of Ngo Dinh Diem, i.e., before the military coup of November, 1964. Several other countries mentioned below (Nigeria, for example) would also have to be reclassified, usually in the direction of greater military participation. — Ed.]

tion decreases; and it is appropriate to describe such a pattern as a (4) *civil-military coalition*, because of the crucial role of the armed forces. Here the military serves as an active political bloc in its support of civilian parties and other bureaucratic power groups. The civilian group is in power because of the assistance of the military. Indonesia provides an example of such political intervention. The military may act as an informal, or even explicit, umpire between competing political parties and political groups as it does in, for example, Turkey. The military may, at this level, be forced to establish a caretaker government, with a view to returning power to civilian political groups. Such were the intention and practice of the first Burmese military government and the intention of Pakistani military leaders. These alliances and caretaker governments are unstable; they frequently lead to a third and wider level of involvement, where the military sets itself up as the political ruling group as in, for example, Thailand, Egypt, and Sudan. The result is a (5) *military oligarchy*, because for a limited time, at least, the poltical initiative passes to the military. When an actual takeover occurs and the military becomes the ruling group, civilian political activity is transformed, constricted, and repressed.

But it is our basic assumption that the military operates at each level of political intervention, including the takeover of political power, as incomplete agents of political change. Thus, an additional type of civil-military relations, in part hypothetical, and to some degree actually emerging, must be postulated. After "takeover," the military regime can begin to recognize the task of supplying national political leaders. At this level, the military recognizes the needs for a mass political base. It seeks to develop a broader political apparatus, either with its own personnel, under their direct supervision, or through a system of alliances with civilians. Trends in this direction already can be noted in Egypt, South Korea, and, to a lesser extent, in Pakistan.

There is no evolutionary process by which a new nation passes from one level of intervention to another, although a pattern of broadening commitments is discernible. It may well be possible for the military in some nations to limit its intervention to that of an active political bloc, along with other groups, and avoid becoming the political ruling group. But the task remains of clarifying the contributions of professional military to these different patterns of domestic politics, since these types give more concrete meaning to the forms of militarism in the new nations.

HISTORICAL AND ECONOMIC DIMENSIONS

The initial step in the comparative analysis of the military in the political development of new nations is to examine, even briefly, the historical and economic factors which fashioned these military establishments. That the objects of our analysis are highly diverse is an obvious fact, but one which complicates our task. The population range of new nations in 1960 varied from India with over 400 million to Gabon with less than 0.5 million. *The United Nations Demographic Yearbook* for 1960 lists, for Africa and Asia, sixty-four political reporting units with a population of over 1 million inhabitants, if China, Taiwan, Japan, and the Union of South Africa are excluded as special cases. From a population basis, is there a minimum level required to support, even with outside assistance, a military establishment which has internal political consequences? The level of 1 million population seems to include all the smaller nations with politically relevant military establishments, even though some of these establishments may be dependent on foreign assistance.

All these sixty-four political reporting units have armed forces, although some as yet have not developed self-contained military establishments with indigenous officers. Ten of them were at that time still colonial dependencies, two are Soviet bloc allies (North Korea and North Vietnam), and one is semi-internationalized (Laos), with the result that the analysis is limited to fifty-one nations for comparative purposes.[6] (See Table 1 for a list of these countries and some basic characteristics of their armed forces.)

For comparative purposes, historical background involves two crucial aspects: differences in cultural-geographical area and variation in the natural history of the armed forces. The armed forces of new nations can be grouped into three vast cultural-geographical areas which reflect pervasive political and underlying social structural differences: South and Southeast Asia, the Middle East and North Africa, and Sub-Sahara Africa. Obviously, differences within each of these areas are marked, but in each there is a historical unity based on the aftermath of colonial rule.

In South and Southeast Asia, indigenous military institutions, with the exception of those of Thailand, were eliminated, transformed, or replaced by the metropolitan powers. Despite different forms of political rule and economic organization, South and Southeast Asia were the areas of maximum impact of colonial rule. Colonial rule rested on military force, but colonialism is not a form of direct military government. Japanese occupation in many areas did introduce military intervention in domestic politics for a brief but sometimes decisive period. However, the armies that were left behind by the colonial regimes or that came into being during World War II had to be articulated with civilian political institu-

---

[6] South Korea and South Vietnam were included, since in these countries the military is active in the domestic political life of the nation despite the presence of United Nations and American military formations. Although the armed forces of the Congo (Leopoldville) disintegrated after liberation, that country is included because United Nations assistance has reconstructed it to the point where it is of some political importance. The African nations of the so-called French community are also included, despite their defense treaty with France.

tions. The nations of this area emerged from a historical tradition of colonial rule and not of military rule. Their political heritage — except for the impact of the Japanese occupation — was not that of the military in politics.

In the Middle East and North Africa, the indigenous Ottoman tradition and the political heritage of the Ottoman Empire were of political involvement and political rule by military officers. Moreover, the impact of colonial rule — as compared with Southeast Asia — was less extensive and less direct. Although there was warfare and violence, military institutions were not radically transformed but only gradually adapted and accommodated to the influence of modernization. Even after liberation, the modernization and professionalization of the military in many countries of this area had to confront the residues of older officer elements. For the military after national liberation, political involvement was a tradition and not an innovation or exception.

In Sub-Sahara Africa, there is a still different historical tradition. The colonial governments easily destroyed indigenous miltary institutions, and, by contrast with other colonial areas, the area was relatively demilitarized. The metropolitan governments ruled with tiny colonial armed forces and, except for short periods of warfare during World War I and World War II, did not mobilize military manpower of consequence. Moreover, independence was granted without resort to violence or military force. The new nations of the Sub-Sahara region face the problem of creating new institutions and new traditions because of the very absence of extensive military institutions at the time of independence.

When new nations are classified into the three cultural-geographical areas, marked differences emerge in the contemporary political role of the military that can be linked to these historical trends (see Table 1). The most extensive political involvement is in the Middle East and North Africa, where, of the twelve countries with modern armies of a professional type, the military constitutes the political ruling group or military oligarchy in four. The military is actively involved in civil-military coalitions in six, and in only two is the military limited to a non-partisan (mark of sovereignty) role. For the Asian countries, four armies have politically expanded roles, while the other eight have limited roles. These latter, with the exception of India and the Philippines, are in the smaller countries without competitive political systems. In Africa, most of the new nations have had independence for such a short time that the non-partisan role of the military reflects its limited and primitive resources and the newness of the country.

Another approach to classifying new nations is according to the natural history or origin of the military, which again reflects differing colonial practices and the political conditions of liberation. It is possible to speak

TABLE 1. BASIC DATA ON ARMED FORCES OF NEW NATIONS

Country	Population (Millions)	Date of Independence	Civil-Military Model	Political Role	Origin of Armed Forces
SOUTH AND SOUTHEAST ASIA					
India	402,600	1947	Democratic-competitive	Mark of sovereignty	Ex-colonial
Indonesia	90,000	1949	Civil-military coalition	Political bloc	National liberation*
Philippines	24,718	1946	Democratic-competitive	Mark of sovereignty	Ex-colonial
South Korea	23,848	1945	Military oligarchy	Political ruling group	Post-liberation*
Thailand	21,881	Non-col.	Military oligarchy	Political ruling group	Non-colonial
Burma	20,457	1948	Military oligarchy	Political ruling group	National liberation
South Vietnam	13,790	1954	Authoritarian-personal control	Mark of sovereignty	Ex-colonial†
Afghanistan	13,150	Non-col.	Authoritarian-personal control	Mark of sovereignty	Non-colonial
Ceylon	9,612	1948	Democratic competitive	Mark of sovereignty	Ex-colonial
Nepal	9,044	1951	Authoritarian-personal control	Mark of sovereignty	Ex-colonial
Malaya	6,698	1957	Democratic-competitive	Mark of sovereignty	Ex-colonial
Cambodia	4,845	1953	Authoritarian-personal control	Mark of sovereignty	Ex-colonial
MIDDLE EAST AND NORTH AFRICA					
Pakistan	86,823	1947	Military oligarchy	Political ruling group	Ex-colonial
Turkey	26,881	Non-col.	Civil-military coalition	Political bloc	Non-colonial
Egypt	25,365	1952	Military oligarchy	Political ruling group	Ex-colonial
Iran	20,457	1945	Civil-military coalition	Political bloc	Non-colonial
Morocco	10,550	1956	Democratic-competitive‡	Mark of sovereignty	Ex-colonial§
Algeria	10,930	1962	Civil-military coalition	Political bloc	National liberation
Iraq	6,952	1932	Military oligarchy	Political ruling group	Ex-colonial
Saudi Arabia	6,000 est.	Non-col.	Authoritarian-personal control	Mark of sovereignty	Non-colonial
Yemen	4,500 est.	Non-col.	Military oligarchy	Political ruling group	Non-colonial
Syria	4,539	1946	Civil-military coalition	Political ruling group	Ex-colonial
Tunisia	3,935	1956	Democratic-competitive‡	Mark of sovereignty	Ex-colonial
Israel	2,061	1948	Democratic-competitive	Mark of sovereignty	National liberation
Jordan	1,636	1946	Civil-military coalition	Political bloc	Ex-colonial
Lebanon	1,550	1941	Democratic-competitive	Political bloc	Ex-colonial

SUB-SAHARA AFRICA

Nigeria	35,400	1960	Democratic-competitive	Mark of sovereignty	Post-liberation
Ethiopia	21,000	Non-col.	Authoritarian-personal control	Mark of sovereignty	Non-colonial
Congo (Leopoldville)	13,652	1960	Civil-military coalition	Political bloc	Post-liberation
Sudan	10,262	1956	Military oligarchy	Political ruling group	Ex-colonial
Tanganyika	9,238	1962	Democratic-competitive‡	Mark of sovereignty	Post-liberation
Ghana	6,690	1957	Authoritarian-mass party	Mark of sovereignty	Ex-colonial
Madagascar	5,239	1960	Not classified	Mark of sovereignty	Post-liberation
Mali	4,300	1960	Authoritarian-mass party	Mark of sovereignty	Post-liberation
Upper Volta	3,537	1960	#	Mark of sovereignty	Post-liberation
Cameroun	3,225	1960	#	Mark of sovereignty	Post-liberation
Ivory Coast	3,103	1960	#	Mark of sovereignty	Post-liberation
Guinea	2,727	1958	Authoritarian-mass party	Mark of sovereignty	Post-liberation
Chad	2,730	1960	#	Mark of sovereignty	Post-liberation
Ruanda	2,634	1962	Not classified	Mark of sovereignty	Post-liberation
Niger	2,550	1960	#	Mark of sovereignty	Post-liberation
Senegal	2,550	1960	#	Mark of sovereignty	Post-liberation
Sierra Leone	2,400	1961	Democratic-competitive‡	Mark of sovereignty	Ex-colonial
Burundi	2,213	1962	Not classified	Mark of sovereignty	Post-liberation
Dahomey	2,000	1960	#	Mark of sovereignty	Post-liberation
Somali	1,990	1960	Authoritarian personal control	Mark of sovereignty	Post-liberation
Togo	1,642	1960	**	Mark of sovereignty**	Post-liberation
Cameroons	1,621	1960	Not classified	Mark of sovereignty	Post-liberation
Liberia	1,500	Non-col.	Authoritarian-personal control	Mark of sovereignty	Non-colonial
Central African Republic	1,185	1960	#	Mark of sovereignty	Post-liberation
Libya	1,172	1951	Authoritarian-personal control	Mark of sovereignty	Post-liberation

* A significant ex-colonial element from the Japanese army is included.
† Ex-colonial cadres from the French period were joined with post-liberation forces.
‡ Civilian control is based on semicompetitive political institutions.
§ An important national liberation component, which served as a guerrila force, is included.
# Not classified as a civil-military model, since the armed forces are not integral groups because of defense treaty with France.
** Military revolt in 1963 resulted in the army assuming the role of political bloc.
Not classified cases imply either absence of data or indeterminacy of situation because of recent independence.

of four different types. In the few that never experienced colonial rule, or even indirect rule, the armies were the direct outgrowth of self-managed change of a traditional institution. There are three such military establishments, one in each of the cultural-geographical areas, that can be called *non-colonial* military forces in order to emphasize their continuity with the past: those of Thailand, Turkey, and Ethiopia. Liberia's is a variant of this type. Afghanistan's is also close to this type, because the impact of indirect rule was so limited. Saudi Arabia and Yemen have a military which should be called traditional, because of the personal and non-professional character of military services in these countries.

But most armies in these new nations can be classified as either *ex-colonial* armed forces, armed forces established during the struggle for *national liberation*, or *post-liberation* armies, since they were, in essence, established after independence. In number, the *ex-colonial* armies total sixteen, or about one-third; the armies of *national liberation* are only four, or less than 10 per cent; while the most numerous are the *post-liberation* formations, which add up to twenty-seven, or about half the nations.

These types exist not only because Great Britain had a different set of policies from France and the other colonial powers, but also because the British varied their policies in the three cultural-geographical areas. The ex-colonial army, with a cadre of modernly-trained indigenous officers who were available at the time of independence, is a product of British policy in South and Southeast Asia and to a limited extent also in North Africa. The British objective was to create institutions which ultimately would lead to some form of political autonomy within the imperial system. This meant that there was a very slow but gradual process of developing indigenous officer cadres, where political conditions permitted the British to pursue such policies. By contrast, the French were concerned with the political assimilation of the colonial nations into the French polity. As a result, where the French exercised direct rule, as in Indo-China, they were less interested in developing indigenous officers, although they made extensive use of native enlisted personnel. Since the Dutch, Belgians, Spaniards, and Portuguese assumed that colonial rule would continue indefinitely, they did not take steps to create such officer cadres.

But in parts of the Middle East, the British and French also exercised indirect rule, with the result that ex-colonial armies emerging from such indirect rule often have a different character. In these areas, the colonial powers did not build these armies up anew from the bottom but rather sought to refashion them. As a result, the professional standards were often relatively low and the officer corps was often enmeshed in the politics of traditional groups, as in, e.g., Syria and Iraq. These armies seem to emerge after independence with less internal and professional cohesion. The introduction of Western military values, in particular public service traditions and technocratic perspectives, proceeded much more slowly than in Southeast Asia, where the armies were being fashioned after the European models and where the break with the past was more clear-cut.

Variants of the ex-colonial army include those in Israel, South Korea, and South Vietnam. Since 1936, the British had given de facto recognition to the Jewish defense forces, and cadres of the Israeli army were trained and fought under British command during World War II. The South Korean army, after 1945, was built from Japanese-trained officers, while South Vietnamese forces established after 1955 included personnel who had served under the French.

By contrast, the result of colonial rule in Sub-Sahara Africa produced *post-liberation armies*. While the colonial powers mobilized African man-power during World War I and World War II, the style of colonial rule, even for the British, did not result in the building up of an indigenous professional cadre until just before independence. In these former British colonies, the transfer of power was accompanied by positive steps to develop rapidly all the institutions of a nation-state, including a complete and self-contained armed force. Central police forces were in existence, and there was sufficient political stability so that these very small military establishments could be expanded and the officer corps could be rapidly Africanized from the bottom up. The French pattern has been different in that even after independence there remain important residues of inte-gration with French military institutions. In the former French colonies — except for Mali and Guinea, which have severed political ties and turned to the Soviet bloc for assistance — political leaders have formed mutual military alliances with France, with the result that French officers play a crucial role and Africanization is proceeding very gradually.

The natural history of the origins of the military in new nations is not a very good indicator of political roles after independence. Clearly, mili-tary formations born in the struggle for national liberation have main-tained wide political involvements. Each of the four armies created as a force of national liberation has expanded its political role. While the post-liberation armies are too new to be effective or tested, the ex-colonial armies are divided, about equally, between those which have remained as instruments of national sovereignty and those which have intervened in domestic politics. In other words, ex-colonial armies, including those with high professional standards built by direct British rule and trained under British traditions, have demonstrated a capacity to assume domestic political responsibilities with rapidity (as in Pakistan and Sudan, for example). Ex-colonial origin hardly insures that the military will limit its role to that of the mark of sovereignty.

Yet, the influence of Western professional forms in inhibiting the political aspirations of the military of new nations is not to be dismissed. When the political behavior of the ex-colonial armies is examined in detail, including the conditions under which they become the ruling political group, there is at least an absence of designed militarism, especially in the case of those armies built up by direct British colonial rule. By "designed militarism" we mean the positive and premeditated intent to intervene in domestic politics and to follow expansionist foreign policies. Prussian militarism is the classic case of designed militarism. Instead these armies display reactive militarism; their political behavior is in part generated by the weakness of civilian institutions and the direct pressure of civilian groups which seek to co-opt and enlarge the role of the military establishment. Of the sixteen ex-colonial armies, elements of designed militarism with its expansive overtones are to be found only in two Middle Eastern countries, Egypt and Iraq, and in these nations, the consequences of the Israeli wars contribute to this positive militarism. In most of the other countries, the military has been drawn into domestic politics because of the weakness of civilian institutions and the positive pressures by civilian groups to expand its role to meet internal political crises.

Another aspect of historical development is the link between political roles of the military and length of time since independence. Leaving aside the Sub-Sahara countries, because of the recency of their independence, there is an apparent but not profoundly explanatory relation between the length of time that a new nation has been independent and the increased political role of the military. Of the countries in which the military has constituted the political ruling group, all but one have had independence for more than ten years. The same pattern holds for those countries in which the military has expanded to become an active coalition ingredient in the domestic political process. But, for those countries where the military is limited to the mark of sovereignty, there has been no consistent pattern since independence; some are relatively new and some relatively old by the standards of new nations. In short, the chance of political involvement increases year by year after independence, while the contraction of the military's political role remains a highly problematic issue (see Table 1).

An alternative basis for grouping new nations and their military establishments is in terms of demographic and economic measures. First, the range in population and size of the military establishment is indeed marked (see Table 2).[7] The Libyan army of 4,500, composed almost

[7] Statistics on the military forces of new nations are often not reliable. The materials presented in Table 2 are based on the evaluation and synthesis of a large variety of sources. They represent an effort to arrive at the best possible estimate of the situation as of January, 1963. Special reliance was placed on unpublished data supplied by social scientists who have had direct contact with particular

exclusively of infantry troops, is hardly the same type of administrative organization as the Indian defense forces of over 500,000, with the first-line jet planes and naval units. In the top ranks are the three "super-states" among the new nations — India, Indonesia, and Pakistan — which constitutes over 60 per cent of the population of this group of new nations. The second-order countries are the nine nations which can be considered large by new nations' standards, because they have populations of over twenty million. (In Southeast Asia, the Philippines, Thailand, Burma, and South Korea; in the Middle East and North Africa, Turkey, Egypt, and Iran; and in Sub-Sahara Africa, Nigeria and Ethiopia.) In effect, the typical new nation is a small country; of the remaining thirty-nine nations, twenty-one have populations under four million.

Second, while new nations with the most modern technology are likely to have the most efficient military establishments, there is no relationship between per capita gross national product and the size of the military establishment. The size of the military is less related to economic base than to total population. In other words, new nations must allocate their resources, and military expenditures are relatively fixed costs. A military establishment appears indispensable, and even the poorest countries are involved in developing a military. (The poorest and least economically developed can create a military establishment with limited modern technology, and they have the advantage of surplus manpower for this purpose.) Nations with larger populations seem to be required to have relatively larger armies — for both domestic and international reasons — and they are forced to allocate resources regardless of their economic position. Thus, investment in the military is hardly the result of disposable capital but is rather a fundamental cost which new nations are prepared to extract, whatever their economic ability to pay.

Third, the costs of a military establishment are, in proportion to per capita income, high for a new nation. In particular, military expenditures take a large portion of the public budget. If a nation spends more than 40 per cent of its public budget, it is classified as in the very high category, and in the high category if the figure is more than 25 per cent (see Table 2). Of course, the official public budget often markedly under-represents military expenditures, which can go unreported or be carried on civilian agency budgets. These expenditures also seem to be rising.

---

military establishments. In this connection, I wish to acknowledge the assistance of Professors William J. Foltz, Yale University; Arthur T. Porter, the University College of Sierra Leone; P. J. Vatikiotis, University of Indiana; David Wilson, University of California at Los Angeles; Drs. Eric du Dampierre, Centre d'Etudes Sociologiques, and Herbert F. Weiss, Columbia University. Relevant publications include *The Statesman's Year Book* and John J. Johnson, *The Role of the Military in Underdeveloped Countries* (Princeton, N.J.: Princeton University Press, 1962), as well as numerous journalistic sources.

TABLE 2. BASIC DATA ON ARMED FORCES OF NEW NATIONS

Country	Population (Millions)	Total* Armed Forces	Total Officers	Per Cent Army	Level of Expenditure (Per Cent)	Economic Development Index†
SOUTH AND SOUTHEAST ASIA						
India	402,600	550,000	—	88	High (25)	2
Indonesia	90,000	350,000	15,000	88	High (30)	2
Philippines	24,718	21,500	—	97	Moderate (16)	2
South Korea	23,848	650,000	—	—	Very high (40)	—
Thailand	21,881	134,000	—	80	Moderate (22)	2
Burma	20,457	149,000‡	5,000	94	High (31)	2
South Vietnam	13,790	205,000	—	96	Very high (45)	2
Afghanistan	13,150	90,000	—	100	Very high (40)	3
Ceylon	9,612	8,881	548	61	Moderate (18)	2
Nepal	9,044	45,000	—	100	High (30)	—
Malaya	6,698	8,000	—	98	High (25)	1
Cambodia	4,845	28,000	2,000	97	Moderate (22)	3
MIDDLE EAST AND NORTH AFRICA						
Pakistan	86,823	260,000	13,000	90	Very high (50)	3
Turkey	26,881	428,500	25,500	88	High (25)	2
Egypt	25,365	80,000	4,000	90	High (24)	1
Iran	20,457	150,000	11,000	96	High (38)	2
Morocco	10,550	35,000	—	94	Moderate (20)	2
Algeria	10,930	65,000	—	100	—	1
Iraq	6,952	60,000	—	—	High (37)	2
Saudi Arabia	6,000 est.	30,000	—	98	—	2
Yemen	4,500 est.	10,000	—	—	—	3 est.
Syria	4,539	45,000	2,000	—	Very high (45)	1
Tunisia	3,935	20,000	—	99	Low (10)	2
Israel	2,061	75,000	—	85	High (34)	1
Jordan	1,636	35,000	1,700	99	Very high (40)	2
Lebanon	1,550	10,800	300	92	Moderate (19)	1

SUB-SAHARA AFRICA

Nigeria	35,400	7,500	350	97	Low (8)	3
Ethiopia	21,000	30,000	—	97	High (27)	3
Congo (Leopoldville)	13,652	31,600	—	—	—	2
Sudan	10,262	12,000	—	—	—	3
Tanganyika	9,238	1,000	—	99	Low (12)	3
Ghana	6,690	6,500	—	95	Low (3)	3
Madagascar	5,234	9,000	—	—	Low (10)	2
Mali	4,300	3,000	—	—	—	—
Upper Volta	3,537	6,000	—	—	—	3
Cameroun	3,225	2,000	—	—	—	3
Ivory Coast	3,103	1,500	—	—	—	3
Guinea	2,727	2,000	—	—	Low (10)	3
Chad	2,730	1,500	—	—	—	3
Ruanda	2,634	1,000	50	—	—	3
Burundi	2,213	1,000	50	—	—	3
Senegal	2,550	7,000	—	—	—	3
Niger	2,550	2,000	—	—	—	3
Sierra Leone	2,400	1,300	50	—	—	3
Dahomey	2,000	—	—	—	—	3
Somali	1,990	6,000	—	—	—	3
Togo	1,642	200 §	—	—	—	3
Cameroons	1,621	—	—	—	—	3
Liberia	1,500	5,000	—	—	—	2
Central African Republic	1,185	4,500	—	99	—	3
Libya	1,172	5,000	—	—	—	2

* Includes regular army, navy, and air force personnel who are on active duty and does not include different types of auxiliary reserves, civilian defense forces, or special frontier guards and national police units, which are very large in some countries.

† James Coleman, *op. cit.* (n. 9 above), p. 543.

‡ Includes military police units.

§ Five hundred additional volunteers who served in the French army claim to be members of the armed forces.

The next step is to explore whether there is any relationship between economic development or its absence and the political role of the military in new nations. The results again are mainly negative. Students of comparative politics have offered the proposition that there is a positive association between economic development and democratic political competitiveness. By inference, the more economically developed a new nation is, the less likely it is that the military could hinder the competitive process in politics.

S. M. Lipset made use of selected indices of economic development to compare Western European and Latin American democracies as a basis for testing this hypothesis concerning the positive association between economic development and political competitiveness.[8] James Coleman employed the same type of analysis for the new nations of Asia, the Middle East, and Africa and concluded that "the major hypothesis that economic development and competitiveness are positively correlated is validated when countries are grouped into major differentiating categories of competitiveness and when mean scores of economic development are employed."[9] Coleman presses the analysis further for his group of nations when he adds that "the hypothesis is weakened by negative correlations found when the economic scores and relative competitiveness of individual countries are considered." In the end there are so many countries which are "deviant cases" that the analysis of the deviant cases instead of the original hypothesis about economic development and democratic competitiveness becomes the main and rewarding focus of his analysis.

In any case, this type of analysis appears to have limited relevance for understanding, on a comparative basis, the dynamic relationship between economic development and political forms, especially for the group of fifty-one new nations of this analysis. First, on purely statistical grounds, the support for this basic proposition in the new nations — Asia, North Africa, and Sub-Sahara Africa — is not impressive.[10] Second, in order

[8] S. M. Lipset, "Some Social Requisites of Democracy: Economic Development and Political Legitimacy," *American Political Science Review*, LIII (March, 1959), 69-105. For purposes of investigating this proposition, the degrees of competitiveness are limited to three: competitive, semi-competitive, and authoritarian. While the concept of competitiveness involves a political or electoral system, these three degrees of competitiveness can be assumed to be broad enough to encompass alternative institutional arrangements for developing political consensus without recourse to coercion.

[9] James S. Coleman, "The Political Systems of the Developing Areas," *The Politics of the Developing Areas*, ed. Gabriel A. Almond and James S. Coleman (Princeton, N.J.: Princeton University Press, 1960), pp. 532-44. It is possible to accept his request to leave aside questions of "accuracy, comparability, and significance of available economic statistics, as well as the validity of gross judgments regarding the competitive or authoritarian character of political systems."

[10] Coleman himself acknowledges this when he points out that the hypothesis is weakened when the economic scores and relative political competitiveness of

to avoid a mechanical test of the proposition, one would expect that the changes in political competitiveness, since the publication of the data for both Latin America and the new nations of Africa and Asia, would at least be congruent with the basic proposition. This means that those nations high on the economic development index should have moved toward more competitiveness. For Latin American, the trend has been toward less competitiveness, and this trend cannot be directly related to the level of economic development; in some cases, it is inversely related.[11] Of the new nations included in this analysis, since the publication of Coleman's data, seven have also become less competitive. Of these seven, one was at the high economic development category level, three were in the middle, and three were at the lower level of the scale. Such data are not evidence in support of the basic hypothesis.

The weakness of this type of statistical analysis rests in the artificial character of the basic categories of competitive, semi-competitive, and authoritarian groups. To group together as authoritarian the political systems of Afghanistan, where the exercise of power is based upon personal rule, and of Sudan, where the authoritarian regime is the result of a coup d'état by a professional military group, is to obscure comparative analysis.

Thus it becomes more relevant to relate economic development to the more refined five types of civil-military relations of this essay (democratic-competitive, authoritarian-personal, authoritarian-mass party, civil-military coalition, and military oligarchy). Using these categories, there is no basis for asserting that, with higher levels of economic development, there is a movement toward more competitive political systems. In fact, among those nations with the highest level of economic development, the absence of democratic competitive systems is more noteworthy than their presence, since competitive systems are concentrated in the middle level of economic development. But the analysis is not without meaning if the general hypothesis is abandoned and the underlying process examined. Authoritarian-personal regimes are heavily concentrated among the nations with low economic development, for these nations are just embarking on economic development. These nations have a pattern of

individual countries are considered. This is in part due to the fact that a limited number of cases are employed and even a minor redefinition of the universe markedly alters the statistical conclusions. Thus, if, instead of forty-six political units, the fifty-one units of this analysis are utilized, the over-all test of the hypothesis is barely confirmed. This procedure removed political units which still have colonial status and treated each of the eight territories of French West Africa and the four territories of French Equatorial Africa as independent units.

[11] See Dwaine Marvick, "Correlates of Democracy in Latin America," paper delivered at the 57th Annual Meeting of the American Sociological Association, Washington, D.C., September, 1962, for an analysis oriented toward the processes of social and economic change.

civil-military relations which reflects the past, for this is essentially the character of their authoritarian regimes. Moreover, it is true that there are no democratic-competitive regimes at the very bottom of the economic ladder. But the economic threshold is rather low for a democratic-competitive system. The basic conclusion is that, with higher economic levels, the outcome is as likely as not to be in the direction of military oligarchy, and perhaps somewhat more likely. Thus, factors such as natural history of origin, time since independence, or level of economic development supply, at best, a limited point of entrance for understanding differences in the political role of the military in the new nations.

SOCIAL STRUCTURE AND
MILITARY ORGANIZATION

By what intellectual strategy can comparative analysis of the military be pursued if there is such marked variation between cultural-geographic area, natural history of origin, and sheer size? There are two strategies for extending the analysis beyond the case-study level. One approach is to focus on paired comparisons of two countries which have important similarities and yet have emerged with marked differences in civil-military relations: India and Pakistan, Nigeria and Ghana, Morocco and Indonesia. Despite the complexities, the alternative approach pursued in this essay is to make some simplifying assumptions and to extend the range of analysis to a very wide, if not the full, range of new nations.

Basically, the analysis rests on two pervasive assumptions about social structure and military organization. One focuses on the common societal context of the military in new nations; namely, new nations have chosen without exception the goal of modernization. They have embarked in varying degree on programs of managed rapid modernization and social change designed to transform their traditional social structure. Thus, despite differences in national culture and history, from this point of view it is assumed that the military is operating in societies which are confronted with rather similar political, economic, and social requirements. Second, as compared with other institutions and bureaucracies, it is assumed that the military establishment has a variety of common organizational features. These common features condition and limit the capacity of the military profession to exercise political power. . . .

The following illustrative propositions about internal organization are offered to help explain the patterns of political behavior of the military in new nations as compared with industrialized nations, on the basis of available data. They are also designed to throw light on differences among the new nations and on the difficulties which confront the military when it becomes the ruling group and must seek to develop mass political support.

1. *Organizational Format.* The capacity of the military establishment in new nations to intervene in domestic politics derives from its distinctive military format, namely, its control of the instruments of violence; its ethos of public service and national identification; and its skill structure, which combines managerial ability with a heroic posture. (In part, this proposition is designed to help explain the greater initial political capacity of the military in comparison with other civilian groups.)

2. *Skill Structure and Career Lines.* While there has been a trend toward "civilianizing" the military profession, the officer corps in the new nations have important limitations in producing those leadership skills in bargaining and political communication that are required for sustained political leadership. These limitations include the absence of a tradition for dealing with clients and publics outside of the military. (While this proposition applies to both industrialized and new nations, it has particular relevance to new nations because of the relative absence of parliamentary and legal institutions for controlling the military.)

3. *Social Recruitment and Education.* In the new nations, the military establishment is recruited from the middle and lower-middle classes, drawn mainly from rural areas or hinterlands. In comparison with Western European professional armies, there is a marked absence of a history of feudal domination. As a result, the military profession does not have strong allegiance to an integrated upper class which it accepts as its political leader nor does it have a pervasive conservative outlook. Military education contributed to an innovating outlook toward modernization. (This proposition helps to account for the differences between "army and society" in the new nations and the industrialized ones.)

4. *Professional and Political Ideology.* While it is impossible to identify a military ideology in the new nations, common ideological themes are found which help to explain the professional officer's political behavior. These include a strong sense of nationalism, a puritanical outlook, acceptance of extensive government control of social and economic change, and a deep distrust of organized civilian politics. As a result of social background, education, and career experiences, military personnel of the new nations become interested in politics, but they maintain a strong distrust of organized politics and civilian political leaders. (As in the case of social recruitment and education, the analysis of political ideology presents a proposition which contrast the military of industrialized nations with those of the new nations.)

5. *Social Cohesion.* The ability of officers to intervene in domestic politics and produce stable leadership is related to internal social cohesion. The military establishments of new nations differ markedly in their internal social cohesion because of differences in training,

indoctrination, operational experience, and intergenerational cleavages. (This proposition relates to differences among the armed forces of the various new nations.)

6. *Political Intervention.* The "takeover" of power by the military in new nations has generally followed the collapse of efforts to create democratic-type institutions; the military has tended not to displace the single mass-party authoritarian political regimes. After "takeover," the military regime faces the task of supplying national political leadership and of developing mass support for its programs. While this phase is only emerging, the evidence seems to indicate that, if the military is to succeed in this political goal, it must develop a political apparatus outside of the military establishment but under its direct domination. (Comparative analysis in the case of this proposition is designed to help clarify the conditions under which the military comes to recognize the need of mass political support and is able to develop it.)

The Satisfaction of Members as Output

Our decision to regard the satisfaction of individuals who staff organizations as one of their outputs could easily be interpreted in an oversimplified fashion. The article by Williams, Whyte, and Green asks how the satisfaction of workers in one culture can be compared with those of another when their psychological needs may be quite different. Workers in one culture may not like close supervision and may look for close colleague relationships while those in another culture make quite different demands on their environment and are therefore satisfied by very different organizational situations.

Our concluding selection, by Inkeles, stresses that in certain specified ways, organizations are similar from one culture to another. Their output in terms of individual satisfaction and happiness, and in terms of more general world views, is similar at least in the sense that higher level personnel seem to be different from lower level personnel in equivalent ways. Even though Inkeles uses occupation rather than organizational position specifically, we may regard the two as roughly parallel. Inkeles does not deny that in addition to similarities, there may be differences due to culture as portrayed by Williams, Whyte, and Green. But by stressing similarities, we are brought face to face with the problem of the "organizational society" and the question of whether this post-industrial phenomenon will make the characteristics of different societies converge.

16   LAWRENCE K. WILLIAMS,
      WILLIAM F. WHYTE, AND
      CHARLES S. GREEN

*Do Cultural Differences
Affect Workers' Attitudes?*

Are the principles of human relations, inferred from research in the United States, generally applicable to supervisor-worker relations in other countries? We shall present findings from a field study in Peru to indicate some of the ways in which culture affects worker responses to supervisors.

Different cultures may be expected to have differential effects on personality formation. Will measures of certain dimensions of personality provide the analytical connecting link between reactions to authority and culture? Data will be presented indicating how such a connecting link may be established.

REVIEW OF PREVIOUS STUDIES

Over several decades the man-boss relationship has been the most popular topic of research in organizational behavior. Many studies have been concerned with the relationship between supervisory style of leadership, productivity, and worker attitudes toward the supervisor.

The survey Research Center at the University of Michigan first focused its analyses on the dichotomy between employee-centered and produc-

Reprinted by permission of the authors and publisher from *Industrial Relations,* 5 (May 1966), pp. 105-117.

tion-centered supervisors.[1] The Ohio State studies of worker perceptions of supervisors resulted in the discovery of two dimensions identified as "initiating structure" and "consideration."[2] Recently there has been a convergence between these two research groups, with Michigan now using the dimensions of human relations (closely allied with consideration) and technical and administrative activities (roughly equivalent to initiating structure).

Although these approaches have recognized that a good supervisor must provide his group with a certain minimum of initiating structure or technical and administrative activities, the primary research emphasis has been put upon the other dimension of human relations, consideration. At least it is assumed that the good supervisor should do his structuring in a participative, democratic fashion, consulting his subordinates, holding group meetings, responding to suggestions, and so on. Out of such approaches to the study of supervisory leadership have arisen a hero, the democratic participative supervisor, and also a villain, the authoritarian supervisor.

Perhaps it is because there is such a "good fit" between the notion of participative management and the democratic values of our culture that few have questioned the validity of the research conclusions supporting participative management or even explored the general applicability of the notion or its limiting conditions. Researchers are just beginning to look to such factors as personality and cultural differences for clues as to the applicability and limiting conditions for leadership theory.

In research within the United States, Vroom found that those who ranked low in need for independence and high on authoritarianism preferred a relatively authoritarian type of leadership.[3] Goldsen and others established a connection between the F scale (which rates individuals on a permissive-authoritarian spectrum) and a scale of faith in people (or interpersonal trust).[4] They found a syndrome of dogmatism, misanthropy, and xenophobia associated with authoritarianism and with low interpersonal trust. Those low in trust were also found to have a desire for stricter controls of labor unions, of religions, and of the right to run for office. Although these studies were not focused on any organization in which the informants held membership, the response pattern suggested that informants low in interpersonal trust might prefer authoritarian leadership within their own organizations.

The personality-leadership style relationship was explored in another

[1] See R. Likert, *New Patterns of Management* (New York: McGraw-Hill, 1961).

[2] See, for example, E. A. Fleishman, "The Description of Supervising Behavior," *Journal of Applied Psychology*, XXXVI (June, 1953), 153-158.

[3] V. H. Vroom, "Some Personality Determinants of the Effects of Participation," *Journal of Abnormal and Social Psychology*, LIX (1959), 322-327.

[4] R. Goldsen and others, *What College Students Think* (Princeton, N.J.: Van Nostrand, 1960).

culture by Foa.[5] In a study of officers and men in the Israeli Merchant Marine, he found authoritarian-type subordinates expressing a preference for authoritarian officers.

To our knowledge, the first study demonstrating certain broad culturally based influences on reactions to supervisory leadership was the replication of the famous Coch-French participation experiment in a Norwegian factory.[6] In Norway, French and his associates found that the participative approach did not elicit the same responses they had found in a U.S. experiment. Instead, they found that workers who considered participation in decision-making legitimate *did* react favorably, whereas those who had no such views of participation did not so react. These expectations, of course, grew out of their life experiences and can therefore be considered cultural products.

THE PERU-UNITED STATES COMPARISON

Our own cross-cultural study involved a comparison between two large electrical utility companies, one in the United States, the other in Peru. Parts of the questionnaire developed and used by Williams for research in the U.S. company were translated to make up a questionnaire which Whyte applied to 364 blue-collar workers and 202 white-collar workers in the Peruvian company.

A previous report on this study presents our findings in detail.[7] In the present article, we will briefly summarize only those aspects of the survey which reveal cross-cultural differences in worker attitude toward, and perception of, supervisors.

1. For both our white-collar and blue-collar Peruvian samples, we fund a small but significant positive correlation (approximately .20) between perceived closeness of supervision and general satisfaction with the supervisor. In our U.S. company, the correlations were at about the same level, but negative (white collar —.17; blue collar —.23). In other words, there was some tendency for these Peruvian workers to prefer the boss who supervised them closely, whereas the U.S. workers leaned toward the one who exercised more general supervision. Similiar preferences for general supervision have been reported in many U.S. studies.

2. "How much emphasis does your supervisor put on getting out a lot of work?" Here again we found a positive correlation between pro-

[5] V. G. Foa, "Relation of Workers Expectations to Satisfaction With Supervisor," *Personnel Psychology*, X (Summer, 1957), 161-168.

[6] J. R. P. French, J. Israel, and D. Ås, "An Experiment on Participation in a Norwegian Factory: Interpersonal Dimensions of Decision-Making," *Human Relations*, XIII (February, 1960), 3-19.

[7] W. F. Whyte and L. K. Williams, "Supervisory Leadership: An International Comparison," *Proceedings of the Thirteenth International Management Congress* (1963), pp. 481-488.

254 WILLIAMS, WHYTE, GREEN

duction emphasis and satisfaction with supervisor, and at a substantially higher level (.39 for white-collar workers and .41 for blue-collar workers). The question was not asked of blue-collar workers in our U.S. company, but for white-collar workers we found a smaller but significant negative correlation (−.20), which again is in accord with many U.S. studies. Apparently Peruvian workers find pressure for production more acceptable than do U.S. workers.

3. "Does your supervisor let his superiors know how members of his work group feel?" Interestingly a high percentage of our Peruvians checked, "I don't know" (57 per cent for white-collar and 48 per cent for blue-collar workers). We have no exact comparison with the U.S. here, since the alternative of "I don't know" was not offered in our U.S. company. However, U.S. workers were free to leave the question blank, and yet very few of them did so. It is our experience that U.S. workers generally think they know the answer to this question, whereas a number of Peruvians asked us, "How should I know?"

"He lets his superiors know how his employees feel only when he feels his superiors will agree with him." In the United States, when a worker checked this alternative, we could be almost certain that he would give a negative evaluation of his supervisor. Not so in Peru. Those checking this item were somewhat more likely than those who did not to give a favorable evaluation of the supervisor. On the question as a whole, in the U.S. company there was a relatively high correlation (.58) between the supervisor's letting his superior know work-group feelings and satisfaction with the supervisor. For the Peruvian white-collar workers, there was an insignificant (.03) correlation, while for the blue-collar workers we found an almost significant negative relationship (−.10).

4. We used the following participation items: How often are there group meetings in which the employees can discuss things with their supervisor? If you have group meetings in which the employees can discuss things with their supervisor, do they do any good? When there is a change to be made in your job, does your supervisor discuss it with you before he puts it into practice? How much do you and other people of your work group have to say about how things are done in your work group?

Here we did not find the reverse relationships noted earlier, but we did find marked differences in the degree of association with satisfaction with the supervisor. In the U.S. study all four items showed positive correlations of .50 or more. In the first three items for Peru, correlations ranged between .12 and .17 for blue-collar workers and between .35 and .37 for white-collar workers. On the last item, the Peruvian correlation approximately equalled that for the U.S. (about .50).

The results suggest that, although Peruvians are just as concerned as U.S. workers about having some power and influence over their work, they are not nearly so inclined to see this power and influence as being related to the participative communication practices of the supervisor.

DESIGN OF THE PRESENT ANALYSIS

On the basis of these results, we felt that we had demonstrated the existence of systematic cross-cultural differences in responses to industrial supervisors. The fact that the findings for both blue- and white-collar workers in Peru presented basically the same contrast added to our confidence in this general conclusion. The conclusion seems to us of theoretical importance, for it suggests the necessity of re-examining all theories of organizational behavior in order to take into account the influence of the underlying culture within which the organization is found.

Nevertheless, the demonstration that differences exist is only a first step. We also wanted to see whether the data available from our first cross-cultural study might enable us to probe beneath the patterns observed to learn something of the way in which a culture may condition responses to organizational authority.

It should be noted that this second type of analysis was made entirely on a post hoc basis. We regarded the questionnaire study in Peru as a broad exploratory effort that might help us to focus our intercultural research more sharply in the future. The present paper analyzes the U.S. and Peruvian reactions to supervisors in the context of one dimension of personality and one further dimension of perceptions of the organization.

The personality dimension is that of faith in people or interpersonal trust. In a report on a values study of Peruvian high school seniors, Whyte pointed out that, compared with the United States, Peruvians tend to show a very low level of faith in people. The study involved a comparison of the attitudes of 2,975 American students included in the Cornell Values Study with those of 1,833 Peruvian school boys.[8]

FINDINGS

As we examined these same faith-in-people items for our Peruvian white-collar workers, we found the results very close to those for our Peruvian school boy sample and far away from those for the U.S. comparison group. To make our questionnaire manageable at the lower educational level of our Peruvian blue-collar workers, we eliminated many items included in the white-collar questionnaire — including the faith-in-people questions. For this reason, the following discussion relates entirely to white-collar workers.

Table 1 presents the comparisons among U.S. college students, Peru-

[8] W. F. Whyte, "Culture, Industrial Relations and Economic Development: The Case of Peru," *Industrial and Labor Relations Review*, XVI (July, 1963), 583-593.

TABLE 1. COMPARISON OF THE RESPONSES OF AMERICAN
COLLEGE STUDENTS, PERUVIAN SCHOOL BOYS, AND
PERUVIAN WHITE-COLLAR WORKERS TO INTERPERSONAL
TRUST (FAITH-IN-HUMAN-NATURE) ITEMS

Item	American College Students N = 2,975	Peruvian School Boys N = 1,833	Peruvian White-Collar Workers N = 202
Some people say that most people can be trusted. Others say you can't trust people. How do you feel about it?[a]			
1. Most people can be trusted	81%	31%	37%
2. Can't be trusted	19	69	60
0. No answer	—	—	3
These days a person doesn't really know whom he can count on.			
1. I agree	24	48	43
2. I agree in part	8	33	45
3. I don't agree	67	18	12
0. No answer	1	1	2
Every man is out for himself.			
1. I agree	Item not	48	37
2. I agree in part	included	32	29
3. I don't agree	In Cornell	20	23
0. No answer	Values Study	—	—
No one is going to care much what happens to you when you get right down to it.			
1. I agree	31	41	43
2. I agree in part	9	29	36
3. I don't agree	60	30	21

[a] In the Cornell Values Study the second alternative was, "Others say you can't be too careful in your relations with other people." That proved practically untranslatable into Spanish, so we substituted the flat statement, "You can't trust people," which seems to us an even stronger statement of mistrust. Agreement with this statement might indicate even greater mistrust than agreement with its English counterpart.

vian school boys, and Peruvian white-collar workers for the four items we used for our faith-in-people scale. On the basis of this four-item scale, we divided our 202 white-collar workers into three groups. Those who gave trusting answers to all four items we called "high trust." Those who gave two to three trusting answers we called "medium trust." Those with a score of 0 or 1 fell into our "low trust" group. Did this sorting, in terms of trust, yield differences in responses to supervisory style? Before we seek to answer that question, let us consider a dimension of organizational life that proved to be highly related to trust.

The dimension is that of work group cohesion. Research in the United States has been characterized by a high level of interest in the work group. In fact, theories of participative management are more concerned with the relationship between the supervisor and the work group than they are with the man-boss pair relationship. Belonging to much the same culture as those who study them, U.S. workers seem to have no difficulty in thinking of themselves as members of a work group and in responding to questions about this group.

When we applied these same questions relating to work group cohesion to our Peruvian workers, the results were quite different. The questions were answered, but the replies did not fit into any pattern that we have yet been able to discover. The Peruvian cohesion scores showed no relationship to satisfaction with the supervisor, with the job, with the company, or indeed with anything else in the questionnaire.

One of two conclusions seem plausible: (1) Peruvian workers have quite a different conception of the nature of a work group, or (2) Peruvian workers tend to identify themselves much less than U.S. workers with a work group. A modification introduced into our questionnaire at the insistence of the company management has provided us evidence in support of the second explanation. Our management advisors argued that many of their workers would not be able to think of themselves as members of a group. They persuaded us to add to our categories of response, "I do not work with a group."

In a sense, we were subjecting our informants to contradictory stimuli. Immediately below the subject heading, "About your work group," we presented the following definition: "The work group refers to all the people you work with who report to your immediate supervisor." By defining the group in terms of all those under the same immediate supervisor, we declared that every one of our informants belonged to a work group. Nevertheless, for those who were insistent on the matter, we did provide the escape of, "I do not work with a group."

Twenty-six per cent of the Peruvian white-collar workers chose this response. An exact comparison with the U.S. findings is not possible, since the U.S. questionnaire did not include this response category. However, those who had difficulty in answering the question could have left it blank. In our U.S. study and in a number of others, the percentage of *no* answers was so low as to confirm our impression that the U.S. workers had no difficulty in thinking of themselves as members of a work group.

Even more interesting than the absolute percentage of Peruvians denying work group membership was the differential distribution found when informants were sorted according to trust score. The proportions of individuals reporting that they did not belong to a work group for high-, medium-, and low-trust groups were 18, 25, and 44 per cent respectively. The differences between high- and low-trust and medium- and low-trust groups are significant beyond the .05 level. There is, apparently, a marked relationship between faith in people and identification with a group.

Because of the marked differences in both the personality area of interpersonal trust or faith in people and the workers' perceptions about their supervisor, it can be reasoned that the man-to-group, human relations approach, as advocated in the United States, is of limited value in Peru and perhaps other Latin American cultures. In other words, a man who does not expect to be consulted by his superior and is not inclined to trust either his superior or his peers will see little value in participating in decisions on a man-to-group basis.

In view of the differences among Peruvian workers with regard to trust or faith in human nature, we might expect that those who were, like U.S. workers, high in interpersonal trust or in faith in people would have similar expectations with regard to man-group relationships. In other words, our hypothesis then becomes: Individuals who are high in interpersonal trust will expect and appreciate a leader-group climate which is democratic and participative as contrasted with those who are very low in interpersonal trust, who will anticipate a more authoritarian and non-participative climate and, therefore, will be satisfied with supervisors as long as they provide the structure in which work can be done.

We then sorted the Peruvian workers in terms of their positions on an interpersonal trust scale. A separate factor analysis of supervisory behavior and climate items was conducted for each subgroup of high-, medium-, and low-trust individuals. If our hypothesis was to be supported, separate factors should be associated with different personality types, with the factors for high-trust individuals most resembling those found in comparable United States studies.

The items used to obtain description of supervisor behavior and attitudes toward supervision are presented in Table 2. In each case, a five-point, Likert-type response category was provided. The items are designed to reflect technical, administrative, and human relations components of a supervisory job. These items can also be considered as being relevant to the consideration-initiating structure concept of leadership.

Table 3 represents the first factor loadings (Quartimax rotation) as a function of the trust score. Looking first at the low-trust score respondents, it should be noted that the highest loadings on this factor relate to the supervisor's attention to training and his technical ability, followed closely by his administrative ability in planning and organization and the summary supervision satisfaction item. Parenthetically, it should be noted that the general satisfaction item should appear in the first factor for all subgroups, and it was presumed that the first factor would involve all items which helped determine an individual's evaluation of his superior. A total of 11 items appeared in the first factor, with technical and administrative items having the highest loadings. Only factor loadings in excess of .40 are shown in the table.

The human relations items include understanding work problems, discussing the job, and a general question having to do with handling people. Each of these human relations items, referring to a relationship between the individual and his superior, concerns man-to-man considerations rather than man-to-group relationships.

Finally, an important item, whether or not the supervisor lets his superior know how members of his work group feel, is positively related to satisfaction with the supervisor. This is contrary to the general findings in this study and to our hypothesis. However, more than half of the respondents in this group indicated that they did not know how their supervisor would relate to his superior. Thus, the significance of this positive relationship for the low-trust group must be regarded with skepticism until further research has shed light on the reasons for the large number of nonresponses.

Somewhat more positive results for the human relations items are found for the medium-trust group. On the other hand, emphasizing the

TABLE 2

1. How good is your supervisor at handling people? (HR[a])
2. Do you feel that your supervisor will stand up for you in front of his superiors? (HR)
3. How free do you feel to discuss important things about your job with your supervisor? (HR, A)
4. How free do you feel to discuss your personal problems with your supervisor?
5. How closely does your supervisor supervise your group? (HR, A)
6. How much attention does your supervisor give to training you and the other people under him? (T, A)
7. How often are there group meetings in which the employees can discuss things with their supervisors? (A, HR)
8. When there is a change to be made in your job, does your supervisor discuss it with you before he puts it into practice? (A, HR)
9. If you have group meetings in which the employees can discuss things with the supervisor, do they do any good? (HR, A)
10. In general, how much do you and the other people of your work group have to say about how things are done in your group? (HR)
11. How much emphasis does your supervisor put on getting out a lot of work? (A, HR)
12. Does your supervisor let his superiors know how members of his work group feel? (A, HR)
13. How good is your supervisor at getting what he wants with his superiors or the other department heads? (A)
14. Your supervisor's part of the job having to do with *working with employees,* how well does he do it? (HR)
15. How well does your supervisor plan and organize the work? (A)
16. How well does your supervisor handle the technical side of the job? (T)
17. On the whole, to what extent does your supervisor appreciate and understand the work problems and needs of his employees? (HR, T)
18. Taking all things into consideration, how satisfied are you with your supervisor? (Summary satisfaction item)

[a]Notations HR, A, T indicate Human Relations; Administrative, and Technical items. Some items imply administrative or technical activities that can differ in terms of the human relations orientation of the leaders.

260   WILLIAMS, WHYTE, GREEN

TABLE 3. FIRST FACTOR LOADINGS AS A FUNCTION OF
TRUST SCORE AND CORRELATIONS WITH SUMMARY
SATISFACTION ITEM[a]

| | Trust Score | | |
	Low (N = 44)	Medium (N = 81)	High (N = 77)
Summary satisfaction (18)[b]	.82	.86	.88
Technical ability (16)	.85 78	.75 64	.65 50
Training (6)	.90 78	.61 43	.73 64
Planning and organizing (15)	.84 81	.68 57	.70 62
Understand work problems (17)	.80 74	.73 70	.74 71
Emphasis on work (11)	.68 54	.46 33	.52 42
Stand up for employees (2)	.66 55	.71 54	.82 72
Discuss job (3)	.59 53	.47 41	.55 43
Handle people (1)	.74 62	.75 69	.78 66
Working with employees (14)	.76 63	.60 49	.71 60
Tell superior (12)	.51 16	− 07	.58 62
Frequency of group meetings (7)	n 27	.55 41	.61 51
Discuss job change (8)	n 20	.51 44	.70 53
Say of group (10)	n 36	.75 64	.68 61
Group discussion evaluation (9)	n 33	n 29	.52 43
Discuss personal problems (4)	n 27	n 28	.44 39

[a]The table shows factor loadings in excess of .40; correlations with the "summary satisfaction" item appear in italics.
[b]Numbers in parentheses refer to items in Table 2.

work and planning and organizing, along with other technical factors, tend to receive lower factor loadings. Additional items receiving factor loading above .40 reflect more emphasis on man-to-group human relations content, including having meetings and the amount of say the group has about how things will be done in the work group. The important human relations dimension of discussing job changes in advance also becomes relevant in the appraisal of the superior.

And then, for those high in interpersonal trust, factor loadings in excess of .40 occur for two items not found in the previous two groups — evaluation of whether group discussions do any good or not and the discussing of personal problems with the supervisor. As was the case with the medium-trust group, the additional items involve human relations or consideration content. Moreover, nearly all items having a human relations content load higher on the satisfaction factor for the high-trust group than they do for the low-trust group. By contrast, for the low-trust group, items having to do with initiating structure or technical and administrative ability load higher on the general satisfaction factor than they do for high-trust respondents. It should also be noted that, as a result of using the criterion of a factor loading of .40 or greater for inclusion, no second factor was found for the medium- or high-trust groups. A second significant factor was produced for the low-trust groups. This was a four-item factor consisting of evaluations of whether group meetings did any good or not, the amount of say the work group had on how things were done in the work group, freedom to discuss personal problems with the supervisor, and whether the supervisor discussed job changes in advance.

That these items were rather independent of their general evaluation of the supervisor is indicated by the fact that the factor loading of the summary supervisory item on factor 2 was −.06. The data in Table 3, then, tend to support the hypothesis that, with greater levels of inter-personal trust, the more human relations or man-to-group functions will be anticipated and appreciated on the part of employees as they view their supervisor.

Table 4 presents the factor loadings on the supervisory items for a group of United States white-collar workers, contrasted with the factor loadings on these items for the high-trust Peruvian group. It can be seen that there is a close similarity between the general supervisory satis-faction factor for Peruvian workers and for equivalent white-collar workers in the United States. Two items are loaded in the general super-vision factor for the Peruvians which are not found in the U.S. results. The item having to do with emphasizing work occurred only as a second factor for the U.S. workers, along with the item on closeness of super-vision. Of interest is the fact that, for the U.S. workers, there was a nega-tive relationship between closeness of supervision and satisfaction, while a positive relationship was found in the Peruvian data. Moreover, the

TABLE 4. COMPARISON OF FIRST FACTOR LOADINGS FOR PERUVIAN (HIGH-TRUST) AND UNITED STATES WORKERS[a]

	Peruvian (High-Trust) Workers N = 77	United States Workers N = 590
Summary satisfaction	.88	.87
Technical ability	.65	.68
Training	.73	.67
Planning and organizing	.70	.74
Understand work problems	.74	.83
Emphasis on work	.52	n
Stand up for employees	.82	.81
Discuss job	.55	.70
Handle people	.78	.85
Working with employees	.71	.83
Tell superior	.58	.68
Frequency of group meetings	.61	n
Discuss job change	.70	.48
Say of group	.75	.62
Group discussion evaluation	.52	.61
Discuss personal problems	.44	.64

[a]The table shows loadings in excess of .40.

item relating to the number or frequency of group meetings also was an independent third factor for American workers, which seems to indicate a more sophisticated expectation — that it was not the frequency of meetings but whether meetings did any good which conditioned their response in terms of satisfaction with their supervisor.

In the U.S. data, there is also an indication that items involving a human relations content and a man-to-group orientation are even more highly loaded than they are for the high-trust Peruvian group. In particular, such items as working with the employees, which has a group referent, and the conducting of good group meetings are more highly loaded for the U.S. workers than for the high-trust Peruvian group. In general, however, there is a high degree of similarity between the general satisfaction factor derived for U.S. and high-trust Peruvian workers.

SUMMARY AND DISCUSSION

The data generally support the hypothesis that individuals with low trust, in a sample of Peruvian white-collar workers, tend to evaluate their supervisor in terms of his administrative and technical or initiating structure ability. With succeeding levels of trust, greater appreciation of human relations content does appear in relation to satisfaction with the supervisor, and the results for high-trust Peruvians are very close to those for American workers.

The greatest difference between the American workers and high-trust Peruvians was with regard to emphasis on production and closeness of supervision. Again, these data, like the findings discussed in the introduction, support the conclusion that the values of subordinates greatly affect their evaluations of superiors, and that, in a highly distrustful society marked by authoritarianism, certain participation forms which involve man-to-group relationships will probably not be successful when they are initiated.

Our findings suggest that the uniformities reported in the U.S. literature must be seen in the context of the culture of the United States. Our democratic ideology encourages a pattern of relations which de-emphasizes the authority of the supervisor and legitimizes the direct thrashing out of differences between the supervisor and the work group.

Although much has been said about individualism in the United States, our understanding has been obscured by an ideology which fails to distinguish between the taking of individual initiative and identification with a group. A widely accepted assumption in the United States, and, in fact, an entire movement of human relations, is based on the notion that a group of workers placed in a similiar work-group surrounding, reporting to the same superior, will start to develop certain kinds of group ties. Although studies of cohesiveness have sometimes indicated that this has not happened — that cliques form within formal groups or that work organizations fail to develop any spirit — supervisory training tends to be based on the expectation that individuals will respond as a group to certain forms of leadership. Our culture tends to stimulate the individual to take initiative toward change in his organizational situation, but, at the same time, the worker tends to think and act as a member of a group and to channel his initiative through the group.

The individualism of the Peruvian seems to be a different sort of phenomenon. His organizational relations tend to be polarized in relation to a more authoritarian management, which seems to result in isolation of the individual worker from his fellows. The worker does not see the work group in terms of psychological identification or of practical support to nearly the same extent as does the U.S. worker. A high faith-in-people orientation seems to go with integration of the individual into the group and confidence in being able to solve problems through the group.

These interpretations go beyond the data reported here and are presented tentatively for further testing. The testing will not be limited to new questionnaires exploring the nature of individual-group relationships and worker-supervisor relationships. We hope to observe groups at the work place and to interview workers and supervisors at some length regarding what their work groups mean to them. Only as we combine questionnaire techniques with observational and interviewing approaches can we go much beyond our present point of demonstrating the existence of broad cultural differences which affect worker perceptions and attitudes.

Industrial Man: The Relation of Status to Experience, Perception, and Value

Ever larger segments of the world's population are living and will come to live in what is now commonly called "industrial society." The standard complex of institutions — most notably the factory — associated with this system daily becomes more widely diffused into a variety of traditional and even "primitive" cultural contexts. These institutions rather rigorously prescribe a set of norms, with regard to such matters as dress, time, order, and authority, which must be conformed to, at least during the time that individuals are engaged in their industrial and related occupations. This aspect of the diffusion of the industrial order is easily recognized.

It is less evident that the distinctive roles of the industrial system also foster typical patterns of perception, opinions, beliefs, and values which are not institutionally prescribed but arise spontaneously as new subcultures in response to the institutional conditions provided by the typically differentiated role-structure of modern industrial society. This paper reports an exploratory comparative study of the influence of these standard environments on attitudes, which yielded considerable evidence that the process is effective and pervasive.

In this investigation I take the institutional pattern or setting as given and the responses to it, particularly those not explicitly required

Reprinted with the permission of the author and publisher from Alex Inkeles, "Industrial Man: The Relation of Status to Experience, Perception, and Value," *The American Journal of Sociology*, Volume 66, July 1960, pp. 1-31. The article is reprinted as abridged with the permission of the author and the holder of the copyright, the University of Chicago Press.

This is a revised and somewhat abridged version of a report prepared for the Conference on Political Modernization which met in June, 1959, under the auspices of the Committee on Comparative Politics of the Social Science Research Council. I am particularly indebted to the Committee's chairman, Professor Gabriel Almond, for support and encouragement. The data were assembled with the aid of a grant from the Ford Foundation, supplemented by the Russian Research Center at Harvard. Dr. Elmo C. Wilson generously made available special tabulations from studies undertaken by International Research Associates, Inc. Jay Greenfield rendered creative research assistance.

by the institutional forms, as the dependent variable. The individual and groups of individuals, not institutions, are the central concern, and we study variation not in formal institutional arrangements but in individual and collective social perception and action. Only one institutional complex is considered here, namely, that which characterizes the modern large-scale, bureaucratic industrial system. What is not given, namely the response to it, will be sought in a number of different realms but in each case will be measured through reported experiences and expressed attitudes and values.

The underlying theory is very simple. It is assumed that people have experiences, develop attitudes, and form values in response to the forces or pressures which their environment creates. By "environment" we mean, particularly, networks of interpersonal relations and the patterns of reward and punishment one normally experiences in them. They include not only access to facilities and items of consumption, necessary and conspicuous, but also such intangibles as prestige, the comforts of security, respectful treatment, calculability in the actions of significant others, and so on. The theory holds that, within broad limits, the same situational pressures, the same framework for living, will be experienced as similar and will generate the same or similar response by people from different countries. This is, of course, not a denial of individual variation, of personality as a determinant of perception, cognition, or affect. Neither is it meant to deny the effect of traditional cultural ways on behavior. These will mute the independent effect of the industrial institutional environment, but it is assumed that they cannot eliminate it. Rather, its force is sufficiently great to assert itself clearly despite the countervailing influence of personal idiosyncracy and traditional cultural ways of thinking and feeling. Insofar as industrialization, urbanization, and the development of large-scale bureaucratic structures and their usual accompaniments create a standard environment with standard institutional pressures for particular groups, to that degree should they produce relatively standard patterns of experience, attitude, and value — standard, not uniform, pressures. The situation of worker and manager may be relatively standard in the factory, wherever it is located, but relative to each other these positions are by no means uniform.

The test of the assumption is very simple. It is made by comparing the perceptions, attitudes, and values of those in comparable positions in the typical hierarchies of modern society, in particular the occupational, educational, and socioeconomic. If the "foreign" (read: "industrial"), externally introduced institutional environment plays no role, there should be no pattern or similarity in the response of incumbents of a given type of position from country to country. If there is such a pattern — if, for example, workers are everywhere less "happy" or "optimistic," or more insistent on obedience in children, than are engineers —

this can come only from the similarity of their situation in the hierarchical setting of occupation, income, or education, since on the basis of their nationality or culture alone they should obviously differ.

To discern this influence of the industrial environment is, of course, not the same as determining either its extent or its intensity. The pressure generated by the institutional setting of industrialism may affect only a narrow range of experience and attitude — possibly only that relating to work experience. It may exert only a moderate influence, producing only a small part of the variance, the main part being accounted for by other factors, such as traditional cultural orientations. These are important problems for further elucidation. For now, we restrict ourselves to a statement of the main proposition — *that men's environment, as expressed in the institutional patterns they adopt or have introduced to them, shapes their experience, and through this their perceptions, attitudes and values, in standardized ways which are manifest from country to country, despite the countervailing randomizing influence of traditional cultural patterns.* I trust it will be understood without great elaboration that this proposition is stated so unequivocally only to facilitate clear exposition. The hypothesis is tentative, a guide to the exploration which this paper reports and not a dictum or an empirically established fact. We are equally interested in proof and disproof and must expect to find both supporting, negating, and ambiguous evidence.

I can hardly claim novelty for the proposition. The idea that the institutions in which men live shape their character and their views is old indeed. So is the more refined notion that a man's distinctive standing and role within the social structure will influence not only his perspective on the world but his wishes, beliefs, and values as well. Probably very few will argue that any people can indefinitely, or even for very long, utilize the material and institutional forms of industrial society without also absorbing some of its culture. At the same time, very few will argue that the industrial system is indeed so standardized or its influence so compelling as to permit no variation in the culture of those who share it. The obvious task of serious investigation, therefore, is to determine with some degree of precision where and how far the institutions of industrial society impose or foster the development of new subcultures wherever they are introduced and in what realms of life and to what degree traditional patterns maintain a relative independence of or immunity to the influence of the industrial institutional system.

There are two main avenues open to us. The first would be to designate certain attitudes or values as indexes of the industrial "subculture" and then to test the degree of association between these indexes and the level of industrialization in various countries. This is essentially the path taken by Davis and Lipset in their comparative studies. Both used the percentage of males engaged in non-agricultural pursuits, and the per capita consumption of energy, as indexes of industrialization. For his dependent variable, Davis studied the degree of urbanization; Lipset, the extent and stability of democratic political processes.[1] If we were to follow this path, our dependent variable would be the proportion of the population in each country holding a certain belief or sharing a particular value presumed to be fostered by the industrial milieu — for example, the belief that most human problems can ultimately be solved by technological advances.

There are several reasons for not adopting this procedure. Indexes of industrialization tend to generalize to the population, as a whole, characteristics which may in fact be intensely developed in only one segment. An outstanding example would be the Soviet Union, which is highly and intensely industrialized, but in which about half the population is engaged in agriculture. In such cases a nationwide index of the industrial subculture might be low, not because the industrialized segment of the population failed to show the expected characteristic, but because so large a part of the population was not integrated into the industrial structure. Our theory applies only to those segments of the population whose life conditions are standardized through industrial or other large-scale bureaucratic organizations.

Another reason for not adopting this method is that the average level of response for a nation may so heavily reflect traditional cultural orientations, or recent events, as to mask the independent influence of the industrial environment. To control this would require matching countries sharing the same traditional culture but varying in degree of industrialization. On the face of it, many would deny the possibility of meaningfully accomplishing this, even if the pool of countries available for matching were much larger than it is.

The most compelling reason for not relying on a single national average as an index of the industrial subculture, however, lies in the nature of the theory being tested. The idea that the industrial institutional order carries with it a distinctive industrial culture does not necessarily mean that the culture is the same for all who live in industrial society. This commonly made assumption can be quite misleading. We should, rather, expect that, in accord with the differences among positions in the modern occupational hierarchy, the different occupational groups will have differentiated attitudes and values. What is likely to be common to industrial societies, therefore, is not a single idea or a

---

[1] Kingsley Davis and Hilda H. Golden, "Urbanization and the Development of Pre-Industrial Areas," in Paul K. Hatt and Albert J. Reiss, Jr. (eds.), *Cities and Society* (rev. ed.; Glencoe, Ill.: Free Press, 1957), pp. 120-40; Seymour M. Lipset, "Some Social Requisites of Democracy: Economic Development and Political Legitimacy," *American Political Science Review*, LIII (March, 1959), 69-105.

set of commonly held ideas but a particular *structure* of experience, attitude, and value which takes its form from the occupational structure.

Our expectation, that the distinctive feature of the industrial culture is a structure of response characteristic of the occupational hierarchy as a whole, also accounts for our not adopting the simple alternative of studying just one distinctive group, such as factory workers. From country to country the proportion of factory workers giving a particular answer might be quite different, yet in each country the workers might stand in a fixed relation to the other strata. This regularity would not be evident at all if we studied only one typical occupational group in different societies. We therefore take as our unit of analysis not a national average or a score for a particular group but the structure of response in some status hierarchy representing the entire nation or, at least, its industrialized segment.

We will speak of the existence of a structure of response when the proportion in each stratum (occupation, prestige, income, or educational group) reporting certain experiences or holding particular views rises or falls more or less regularly as we ascend or descend the hierarchy. We will speak of a cross-national *pattern*, with which we are most concerned, when the structure of response is more or less the same as we move from country to country — that is, when the direction and, to some degree, the magnitude of the changes in proportion are similar in different national populations.

We assume that the industrial order fixes the situation of different groups relative to each other in a more or less invariant fashion. We also assume that occupational groups, as units, respond distinctively to their occupational environment and the world outside it according to their situation and the characteristic pressures it generates. Insofar as these assumptions are correct, we should expect to find a cross-national pattern of response on many issues directly and indirectly related to the typical pattern of experience in the roles common in industrial society. The similarity in the structure of response as we move from country to country may exist, even though the average response varies widely from one nation to another. The typical response of any population may be strongly shaped by its traditional culture, and that of any particular group in some country may be influenced by a unique local situation. But, by focusing on the occupational hierarchy as a whole, country by country, we at once control both the effect of traditional culture at the national level and the special circumstances affecting one or another occupational group at the "local" level.

To test these assumptions, we should, ideally, have data gathered for this specific purpose. Our samples should come from a variety of countries selected to represent diverse cultural traditions, and the sample from each country should be restricted to those holding strictly comparable positions in each respective society's industrial sector. The questionnaires would be carefully translated to insure comparability of meaning. But what is actually available is very far from meeting the optimum requirements. I have had to rely on already completed studies drawn from a file of the reports of various national survey agencies,[2] the one major international compilation edited by Hadley Cantril,[3] the few, more systematic, comparative studies such as those undertaken by UNESCO[4] and International Research Associates, Inc. (INRA),[5] and sundry other scattered sources. None of these studies was designed for the purpose for which we wish to use them. The selection of countries is highly variable. The sample subgroups are frequently not equivalent from country to country, and it has been necessary to use other criteria of stratification than occupational status, which is most relevant to our theory. The questions used in different countries are often only very approximate equivalents. Under the circumstances, failure to find the expected patterns would be somewhat inconclusive as a test of our hypothesis. On the other hand, the presence of so many potentially randomizing influences in the data means that the emergence of the expected pattern, even if weakly manifested, may be taken as highly suggestive of the probable predictive power of the theory.

THE REALM OF WORK

If our theory holds at all, it should be most effective in ordering information in the realm in which it has most direct and immediate applicability, namely, within the industrial enterprise. Wherever the factory or the large-scale organization exists, there will be a clearly stratified hierarchy of authority and of technical competence. A hierarchy of income, prestige, and other rewards will also be found following the main lines of the hierarchy of authority and technical competence. There is, naturally, a great deal of variation, but the general pattern is seldom departed from in fundamentals.

[2] Particularly useful were the Italian agency *Doxa Bolletino published in Milan* (hereinafter cited as "*Doxa*"), the releases of the Netherlands Institute of Public Opinion in Amsterdam (hereinafter cited as "NIPO"), and the bulletins of the Australian Gallup Polls of Melbourne (hereinafter cited as "AGP").

[3] Hadley W. Cantril (ed.), *Public Opinion, 1935-1946* (Princeton, N.J.: Princeton University Press, 1951).

[4] William Buchanan and Hadley Cantril, *How Nations See Each Other* (Urbana: University of Illinois Press, 1953).

[5] During 1958 they undertook a substantial number of comparative surveys, released through the *New York Herald Tribune*. Additional tabulations were made available through the courtesy and cooperation of Dr. Elmo Wilson. Although the Gallup affiliates in various countries often ask the same question at more or less the same time, detailed consolidated results suitable for comparative study are generally not available. Some reconstruction is possible from the bulletins released by the individual affiliates.

Our problem, then, is this: In what ways and to what extent does this objective hierarchy, this standardization of external conditions of work and pay, shape the attitudes and feelings of the incumbents of the commonly differentiated positions? We may begin with the simplest and perhaps most obvious of examples — that relating to job satisfaction, or the sense of pleasure or gratification a man finds in his work. Since those in certain positions, such as managers and engineers, are almost always better paid, given more security, granted more respect, and perhaps also allowed more freedom and autonomy, we may reasonably expect that they will more often express satisfaction.

As Table 1 reveals, this expectation is indeed borne out. We have in hand fairly good data on job satisfaction in six countries, covering a fair range of situations. There is a definite and unmistakable structure in the responses manifested from country to country. Those standing at the

TABLE 1. NATIONAL COMPARISONS OF JOB SATISFACTION, BY OCCUPATION

PERCENTAGE SATISFIED*					
U.S.S.R.		U.S.		Germany	
		Large business	100		
		Small business	91		
Administrative, professional	77	Professional	82	Professional	75
Semiprofessional	70			Upper white collar	65
White collar	60	White collar	82	Civil servants	51
				Lower white collar	33
Skilled worker	62	Skilled manual	84	Skilled worker	47
Semiskilled	45	Semiskilled	76	Semiskilled	21
Unskilled	23	Unskilled	72	Unskilled	11
Peasant	12			Farm labor	23

PERCENTAGE SATISFIED*					
Italy		Sweden		Norway	
		Upper class	84	Upper class	93
		Middle class	72	Middle class	88
Skilled worker	68				
Artisan	62	Working class	69	Working class	83
Unskilled	57				
Farm labor	43				

*U.S.S.R. — percentage answering "Yes" to: Did you like the job you held in 1940?" (Soviet refugee data, Russian Research Center, Harvard University). U.S. — percentage answering "Yes" to: "Are you satisfied or dissatisfied with your present job?" (Richard Centers, "Motivational Aspects of Occupational Stratification," Journal of Social Psychology, XXVII [1948], 100). Germany — percentage who would choose present occupation in response to: "If you were again 15 years old and could start again, would you choose your present occupation or another one?" (from German poll data, courtesy of S. M. Lipset). Italy — those "satisfied" or "fairly satisfied" with work (Doxa Bolletino). Sweden and Norway — percentage giving "satisfied" in response to question: "Are you satisfied with your present occupation, or do you think that something else would suit you better?" (Hadley W. Cantril [ed.], Public Opinion, 1935-1946 [Princeton, N.J.: Princeton University Press, 1951], p. 535).

top are, as a rule, more satisfied than those in the lower positions. Indeed, in every country the proportion who report job satisfaction decreases quite regularly as we descend the steps of the standard occupational hierarchy. Even the departures from the strict step pattern appear to be the same, at least in those countries where the data permit a comparison. Thus, in each of the three countries for which we have the more refined data (United States, U.S.S.R., Germany), the skilled manual workers are slightly more often found among the satisfied than are the rank-and-file white-collar workers. This presumably reflects the fact that, generally, the pay and often the prestige accorded the skilled worker exceeds that of ordinary white-collar personnel.

There are, of course, some other departures from the standard pattern which could not be so easily explained. Note, for example, that in Germany the group with the smallest proportion satisfied are the unskilled workers, whereas the farm laborers are twice as often satisfied men. The latter are disgruntled only as often as the semiskilled workers. By contrast, in the Soviet group the situation is reversed. The man least often satisfied is the peasant.

Such variations, or departures from a standard, point to quite important differentation in the relative positions of particular occupational groups in different countries. Consequently, our method, far from covering up or glossing over the differences between countries, can serve as a definite pointer for locating precisely what is distinctive in the situation of a particular group in a given country.

The data on job satisfaction illustrate well the appropriateness of the model of analysis sketched in the preceding section. Although all the countries are advanced, well-to-do representatives of the West European complex of industrial nations, the *average* level of satisfaction in each is markedly different. For example, in the United States the national average would clearly be over 80 per cent satisfied, whereas in Germany it would be closer to 40 per cent. Similarly, if only one particular occupational group, such as the semiskilled workers, were considered, one would be led to conclude that their shared status by no means produced a shared or standard effect, regardless of nationality. On the contrary, the proportion satisfied among the semiskilled ranges from 21 per cent in Germany to 76 per cent in the United States. Yet, as we have seen in Table 1, there *is* a definite, unmistakable, and obviously quite meaningful pattern in the experience of job satisfaction which is uniform from country to country. But that, to repeat, emerges only when the unit of analysis is the occupational hierarchy as a whole and when attention is on the pattern of response within it rather than on the data, country by country or group by group.

It may seem obvious that, in all the countries for which we have data, job satisfaction is structured, with those higher in the hierarchy of occupations more often satisfied. Of course, those who are not ready to take a close look at the obvious have little need for science. Certainly it is less pejorative to say the example is striking rather than obvious. In any event, it is not presented first as definitive proof of the theory but rather because it so clearly illustrates the mode of analysis to be used later in assessing reactions which are not so "obviously" derivable from the external conditions of the individual's situation at work.

A more serious criticism is that we unduly stress the regularity in the pattern across national lines while slighting the impressive differences in the absolute proportion satisfied in the several countries. Choice of emphasis is largely a consequence of one's purpose; the concern here is to discover regularity in human social behavior in response to standard stimulus conditions, something which seems rather more difficult to find than examples of diversity. This is not to say that for some purposes the location and analysis of differences is not more important. For example, if you wished to predict whether unskilled workers in Europe were more likely to vote communist, or for whatever was the legal party of the far left, it would be quite important to know that, compared to unskilled workers in the United States, they are seldom satisfied on the job. But, even here, it is only when you have the comparative data that you are alerted to take special notice of the German or Italian workers' response. Furthermore, the signal does not rest mainly on comparing German and American *workers*. The striking nature of the German response is evident only when we realize that German professionals and businessmen were satisfied about as often as were their American counterparts, whereas this is *not* true of workers. If Germans in all occupational groups characteristically reported job satisfaction less often than their opposite numbers in other countries, we would have to assume that some economic or cultural factor common to all Germans, or something peculiar or distinctive in the question put to them, accounted for the difference. Indeed, if we found such homogeneity *within* nations existing simultaneously with substantial differences among nations in the response to questions which, on theoretical grounds, we expected to show the predicted step pattern, that would constitute evidence refuting our hypothesis.

Finally, in assessing average or typical responses from country to country, we should keep in mind the possibility that these differences may be not so much a reflection of real differences in sentiments as an artifact of technique. We must take account of the marked effect produced by changes in question wording, differences in meaning introduced through translation, and variations in the conventions used for reporting answers to a question. In many of the comparisons made in this paper the questions used were only approximate equivalents. Thus, to assess job satisfaction, we might for one country have the question, "Do you like your job?"; for another, "Do you enjoy your work?"; and for a third, "Would you take the same job again if you started over?" Each may legitimately be taken as a measure of job satisfaction. Yet, if asked of a single population in one country, they would probably yield quite different proportions of "satisfied" workers. Nevertheless, the underlying structure of response would undoubtedly be similar for all three measures, with each showing the professional managerial groups most satisfied, the workers and farm laborers least so. This is not a purely hypothetical example. It can clearly be demonstrated on the basis of data available for the United States, the U.S.S.R., and other countries. Even in more systematic international polls the translation of the questions often gives them special meanings which influence the level of response in different countries. In addition, different conventions used in asking the questions and reporting the answers further influence the picture. In one case the alternatives offered may be only "I like my job" or "I don't like my job." But another study may include a third alternative, such as "I like it somewhat." These variations can obviously have a marked effect on the absolute proportion considered "satisfied" in one or another country.

If job satisfaction is a response to the "objective" factors which characterize the job as a whole, it should also respond to variations in the individual factors which make up the job complex. One of the most obvious determinants of job satisfaction, therefore, should be the salary or wage it carries. Data for the United States and the Soviet Union suggest a very direct connection. The higher the job in the hierarchy of power and prestige, the more often will the incumbents be satisfied with their pay. This is in good part, though not exclusively, because the pay is generally greater for jobs high in the hierarchy. Yet pay alone is not sufficient to account for reported job satisfaction. If it were the step pattern shown in Table 1, it should be fairly uniform for all the countries. In fact, it is not.

In both the Soviet Union and Germany, as against the United States, there are sharp breaks or discontinuities. For example, the proportion satisfied falls off precipitously between the skilled and semiskilled. There is another sharp drop in going from semiskilled to the unskilled, and again in going from semiskilled to the peasants. An initial exploration suggests the cause is not a difference in the structure of the wage scales, which are relatively similar in these countries. It seems instead to have to do with the "absolute" meaning of the very low pay received by those at the bottom in Germany and the U.S.S.R. as against the standard of living possible to the unskilled American worker even when he *is* at the bottom. In addition, differences in the absolute levels of prestige and self-respect which those at the bottom can command also seem to play a role.

Values About Jobs

It may be obvious that position in the occupational hierarchy, because it determines income and psychic reward, should influence the sense of job satisfaction. But what about *values?* Should the things people want from jobs also be so determined? We might reasonably make any one of three assumptions. Since values are presumably what is "shared" in any culture, we might expect that in each country everyone would want pretty much the same qualities in a job, with more or less the same intensity. On the other hand, if we assume that what people want is determined by what their life situation induces them to desire, we will expect systematic variation in the values reflected in job evaluations made by those at different levels of the occupational hierarchy. A third possibility would be that what men will want in a job will be determined by the kinds of men they are, that is, by their personality or training.

These three theories are not necessarily totally independent of each other, and only a full-scale analysis with data of good quality could settle the issue by revealing the relative weight of the factors and their interrelations. The scattered data in hand suggest that there are definitely some common values about the occupational realm shared not only within particular countries but in all modern, large-scale, more or less industrial societies, without much differentiation within the population by occupational group. Inkeles and Rossi located and analyzed the relative standing of lists of occupations in six industrial countries.[6] To an extraordinary degree the occupations were ranked in the same order. More important for us, they found very little variation in the evaluation of these occupations from one subgroup of the population to another. In other words, whether a worker or a professor does the rating, both place the doctor, lawyer, and engineer very near the top of the list, the ordinary worker about two-thirds of the way down, and the shoe-shine boy or garbage man at the bottom. This seems to be true for all countries, although there are some interesting variations which cannot be gone into here.

In the light of these findings, are we not forced to restate the theory

[6] A. Inkeles and P. Rossi, "National Comparisons of Occupational Prestige," *American Journal of Sociology*, LXI (1956), 329-39. These values may also be shared in countries not so highly industrialized but already incorporated into or influenced by currents of modernization (see E. Tiryakian, "The Prestige Evaluation of Occupations in an Underdeveloped Country: The Philippines," *American Journal of Sociology*, LXIII [1958], 390-99).

with which we started? The evaluation of occupations seems not to be influenced by differential situational pressures. At least the rater's own position in the occupational structure seems to make no fundamental difference in how he evaluates the standing or prestige of occupations. It might be objected that, after all, a man's standing in the community is a pretty "objective" thing. Anyone can see how much respect a doctor gets from everyone else. The fact that people agree on his standing is therefore "natural." But even so this requires that we reformulate our theory to say that a rater's own position or situation can be expected to influence only his *subjective* judgments—those statements in which he reports what *he* feels, or what he wants or likes. This is, however, a very confining assumption and more conservative than is strictly necessary. For we will see that certain estimates made by people about situations which are as "objective" and "external" as the standing of an occupation *are* influenced by the position of the observer, just as the experiments of Solomon Asch have shown that interpersonal situations can have a marked effect on the reported perception of such objective physical facts as the length of a line. But it may be that situationally determined perceptions of "objective" facts are not common and partake of a special nature. For the present, then, let us make the more conservative assumption that only intrinsically "subjective" reactions will be shaped by one's position in the social structure.

The qualities a man desires in his job certainly may be regarded as personal and subjective choices. Such desires may be assumed to reflect deeper values. Do those in different positions in the occupational hierarchy then wish for different qualities in a job? The relevant question has been asked in a number of countries, but I have located appropriate cross-tabulations for only two. The results suggest that there are some patterns which hold up across national lines. But there is also substantial variation, an absence of pattern, with regard to certain classes and dimensions, which obviously reflects very important differences in the general state of affairs within the two countries and in the relative position of certain special groups within each.

We may begin with the more regular patterns (Table 2). In both the United States and the Soviet refugee sample, those who hold jobs of higher status are much more likely to be concerned about having a job which is "interesting," stimulating, challenging, permits self-expression, and so on. The proportion of professionals desiring this quality, as against the proportion of unskilled workers citing it, produces a ratio of about 3:1 in both countries.

But the role of large income is quite different in the two countries. In the United States it is a factor in the "free choice" of a *job* for only 3 to 8 per cent, and there is no step pattern. In the Soviet Union, by contrast, the responses are highly patterned. Large earnings are the primary consideration for 57 per cent of the peasants and only 8 per cent of the intelligentsia. This may be striking evidence that in the United States, at least in 1948 and perhaps beyond, pay was no longer so desperately problematical an issue for the working class as it was in many other countries. Americans seem sure that if they have work their pay will be decently adequate. Additional evidence for this conclusion lies in the fact that, when Americans cited their reasons for being dissatisfied with a job, low pay accounted for only one-fifth of the complaints and was actually cited more often by white-collar than manual workers, whereas in the Soviet sample more than two-thirds of the dissatisfied workers and peasants cited low pay as the reason for their dissatisfaction and did so much more often than ordinary white-collar workers.

Our impression — that workers are generally concerned to increase their pay, while those more highly placed care more about interesting work[7] — must be tempered by the consideration of security. As between still more pay or still more interesting work, it seems that those higher in the scale will vote for increased interest, the worker for more pay. But what about security, or certainty, *as against* more pay linked to uncertainty? A number of questions asked in different countries bear on this issue. They all suggest that workers, more often than the middle classes, will choose certainty of income, or security, over more money with less security.

Thus in the Soviet-American comparison (Table 2) it is evident that security is much more a concern for the American workers than it is for professional-administrative people. Unskilled workers cited security as the basis for choosing a job in 29 per cent of the cases as against 2 per cent among those in more favored occupations. The Soviet data are not strictly comparable, since, in that context, security meant mainly freedom from fear of the secret police. Even so, it is striking that the intelligentsia, which experienced by far the highest rate of political arrest, nevertheless cited freedom from fear as the quality "most desired" in a job only one-half as often as did the ordinary workers.

In Australia, people were asked to choose between a straight raise or an incentive award. Among employers, 76 per cent chose the riskier incentive award, but only about 50 per cent of the workers did so.[8] The

[7] In the Netherlands (NIPO, Ballot 118, November, 1948) the question was asked: "Could you tell me for what purpose you work?" A break by socioeconomic standing revealed little patterning. "For family and children" was the chief reason given by all groups, and "money" next. The relative importance of money as against family and children was actually greatest among the well-to-do. Whether this is mainly a result of the difference in the question, or is evidence that there is no pattern here which can be expected cross-nationally, cannot be said on the basis of present evidence.

[8] Reported in *Doxa*, IV, No. 23-24 (December, 1950). This size of the plant

TABLE 2. QUALITY MOST DESIRED IN A WORK SITUATION, IN PERCENTAGES BY COUNTRY AND OCCUPATION

Occupation	Preferences of Sample of Soviet Refugees*				
	Adequate Pay	Interesting Work	Free of Fear	All Others	N
Intelligentsia	8	62	6	24	95
White collar	23	31	13	33	62
Skilled workers	22	27	15	36	33
Ordinary workers	48	20	13	19	56
Peasants	57	9	17	17	35

Occupation	Preferences of Sample in United States†				
	High Pay	Interesting Work ‡	Security	Independence	Other
Large business	6	52	2	7	33
Professional	3	50	3	12	32
Small business	6	41	5	22	26
White collar	7	42	12	17	22
Skilled manual	4	36	13	22	25
Semiskilled	6	20	26	24	24
Unskilled	8	19	29	15	29
Farm tenant and laborer	12	21	20	18	29

*Based on coding of qualitative personal interviews from the Harvard Project on the Soviet Social System.

†Based on R. Centers, "Motivational Aspects of Occupational Stratification," *Journal of Social Psychology*, XXVIII (November, 1948), 187-218, Table II.

‡Includes: "A very interesting job" and "A job where you could express your feelings, ideas, talent, or skill."

issue of security is only indirectly raised here. But in a number of cases the choice between more money and less security, or the reverse, has been put more directly, although the results are unfortunately not always reported with a class break.[9] In three out of four cases where this break is available, the choice of security over earnings is more often favored by workers than by those higher in the occupational or income hierarchy. The question has been asked in the United States a number of times in slightly different form. In 1940 the choice was between "a steady job earning just enough to get by on, with no prospect for ad-

---

in which the worker is employed seems to play a role here. In smaller plants (fifty or fewer employees) 56 per cent chose the incentive pay, but in larger plants only 45 per cent would take the risk. Size of plant seems an important factor in shaping the workers' perception and attitudes, and we should give it more systematic treatment in future studies. S. M. Lipset and Juan Linz, in their unpublished study, "The Social Bases of Political Diversity in Western Democracies," have noted several German studies which reveal that the larger the factory, the more radical will be the workers in it.

[9] In Denmark, NIPO, Ballot of April 11, 1943, for example.

vancement," as against "a job that pays a high wage, but with a 50/50 chance of getting promoted or fired." Forty-five per cent of factory labor as against a mere 8 per cent of executives chose the low-income–high-security alternative![10] On another form of the question, 64 per cent of professionals and executives were willing to risk all their savings on a promising venture, whereas only 40 per cent of unemployed workers inclined to this course as against sticking to "a good steady job."[11]

These results are congruent with those from the Soviet Union. Here the alternatives offered were: "A job that pays fairly well and is secure, but offers little opportunity for advancement," as against: "A job that pays less well and is not secure, but offers good opportunities for advancement." In the Soviet-refugee sample, among men under 40, the proportion preferring advancement over security falls from 50 per cent in the intelligentsia to about 23 per cent among workers and peasants. The ratio of preference for security over advancement is about 4:5 in the intelligentsia, but the preference for security increases to 3:1 among workers.

The evidence seems strong that, when offered the incentive of promotion or success at the risk of security, those in high-status occupations are willing to take risks which are shunned by the manual classes, who favor security above all else. But we are brought up short by the fact that in both Britain and Australia the same occupational differentiation is not noted in response to a seemingly similar question: "Which is more important in a job — as high wages as possible or security with lower wages?" In the British sample security was chosen over high wages by at least 2:1 *in all groups*. Indeed, the preference for security was strongest among salaried clerical and professional executive groups.[12] For Australia we do not have the exact percentage but are told "all occupational groups have similar ideas" in overwhelmingly preferring security to the better-paying but presumably insecure job.[13]

The conflict between these results and those reported for the U.S. and U.S.S.R. may be less glaring than appears at first glance. It should be observed that in both the American and Soviet studies there was an added element not present in the British and Australian question, namely, the prospect of promotion or "advancement." It may be that our initial formulation was either too sweeping or too imprecise. Perhaps we should

[10] Cantril (ed.), *op. cit.*, p. 530.
[11] *Public Opinion Quarterly*, XIV (Spring, 1950), 182.
[12] Cantril (ed.), *op. cit.*, p. 1016.
[13] AGP, Nos. 579-89 (March-April, 1949). This issue also reports that at that time Gallup asked the same question in a number of other countries, but the results are not reported with class breaks. The proportion of the total samples choosing the steady job is so high in Canada (85 per cent), Holland (79 per cent), and Sweden (71 per cent) that we must assume that in those countries as well the steady job was the overwhelming favorite in all groups.

have said that, where there is a prospect of advancement, a promise of special success, then those in the occupations of higher status will more readily take risks, but, where security is balanced against high earnings alone, they will act like most others in preferring security. Formulated thus, our expectation is more congruent with relevant psychological theory treating "need achievement" as a risk-taking propensity[14] and with the evidence that it is much more common among those higher in the occupational hierarchy.[15]

This formulation is also more in line with our earlier finding that in judging the qualities of a job those in the positions of higher status were not particularly preoccupied with high earnings. Fortunately, we have a partial test of the soundness of our shift in emphasis, since an American sample was also asked a question similar to the one used in Britain and Australia.[16] Under this condition, *with no mention of advancement*, the response was markedly different from that reported above. Although there was still some structured occupational differentiation, it was very slight compared to that observed when the hope of advancement was one of the conditions. With the question in this form the overwhelming majority of Americans at all occupational levels chose the secure job, as had their opposite numbers in Britain and Australia.

That seemingly so slight a difference in wording a question can produce so marked a difference in the structure of response must give us real pause about this whole enterprise. It warns against interpreting all the scattered and limited findings we have and demonstrates the great importance of doing carefully designed, focused, informed, special studies of our own as soon as possible. But it should not discourage us. It does not cast serious doubt upon the basic theory. In the case just discussed, for example, we did not refute the general proposition that the higher status groups respond in a different way than those of lower status when confronted with certain alternative choices in the job realm. But we did see the necessity for refinement in delineating precisely what has special appeal to these groups and wherein they share values in common. The theory therefore becomes less global, less "omnipredictive," but, in the long run, more interesting and more suggestive for future work.

[14] See J. W. Atkinson, "Motivational Determinants of Risk-taking Behavior," *Psychological Review*, LXIV (1957), 359-72.

[15] This is suggested by a number of the studies in J. W. Atkinson (ed.), *Motives in Fantasy, Action, and Society* (Princeton, N.J.: D. Van Nostrand Co., 1958). Definitive evidence based on a national sample has been collected by the Survey Research Center at the University of Michigan in a study, directed by Gerald Gurin and Joseph Veroff, to be published soon.

[16] It was worded as follows: "Some people prefer a job which pays very well even though it may not be so secure (permanent). Other people prefer a steady job even though it may not pay so much. Which would you, yourself, prefer—the steady job or the better-paying one?" (*Public Opinion Quarterly*, XIII [Fall, 1949], 553).

To sum up our findings in the realm of work: We see striking confirmation of the differential effect of the job situation on the perception of one's experience in it. The evidence is powerful and unmistakable that satisfaction with one's job is differentially experienced by those in the several standard occupational positions. From country to country, we observe a clear positive correlation between the over-all status of occupations and the experience of satisfaction in them. This seems to hold, as well, for the relation between satisfaction and the components of the job, such as the pay, but the evidence is thinner here. We may expect that the relationship will hold for other components, such as the prestige of the job and the autonomy or independence it affords. Job situation appears also to pattern many values germane to the occupational realm, such as the qualities most desired in a job and the image of a good or bad boss.[17]

At the same time, we note that there are certain attitudes which position in the occupational hierarchy does not seem to influence. For example, all occupational groups agree on the relative ranking of the status or desirability of different jobs. And they seem to agree in favoring job security at less pay over a better-paying but less secure job. Yet in the latter realm we discover an interesting fact. When we add the special ingredient of a promise of success, promotion or advancement, we trigger a special propensity to risk-taking in those in more esteemed occupations, whereas those in the manual classes remain unmoved and stick to security. This alerts us to the importance of precision and refinement in seeking the exact nature of the values and beliefs which differentiate the social groups on the basis of position in the occupational hierarchy, as against those which they share in common with all of their nationality or all who participate in modern society. . . .

THE MASTERY-OPTIMISM COMPLEX

Those lower in the occupational hierarchy bring certain important personal characteristics or propensities to their typical "assignments" in life, which tendencies are reinforced by conditions of their characteristic setting. Their education is limited, they generally will not have benefited from travel, and they confront most of the challenges of the outside world with minimum training or skill. Their home environment, particularly the example of the father, will probably have taught blind obedience to authority, if not as a virtue, at least as necessity.[18] Even

---

[17] For lack of space the relevant evidence with regard to images of the good and bad boss has not been presented.

[18] But not necessarily respect. Indeed, the experience of the harsh and peremptory demands for obedience experienced by those at lower status levels more often breeds surface conformity and, beneath that, a smoldering hatred or disrespect for authority, except when so strong as to compel or win blind allegiance.

before he goes to work, the factory will have been described to the working-class boy: its great power, its vast size, the impersonality of its processes, and the mystery of the forces which move within it. On arriving at the plant, the young worker will find many of his images and expectations confirmed. Personnel clerks will treat him as something to be fitted into impersonal categories. If there is a doctor who passes on his fitness, the worker may well sense that he is treated as an object assessed, not as a person examined. The foreman will probably be a tough character who makes it clear who is boss, what is expected, what happens to those who step out of line. All the force and power that the lowly employee sees around him will appear to be under the control of people distant and not highly visible who are controlled by others more distant, more powerful, and still more invisible. The other workers, if not initially suspicious, perhaps will immediately begin a briefing on how to stay out of trouble, replete with accounts of unpleasant things which happened to people who could not stay out of trouble, and other tales which make evident the workers' helplessness. If he is too energetic, the new worker will soon be taught by the others, by force if necessary, to restrict his output, to "play it safe," and to be cautious.

These forces conspire to impress upon the worker a particular view of himself and his relation to the world of work and beyond. His image of the world is, as a result, likely to be that of a place of great complexity whose workings are not too easily comprehended by the common man. He has rights, but he needs friends who are more powerful or knowledgeable, who can explain things, tell him where to go, or help him by putting in a good word in the right place, like a key in a special lock which opens closed doors. For his own part, he feels he should stick to his job, not ask too many questions, and stay out of trouble. Part of staying out of trouble involves keeping one's workmates assured of one's sense of solidarity with them; group loyalty must be placed above personal ambition and self-aggrandizement. But the requirement to conform to orders from above and, at the same time, to pressures from one's equals encourages his impression of other people as unreliable, untrustworthy, and out to do for themselves first. The one thing a man can really count on are his own sensations, and this fosters a certain hedonism: "Eat, drink, (fornicate) and be merry." These impulses, can, however, be gratified only sporadically because of one's dependency, insecurity, and liability to punishment by powers which do not favor too many riotous good times.

A comparable profile for someone at the other end of the occupational hierarchy would presumably be quite different, if not always polar. It is this relative polarization, and the steady gradations as we move from one extreme to the other, which cause the step pattern of experiences and reactions which we have observed and on the basis of which we could generate a host of specific propositions and predictions. For nine-tenths of the propositions there would be no data with which to test them. It will be more economical, therefore, to assemble all the seemingly relevant comparative materials available and to select the topics for investigation in accord with them. We have good comparative data on feelings of personal competence, on images of human nature and its malleability, and on several questions which may be taken as alternative measures of optimism.

Personal Competence

Lacking skills, education, and training, directed by people who have more power than he has and who exercise it effectively over him, the member of the lower classes may be expected less often than others to have self-confidence, that is, a favorable assessment of his competence and capacity. This feeling could presumably be tapped by a single general question. More specific questions, separately testing self-confidence about technical or managerial ability in, say, hospitals, courts, or schools, would presumably produce sharper differentiation. At the same time, there might be some areas where those of lower status typically felt more competent or at least less in conflict. For example, the staff at the University of Michigan Survey Research Center reports in an informal communication that their data suggest middle-class men are more often insecure in their performance as husbands than are lower-class men.

Asked point-blank: "Are you troubled with feelings that you can't do things as well as others can?" — most people in most countries said "No." But the proportion who said they were troubled by feelings of inadequacy rose as high as 59 per cent (in the lower class in Brazil); the question is clearly worth examining. The only break available is by socioeconomic status.[19] It provides some, but only modest, corroboration of our expectation. Of twelve countries reporting, the expected pattern is clear-cut and moderately strong only in Denmark and Brazil. In the latter the proportion who feel less competent rises from 43 per cent in the upper class, to 52 per cent in the middle class, and then to 59 per cent in the lower class. But these cases are offset by Australia, which clearly reverses the predicted direction. Even if we adopt the crude standard of qualifying all countries in which the lower class had the highest proportion troubled by feelings of inadequacy, only seven of the twelve countries qualify.

This is hardly impressive support for our theory. One reason for this outcome may be the ambiguity of the referent "others." The theory predicts mainly that those in the lower strata will feel less competent than "others" who are *above* them. But many answering the question

[19] Table not shown. I am indebted to Dr. Elmo Wilson and the International Research Associates for the data.

undoubtedly took as their referent "others" on the same level. Insofar as this was the case, it would obviously reduce the differentiation between classes. The results may also have been influenced by ambiguity as to the types of competence the questioner had in mind. There are, of course, some areas where lower-class people may generally feel quite competent, or at least not disposed to question their own competence. If they had such areas in mind, they would be less likely to say "Yes" to the question.

We may then say that there is some slight evidence that groups of lower status tend in many countries to be the least often assured about their own general competence. Very rarely are they the group with the most pervasive feeling of adequacy. But the issue is not simple, and the response depends upon the area of life. Our main gain here, then, is perhaps increased awareness of the complexity or subtlety of the issue.

Child-rearing Values

Not only is the horizon restricted for the individual of lower status, himself; he also tends to insure his self-perpetuation by restricting the horizon of his children and others who share his disadvantaged status. Less well equipped with education and experience than those in more favored positions, he learns that a little bit of security is a good thing and that it is wiser to choose what is certain than to strive for the perhaps unattainable. Consequently, we may expect him to be much less likely than persons of middle or upper status to urge a young man to strive for an occupation with high status which may not be easily obtained, and much more likely to urge the young man to go after a well-paid, secure job at the working-class level. This is true not only in everyday practice but holds even under the stimulus of a white-collar interviewer who saves the interviewee further embarrassment by offering him conditions free of the objective restrictions he may know actually exist. In one International Research Associates poll in nine countries, the question was put: "If an *intelligent young man who seemed suited for almost any line of work* asked your advice, what occupation would you be most likely to recommend for him?" (Italics supplied.) Rather consistently from country to country, people of lower socioeconomic status choose the modest goal of "skilled labor" for such a boy much more often than do the more advantaged classes (Table 3). Very similar results were obtained with comparable questions in the United States, in Italy, and with Soviet refugees.

We might again say that this is obvious. It is, furthermore, objective and realistic to advise the working-class boy to set his job sights low. But should we assume that a father's occupational position influences his values in child-rearing only in regard to the "objective" realm of job choices? The influence of the father's life situation may be expected

TABLE 3. OCCUPATIONS RECOMMENDED TO YOUNG MEN IN
PERCENTAGES BY COUNTRY AND OCCUPATION*

Country and Occupation Recommended	Respondent's Occupation		
	Executive, Professional	White Collar	Wage Earner
Australia:			
Engineering, science	24	26	20
Skilled labor	10	11	28
Belgium:			
Engineering, science	43	52	28
Skilled labor	8	11	33
Britain:			
Engineering, science	54	50	48
Skilled labor	7	6	9
Denmark:			
Engineering, science	8	15	8
Skilled labor	7	7	17
France:			
Engineering, science	20	30	19
Skilled labor	8	5	11
Japan:			
Engineering, science	24	22	26
Skilled labor	1	—	2
Netherlands:			
Engineering, science	33	39	22
Skilled labor	7	5	13
Norway:			
Engineering, science	11	17	19
Skilled labor	15	18	16
Sweden:			
Engineering, science	12	19	15
Skilled labor	8	8	15

*Adapted from data made available by International Research Associates through the courtesy of Dr. Elmo Wilson.

to flow over into other areas; ambition itself may be affected. And not only ambition, but a number of other values which guide child-rearing may well fall into class-determined patterns.

An International Research Associates study inquired which value is the most important to teach to children and offered as choices: "To be ambitious and get ahead"; "To obey parents"; "To enjoy themselves"; "To place their trust in God"; and "To be decent and honest." Since in our Soviet-refugee study we had already investigated very similar values and had found patterns broadly congruent with the theory underlying the thinking in this report,[20] I undertook to predict the outcome of the INRA inquiry. The main assumption, following from general theory and supported by the earlier study, was that traditional, restrictive, cautious, conventional values are much stronger among manual

[20] Alex Inkeles, "Social Change and Social Character: The Role of Parental Mediation," *Journal of Social Issues*, XI, No. 2 (1955), 12-23.

workers, whereas the belief in effort, striving, energetic mastery, and the sacrifice necessary to those ends is much stronger in the middle class. On the basis of this fundamental assumption, I predicted for the INRA study that ambition would be more stressed by the middle class, obedience to parents by the working class. A secondary prediction was that the values focused on personal qualities produced by careful training, such as decency and honesty, would be more stressed by the middle classes. Although predicting emphasis on religion was obviously complicated, I assumed that trust in God, taken as an *external* source of authority and power, would be stronger among manual workers. Finally, I anticipated that stress on enjoyment would be more evident in the working class, presumably as compensation for past and present frustrations and anticipated future deprivations.

These predictions are generally, but not consistently, borne out by the data. . . . The working class does have the lowest proportion stressing ambition in six of eleven countries and is tied in a seventh, a position held only twice each by the middle and upper socioeconomic groups. Only three countries show the usual step pattern, however, and there are two clear-cut reversals to offset them. The absence of pattern is largely a result of the tendency, perhaps not surprising, of the middle class to exceed the upper classes in stressing ambition in rearing children.

Our prediction with regard to emphasis on obedience is more firmly supported. The lower class has the highest proportion stressing it in eight of eleven cases, and it took no less than second place in the remaining three countries. In six the expected step pattern is clearly manifested, and there are no reversals.

Among the second-line predictions, the estimate with regard to decency and honesty was relatively correct. In seven of eleven countries, the higher the socioeconomic status, the greater the proportion emphasizing it. In an eighth case the lower class behaves as expected, but the middle class is out of line. In addition to one unpatterned case, however, there are two clear reversals. The prediction with regard to trust in God was not confirmed: the lower class did most often have the highest proportion, but it also was most often in last place; in general, there was almost a complete lack of pattern from country to country. We may note, finally, that not much can be said about the theme of enjoying one's self, since it was mentioned by only 1 or 2 per cent in most countries.

In general, the class patterning in which we are interested manifests itself again, but the patterns are not strong. In most cases only a few percentage points separated one class from the other. In values in child-rearing, cultural forces — particularly those deriving from ethnic and religious membership — play a powerful role and may, indeed, be the prime movers. Yet the fact that in this initial and unrefined procedure

we can see a definite patterning of values that fit the expectations derived from our general theory is encouraging and recommends us to
further and fuller exploration. . . .

. . . The following statements seem justified by our experience:

There is substantial evidence, over a wide attitudinal and experiential
range, that perceptions, opinions, and values are systematically ordered
in modern societies. The proportion of people who give a particular
response increases or decreases fairly regularly as we move up or down
the typical status ladders of occupation, income, education, and prestige.
These patterns emerge not only in realms which are obviously closely
related to status pressures but also in areas seemingly far removed. In
every country the average or typical response may be distinctive, but
the same order or structure is manifested within *each*, even though
they vary widely in their economic and political development and have
unique cultural histories. This similarity in the patterning of response
seems best explained by assuming that, in significant degree, perceptions,
attitudes and values are shaped by the networks of interpersonal relations
in which individuals are enmeshed and particularly by rewards and
punishments.

It follows that a careful study of the specific external situation of the
major subgroups in any country would enable one to deduce the distinctive internal life — the perceptions, attitudes, and values — of those
groups relative to each other. This makes the very large assumption,
however, that one is equipped with a great battery of subtheories which
specify the probable psychological outcome of a very wide range of
diverse external situations, taken alone and in numerous combinations.
With or without the requisite battery of subtheories, this is, in effect,
what historians, anthropologists, and sociologists frequently attempt to
do when they analyze life in some one nation or culture. However, the
uniqueness of the external situation studied in each case, and the *ad
hoc* nature of the theory used, make it difficult to test and refine theory
and on this basis to accumulate firm empirical knowledge.

The cross-national or comparative approach permits concentration on
a few widely present situational forces and facilitates the systematic testing and validation of theory. This paper's concentration on modern
industrial society should not be understood, however, as suggesting it to
be the only realm in which the theory sketched here is applicable. On
the contrary, we expect that, whenever any set of nations places major
social strata in a structure highly comparable from society to society, a
cross-national attitudinal pattern similar to the one we observed will
also be found. Theoretically, a parallel analysis could be made for the
various strata of medieval European societies, of the traditional mon-
archies of the eighteenth century, or of the underdeveloped nations of

the early twentieth century. In fact, any such effort would probably founder, either because we could not secure adequate information on the specific distribution of attitudes or because we could not satisfy the requirement that the situation of the subgroups, and the hierarchies in which they were organized, be strictly comparable from one society to the next.

The choice of industrial society as a field of investigation is therefore not based solely on grounds of methodological expediency or political interest. It is the only setting which relatively unambiguously satisfies the conditions to which the theory has critical relevance. Modern society, most notably in the factory system, and secondarily in large-scale bureaucratic organizations in business, government, and other fields, is more or less unique in the extent to which it produces standardized contexts of experience. These are exportable, and are sought after to a degree which far exceeds the exportability of most other culture complexes. And to an extent far beyond what is true of other complexes, these resist being reformulated, changed, or adapted to suit the larger sociocultural environment into which they bluntly intrude or are invited or accepted.

The patterns of reaction we have observed are to be expected, however, only insofar as the hierarchies in the different countries are equivalent, not merely in the positions recognized, but also in the conditions of existence they provide for the incumbents of those statuses. Departures from the standard pattern (as distinguished from differences in the average response for any country) must in all cases be assumed to arise from empirically discoverable variations in the conditions of existence, by status. It follows, therefore, that, to the degree a nation's social structure approximates the model of a full-scale primary industrial society, to that degree will it more clearly show the differentiated structure of response we have delineated, and do so over a wider range of topics, problems, or areas of experience. There are, of course, many theoretical and methodological difficulties in developing a model of industrial society, which we cannot go into here. Suffice it to say that England before World War I, the United States between World Wars I and II, the Soviet Union and Western Germany after World War II all can be shown to have approximated the model in important respects. My anticipation is that all the currently developed nations and all those on the verge of developing will at some point approximate the model and will at that point show most clearly the patterns we have described.

This brings us to the often cited tendencies toward homogenization of experience in the most advanced industrial countries, notably the United States. If our general theory is valid, then to the extent that the conditions of life, the network of interpersonal relations in which people work, the patterns of reward and punishment, come to be more and more alike regardless of status and situs, to that degree should their perceptions, attitudes, and values become similar. In other words, the typical step pattern we observed would become less and less evident and might eventually disappear altogether. Furthermore, to the degree that similar conditions came to prevail in other countries, the same process of homogenization could be expected to manifest itself there as well. Indeed, although it seems far off and far-fetched, it could very well be that we will, in the future, come to have a fairly uniform world culture, in which not only nations but groups within nations will have lost their distinctive subcultures. In important respects — exclusive of such elements as language — most people might come to share a uniform, homogeneous culture as citizens of the world. This culture might make them, at least as group members, more or less indistinguishable in perceptual tendency, opinion, and belief not only from their fellow citizens in the same nation and their occupational peers in other nations but from all men everywhere.[21]

Such speculation of course goes far beyond what our data can at present support even remotely. The data are, furthermore, by no means unambiguous. The questions put in different countries, for one thing, are not comparable. But it is highly improbable that ambiguity in the stimulus would generate agreement in the response pattern. On the contrary, the likelihood is vastly greater that any consistent pattern really there would be muted or muffled by questions which put, in effect, a randomly varying stimulus to respondents in the different countries. There is also the substantial problem that *within* any country a question in the same language may have quite different meaning for people with markedly dissimilar education. We obviously need to develop methods which insure that our questions, *as understood* by respondents of different countries and classes, are more strictly equivalent. We have methods which can satisfy this requirement in substantial degree. They are moderately costly, and require time, but the advantage of using them in scientific, as contrasted with the commercial, studies is great enough to warrant the cost.

Another difficulty arises with regard to the criteria to be used in determining when opinions are structured in any country and patterned across national boundaries. The usual statistical tests are not automatically applicable. In any event, for purposes of this exploratory study I have adopted a liberal and flexible definition. But in later, more systematic studies we must be prepared to specify our criteria more precisely and to apply them more rigorously.

A more imposing challenge to our findings is that in a great many

[21] For a forceful—indeed extreme—argument of this position, including an exposition of the forces working to bring it about, see Roderick Seidenberg, *Posthistoric Man: An Inquiry* (Boston: Beacon Press, 1957).

items the variation in the average or typical response for different countries is so great as to dwarf into insignificance the similarity in pattern from nation to nation. The occupational or other hierarchy, in other words, often explains only a small part of the variance, at least as compared to dimensions like nationality, citizenship, or ethnicity. We should, perhaps, be pleased to have discovered *any* regularity in human behavior which persists across national boundaries, even if it is only "minor." It is also possible that often the seemingly great size of these differences among nations is more spurious than real and arises mainly from the fact that the questions used are not really comparable stimuli for the various respondents. The differences may, however, be very real indeed. If they are, then we will still have to choose between alternative explanations — the distinctive cultural tradition of a nation, on the one hand, and its level and style of economic and political development, on the other. Undoubtedly both factors exert major influence, and often they will be so intertwined as to make it impossible to assign separate weights to them. But careful selection of the countries to be studied — perhaps even matching countries with similar traditions but different economic or political development, and vice versa — would yield interesting results. It will be particularly important to seek to discover those realms of perception, opinion, and value which seem most influenced by the industrial social order, as against those which are relatively more tightly integrated in an autonomous pattern of traditional culture and hence more immune, or at least resistant, to change even in the presence of the standard industrial environment.

One last reservation is the claim that these data are subject to quite different explanations than those here offered. For example, the pattern can be explained as arising mainly from educational differences — not an alternative explanation, but really an integral part of my argument. The theory stresses that people are ordered in modern society in hierarchies of power, responsibility, prestige, income, and education. The amount of education a man receives is part of the structure of rewards. It also is a major element in determining his occupational status. As such it can be seen as merely an integral, although alternative, *index* of his *situation* rather than as an independent and alternative *explanation* of his *behavior*. But, quite apart from this, the theory holds that situational pressures exert an influence independent of the education of the incumbents of the position. To test this assumption and to discover how great is the independent influence of education, we would, of course, need to compare the responses of people with comparable education who occupied systematically different positions, and vice versa.

We obviously need more and better research on the important problem this initial exploration has barely opened up. It is to be doubted, however, that merely by collecting more data of the type now in hand we can settle many of the issues. But through carefully designed studies, building on the experience of this exploration and sharply focused on some of the issues raised by it, we may expect to make substantial progress. We would hope to insure comparability in the meaning of the questions from country to country and from class to class. Instability and unreliability in the findings could further be greatly reduced by the use of scales to measure important universes of attitudes, in place of the single question which has been the standard in the past. Rather than gathering scattered bits and snippets of information from numerous different samples, we should aim to secure a rich set of responses from the *same* set of respondents in each country, thus providing the basis for studying patterns of interrelation among sets of perceptions, opinions and values. To aid in resolving some of the difficult problems of interpreting the findings we have so far accumulated, the countries studied should represent a wide range of stages and forms of economic development and cultural type. And the samples drawn from each should be not the bare minimum representative sample but, rather, carefully stratified and, where necessary, extensively overrepresented to provide subsamples large enough to permit complex internal comparisons. With sufficient resources we could reasonably hope to make substantial strides toward developing a respectable social psychology of industrial society.